The Soviet Union 1984/85

About the Book

In 1984 and 1985, the swift succession in the USSR's leadership affected all levels of Soviet society. This eighth volume in a series of biennial reports on the Soviet Union analyzes domestic affairs, economics, and foreign policy in light of that succession. Power struggles within the highest echelons of the Soviet communist party are examined. Contributors evaluate prospects for the attempted economic modernization in a system that leaves little room for radical reform. Moscow's swings between extremes of self-isolation and readiness to talk raise questions about foreign and security policy during the transitional period. The contributors also identify perspectives, priorities, and trends for the future of Soviet politics, economics, and social developments.

The Federal Institute for East European and International Studies in Cologne was established in 1961 as an academically autonomous research institution. It operates under the administrative and financial authority of Germany's Federal Ministry of the Interior.

Published in cooperation with
das Bundesinstitut für ostwissenschaftliche
und internationale Studien/
the Federal Institute for East European
and International Studies

The Soviet Union 1984/85
Events, Problems, Perspectives

edited by
the Federal Institute for
East European and International Studies

Westview Press / Boulder and London

Westview Special Studies on the Soviet Union and Eastern Europe

This Westview softcover edition was manufactured on our own premises using equipment and methods that allow us to keep even specialized books in stock. It is printed on acid-free paper and bound in softcovers that carry the highest rating of the National Association of State Textbook Administrators, in consultation with the Association of American Publishers and the Book Manufacturers' Institute.

Published in 1986 in the United States of America by Westview Press, Inc.; Frederick A. Praeger, Publisher; 5500 Central Avenue, Boulder, Colorado 80301

Library of Congress ISSN: 0163-6057
ISBN: 0-8133-0416-4

This book was produced without formal editing by the publisher.

Printed and bound in the United States of America

(∞) The paper used in this publication meets the requirements of the American National Standard for Permanence of Paper for Printed Library Materials Z39.48-1984.

6 5 4 3 2 1

Contents

Tables and Figures

Tables

Figures

Foreword to the US Edition

Not only the informed layman but even the university student and the professional scholar, journalist, reference librarian, and government specialist are bound to have difficulty keeping up with the changing Soviet scene. This is but a more extreme case of the more general phenomenon regarding states and societies where access to information is controlled and available data are incomplete or unreliable; it is essential for the observer to have a grounding in the political context, the political culture, and the political jargon to understand the course of events.

What can we do to bridge the gap? Although the US reader has the opportunity to consult authoritative translations from the Soviet press and, selectively, from Soviet radio and television,[1] these sources—valuable as they are—are often apt to be frustrating. These are, after all, official sources. For certain purposes, such as the dissemination of government and Party pronouncements, this authenticity is an essential attribute. But the official sources are not calculated to provide independent judgments about trends and developments in Soviet politics, economy, technology, foreign affairs, cultural policy, secret police, civil-military relations, and resource utilization. Despite the profusion of English-language periodicals dealing with Soviet affairs—some of them excellent[2]—none has chosen to provide systematically and regularly the sort of factual information and authoritative, integrated interpretation essential for an understanding of current affairs that goes beyond the reporting of the daily or weekly press. Research papers produced by most agencies, both governmental and nongovernmental, are generally either not available to the public or published only after considerable delays and significant excisions.[3] The work of certain other research institutes is perceived to reflect special political pleading or the views of particular opinion groups and, perhaps, to suffer from some unwitting selectivity of data. The products of such organizations all deserve to be studied and consulted by the serious student. But none alone quite does the job.

All these considerations make the appearance in English of the present volume and others in this series particularly welcome. Das Bundesinstitut für ostwissenschaftliche und internationale Studien (the Federal Institute for East European and International Studies) in Cologne has in the past decade emerged as perhaps the leading West European research center on the contemporary Soviet Union and Eastern Europe. Its papers and studies stand out by their factual reliability and the objectivity of analysis. Its staff is remarkably well informed, and although the interpretation of Soviet trends is always a matter of some intuition and subjective judgment, we can feel secure in the knowledge that in this instance the judgments are made by a team of skilled, informed, and seasoned specialists, without ax-grinding or political preconceptions.

The latter is particularly important in recommending a West German perspective to the US reader. On most matters of broad interpretation of Soviet developments, North American and West German specialists are normally very similar—or rather, normally show roughly the same spectrum of divergent opinions. But on a few issues—be it foreign trade or the prospects for change in the Soviet system—the German, or more generally the West European, perspective is at times apt to differ from that of Washington. At the very least it deserves a serious hearing. At times, it has proven far more accurate than the US view; on other occasions, it has served as a useful corrective.

The present volume—the eighth in this biennial series—provides, as it were, a benchmark at the start of the Gorbachev era. The contributors review, topic by topic, the developments in Soviet domestic politics, the economy, and foreign policy during the interregnum between Brezhnev and Gorbachev. They analyze debates among the Soviet elite, successes and failures, pressures and constraints, and the options open to the decision-makers. One can of course dispute some of the views expressed in the various contributions to this volume; in fact, some of the contributors may well disagree with each other. But the thoroughly documented picture of the USSR as it emerges from these pages is valuable not only because of what it offers the reader but also because it avoids several frequent and characteristic missteps and misconceptions.

The authors and editors are seasoned enough not to be taken in naively by Soviet assertions and statistics. Economic growth rates and social tensions are just two examples of areas where foreign specialists must reach their own independent conclusions, though naturally using Soviet information wherever they can.

At the same time, the contributors avoid the two equally inaccurate images of the Soviet Union as either "ten feet tall" or on the verge of crisis and collapse. Both of these views, in large measure ideologically driven, have in fact rendered a serious disservice to those who wish to deal earnestly and realistically with the Soviet challenge.

The image of Soviet totalitarian omnipotence (often couched in the assertion of resurgent neo-Stalinism) ignores a variety of recent trends. The serious shortcomings in productivity, efficiency, and technological innovation have been discussed with a good deal of candor in the Soviet press. Resource constraints are real and increasingly severe. Social trends and social problems—beginning with pandemic corruption and civic malaise—increasingly appear to lie beyond the effective control of the political authorities. Elite politics reflect not only rival ambitions but also divergent values, norms, and policy preferences. There is considerable uncertainty about the proper policies to pursue in a great number of issue areas, from Soviet involvement in the Third World to the toleration (or even encouragement) of private plots in agriculture. The speculation abroad, in the Andropov and Chernenko years, about the ostensible takeover in Moscow by either the secret police or the military, has of course proved to be misleading nonsense.

The alternative vision of doom (particularly popular among foreign observers who delight in rhetorically relegating the communist system to the trash can of history) fails to give adequate weight to the remarkable stability of the Soviet system. At an admittedly high price, the regime has built up an unprecedentedly powerful military machine. Despite episodic dissidence and a multiplicity of grievances, the fundamental loyalty and perceived legitimacy of the system in the eyes of the bulk of the population are scarcely in doubt. The virtually routine fashion in which the three recent successions at the top of the political pyramid were accomplished only testifies to the solidity of the system. Whatever else, its leadership has accumulated three generations of experience in dealing with a great variety of crises, predicaments, shortcomings, and challenges—many of them far more dramatic and extreme than those that the Soviet Union is apt to face at this time. Nor is there any evidence that the system can be bankrupted by US efforts to step up the arms race, disintegrated by attempts from abroad to appeal to ethnic groups within the USSR, or subverted by intimations of Western consumerism (attractive though many of its products may be to potential Soviet purchasers).

The Soviet Union faces the Gorbachev era, at home and abroad, with a novel and perhaps unique combination of difficulties and opportunities. The headlines inform us of some of the ways in which the new leadership in the Kremlin is seeking to deal with them. This volume provides valuable background and analyses, as well as reference information, to follow these and future developments with far better understanding.

Alexander Dallin

Notes

1. *The Current Digest of the Soviet Press* (weekly, Columbus, Ohio; and Federal Broadcast Intelligence Service (FBIS)), *Daily Report: USSR.*

2. *Slavic Review* (Austin, Texas), *Soviet Studies* (Glasgow, Scotland), *Russian Review* (Syracuse, New York), *Problems of Communism* (Washington, D.C.), and others.

3. E.g., US Congress, Joint Economic Committee reports and hearings on the Soviet economy; also reports of the Congressional Research Service (Washington, D.C.); Rand Corporation papers and reports (Santa Monica, California); Brookings Institution publications (Washington, D.C.); Radio Liberty Research Bulletin (New York and Munich); United States Information Agency (USIA), Research reports (Washington, D.C.); and others.

Editors and Contributors

Editors

Heinz Timmermann (chief editor), Wolfgang Berner, Heinz Brahm, Hans Bräker, Arnold Buchholz, Helmut Dahm, Hans-Hermann Höhmann, Barbara Langer, Gerd Linde, Karin Schmid, Gertraud Seidenstecher, Heinrich Vogel.

Contributors

Oskar Anweiler, Bernd Bentlin, Wolfgang Berner, Dieter Bingen, Astrid von Borcke, Heinz Brahm, Hans Bräker, Christel Brückner, Arnold Buchholz, Hung-hsiang Chou, Hermann Clement, Helmut Dahm, Stefan Donew, Joachim Glaubitz, Brigitta Godel, Manfred Görtemaker, Dieter Heinzig, Hans-Hermann Höhmann, Peter Hübner, Gyula Józsa, Bernd Knabe, Peter Kruschin, Friedrich Kuebart, Thomas Kussmann, Barbara Langer, Gerd Linde, Christian Meier, Fred Oldenburg, Wolf Oschlies, Alexander Rahr, Boris Rumer, Thomas Scharping, Karin Schmid, Eberhard Schneider, Alarich Scholz, Gertraud Seidenstecher, Gerhard Simon, Gerd Stricker, Heinz Timmermann, Heinrich Vogel, Franz Walter, Gerhard Wettig.

This edition was translated by Roger A. Clarke and Ulrich Strempel and edited by Harry G. Shaffer

Introduction

Heinz Timmermann

The Soviet Union 1984/85 is the eighth in the series in which the Federal Institute for East European and International Studies in Cologne reports on developments in the Soviet Union. Three comprehensive surveys and 25 essays examine events, problems, and perspectives of Soviet politics, each contribution bearing the mark both of the scholarly competence and insight as well as the specific assessment of the respective author.

Andropov's and Chernenko's years in office that fall within the period covered here can be characterized as a phase of transition—a transition from the immobilism of the late Brezhnev era to a new energetic attempt at a modernization of the Soviet Union (though in conformity with its system) under Gorbachev. (Of course, Brezhnev and Chernenko—much like Gorbachev's mentor Andropov—had also advocated modernization in rudiments and using terms such as "perfection," "modification," and "intensification.") Soviet leadership's historical optimism has given way to a growing awareness that, without a thorough overhaul of its internal structures, the USSR could end up in an even more difficult situation. The myth woven around the "modernist" Andropov, even in the Soviet Union, can really be explained only by this general awareness of crisis and by the fact that he especially was believed capable of engineering a corresponding about-face.

The election of the "Andropovist" Gorbachev points in the same direction: toward a certain consensus among large parts of the leadership and populace regarding the necessity of relaxing the administrative-bureaucratic fetters of a centralized command structure in specific areas. This is meant to give new impulses to the economy and to motivate the people anew. Even the majority of traditionalists should be aware that without certain structural changes, the Soviet Union could not maintain (much less raise) its level of development and at the same time would run the risk of falling even further behind those Western industrialized states considered most dynamic and innovative, especially in economic-military terms. The rapid development of high technology in the West and the determination of the competing superpower, the USA, to use it militarily in the form of new space-weapons-systems—all this reactivated the historic trauma of Russia's technological backwardness and fostered the urge to modernize the country.

Andropov's and Chernenko's brief periods in office confirmed this impression. Significantly, Brezhnev who, after all, had ruled for 18 years but had finally turned into a symbol of stagnation, was hardly ever mentioned throughout their interregnum. At the same time, though, these interludes with their differing emphases indicate that the Soviet leadership is far from agreed on methods, instruments, and limits of such a modernization. Symptomatic of this was the Central Committee's resistance to Gorbachev's election, which only Gromyko's vigorous championship of the new secretary general could overcome. This resistance was less concerned with the "inexperience" of the comparatively young Gorbachev (born in 1931); rather, it resulted from a critical attitude towards the new secretary general's political concept, its contours already discernible today, and from anxiety lest he take too far the "purge" of the cadres in the process. To be sure, none of this means that Gorbachev's concept has already become a reality, especially since his predecessors had also voiced similar intentions. The new secretary general's term, after all, has only just begun and it should take some time before Gorbachev's real profile becomes apparent.

Like any transitional phase, the period of Moscow's interregnum with its inevitable diffusion of power afforded an exceptionally good glimpse of the discussions among the Soviet leadership and the manifoldness of the resultant conflicts. For instance, the following questions came up: Is the ideology capable of molding the "new man"? Is it therefore one of the Party's paramount tasks to purposefully alter social conscience and control its transformation, as Chernenko had demanded and as Brezhnev and Suslov had before him? Or will the people be motivated to superior performance only if the Party emphasizes the increase in efficiency in the economic realm that Andropov and Gorbachev had intended? Are there universal truths (Chernenko), or should the Party admit that in many areas of theory and practice it does not have ready concepts at its command and that it must steadily continue learning (Andropov and then Gorbachev)? Toward this increase in efficiency, should technocratic streamlining measures be taken, or should decentralizing reforms be initiated? Should the intensification required to overcome the agricultural crisis be achieved above all through melioration projects, i.e., a policy of large-scale investment, or instead should new forms of organization be applied? Ought the economy to be drawn upon even more for armaments, or does the past supply of new equipment suffice to meet the military tasks? Should the economy rather bet on autarchy or on further integration into the world market? And finally, in the dialogue with the West, assuming its resumption is deemed useful in the first place, should one concentrate on the US or should one, in a parallel way, include the Western Europeans as important components?

This is far from an exhaustive list of differing positons advanced during the transitional phase from Brezhnev to Gorbachev. Incidentally, it is reflected (in a considerably heated way at times) in academia and journalism, in their contributions to the discussion of economic reform (though for the most part the term reform is avoided), or in controversies regarding the possibility of "antagonistic contradictions" arising in Soviet communist-type societies. The positions emerging from all this are, of course, difficult to link to particular individuals (or groups of individuals), the more so since these often act flexibly (e.g., Gromyko in his plea for Gorbachev). Moreover, the lines of conflict frequently cut straight across interest groups and are not simply drawn between them. Nevertheless, the contours of a new political concept emerged in early 1983 under Andropov, and more clearly yet following Gorbachev's de facto assumption of power in the late fall of 1984. In East-West relations—and particularly in regard to efforts to resume the dialogue of detente—this concept (supported, incidentally, by Chernenko) maintains the Brezhnev era's course of important action and behavior patterns. In domestic and economic policies, however, Andropov, and even more plainly Gorbachev, developed a concept markedly different from the line pursued by Brezhnev.

At the core of this contrasting concept is the demand for an intensification of the economy, for a "radical modification" of its planning and management mechanism. It starts out with the necessity of an accelerated introduction of modern technologies and calls on Soviet citizens to put forth an effort comparable to the industrialization of the 1930s. Not only is the modernization of the economy considered the precondition for a further rise in the standard of living; on its success hinges also the answer to the question of whether or not the Soviet Union will be able to retain her position as a superpower equal to the US in world politics. In short, the success of modernization determines the USSR's capacity, says Gorbachev, "to enter the new millennium as a great and burgeoning power."

Now, this concept certainly does not represent aspirations towards systemic change modelled on the "Prague Spring." The current economic system, after all, has been developing continuously for some 60 years—not least as an instrument to secure Party rule—and is firmly anchored in people's acquired behavior patterns. Moreover, it is not merely in the perception of the leadership that the Soviet communist-type centrally planned economy is associated with the USSR's successful rise to world power.

All told, therefore, the Gorbachev-concept rather aims at modernization without thoroughgoing reforms in the Western sense. It aspires to a basic improvement of efficiency, to a streamlining of the overall economic system, resting on the central elements of discipline and order (in bureaucracy and at work), to decentralization and enlarged decisionmaking power for enterprise management (by reducing the authority of the ministries and curtailing the Party's operative influence) and to enhancement of the motivation and material interest of the individual (by forming increasingly autonomous work collectives and brigades in industry as well as agriculture). Corresponding measures and experiments were initiated under Andropov and are further promoted under Gorbachev. No consideration is given to an introduction of market mechanisms nor to a promotion of private initiative beyond limited corrections in the agricultural and perhaps the service sectors. On the contrary, at his election as secretary general, Gorbachev expressly spoke of the necessity "to realize the economy's planned development and consolidate socialist ownership." His maxim is: centralized planning—yes, but relieved by effective decentralization (to varying extent, depending on the economic sector).

An interesting part of this process is the ideology's change beyond its continuingly indispensable role as the source from which Party rule is legitimized. Under Brezhnev and Suslov ideology had degenerated into an ultimately ineffective campaign instrument; by way of resuscitation, Chernenko had restricted himself to enriching it with some populist elements. Gorbachev, on the other hand, picked up on Andropov's endeavors to strip the ideology of its abstract character and to associate it directly with the concept of economic modernization. Bureaucratic arbitrariness, incompetence, corruption, both concluded, had deprived ideology of its credibility and thus of its bonding effect; patronizing and gilding by bureaucracy and mass media was driving people into passivity. In short the level of sociopolitical organization (or productive relationships) had fallen behind the level of economic development (or productive forces).

From this approach Gorbachev developed a concept of "perfecting" socialist democracy along Andropov's line. This concept was designed to enlist popular support for his concept of economic modernization. It envisages greater participatory rights for Soviet citizens, greater autonomy for plant collectives, greater transparency in political decisionmaking (also regarding Party decisions), and more realistic news broadcasting in the media. Citing the classicists of Marxism-Leninism, Gorbachev rated "administrative autonomy" highly in the overall system of social relations.

For all that, since Andropov (and especially in scholarly publications), those doing political-ideological work have strongly emphasized the need for increasing consideration of various social groups' interests. Quite evidently, this too is closely related to the aim of intensifying economic activity: The Brezhnev era's populist "levelling" is supposed to give way to a policy of "social justice" in distributive relations in order to reward performance and competency as well as to punish "passivity at work, parasitism, and moral nihilism." The contradictions and conflicts between groups oriented towards productivity on the one hand, and interests bent on obstructing efficiency on the other, are to be resolved openly at the expense of the latter and put to use, as it were, as generators of economic dynamization.

For the time being, of course, all this is but a concept which, incidentally, Brezhnev and Chernenko had also proclaimed in some areas, e.g., in regard to an increase of citizens' participatory rights, improved transparency of political decisionmaking or a "modification" of the economic mechanism. Even if realized only to a limited extent, this would in effect amount to thoroughgoing changes especially of the USSR's economic structures. Gorbachev's chances rest on a certain awakening that has seized Party and population, and they rest on an evidently widespread awareness that without the transformation projected, the Soviet Union is faced with a long period of stagnation and crisis and would scarcely be able to enter the next millenium as a "great and burgeoning power," actually equal to the US. The approval Khrushchev encountered in the first phase of his rule with his de-Stalinization policy exemplifies that even in the Soviet Union a determined Party leader can put his mark upon developments, provided his program is carried by a broad ground swell.

But the example of Khrushchev also shows the obstacles in the way of a modernizing course—and of any incisive change, for that matter—in the Soviet Union. The Brezhnev era (including its epilogue under Chernenko) was characterized by the leadership seeking to take all interests—those of various social groups as much as those of the economic establishment, the military, and Party and state bureaucracies—into consideration and integrate them into its project of perfecting socialism. The extent to which influence and self-confidence of the large apparatuses had grown under the protection of the "cadre stability" formula was evidenced not least by the fact that despite lengthy incapacitation of two secretaries general, the Soviet machinery continued to run relatively smoothly.

For now, Gorbachev remains tied into a collective leadership whose decisions he has supported since 1978 and within which he will be able to expand his room for maneuver only one step at a time. He must make allowance for numerous interest groups, such as, for example, the military. From the increase in efficiency, they expect primarily a rise in their budget. According to CIA estimates, at an annual average growth of two percent since 1976 this budget has merely grown at half the rate of the 1971 to 1976 period. Sooner or later, he will have to start treading on the nomenklatura's established interests which—embedded in Stalinist structures and filtered through the apparatuses—has acquired a large weight of its own, impeding innovation. Thus it represents a heavy burden for the modernization envisaged. In fact, the solution to this problem constitutes a central element of Gorbachev's concept: What mattered, he observed at the April 1985 plenary session of the CC, was to avoid any "immobility of cadre movement" and to "complement" the Party's leading organs with better qualified "fresh forces."

From this perspective also, the new secretary general's positive assessment of non-antagonistic contradictions in real socialism makes sense: It serves as theoretical background for his intention of aiding, in the altercations interpreted as conflicts of interests (and not class conflict) within the various groups, in the breakthrough of those interests and tendencies that support Gorbachev's course of innovation and of increasing efficiency and competency. Hence, the project of modernization is a long-term one. As Khrushchev's fate has shown, it stands a chance of success only if Gorbachev manages to maintain his line consistently, to isolate resisting tendencies, and to secure for his policy the lasting broad approval of reform-oriented forces. Given the system-determined narrow margins for reform, such prospects for success must be rated rather skeptically. The Twenty-seventh CPSU Congress, planned for February 1986, which will have to pass a new Party program and elect a new CC, will be a central indicator of the assertive force of Gorbachev's concept in terms of content and personnel.

This also applies to Soviet foreign and security policy. Following the failure of the INF-talks and the beginning of intermediate-range missile deployment by NATO (November 1983), Moscow broke off the Geneva INF and START negotiations and, with Foreign Minister Gromyko in charge, embarked upon a course of comprehensive refusal to communicate—incidentally applied to China as well—excluding only economic relations. This line of de facto self-isolation was contrary not only to all previously held principles of a "Leninist foreign policy," but also to the pragmatic rule of cultivating the dialogue with the US, which is at once the most important opponent and most desirable partner for cooperation, as well as talks with the Western Europeans (and the Chinese), i.e., to exploit to the fullest all differences inside the "imperialist" camp and generally to keep all options open.

Designed as a demonstration of firmness and strength, this course, to be explained politically-psychologically only by feelings of disappointment, insecurity, and inferiority complexes, had extremely negative consequences for Soviet foreign policy and fostered the very reactions and developments Moscow had always sought to prevent. In other words, the considerable difficulties (instability in Poland, war in Afghanistan, tensions in the relations with China) were now joined by further grave problems: The US could continue unchecked its program of military rearmament and modernization by pointing to further military growth in the Soviet Union; the allies of the US (including Japan) were induced to close ranks even more tightly with the competing superpower. Even in its own camp, Soviet intransigence caused anxiety and partially even open criticism: Apart from Romania, traditionally bent on an independent foreign policy, even the GDR and Hungary now undertook autonomous initiatives and through intensive use of all-European channels of communications tried to make a contribution towards overcoming the East-West no-talk state of affairs.

In this situation, the US project to create a space-based anti-missile system (Strategic Defense Initiative, SDI) offered a welcome opportunity for the Soviets to escape their self-induced isolation again and to pick up the thread of talks with the US. Under Chernenko, the Soviet leadership had already stressed the necessity of an "about-face" in East-West relations, and Gromyko's visit to the White House (September 1984) signalled their interest in comprehensive negotiations with the US. At their Geneva meeting of January 1985, foreign minister Gromyko and Secretary Shultz agreed to resume disarmament negotiations between the US and the Soviet Union in March 1985 and to tie up the three components of space weaponry, intercontinental and continental systems into one package.

This development placed Gorbachev at the "outer front" in a more propitious starting position than that found by Secretaries General Andropov and Chernenko when they took office. Like his predecessors, his system of foreign policy priorities is headed by the consolidation of Soviet rule in Eastern Europe as the base of the USSR's world power position. Such consolidation, however, does not seem linked to any intention of adjusting these countries' politics and domestic structures in every detail to the Soviet model. Rather, pursuant to Andropov's concepts, Gorbachev appears willing to leave the Eastern European countries some margin for action in accordance with their respective specific traditions, conditions, and interests—provided they support the basic thrust of Soviet foreign and security policy and do not cross the system boundaries laid down by Moscow.

An understanding with the US is a similarly high priority for the new secretary general. Here, the focus is on efforts towards an agreement for the prevention of the militarization of space. Not coincidentally Gorbachev deems this to be of "key importance" for the future character of East-West-relations. Quite obviously the Soviets view SDI as an attempt by the US to apply their powers of technological innovation, which are far in excess of the USSR's capabilities, in an effort to regain military-strategic superiority and thereby annul (to the Soviet Union's disadvantage) the principle of equality and equal security of the superpowers. This equality had been fought for with great effort by Moscow and was codified in 1972. Accordingly, a noticeable warming of the East-West climate is highly dependent on an agreement on the issue of space weaponry.

Gorbachev's endorsement of discrimination in detente initiatives must be placed in this context, i.e., of a line that can overcome Gromyko's one-sided fixation on the US and on activating relations with the West Europeans. During his visit to Great Britain (December 1984) he spoke of Europe as the "common home," implicitly picking up, by the way, on a similar utterance by Brezhnev during the latter's last stay in Bonn in 1981. As in the 1970s, Soviet leadership is not likely given to any illusions that it could succeed in detaching Western Europe from the US. Rather, the efforts seem designed to press West Europeans to voice their specific interests more emphatically vis-à-vis Washington. The USSR also hoped that West European economic power and technology might increasingly be enlisted for the envisaged modernization of the Soviet economy.

To be sure, none of this means that the new Soviet leadership will cease to cast its foreign and security policy into Marxist-Leninist ideological categories of a world historical struggle between capitalism/imperialism and socialism. Possibly the new beginnings of the Gorbachev course that had already emerged under Andropov are entirely tactical in nature, designed only to slow down US innovative dynamics in the armaments sector and to gain time to modernize the Soviet economy. In any event it is improbable that the Soviet Union, like the Chinese, could start concentrating its energy and resources chiefly on the civilian sector since this would undermine its claim to military strategic parity with the US.

Just possibly there is more to Gorbachev's security policy concept—namely the idea that in the nuclear age any aspiration to military superiority bears incalculable dangers for all mankind. Thus, it certainly is no coincidence that for some years the Soviets have referred to the offensive aim of "changing power relations to the advantage of socialism" but somewhat defensively moved "securing world peace" to the fore. Gorbachev's proposal to seek "sensible compromises" in East-West relationis and to strengthen "mutual understanding and trust" follows the same line. With the formulation that nowadays "no one can guarantee his own security to the detriment of the security of other states," he even seized upon a core element of Western security philosophy. Certainly, as the Soviet Union's spokesmen themselves frequently reproach the US, words must not be taken for deeds. Still, partially novel thought patterns are emerging here, and it is worth the West's while to test their substance.

Thus, the Soviet Union presents a picture of a superpower afflicted with domestic troubles, but one that has nevertheless been set into motion. Especially in the fields of domestic and economic policy, the future course is contested by "traditionalist" forces and "modernist" tendencies. The outcome is as yet quite uncertain and will be determined only in the medium-term.

New opportunities for Western policy might arise from this situation provided concrete possibilities are examined and misinterpretations are avoided. Thus, the "modernists" by no means qualify as reformers in the Western sense. They are instead efficiency-oriented technocrats pleading for structural changes and expanded participatory rights. Their view is exclusively toward improvement of the economic mechanism with no questioning of the Party's exclusive power to determine the country's basic course. The repression of dissidents and any opposition has probably even been stepped up since the Andropov-year, 1983. Gorbachev has called for ideological "vigilance and intransigence" towards foreign views alien to the Soviet Union. These steps are ample warning to Soviet citizens not to mistake endeavors to improve efficiency for increased tolerance of democracy and pluralist leanings. Seen from this angle the dispute on human rights will continue to be a central point at issue between East and West.

On the other hand, one must guard against speaking rashly of the Soviet Union's inevitable historic decline—even if the "modernists" should prove unable really to assert themselves. The USSR has undoubtedly reached certain limits, and its leadership has been aware of this since the end of the Brezhnev era. However, under the banner of Soviet patriotism, which is being propagated more vigorously again these days, the Kremlin has repeatedly managed to mobilize considerable resources. Therefore, even in case of a further decline or stagnation of economic growth, for some time the Soviet leadership would likely remain in a position to safeguard the USSR's internal stability and maintain its superpower status. All neighbors of the Soviet state, East and West, North and South, are well advised to adjust to such a perspective.

Part One

Domestic Politics

1
Secretaries General Come and Go

Heinz Brahm

Figurehead or Helmsman?

Within 28 months, the Soviet Union experienced four secretaries general. The USSR underwent no radical changes from Brezhnev to Andropov and from Andropov to Chernenko. This, however, is not to say that the Soviet Party leader is always a figurehead on the ship of state or that invisible forces keep the ship on a course predetermined since time immemorial. At the very least, both Andropov and Chernenko had a go at resetting the course of Soviet domestic and foreign policies in their own way.

If, for all that, only adjustments in the course and no fundamental changes were made, it was not only because of the advanced age of the secretaries general and the immobility caused by their illnesses. It also resulted from the ossified ideology of Marxism-Leninism and, not least, to the inertia of the central power-bureaucracy upon which a Party leader is dependent. After all, the Party apparatus has at its mercy any secretary general without widely acknowledged authority. Though Andropov tried to revamp this apparatus, the attempt obviously took him to the limits of his power. Because Brezhnev, Andropov, and Chernenko were often incapacitated by their physical ailments, the bureaucracy was able to usurp a large part of their authority. As it turned out, a secretary general's line was seemingly pursued unerringly even if he dropped out of sight for months on end. Throughout the thirteen months of Chernenko's tenure as secretary general, it appeared that the new Party leader had divested himself, or was forced to divest himself, of some of his power.

As a rule, a secretary general has considerable influence. Once elected secretary general by a majority of the Politburo, he can hope in time to expand his power base. As expressed by the title "secretary general," he is the ranking representative of the CC-Secretariat and thus of the entire Party apparatus. He is ex officio chairman of the Politburo and hence inevitably assumes the role of supreme coordinator. Since all strands of information converge in his outer offices, and chiefly in the CC's "General Department," his knowledge puts him ahead of all other Politburo members.

If in addition the CC secretary in charge of cadres is on his side, he enjoys a certain preponderance in the appointment and removal of top functionaries. This evidently causes the functionaries to adapt to the secretary general, the more so if they feel far from secure in their positions.

In practice, however, secretaries general have had to negotiate around more stumbling-blocks than suggested by this idealized description of their office. Since the early 1980s there has been a lack of broad consensus among the leadership; Brezhnev, Andropov, and Chernenko had to submit to the respective majorities. For understandable reasons, the younger functionaries are unlikely to have thought it advisable at all times to throw in their lot for better or for worse with an ailing secretary general.

Andropov at the Top

In May 1982, Brezhnev's personnel politics were dealt a severe blow when Andropov, supported by a faction including Defense Minister Ustinov and Foreign Minister Gromyko, returned to the CC-Secretariat, thereby disputing the succession of Chernenko's heir apparent. At the highest levels, displeasure with the Party leader's slack grip on the reins had probably grown by the end of his rule. Possibly Brezhnev was held more or less responsible for the failures of Soviet policy.

Since the late 1970s, the Soviet economy has experienced a distinct recession. In 1979 a series of poor harvests began. That year, the growth rate of the real gross national product amounted to a mere 0.7 percent compared to 4.3 percent in 1976. Sagging work morale, growing disinterest in the ideology, and potential discontent at supply bottlenecks were of concern to the innermost circle of power. The end of the Brezhnev era had left foreign policy in a shambles. The Soviet Union was embroiled in an undeclared war in Afghanistan. In Poland the Solidarnosz-movement with some ten million members had demonstrated to the Soviets how vulnerable the socialist camp was. Romania went its own way in foreign policy, Hungary in economics. Finally, East-West relations dangerously approached the freezing point. The Politburo perceived of NATO's modernization as a great challenge, possibly even a severe blow.

Those critical of Brezhnev's detente policy likely gained the upper hand at that time. Tighter reins were demanded not only in foreign policy, but in domestic politics as well. Brezhnev himself still initiated, or was forced to initiate, the turnabout to the harsher course, but his opponents felt he pursued it merely halfheartedly. Therefore, his antagonists set all their hopes on putting a man of their choice into the secretary general's seat. Their preferred candidate was Andropov. Thanks to his intelligence and verve, Andropov was to imbue the country with the stimulus urgently required to overcome stagnation. Chernenko, by contrast, was apparently expected to dawdle on as before, despite his definite attempts to contribute new ideas to the shaping of the Soviet Union.

When Brezhnev died on 10 November 1982, Andropov presumably became secretary general thanks only to massive pressure by Defense Minister

Ustinov. Rumor has it that Chernenko actually commanded a numerical majority in the Politburo.[1] The members of the CC who were to confirm the election of the new Party leader on 12 November might well have been displeased at the manner in which the decision had been made over their heads. Pursuant to the Statutes of the CPSU, it is the CC's right to "elect" the secretary general.

After Andropov had become the Party's leader, he took so firm a stand in public as to suggest he had the support of the entire Party leadership. Really, he probably just took the bull by the horns. Above all, it is unlikely that he was in full control of the central Party apparatus. At the CC session of 12 November 1982 Chernenko unabashedly reminded him of the need for a reliable organization (that is, the Party apparatus) to carry out his intentions.[2] Andropov even had to settle for an old fellow traveller of Chernenko, K. Bogolyubov of all people, assuming the chairmanship of the CC's General Department. Soon after Andropov's enthronement, functionaries in the Party apparatus and in the Council of Ministers were dismissed at a feverish pace, but it is not certain that Andropov was sufficiently familiar with the maze of personnel politics to succeed in filling the vacancies with "his people." Quite evidently the Chernenko group retained great influence in cadre politics.

The coalition including Ustinov and Gromyko, to which Andropov presumably owes his election as secretary general, was likely not without problems, either. In all probability, Andropov's motley crew really saw eye-to-eye on but few questions. Agreement was reached most readily on the need to attack rampant corruption at all levels and to raise working morale through draconian measures. The individual steps, however, were not fully thought through. Raids on shirkers in public transportation, department stores, pools, and at hair dressers, were soon discontinued when their devastating psychological effects were recognized.

Under Andropov, however, there was no consensus in the Politburo on more comprehensive economic measures. In November 1982, the new secretary general declared that there were no ready answers,[3] demonstrating, in essence, his helplessness. Unmistakably, Andropov was not prepared to make do with what had already been achieved in the economy. He restlessly pressed for increased efficiency, disavowed the complacency of earlier times and had nothing but cool irony for the Brezhnev era's slogans ("The economy must become economic"). But even his modest new beginnings were for the most part crushed mercilessly between the millstones of the apparatus.

Should Andropov have intended to revive the policy of detente to a certain extent, as was insinuated and for which there is some evidence, he might have had a hard time with Ustinov and Gromyko. The latter two probably did their bit to have the "walk-in-the-woods-formula" of P. Nitze and Yu. Kvitsinsky dropped. Under Andropov Gromyko gave the impression he was anything but a "dove" in the Kremlin towers.

A mere three months after his inauguration as secretary general, Andropov was put on a dialysis machine for kidney failure. In April 1983, there were rumors in Moscow that Andropov no longer commanded a majority in the Politburo.[4] At the CC plenary session postponed from March to June 1983, Chernenko was the first to take the floor. This was his debut as chief ideologist. His long-winded speech identified him as a dogmatist little different from M. Suslov, the Brezhnev-era's legendary keeper of the Holy Grail of Marxism-Leninism.[5] By 1983, Chernenko had quite evidently become a different man. He stood on preserving the purity of the old teaching.

Since his article in *Kommunist* of April 1982—at that time he was still Brezhnev's favored heir apparent—no "progressive" ideas had been heard from him. Back then, he had turned quite unexpectedly against functionaries who held that there was too much democracy in the Soviet Union.[6] Since spring 1982, he thus seems also to have been swept along by the changing trends in the Politburo. Andropov, who had become a CC secretary in May 1982, had probably already swung onto the harder line earlier. As R. Medvedev once put it, he supposedly was no longer fully supportive of Brezhnev's detente policy and only thus turned into an acceptable coalition partner for Defense Minister Ustinov.[7]

As of Spring 1982, no "soft" line could have stood a chance of success in the Politburo. After Chernenko had become CC Secretary in charge of ideology, presumably in November 1982, he headed a department composed of former members of Suslov's staff. Embedded in this team of dogmatists, even a reform-oriented politician would have had a hard time providing Marxism-Leninism with a modern outlook.

After 18 August 1983 Andropov, who for some time had impressed people he talked to as rather infirm, was no longer seen in public. Soviet functionaries quite seriously attributed his absence from the anniversary celebrations of the October Revolution to a cold. For several weeks "usually well-informed circles" in Moscow continued to announce Andropov's return to active politics without his ever reappearing.

Letters and documents published on Andropov's behalf were meant to keep up the impression of an indefatigably active secretary general. But Andropov probably died without ever fully regaining control of his powers. Now Chernenko's time had come. One of his faithful followers, A.I. Lukyanov, advanced to First Deputy Head of the General Department. Since Bogolyubov, the head of this department, already belonged to the Chernenko group, Andropov's influence could not have been very great at that time.

The plenary session of the CC in December 1984, which resolved major changes in the top leadership, took place without Andropov. M.S. Solomentsev (70), formerly prime minister of the RSFSR and chairman of the Party control committee since June 1983, as well as V.I. Vorotnikov (57), the RSFSR's new prime minister, were made full members. V.M. Chebrikov (60), chief of the KGB since December 1982, became a candidate member of the Politburo. Ye.K. Ligachev (63), who quite surprisingly had moved up from the office of first secretary of the Tomsk Regional Committee to head the CC Department for Party Organization in April 1983, was elevated to the rank of CC secretary. In the West, all four climbers were often styled Andropov's men, which is doubtful in the case of Solomentsev and Chebrikov.

It is also very much open to question whether Ligachev was merely a follower of the moribund Andropov or whether he selected the cadres more or less in agreement with the Chernenko group. In late 1983, there was a quiet purge of Party leaders in the provinces. Of the 159 first secretaries in the obkoms (districts) and kraykoms (regions), thirty-five were replaced under Andropov. This broke the personnel incrustation of the Brezhnev era, but there is no telling which reference persons in the Politburo are attributable to which new *obkom* Party leaders. Since a large number of functionaries had recently been relieved of their offices in the Party apparatus and the Council of Ministers as well, the startled leading cadres, bound to fear for their positions, might have viewed Chernenko as the savior from dire straits.

Chernenko and Gorbachev

Andropov died on 9 February 1984, naturally not of a cold. The medical bulletin published after his death lists various ailments, ranging from diabetes and kidney diseases to cardiac insufficiency. Already the next day, notice was given that Chernenko chaired the funeral commission. Hence, at that time, the selection of the new secretary general must presumably already have been decided on in the Politburo. Had G. Aliev, Solomentsev, and Vorotnikov, who had managed to enter the Politburo under Andrpov, really been Andropov's vassals, Chernenko's nomination would hardly have been conceivable, the more so given his great handicaps: He was more than seventy-two years old; as was alarmingly evident at the time, he was in very poor physical condition, and was so short of breath that he was barely able to read his speeches. On Brezhnev's death, just two days were allowed to pass before the next CC session. This time nearly four days elapsed. This time, then, there would have been ample time to inform the CC members more thoroughly about the succession and the distribution of power.

All his undeniable weaknesses notwithstanding, Chernenko was favored by the majority of the Politburo over the considerably younger Gorbachev. If Chernenko, as can be assumed, had performed the official functions during Andropov's long absence, this naturally made him winner by points. His age was not a drawback for many Politburo members, though his illness was. True, no secretary general so advanced in age had ever been appointed, but one must bear in mind that at seventy-two Chernenko was the youngest in the squad of top dignitaries at the time: Tikhonov was seventy-eight, Ustinov seventy-five, and Gromyko seventy-four. Henceforth this group of four had a row all to themselves in the notables' choir stalls at sessions of the Supreme Soviet—to protocol-conscious Soviet citizens, this was an indication of their outstanding position.

Thus, Defense Minister Ustinov likely abandoned the massive resistance he had mounted against Chernenko's election following the death of Brezhnev. If earlier he had differed on material grounds from Chernenko (for instance on armaments and detente), these differences had probably been cleared away in the meantime. Agreement must have been reached on a common line, meaning presumably that Chernenko had yielded. Surprisingly, Ustinov was the one to deliver the laudation in 1984 at Chernenko's seventy-third birthday.[8]

Gromyko, too, must have come to terms with Chernenko's election, though perhaps only while gritting his teeth. Under the new Party leader he could posture as the spokesman on foreign policy. He was often present when Chernenko received official foreign visitors, not seldom speaking more than he, indeed even interrupting him. He may well have contributed to V. Molotov's readmission to the party. If Gromyko's book *The Foreign Expansion of Capital* is any measure, he is a narrow-minded doctrinaire who simply views the world around him in the narrow categories of a petrified ideology.[9]

Chernenko was truly backed above all by Prime Minister Tikhonov. Furthermore, in the Politburo D.A. Kunayev, V.V. Shcherbitsky, and V.V. Grishin may have been more or less firmly committed to him, perhaps also Aliyev and Solomentsev. Gromyko claimed that Chernenko's election by the Politburo had been unanimous. Even if this had been the case, it is no reflection on the degree of support actually enjoyed by the new secretary general. There is some evidence to indicate that an influential group in the Party leadership would have preferred Gorbachev in Andropov's empty chair, not so much on account of his "youth" but rather because of his more radical program to raise economic efficiency. These young Turks were probably kept still by the appointment of Gorbachev to a position of something like a vice–secretary general, slated to move up immediately in the case of Chernenko's demise.

Many of the older functionaries most likely identified with Chernenko. For years he had been working at the image of a strict but just patron. There were good reasons, then, for Prime Minister Tikhonov to emphasize Chernenko's "benevolent attitude" towards the cadres when he nominated Chernenko at the CC plenary session of 14 February. As secretary general, however, Chernenko was sparing with promises to the cadres. Meanwhile he could no longer express only his own wishes, but had to accommodate the interests of the entire power elite. Above all Gorbachev and his followers put constant pressure on him. It was striking that following Andropov's death the collectivism of leadership was stressed more emphatically than before.

Apart from the secretary general, the Politburo's innermost circle also included Tikhonov, Ustinov, Gromyko, and Gorbachev. In light of Chernenko's evident physical weakness, interested parties in Moscow pointed to Gorbachev not only as second CC secretary, but unofficially also as Chernenko's probable successor. V.G. Afanasyev, editor-in-chief of *Pravda*, had already made less than reverent remarks about Chernenko after Andropov's election as secretary general. After February 1984, he twice pointed out Gorbachev to Western interlocutors in a way sure to catch their attention.

In April 1984, Afanasyev called him second CC secretary supervising the CC Secretariat. In September of that year, when Chernenko had again been absent for some time, he allegedly called Gorbachev the second secretary general.[10]

Not only was the collectivism of leadership particularly emphasized following Chernenko's assumption of office, but so was the continuity of policy. During his few months at the head of the Party, Andropov had managed to set firm bearings, but he was unable to alter in any way he wanted previous CC decisions or targets set by the last Party convention. In the final analysis, what might be termed the Andropov line was nothing but the resultant in the power parallelogram. After Brezhnev's death, all members of the Politburo had agreed on a route and not even Chernenko could simply deviate from it after becoming secretary general. All the new Party leader could do was to correct the course step by step, provided he had strong allies and sufficient time to consolidate his power.

Of course, the economic experiment in the selected five All Union and Republic ministries was continued, as was the quest for new economic methods—although less hectically and, above all, with less propaganda effort. Reading between the lines of prominent politicians' speeches delivered to the Supreme Soviet indicates that younger Politburo members and CC secretaries in particular were in favor of vigorously pursuing the course followed since Andropov to increase economic growth: Gorbachev, Romanov, Vorotnikov, Ligachev, N. Ryzhkov, and possibly V. Dolgikh. By contrast, according to some older top politicians like Tikhonov, D. Kunayev, V. Shcherbitsky, V. Kuznetsov, P. Demichev, and I. Kapitonov, the economic situation appeared satisfactory.[11] It would be far too easy, though, to classify the first group as "Andropovists" or even reformers. The frontlines cross-cutting the Soviet leadership probably shift from issue to issue. The assumption that Chernenko was a dyed-in-the-wool conservative apparatchik who would brook no alterations in the well-tested and proven would also be wrong. The opposite might have been the case. At least as Brezhnev's heir apparent, he displayed great readiness for new ideas. None other than he seems to have raised a protective hand over innovative experiments in Georgia, and especially over the experiments in Abasha and Poti.

In April 1984 Chernenko became president after Chief-of-Staff N. Ogarkov, of all people, had previously spread the word that the new secretary general was also chairman of the Defense Council. Formally, this gave Chernenko the same large number of offices as Brezhnev after 1977 and Andropov after June 1983, but by all evidence, far from the same power and much less authority than his two predecessors. From 15 July to 5 September Chernenko remained invisible, fuelling speculations as to his state of health. Since September 1984, extensive attempts had been made to counteract the impression of leaderlessness which could manifest itself even in the CPSU and its sister parties in socialist countries. On 4 September, East-German Party leader and head of state Honecker had to cancel his impending journey to the Federal Republic, in all likelihood at Moscow's behest. The next day Chernenko reappeared in public. On 6 September the dismissal of Chief-of-Staff Ogarkov and his replacement by S. Akhromeyev was announced. On 9 September Bulgarian head of state and Party leader T. Zhivkov cancelled his trip to the Federal Republic, after Gorbachev had objected to it during a visit to Sofia. On 10 September Moscow announced that Gromyko would meet with US President Reagan.

As at the CC plenary session of April, there were no personnel changes in the Politburo or the CC Secretariat at the October 1984 plenary session either. At the October session, a melioration program was introduced. That the November 1984 winter session of the Supreme Soviet was preceded by a session of the expanded Politburo rather than a CC session was also a deviation from the rule. This alteration may have ensued from the desire to decide the problems at hand in a more intimate circle. Probably, though, it was primarily the reflection of a stalemate within the leadership. It was possibly only Ustinov's death on 20 December 1984 that caused a break in the rigid front. As a career officer, the new Defense Minister, Marshal S. Sokolov, is probably closely associated with the military. The same could not necessarily be said of Ustinov, a civilian with a background in the armaments industry. There seems to have been a tug-of-war over the defense minister's successor months before Ustinov's death. In retrospect, the replacement of Ogarkov seems a gambit to prevent his advance to the head of the Defense Ministry. Sokolov's power falls far short of the authority Ustinov had. A mere candidate member of the Politburo, his direct influence in the leadership is not likely to be very great for the time being. At seventy-three, his prospects of expanding his power base are probably slim.

Since late 1984, Chernenko's state of health must have deteriorated greatly. On 7 February 1985, V.G. Afanasyev declared with unusual straightforwardness of Italian television that the secretary general was ill.[12] Presumably Gorbachev's followers must have been pressing for Chernenko's resignation, in turn causing his partisans to present Chernenko, barely able to stand up, on Soviet television.

Chernenko died on 10 February 1985. The very next day the CC appointed Gorbachev his successor, albeit not unanimously as was customary in the case of a secretary general, but "by common consensus." This indicates that the new secretary general had to overcome resistance. Gromyko's speech before the CC plenary session gave the same impression. He proposed Gorbachev's election so forcefully that one had to take it as wooing, or even as a threat directed at the undecided or reluctant. Gorbachev's first speeches following his election indicate his intention to pursue Andropov's economic policy.

As party leader, Ghernenko did not succeed in filling vacant spots in the Politburo. No sooner was Gorbachev elected than three men moved up into the Politburo. E. Ligachev and N. Ryzhkov, likely two of Gorbachev's allies, became full members—without having been candidate members. By contrast, the promotion of KGB chief Chebrikov, who had been a candidate member, had been expected.

The Apparatuses: Pillars of Power

The secretary general is but one factor in the confusingly complex network of the Soviet system of government. In so far as he wishes to travel new paths, he can do little all by himself. We know from the past that as a rule it takes considerable time before he is firmly in the saddle. To begin with, he must come to terms with the leadership staff taken over from his predecessor. Whether and to what extent he has the four large apparatuses (Party, government, military, and KGB) on his side is crucial to his assertive power.

As the secretary general has always been drawn from the Party's top level, the CC apparatus, he should make sure to have tremendous backing from the start. His power is the greater the more solidly the Party apparatus stands behind him. However, the unity of the CC Secretariat, and thus of the central Party apparatus, has been in a sorry state for some years. When Brezhnev died, there were at hand two aspirants to the office of secretary general: Andropov and Chernenko. Presumably both pretenders commanded their battalions in the Party apparatus, the latter apparently more than the former. There is enough evidence to deduce that Andropov cannot have been the favorite of the entire Party apparatus. No sooner was he elected than the Party apparatus came under attack.[13] That he was indeed dissatisfied with the top Party functionaries is evident because during his rule, seven out of twenty-four CC department heads were replaced, and some two dozen new deputy department heads were appointed. The regional Party apparatuses were similarly purged: 20 percent of *obkom* secretaries lost their offices.

After such drastic treatment, the Andropovists should, for all intents and purposes, have beaten the scattered remnants of Brezhnev's and Chernenko's troops hands down. Curiously, Chernenko's position grew stronger despite all turnabouts. There is no other explanation for his election as secretary general. Chernenko's followers and allies must have managed to fill at least some of the vacant positions with their people. It is assumed here that Gorbachev was assigned as Chernenko's deputy as early as February 1984. This indicates the persistent precariousness of power relations in the Soviet leadership.

When Chernenko headed the Party, cadre politics quieted down. Though the anti-corruption crusade was carried on, meticulous care was taken to avoid further affronts to Party functionaries whom Andropov had stirred up. Chernenko seemed willing again to act under Brezhnev's motto of "confidence in the cadres." He seemed convinced that functionaries could not be spurred to maximum effort by pressure and incessant control from above. Moreover, he proceeded on the assumption that without an apparatus upon which to rely, no changes of any consequence, much less reforms, can be realized. Under Andropov, nineteen of the eighty-six state committee chairmen and ministers in the government apparatus were replaced, under Chernenko there were eight by December 1984.[14] Some new appointments were necessitated by incumbents' deaths. But in many cases, members of the council of ministers were dismissed because they lacked efficiency or were corrupt. Even more than Andropov, Chernenko insisted on greater separation of Party and government duties. In a manner of speaking, the Party's job was to supervise government activities from above. It was not to be constantly bothered with inquiries; it was, rather, to keep its head clear to deliberate on fundamental matters of consequence.

The military and the KGB most certainly constitute important factors in Soviet decisionmaking, but we have little tangible knowledge about these two apparatuses. References in Western writings to Ustinov as Andropov's trailblazer might give objective observers the impression of immense influence exerted by military circles.[15] In point of fact, Ustinov, an esteemed member of the CC Secretariat and the Politburo of long standing, did in all likelihood cast his personal weight onto the scales at the election of Brezhnev's successor. Throughout the existence of the Soviet state, its leaders have felt permanently besieged. On the whole, the Politburo probably thinks very much in terms of military security. As far as can be determined, however, it is by no means hostage to the military-industrial complex. The military has specialized knowledge in its field, but is scarcely fully informed on actual political interrelationships.

Of all apparatuses, the KGB is the most difficult to learn about since by the very nature of things, it operates in secret.[16] For a Party leader, it serves as an early warning device, alerting him in good time to approaching dangers. After his overthrow, Khrushchev is said to have bitterly regretted dropping his protegé, I. Serov, as chief of the KGB and permitting unreliable customers like A. Shelepin and V. Semichastny to supervise the state security service.[17] As secretary general, Andropov was most certainly able to harness the KGB, which he knew from many years' experience, to his cart. Whether he was completely sure of the state security service is open to doubt. Chernenko had probably also managed an arrangement, at least with V. Chebrikov, chief of the KGB.

Unsolved Problems

If the Soviet Union's political, economic, and social rigidity is to give way to new dynamics, the ideology of Marxism-Leninism will first have to be subjected to a rejuvenating cure. The Herculean drive of the earlier revolutionary days has meanwhile abated. The vision of a world completely renewed had inspired the communists when they shouldered the tribulations of civil war and when they pressed on with collectivization and endured Stalinist terror. Today the Soviet Union is beyond its *Sturm-und-Drang* era. It has aged, and with it the ideology, which nevertheless is present and even very effective. This is so partially because decades of indoctrination have made it an integral part of large portions of the population and partially because it has fused with Soviet patriotism.

In the recent past there have been attempts to break out of the ghetto of Marxism-Leninism.[18] Some ideologists have recognized that even under socialism, antagonistic contradictions might arise, i.e., large-scale conflicts such as the ones in Hungary in 1956, in the CSSR in 1968, and in Poland in 1980–1981. Though certainly no sensational insight, this was a cautious approach to reality. But in 1984, the proponents of the theory of antagonistic contradications, whose patron may be said to have been Chernenko, had to strike sail. For a while it even seemed as if the Soviet Union was prepared to permit more outspoken discussion of questions, regarding the purpose of life, but the dogmatists soon throttled a reappraisal. It was generally ordained that the core of the "true teaching" would brook no revision. At the June 1983 plenary session of the CC, Chernenko declared: "But there are truths that are not subject to change, problems that have long since been solved, and unequivocally at that."[19] If this restrictive interpretation of Marxism-Leninism is retained, there can be but a recycling of well-known dogmas. Even when Gorbachev was placed in charge of the ideological sector in 1984, no inkling of greater flexibility was discernible. Meanwhile, a new Party program is in preparation which, compared to Khrushchev's, is to be marked mainly by greater matter-of-factness.

In their times, Lenin and his comrades-in-arms had hoped that the October Revolution would release such creative forces among the working people as to enable the Soviet Union before long to become the vanguard of progress. But sixty-eight years later, Moscow is still forced to admit that labor productivity in the USSR lags far behind that of leading "capitalist" industrialized countries.

Soviet leadership is clearly dissatisfied with the condition of their country's economy, but has thus far shied away from relentlessly exposing the causes for this unsatisfactory state of affairs. Insufficient progress, especially in the administration of state and economy, deficiencies of the planning mechanism, but also human shortcomings are blamed; never, however, the Party's monopoly of power. A reform worthy of its name would have to begin by considerably curtailing the CPSU's claim to infallibility. But if no discussion of the political system is permitted, the leaders can do little else but "improve" upon the execution of Party directives and try in any way it can to stimulate the population to increase productivity.

Steps were taken under Andropov to keep a closer watch on everyone not meeting standards of performance. The campaigns of intimidation and mobilization continued even after his death. Work collectives (above all plant managers) were called upon to maintain strict discipline.[20] What frequently passes for "reforms" in the West were actually mere repairs of a system of management whose engine, the Party, remained unchanged. Consequently, in the Soviet Union one refers only to "improvement" or "perfection" of the economy not to reform.

It is no coincidence that the "human factor" is mentioned so frequently in Soviet papers and periodicals. Time and again Party leadership embarks upon new attempts to raise the educational level of the population. This objective is also served by 1984 measures to improve schooling. These are also referred to *expressis verbis* as "reform," though it is doubtful whether they deserve this label.[21] The main point at issue is a more intensive career orientation, as well as greater civic consciousness and an enhanced sense of responsibility among the students. Years ago, even the highest ranks of the Party apparatus already seem to have become aware that they simply do not know enough about rank-and-file morale. For a while, sociology was not only believed capable of providing information about the population's activities, but also expected to proffer recommendations on how best to keep the citizenry in line. However, sociologists evidently proved to be of little use as the Party's helpmates.[22]

The Soviet Union, we are told, has more scientists than any other country in the world. Since it also claims the most progressive system of government, it is basically incomprehensible why it fails to tower scientifically and economically over all Western industrialized nations.[23] It is officially admitted that the translation into practice of scientific results is too slow. This is a result of the planned economy. To thus must, of course, be added that scientists cannot develop their ideas freely in an atmosphere of constant regimentation.

The West sometimes expects social forces outside the CPSU to provide initiatives for the country's rejuvenation. There is occasional talk of a religious renaissance in the Soviet Union. Indeed, there are numerous signs of remarkable religiosity. But even if there were two or three times as many faithful as there are CPSU members (there are over eighteen million of the latter), they are not a political factor. They are instead a nuisance factor which, to be sure, may still give the communists tremendous headaches.[24]

In the past it was frequently assumed that dissidents would exert strong pressure on political leadership. However, critics of the regime today are reduced to ineffectiveness.[25]

References in the West to necessary "reforms" in the Soviet Union ordinarily address only economic innovations and not a democratization of the country. This shows how little is expected of the Soviet leadership by now. But in a country like the Soviet Union which has long since stamped out hunger, progress should no longer be measured in terms of economic growth rates, but rather by the extent of civil liberties granted the population.

Notes

1. Brown, *The World Today,* No. 4, (1984), p. 137.
2. *Pr,* 13 November 1982.
3. *Pr,* 23 November 1982.
4. Tatu, M, 19 April 1983.
5. *Pr,* 15 June 1983.
6. K, No. 6 (1982), p. 41.
7. J. Kraft, *The New Yorker,* 31 January 1983, p. 106.
8. *Pr,* 28 September 1984.
9. Cf. H. Brahm, *Aktuelle Analysen des BIOst,* No. 31 (1984). Of course, one could assume also that Gromyko only struck such harsh tones to qualify as orthodox in the eyes of the ideological keepers of the Holy Grail.

10. *AFP*, 10 October 1984.

11. E. Teague, *RL*, 8 March 1984, p. 5.

12. NZZ, 8 February 1985.

13. Cf. Gyula Józsa, "The Party Apparatus Under Andropov and Chernenko," in this volume, Chapter 2.

14. Cf. Eberhard Schneider, "The Government Apparatus Under Andropov and Chernenko," in this volume, Chapter 3.

15. Cf. Peter Kruschin, "Military and Political Decisionmaking Processes," in this volume, Chapter 4.

16. On this see Astrid von Borcke, "The Role of the Secret Service," in this volume, Chapter 5.

17. R. Medvedev, *Index on Censorship*, No. 3 (1979), p. 6.

18. On this see Helmut Dahm, "Ideology as a Key to Politics," in this volume, Chapter 6.

19. *Pr*, 15 June 1983.

20. Cf. Bernd Knabe, "How to Mobilize the Soviet Working World: Discipline or Participation?" in this volume, Chapter 7.

21. On this see Oskar Anweiler and Friedrich Kuebart, "The New School Reform," in this volume, Chapter 8.

22. Thomas Kussmann, "Why Does the Party Need Sociologists and Psychologists?" in this volume, Chapter 9.

23. Arnold Buchholz, "Science and Technology," in this volume, Chapter 10. Cf. Ständiges Sekretariat für die Koordinierung der bundesgeförderten Osteuropaforschung, A. Buchholz (ed.), *Die Sowjetunion zwischen Systemerhaltung und Reform*, German-American conference, 21–23 June 1983.

24. Gerd Stricker, "Churches in the Soviet Union," in this volume, Chapter 11.

25. Peter Hübner, "Cultural Policy, Culture, Opposition," in this volume, Chapter 12.

2
The Party Apparatus Under Andropov and Chernenko

Gyula Józsa

The Party Apparatus Remains the System's Main Pillar of Power

As the epigraph for one of his works, Chernenko selected the following dictum by Lenin: "If we study the apparatus well and work at it for years, it will be a major achievement, the basis of our success."[1] Based on decades of work in the Party apparatus he knew how well this statement cuts to the quick of the system. He also knew that internal power struggles in the Soviet Union are won by those who are supported by or control the system's major pillar of power, the Party apparatus.

Chernenko's "failure" right after Brezhnev's death as well as his "success" following Andropov's death confirm this basic rule. Although we are not familiar with the details that regulated the succession after the death of Brezhnev, Andropov, and Chernenko, we can still surmise certain connection: The 1982 decision against Brezhnev's favorite, Chernenko, was reached without much attention paid to the regional Party apparatus. Faced with having to choose a successor in 1984, though, the Politburo apparently felt compelled to take into consideration the largest contingent in the CC, the regional representatives of the Party apparatus. This contingent had been stirred up by Andropov's disciplinary campaign. That Gorbachev's election as the new secretary general in March 1985 was not unanimous but merely "by common consent" (*yedinodushno*) might also be taken as an indication of some opposition to the current Party leader.

Few observers have called in question L. Shapiro's thesis that the communist Party apparatus embodies political power in a communist state.[2] To be sure, there were authors in the late 1960s and early 1970s who assumed that the ruling function of the Party apparatus would gradually turn into a coordinating, consultative-bureaucratic function—for instance in the sense of M. Weber's "rational" concept of bureaucracy. In 1972, J. Hough mentioned the declining share of Party functionaries in the Party's supreme elective and representative body, the CC, from 1956 to 1971. He said this was indicative of a development trend towards a certain "institutional pluralism" in the Soviet system.[3] Since 1971, however, the weight of the Party apparatus relative to other professional groups has not been declining, but has been increasing again.

The numerical preponderance of the Party apparatus in the CC proves that its interests take priority in the Soviet system's hierarchy of interests. This secures the Party apparatus's claim to leadership as much as it does its governing function, rephrased in Party writings as the "growing leadership role of the Party."

The hierarchic steps of the central (Politburo, Secretariat, CC departments) and the regional or local Party apparatus (in the Union republics, regions, territories, districts, cities etc.), where some 500,000 professional Party functionaries work, perform a dual function in the system: Relative to the hierarchically superior Party authorities, they are executive organs (instruments of rule); relative to lower Party authorities and the parallel bureaucracies, they are subordinated subjects. They perform their ruling function by controlling (by means of cadre politics in the context of the nomenklature system) the whole Party and state bureaucracy, by acting as channels of information inside the apparatus hierarchy (from top to bottom and vice versa), and by playing the most important role in the decisionmaking process. Even at the low level of the apparatus hierarchy, in the approximately 4,000 to 5,000 district committees, the Party apparatus has a firm grip on the parallel bureaucracies. Thus, appointments to some 600 to 700 official positions in a district fall within the jurisdiction of the district apparatus.[4]

In the context of the disciplinary campaign, Andropov and his followers did all they could to gain control of the Party apparatus. During Andropov's term in office, a certain trend towards "polycentrism of power at the expense of the partocracy" emerged when certain areas of public administration—chiefly those related to disciplining—moved notably to the fore: KGB, army, public prosecutor's office, etc., as well as Gromyko's Ministry of External Affairs. As shown by the outcome—surprising to many—of the way the succession was handled in February 1984, Andropov's brief tenure was insufficient to take the "fortress of the Party apparatus" by storm.

The Party Apparatus as Catalyst of Bureaucratic Bloating

"The Party leads, the state administers." Since Lenin's time, this principle has implied not only increasing bureaucratization of the system, but also a questioning of the relations between Party apparatus and parallel bureaucracies.[5] Only the decisive problem of relations between the Party apparatus on the one hand and the adminstration of the state and of the economy on the other will be referred to here. The topic is important because the system's tremendous bureaucratization, brought on by the Party apparatus, threatens gradually to limit the Party bureaucracy's hegemonial position and room for manoeuver. Thus it represents a major potential for crisis. On the other hand, it is the Party apparatus that initiates reform under certain circumstances.

As exemplified by Hungary, reforms within the framework of the system are possible only if the Party apparatus, in the interest of the political-ideological hegemony-position transfers decisionmaking power (for instance, to economic experts) for the benefit of economic and bureaucratic rationality. In Hungary this required a jolt to the 1956 system's very existence. So far, the Soviet Union has not experienced a similar crisis in the post-war period. Nevertheless, certain reforms (perhaps similar ones) cannot be ruled out even in the Soviet Union. However, this requires great and prolonged efforts since the resistance put up by established bureaucracies is all but insurmountable (as Khrushchev's fall demonstrates).

The swelling of Party and state bureaucracies has been a function of the mounting chaos about decisionmaking power, of corruption, of negative economic growth, and also of divisive tendencies in the Party apparatus. It was characteristic of the antecedents to the crisis situations in Hungary in 1956, in Czechoslovakia in 1968/69, and also in Poland in 1980. Apparently Chernenko, who was especially anxious about the events in Poland, had recognized the crisis-potential inherent in the expanding Soviet Party and state administration before many of his colleagues.

Both Andropov and Chernenko were aware of the problem of bloating bureaucratic apparatuses, and Gorbachev is also monitoring it with apprehension. The difference between Andropov's concept and Chernenko's was not in the goal of solving the problem somehow, but the methods and instruments of power to be applied: While Andropov made a bid for a certain rationalization within the framework of discipline from above, Chernenko seemed to want an inner renewal of the Party apparatus. That is, he wanted its voluntary return and self-restriction to the main functions of cadre politics and ideology. This would have amounted to a retreat from the economic-adminstrative area of operations and the transfer of responsibilities to the state, economic, and Soviet organs.

However contradictory and difficult this project, the hypothesis that Chernenko's concept bore greater potential for reform than Andropov's is plausible. Reforms within the bounds of the system are apt to succeed only with or through the Party apparatus, but not against it. Even then they can succeed only to the extent that reforms do not significantly restrict the Party bureaucracy's claim to leadership. Forced under the aegis of, say, the KGB or the army, "reforms" of the Party apparatus would tear the system apart. Either the Party bureaucracy, fearing for its "leading role," would nip such reform in the bud, or a crisis situation in domestic and foreign policy would result.

The claim to total control and the conception of a barter economy have resulted in a tendency to create for each task (branches of production, and locations of production) additional administrations and control agencies, even in the Party. But this, in turn, seems to have caused an almost incessant swelling of the Party bureaucracy. External symptoms of this process are the new departments created in the CC apparatus during the last years of Brezhnev's tenure and the creation of agricultural departments in the apparatuses of the Party's over 4,000 district committees. The latter were initiated in 1982 in connection with the food program. This means tens of thousands of new Party functionaries flooding into the Party apparatus.

If Parkinson's law is already disastrous in the Party apparatus, its effects are amplified due to the "catalyst function" of this very apparatus vis-à-vis the state and economic administrations it leads. The Council of Ministers' 1981 decree on the reduction of administrative personnel[6] was evidently unsuccessful. After Chernenko assumed office, remarkable data on the Soviet bureaucracy appeared in the Soviet press. According to these reports, 18.6 million Soviet citizens worked in state and economic administrations in 1984, 15.3 million of these in economic administration alone. That amounts to over 15 percent of the working population. This army of bureaucrats is employed by the 36 councils of ministers, the over 1,000 ministries and state committees, the over 51,700 executive committees of the regional and local soviets, the 44,600 production and scientific-production associations, the 21,600 *sovkhozes,* transportation, construction, trading, and service enterprises, as well as health and educational institutions, etc.[7] These data on the golem that is the Soviet bureaucracy apparently exclude the Party apparatus, army, KGB, border troops, police, the administration of union and *komsomol* organizations (and other social organizations) as well as the *kolkhozes*—on the average consisting of seventy to eighty people.[8] In 1982, M.I. Piskotin deplored the unnecessary bloating of the administrations of state and social organs, stating that 26.1 percent of all the gainfully employed worked in the "non productive sphere."[9]

Furthermore, after Chernenko assumed office, noteworthy facts came to light about the growth of the bureaucracy: The number of civil servants and public employees grew by three million between 1975 and 1980, with clerical and service staff accounting for a mere 3.8 percent. The State Committee for Construction Materials alone employed 160,000 "administrators" in 1984.[10] We are told that the huge avalanche of papers and documents is smothering economic activity (and agriculture, also)[11] and that personnel cutbacks at the lower levels are compensated for at the higher levels (or vice versa).[12]

Not coincidentally, those Soviet scientists—like B.P. Kurashvili—who expressly call for reforms do not propose ingenious economic indices, but instead a decentralization and rationalization of "production relations," i.e., of state and economic administrations.[13] In the face of a mounting labor shortage, both Kurashvili and Piskotin are well aware of where reserves of workers and generally the reserves for rational production and productivity increases are hidden.

The Party Apparatus Under Andropov

"The apparatus often turns into a veritable disaster. For it happens that instead of our leading it, it leads us." Shortly after Andropov's election as secretary general many Western observers—on hints from "highly placed

Soviet circles"—took this sentence by Lenin, quoted in a startling editorial in *Sovietskaya Rossiya*, as a cue to Andropov's budding reforms. As a result of expectations, in part "remote controlled" from Moscow, many Western media developed the ideal image of a new secretary general "addicted to reforms." He would put the encrusted bureaucratic apparatuses in order and after a lengthy period of stagnation, would introduce genuine reforms.

Only too readily forgotten was the simple experience from Soviet history that no newly elected secretary general ever begins his terms with reforms. Rather, he seeks before all else to fulfill his sponsors' mandate and bolster his own position. Projected changes or even reforms can be carried out only after the new secretary general has considerably tightened his grip on the apparatus.

Andropov's "sincere and responsible" sponsors (according to *Pravda*'s editor-in-chief V. Afanasyev), among them, Gromyko and Ustinov, gave him a mandate to establish discipline and order in the country. Indeed, he set out with great energy to fill this mandate. In the process he sought to consolidate his position, especially in the Party apparatus. By means of massive personnel reshuffles in the Party and government apparatus, he did his utmost to keep the "apparatus" from becoming his and his followers' "undoing," as Lenin had feared. Due to his brief period in office and perhaps also because he went at it too ruthlessly, he could not leave his successors a fully "domesticated" Party apparatus.

During his tenure, seven of the 23 CC departments ("superministries of the CC apparatus") received new department heads.[14] Thirty-five of the 159 regional and district secretaries ("provincial princes" or "prefects" of the regional Party apparatus), or over 20 percent, were dismissed.[15] The majority of them were demoted or retired. The cadre department of the CC (Department for Organizational and Party Work) was all but fully reshuffled under Andropov and was particularly active in provincial purges.

Of Brezhnev's aides and advisers who had enjoyed special patronage in 1981, Andropov retained only the specialist on Western policy, A.M. Aleksandrov-Agentov. A.I. Blatov, V.A. Golikov, G.E. Tsukanov, and the adviser Ye.M. Samoteykin, (who was made ambassador to Australia) disappeared from the scene.

China expert V.V. Sharapov, and later also A.I. Volsky (specialist on mechanical engineering) and P.P. Laptev (jurist) emerged as aides to the new secretary general. R. Medvedev, who announced with great fervor in the Western media that Andropov had "a firmly outlined program of economic and political reforms," also named B.G. Vladimirov as an aide to Andropov.[16] Under Chernenko, he became deputy department head in the CC Department for Science and Educational Institutions.

Three CC departments concerned with the economy were reorganized and renamed: The Department for Planning and Finances was newly designated "Department of the Economy," the department for "consumables and food industries" was renamed "Department for Consumables and Consumer Goods Industries," and the agriculture department was renamed "Department for Agriculture and Food Industries."[17]

In mid-1983, it became known that Chernenko had relinquished the direction of the General Department, and presumably had been forced to relinquish it. As confirmed by its current head, K.M. Bogolyubov,[18] this department, directly subordinate to the secretary general, is a key body in the CC apparatus. By all appearances it is even more important than the cadre department, especially in regard to control of the CC apparatus, and perhaps even of the KGB. Though Chernenko had to leave the "Secretariat of the Secretariat and the Politburo," his staff members Bogolyubov and the newly added first deputy, A.I. Lukyanov (who had been part of the circle of well-wishers around 70-year-old Chernenko as early as 1981), continued to represent his interests with verve.

Following Andropov's serious illness, Andropov people were no longer the only ones to have a hand in important personnel decisions. They had originally ignored the Party apparatus' calls for a "policy of confidence in the cadres,"[19] and then Chernenko's influence gradually grew to the point where he was able to assist several hard-pressed functionaries (e.g., in Moldavia).

N.N. Chetverikov's promotion to L.M. Zamyatin's first deputy in the Department for International Information showed that Andropov had started to hoist his proven men from the KGB into ranking positions in the CC apparatus. This operation also shows which side regarded the department that Chernenko saved[20] as a competing institution in need of control. As a KGB agent, N.N. Chetverikov had been expelled from France in 1983 together with forty-six other suspicious Soviet officials.[21] The extent of the turnover in the CC apparatus under Andropov is evidenced by the fact that aside from the seven new department heads, eight first deputies and eighteen new deputies were placed at the head of CC departments.

The Party Apparatus Under Chernenko

In his first statements following his election as secretary general Chernenko emphasized continuity. He also emphasized continuity in discipline. Pursuant to his underlying mandate, however, he also intimated that he would not treat the cadres as rudely as had his precedessor. During his brief tenure, the personnel carousel revolved rather more slowly than under Andropov. Personnel reshuffles in the Party apparatus did not exceed what might be termed "normal" in the event of a change at the top.

Following his first major appearances, Chernenko arranged for a meeting with the staff of the CC apparatus.[22] In a speech published only in part, he implored the Party's management as a "political organ to apply political means" (i.e., cadre politics) and to refrain from operative interference ("podmena") with the administration of state and economy. This was to prevent the "bureaucratic temptations" of the state apparatus from infecting the Party apparatus.

Chernenko apparently made a less radical sweep of the secretary general's assistants than his predecessor. Besides A.M. Aleksandrov-Agentov, he took over from Andropov's cabinet into his personal staff V.V. Sharapov, A.F. Volsky, and also P.P. Laptev. Next to V.V. Pribytkov, his coworker for many years, V.A. Pechenyev appeared at Chernenko's side. Possibly, V.G. Lomonosov was also part of Chernenko's staff.[23]

Under continuing reorganization and redistribution of responsibilities in the CC apparatus, the Department for Heavy Industry was renamed "Department for Heavy Industry and Energetics." V.I. Dolgikh, candidate member of the Politburo and CC secretary, turned over the direction of his department to his previous first deputy, I.P. Yastrebov. After Chernenko assumed office, two new first deputy heads of department appeared: Yu.N. Valov (CC business management) and G.Ye. Tsukanov. As for Brezhnev's long-term chief of cabinet, it is more appropriate to speak of a reappearance.[24] Under Chernenko, eight new deputy heads of departments were placed in the various departments, two of them (B.P. Utkin and D.A. Volkogonov)—probably as part of the efforts to control the army—in the political headquarters of army and navy.

In the regional Party apparatus, where Brezhnev's followers were particularly supportive of Chernenko, the personnel carousel slowed down, however, without coming to a stop. Shortly after the new secretary general took office, the first secretary of the Karelian district (I.I. Senkin) was dismissed. The regions and districts of Primorye, Aktyubinsk, Kara-Kalpak District, Kashkadar, Kzyl-Orda, Kokchetav, Syrdarya, Tashkent, Turgay, Rostov, Khmelnitsky, Chernovtsy, and Checheno-Ingushetia got new first secretaries.

Upon the death (possibly suicide) of the first secretary of Uzbekistan, S.R. Rashidov, it seems that a veritable purge was effected there—in part to prove the continuation of the disciplinary campaign. Apart from the regional secretaries, some fifteen municipal secretaries, several ministers, and hundreds of top functionaries are said to have been dismissed in 1984.[25] At the turn of 1984/1985, Kazakhstan was apparently swept by a similar wave of purges. D.A. Kunayev, Brezhnev's friend, managed to exert his influence—so far, at least—to the extent that his first secretaries overwhelmingly were not dismissed, but substituted for one another.

The Responsibilities of Some CC Secretaries

In 1983 I.V. Kapitonov lost the directorship of the cadre department to the new CC secretary E.A. Ligachev. Kapitonov now supervises the sector governing consumables and consumer goods industries.

There were also critical remarks about cadre politics prior to Andropov's time. For example, there were indications that national sensibilities had not been observed at all times[26] and that in the selection of cadres, the opinion of the lower Party organizations had been ignored. It cannot be ruled out that Kapitonov, who defended "the stability of cadres," had to surrender his authority because of a consensus among the main oligarchs. With such an important decision, however, the prime responsibility was probably the secretary general's. Unlike his colleagues from the Secretariat, Kapitonov did not belong to the funeral commission after Andropov's death. He made more frequent appearances during Chernenko's term. He attended protocol functions, usually ahead of M.V. Zimyanin, his fellow secretary, who, in spite of correct alphabetical order, had been listed ahead of him in early 1983. In February 1985, he was awarded the Lenin prize.

According to *Népszabadsag's* description of responsibilities on 19 January 1985, M.S. Gorbachev was "the CC secretary in charge of ideological questions" under Chernenko. This and other indicators from Moscow prior to his election as secretary general suggested that he had in effect been the Party's second-in-command even before Chernenko died. This assumption was corroborated by Gromyko's presentation of Gorbachev before the CC assembled for the election of the new secretary general.[27] It is relevant for Gorbachev's early period in office that he had been able to expand his decisive influence in cadre politics under Andropov. The deliberations in the CC that initiated the purges in the provinces were chaired by Gorbachev.[28] The failures in agriculture, which he had supervised for seven years, did no damage to the man from the ultimate Party apparatus.

In autumn 1984, when Chernenko energetically moved to the fore for the first time during his brief period in office, Gorbachev seemed to be taking a back seat. He failed to appear either at the plenary session on agriculture in October or at the expanded Politburo session at which the annual plan for 1985 was discussed. In November, Gorbachev was also absent from the joint sessions of the commissions of the two chambers of the Supreme Soviet for external affairs,[29] which he should have chaired ex officio if for no other reason.

Gorbachev's time came in February 1985, when Chernenko passed on. Whether Gorbachev will prove the "reformer" that East and West proclaim him to be is hard to determine at this point, and this hope for a reformer is based more on expectation than facts. If he wants to effect innovations, he must certainly first gain control of the Party apparatus.

The CC plenary session of 1 July 1985 supplied some information about this. For G.V. Romanov (born 1923), first Party secretary of the Leningrad region since September 1970, member of the Politburo since March 1976 (candidate member 1973–76), and secretary of the Central Committee since June 1983, was relieved of his duties in the CPSU's Muscovite governing bodies. Rumor has it that he left on his own request. Rumor also has it he wanted to retire because of his health. He had supervised the armaments industry and presumably been called from Leningrad to Moscow by the late Minister of Defense D.F. Ustinov. The 1984 promotion of G.V. Zakharov from Leningrad to first deputy head of the department for propaganda in Moscow was presumably effected with Romanov's help. The second man in the CC Secretariat worthy of special attention is V.I. Dolgikh from the Krasnoyarsk region. He was patronized by Brezhnev and Chernenko and has so far remained at his post. Dolgikh, who supervises heavy industry and energetics, relinquished the immediate direction of the corresponding

CC department in 1984. In the past, such measures (as in the case of F. Kulakov in 1978) have indicated that the respective CC secretary was earmarked for higher offices.

Notes

1. *PZh* No. 17 (1982), p. 10.
2. Cf. L. Schapiro, in W. Laqueur/L. Labedz, *The Future of Communist Society* (New York, 1962), p. 166.
3. J. Hough, *Problems of Communism*, No. 2 (1972), pp. 25–45.
4. *Sovetskaya Rossiya*, 7 September 1984.
5. Cf. Eberhard Schneider, "The Government Apparatus Under Andropov and Chernenko," in this volume, Chapter 3.
6. On this, see Bernd Knabe, *Berichte des BIOst*, No. 35 (1981), p. 12.
7. M.U. Klimko, *VIKPSS*, No. 11 (1984), p. 16.
8. *Nedelya*, 3–9 September 1984, p. 13.
9. *Sovetskoe gosudarstvo i pravo*, No. 9 (1982), p. 47.
10. *Iz*, 13 May 1984.
11. *Pr*, 26 December 1983 and 25 March 1984.
12. *Pr*, 31 March 1984.
13. *Sovetskoe gosudarstvo i pravo*, No. 6 (1982), pp. 38ff.; cf. also Hans-Hermann Höhmann, "Soviet Economic Reforms: Higher Achievement as a Result of New Premises?" in this volume, Chapter 18.
14. "Andropov Consolidates His Hold on the Central Committee Apparatus," *RL*, 339/83, 9 September 1983.
15. *Le Courrier des Pays de l'Est*, 282 (1984), p. 7; G. Józsa, in H.-J. Veen (ed.), *Wohin entwickelt sich die Sowjetunion?* (Melle, 1984), pp. 198ff.
16. *IHT*, 2 August 1983.
17. A. Rahr, *RS*, 114/83, 10 June 1983.
18. *PZ*, No. 21 (1984), p. 26.
19. V.V. Mikshin, *VIKPSS*, No. 1 (1983), pp. 105ff.
20. On this, see G. Józsa, *Aktuelle Analysen des BIOst*, No. 18 (1983), p. 4.
21. *L'Express*, 8 February 1985, p. 30; *FAZ*, 4 February 1985.
22. *Pr*, 7 March 1984.
23. A. Rahr, *RS*, 210/84, 2 October 1984, p. 2.
24. *M*, 20 March 1984.
25. *Posev*, No. 12 (1984), p. 10.
26. A.M. Korolev, in *Seriya Znanie*, No. 9 (1982), p. 12 and especially pp. 26–29.
27. *K*, No. 5 (1985), p. 6ff.
28. *Pr*, 30 August 1983.
29. *Pr*, 24 November 1984; *NZZ*, 5 December 1984.

3
The Government Apparatus Under Andropov and Chernenko

Eberhard Schneider

Towards the close of the Brezhnev era, the average age of the members of the Council of Ministers of the USSR was 64. Members of government averaged ten years in office. These two pieces of data suffice to indicate the Soviet government's dire need for new personnel. The first thrust in this direction was carried out by Andropov.

Under Andropov

Under Andropov (12 November 1982–10 February 1984), two first deputy chairmen as well as one deputy chairman of the Council of Ministers of the USSR, ten out of a total of sixty-four ministers, and nine out of twenty-two State Committee chairmen were newly appointed. It is to be borne in mind here that under Andropov the number of first deputy chairmen of the Council of Ministers of the USSR was raised from one to three: On 24 November 1982, G.A. Aliyev and on 24 March 1983, A.A. Gromyko, both Politburo members, were appointed to this position. The latter retained his function as foreign minister. At an international press conference in Moscow on 2 April 1983, Gromyko stressed that he would devote himself in his new function to the coordination of foreign policy activity, probably including the Soviet Union's foreign economic activities. Previously, the only Soviet foreign minister also to hold the office of first deputy head of government had been V.M. Molotov (from 1941–1946 and from 1953–1956).

Aliyev's appointment to the government position twelve days after Andropov's election as the new secretary general suggests that the former Azerbaijani Party leader (1969–1982) had already been earmarked for promotion to membership in the Politburo and the Presidium of the Council of Ministers under Brezhnev.[1] Aliyev had been among Brezhnev's proteges. During the reshuffles in the security apparatus initiated by Brezhnev with Andropov's appointment as chief of the KGB, Aliyev advanced from Deputy Chairman (1964–1967) to Chairman of the KGB in Azerbaijan. At the same time, Aliyev must have had good connections to Andropov, for Aliyev's appointment to the KGB chairmanship in Azerbaijan occurred subsequent to Andropov's assumption of the KGB chairmanship in Moscow in 1967. In addition, the new Politburo member Aliyev was appointed chairman of the Politburo commission in charge of developing a complex program for the service sector. It is a fair assumption that these questions fell within the purview of his government function as well.

Moreover, two new state committees were created under Andropov: one for foreign tourism in May 1983 by upgrading the INTOURIST central administration,[2] and one in July 1983 to supervise safety in the nuclear power industry.[3] The proposition by the Council of Ministers of the USSR to establish a state committee for the supervision of safety in the nuclear power industry had been approved by the Politburo a few days earlier. It was to increase "reliability and safety" of nuclear power plants. At the same Politburo session the Committee for Party Control at the CC of the CPSU and the Committee for Popular Control of the USSR reported on "gross breaches of state discipline by various ministries, offices, and their subsidiary organizations in the planning, construction and operation of industrial projects, and of social and cultural institutions in Volgodonsk." Those responsible for these breaches of discipline were said to have been severely punished.[4] According to Western sources the failure to observe construction regulations by "Atommash," the largest Soviet producer of nuclear power plants, has resulted in serious damage to Soviet nuclear power plants from frost.[5] At the same time, I.T. Novikov's retirement as chairman of the State Committee for Construction and as Deputy Chairman of the Council of Ministers of the USSR was made public. Six months later the Minister of Power Engineering, V.V. Krotov, was retired "at his request for health reasons." Early in 1984, B.Ye. Shcherbina took the retired Novikov's place as deputy chairman of the Council of Ministers. The failure of S.V. Bashilov, Novikov's successor as chairman of the State Committee for Construction, to advance to the Presidium of the Council of Ministers shows that membership in this supreme organ of the government is not so much tied to certain functions, but depends rather on the person's qualities. Furthermore, three of fifteen chairmen of Councils of Ministers of the Union republics, who ex officio are also members of the Council of Ministers of the USSR, were newly appointed (RSFSR: V.I. Vorotnikov; Byelorussian SSR: V.I. Brovikov; Estonian SSR: B.E. Saul). All told, twenty-five of 115 members of the Council of Ministers were replaced under Brezhnev's successor (21.7 percent).

Under Chernenko

Chernenko (13 December 1984–10 March 1985) appointed one deputy chairman of the Council of Ministers, eight ministers, two chairmen of state committees, and two chairmen of Union republic Councils of Ministers (Kazakh SSR: N.A. Nazarbayev; Uzbek SSR: G.Kh. Kadyrov), overall thirteen new members of the Council of Ministers of the USSR (11.3 percent).

In late September 1984, Ya.P. Ryabov replaced L.A. Kostandov, who had passed away unexpectedly, as deputy chairman of the Council of Ministers of the USSR. Therefore, he relinquished his chairmanship of the State Committee for Foreign Economic Relations which he had only assumed in late May 1983. The State Committee for Foreign Economic Relations handles Soviet construction projects in the CMEA countries and in addition is also responsible for armaments exports to the Third World.[6]

Quite obviously Andropov replaced more members of the Council of Ministers than Chernenko. The more thorough personnel refurbishment of the Council of Ministers of the USSR was part of the program with which Andropov started out. At the first regular plenary session of the CC following his election as Party leader, he called for a more determined "struggle against any breach of Party, state, and work discipline."[7] Similarly, in his speech immediately upon his election as secretary general, Chernenko emphasized that his "attention" was focused on "improving order and discipline."[8] Mismanagement and corruption in the Soviet Union had spread far too much during Brezhnev's last years for Chernenko to be able to abandon Andropov's disciplinary course. However, Chernenko favored a gentler approach. Addressing his first regular CC plenary session as Party leader, he referred to the cadres as the "golden reserves of Party and State," demanded "a clear and rational system unlike anywhere else in working with the cadres," and indirectly criticized Andropov by turning against "frequent replacement" of cadres.[9]

Reasons for the Departure of Members of the Council of Ministers

The new appointments were necessitated by the retirement of members of the Council of Ministers for reasons of age or health, the "assumption of a new function," or the death of a member of the Council of Ministers (Kostandov, Ustinov). Occasionally a new appointment to the top of a ministry or state committee was preceded by public criticism of the previous incumbent. Thus, in his speech at the CC plenary session of 22 November 1982, Andropov criticized the annual decline in the performance indices of the railroads, notwithstanding the government's "considerable assistance" to the Ministry of Railroads. A week later, the minister of railroads was dismissed. Continuing public criticism of deficiencies in transportation proves that personnel changes at the very top of a ministry do not always solve the problems.[10]

Minister of the Interior N.A. Shchelokov was particularly hard hit as he was not only dismissed as minister soon after Andropov's assumption of power but also expelled six months later from the CC for "permitting errors at work." Finally, on 6 November 1984 the Presidium of the Supreme Soviet of the USSR stripped Brezhnev's former intimate of his rank of army general for "abusing his official position and bringing discredit upon the military rank of a Soviet general." Rumors had connected the minister with embezzlement and abuse of state funds. His death (suicide?) in early December 1984 spared him criminal proceedings which may have been planned. The appointment of a new chairman of the State Committee for Work and Social Questions (Yu.P. Batalin) in April 1983 should probably also be looked at in the context of Andropov's struggle for improved work discipline. Moreover, the appointment of a new minister of Agricultural Construction early in December 1982 (V.D. Danilenko) likely resulted from Andropov's criticism of the organization of construction. On the other hand, the nominal reprimand of the ministers of Light Industries (N.N. Tarasov), of Mechanical Engineering for Consumables and Food Industries, and for Domestic Appliances (I.I. Pudkov), as well as of Chemical Industries (V.V. Listov) has not so far led to their dismissal.[11]

Social Background and Recruitment Patterns of the New Members of the Council of Ministers

Out of a total of thirty-eight new appointments to the Council of Ministers, which do not include a single woman, twenty-four are Russian nationals (63.1 percent), slightly fewer than under Brezhnev in 1981 (67.0 percent). All new members of the Council of Ministers are university graduates, nine have science degrees, and three hold doctorates in economics (Gromyko) or in applied sciences (G.D. Kolmogorov, Chairman of the State Commitee for Standardization, and minister of education S.G. Shcherbakov). Engineers form 68.4 percent of the new members of the Council of Ministers—compared to two-thirds under Brezhnev in 1981[12]—three of the new members studied history and two agricultural science. Only four attended a Party college. The new members of the Council of Ministers averaged fifty-seven years of age at the time of their appointment to government (fifty-four under Brezhnev in 1981). The average age of new members of the Presidium of the Council of Ministers on their appointment is higher, at sixty-four.

Of the new members of the Council of Ministers, 65.8 percent was recruited from the government apparatus (25), 26.3 percent (10) from the Party apparatus, and 7.9 percent (3) from other areas of organization (under Brezhnev in 1981, 62.9 percent from the government apparatus and 22.4 percent from the Party apparatus). Of the three members of the Council of Ministers responsible for the educational sector, the chairman of the State Committee for Vocational Education and the minister of education were replaced. Both organs of the Council of Ministers are concerned with implementing the school and educational reform first addressed by Andropov and Chernenko at the CC plenary session of mid-June 1983. The Party considers this school reform most important, as manifested by the appointment of two former central Party functionaries to head the two organs of the Council of Ministers.[13]

If all state functions, i.e., not just functions in the Council of Ministers, are taken together, then 71.1 percent (27) of the new members of the Council of Ministers came from the state sector and 28.9 percent (11) from the Party and Komsomol apparatus. Prior to their appointment, thirteen new members of the Council of Ministers had been first deputy ministers or first deputy chairmen of state committees, seven had been ministers or chairmen of state committees, and three deputy ministers or deputy chairmen of state committees.

The percent of the new members of the Council of Ministers were recruited from positions at the central level is 78.8, compared to 72.3 percent under Brezhnev in 1981 (excluding the chairmen of the Union republic councils of ministers). With but one exception, the members of the Council of Ministers recruited from the Party apparatus did not come from offices at the central level but from the Union republic, regional, and local level (Party organization of the City of Leningrad). All five new chairmen of the Union republic councils of ministers came from the Party apparatus.

What it all adds up to is this: A switch from Party apparatus to state apparatus occurs relatively seldom. When it does come to pass, it is usually from a lower hierarchical level. At the level of the Union republics, by contrast, it is an opportunity to achieve a ranking position at this hierarchic level and to gain experiences in the state apparatus, preparatory perhaps to the next career move to the apex of the Union republican Party organization. The relative frequency of self-recruitment (from the government apparatus) goes to show that membership in the government is not so much a matter of political office as of a position requiring special expertise. The recruitment patterns that prevailed in 1981 under Brezhnev have not changed under Andropov and Chernenko.

Some 42.1 percent (16) of the new members of the Council of Ministers are full members of the CC (66.1 percent under Brezhnev in 1981), three of them are Politburo members (Gromyko, Aliyev, Vorotnikov), and one is a candidate member (V.M. Chebrikov). One new member of the Council of Ministers is a candidate member of the CC and another a member of the Central Commission of Revision. The members of the Presidium and usually those new members of the Council of Ministers recruited for tasks in the government from the Party apparatus or those who previously held Party functions (Ryabov, Minister of Trade, G.I. Vashchenko, and P.A. Abrasimov, chairman of the State Committee for Foreign Tourism) are CC members. Only S.A. Afanasyev (Minister of Heavy and Transportation Engineering) and Chebrikov entered the CC by virtue of their state functions (as deputy chairman of the Council of Ministers of the RSFSR, and respectively as deputy chairman of the KBG). Following the appointments to the Council of Ministers of the USSR, there were no recruitments into the CC. Except for the Presidium of the Council of Ministers, CC membership of government members in charge of economic departments is not tied to a ministry or state committee. Remarkably, Minister of the Interior Fedorchuk, KGB chief from May to December 1982, to this very day does not belong to any Party body (neither as a member or candidate member of the CC nor as a member of the Central Auditing Commission).

Since the RSFSR does not have any Party organization of its own, the prime minister of the RSFSR functions in practice as the Party leader of the largest Union republic, as well. Vorotnikov became chairman of the Council of Ministers of the RSFSR, as well as candidate member of the Politburo, in June 1983 and full member of the Politburo in December 1983. From 1975 to 1979, he had already been the RSFSR's first deputy head of government but then had to go to Cuba for three years as ambassador. The reasons for this career setback are not known. The fifty-nine-year-old Vorotnikov belongs, like Gorbachev, to the group of prominent economic experts from the generation of fifty-to-sixty-year-olds who are gradually being admitted to the Politburo.

Chebrikov's appointment as chief of the KGB in December 1982 took place more or less routinely after the previous KGB chairman and Andropov's successor in that position, V.V. Fedorchuk, had become minister of the Interior. Chebrikov was a Brezhnev confidant in the KGB apparatus who, after fifteen years of collaboration with Andropov (1967–1982), seems to have won the confidence of Brezhnev's successor also. Under him Chebrikov was head of the KGB cadre administration (1967–1968), deputy (1968–1972), and finally first deputy chief of the KGB (1982). But for the time being, he became a candidate member of the Politburo in late December 1983, to rise to full Politburo membership under Gorbachev in late April 1985. Moreover, he was promoted to army general in November 1983 and awarded the marshal's star accorded this rank in April 1984. In May 1984 the possibility of also awarding the KGB chief the title of generalissimo was even created. Although Chebrikov himself was not promoted to marshal or to generalissimo either, the fact that the KGB's highest ranks became the same as the army's testifies to the expanded influence of the KGB.[14]

Andropov appointed but few proteges to the Council of Ministers, not to mention that—as opposed to Brezhnev—he has at his disposal but a small number of followers. Aliyev, Fedorchuk, and Vorotnikov are among those new members of the Council of Ministers identifiable with some degree of certainty as Andropov's men. Aliyev had a good relationship with Brezhnev, as well.

Chebrikov and Sokolov were Brezhnev's proteges. F.A. Afanasyev and M.A. Sergeychik (chairman of the State Committee for Foreign Economic Relations) were sponsored by Ustinov. It is fair to assume that under Andropov patronage relations, whether with the late Brezhnev, Andropov, or his rival Chernenko, were of little consequence in the selection of new government members. Under Chernenko, Romanov's favorites, Yu. F. Solovyov and S.L. Sokolov, became minister for industrial construction and minister of defense.

As first deputy commander in chief (1964–1965) and as commanding officer of the troops in the Leningrad military district (1965–1967), the new Minister of Defense Sokolov must have had dealings with Romanov who, from 1963 to 1970 was second secretary of the Leningrad Regional Party Committee. That Romanov would become defense minister was not to be expected since that would have required him to give up his position as CC secretary and hence his candidature for Chernenko's succession. In

1976, Brezhnev had already had trouble gaining the military's acceptance of his appointment of the armaments expert but non-soldier Ustinov as minister of defense. Given the military's strong influence in Moscow, it was a fair assumption that following Ustinov's death a professional soldier would head the defense department. The choice of seventy-three-year-old Marshal Sokolov from the First Deputy Ministers of Defense is probably to be seen as an interim solution. Marshal S.F. Akhromeyev, moved to the top of the general staff only in September to succeed N.V. Ogarkov. The latter, to everyone's surprise, had been dismissed. Because of this, Akhromeyev could probably be ruled out as Ustinov's successor. However, another of Ustinov's first deputies would be conceivable as the new minister of defense: Marshal V.G. Kulikov, age sixty-three, commander-in-chief of the Warsaw Pact troops and previously chief of staff.

Party-Government Relations

Both Andropov and Chernenko advocated a clear separation of state and Party functions. At the CC plenary session of June 1983, Andropov deplored that it was "not always" possible to prevent state and Party from doing parallel work, "often leading to a decline in the responsibility of heads of state organs" and to "endeavors to pass this on to the Party organs." In the Party organs, this "could not but give rise to thinking along departmental lines."[15] Immediately following his election as secretary general in mid-February 1984, Chernenko criticized the fact that the "staffs of Soviets, ministries, and plants frequently display a lack of the requisite independence and pass questions, which they should answer by themselves, on to the Party." This not only paralyzed the effectiveness of the cadres but also bore the "danger of weakening the role of the Party committee as an organ of political leadership."[16]

Andropov and Chernenko continued Brezhnev's efforts towards stricter separation of state and Party functions. The Party was to wield political, not administrative, leadership. Reporting on the 1984 Party elections, *Pravda* championed a "clear delineation of the functions of Party committees and state organs."[17] The Party committees were called upon to raise the "effectiveness of political leadership by state and social organizations."

In October 1984, the chairman of the Party Control Committee, Politburo Member M.S. Solomentsev, reminded the Party committees in the ministries that by Party statute they are called upon to control the work of the apparatus relative to the realization of Party and government directives.[18] *Party Control of Administrative Activity*, published in Moscow in 1983, says that the Party organizations in ministries and government offices have "perfected" forms and methods of controlling the apparatus.[19]

Occasionally the Party committee of a ministry is criticized. Thus, in October 1983, a decision by the Central Committee reprimanded the Party committee of the Ministry of Railroads for its complete failure to exert "control over the activity of the apparatus relative to carrying out Party and government directives."[20] On the whole it is fair to say that along with the greater separation of Party and government functions, with the emphasis on the CPSU's claim to political leadership, control of the Party over government activities has been intensified.

Discussion on Reform of the Council of Ministers

There is much evidence that the necessity of reforming the Council of Ministers has been recognized in the Soviet Union and that this was discussed increasingly under Chernenko. Thus, in his address to the CC plenary session of mid-Februray 1984, Chernenko went beyond his predecessor Andropov in stating that the "system of economic management" and the "entire economic mechanism" required a "thorough restructuring."[21] Even more specific was Minister of Electronic Industry, A.I. Shokin's lament that those ministries in charge of a branch of the economy were "too narrowly specialized."[22]

In April 1984, I.O. Bisher continued a series of essays (primarily from 1982) pleading for a reorganization of the system of ministries.[23] The reason why Bisher believes a reorganization of the Council of Ministers to be necessary is that the sectors that manage a ministry are administrative sectors not corresponding to branches and sectors in the economy. Virtually no economic problem could be solved by a branch ministry if the ministry was too specialized. Consequently, these questions would have to be decided at the government level.

According to Bisher, the main tasks of a ministry also include safeguarding the interests of the state as a whole. To this end the ministry must be freed from functions of operative economic organization. Indeed, several ministries today are little more than businesses. In the course of a reorganization they could be transformed into industrial, construction, transport or other associations.

Summary and Prospects

During his 15 months in office Andropov replaced one-fifth of all members of government, Chernenko only one-tenth in nearly the same length of time as Party leader. Social background and recruitment patterns of new members of the Council of Ministers under Andropov and Chernenko resembled those under Brezhnev. Andropov and Chernenko continued Brezhnev's efforts towards a clearer separation of Party and state functions. This was also reflected in personnel terms by the lower percentage of Party functionaries appointed to the Council of Ministers. The necessity for a reform of the Council of Ministers was discussed extensively under Brezhnev's successors.

The new Party leader Gorbachev has called for the creation of an economic mechanism corresponding to the requirements of developed socialism. He has championed a restructuring of the system of cadre training because of the higher demands placed on the cadres by scientific-technical progress. He will presumably continue to restaff the Council of Ministers, and to a far more drastic extent than Andropov did.

Notes

1. *The Christian Science Monitor*, 31 December 1982.
2. *VVS SSSR*, No. 22 (1983), Pos. 343.
3. *VVS SSSR*, No. 30 (1983), Pos. 467.
4. *Pr*, 16 July 1983.
5. *AFP*, 30 December 1983.
6. FAZ, 29 September 1984.
7. *Pr*, 23 November 1982.
8. *Pr*, 14 February 1984.
9. *Pr*, 11 April 1984.
10. *Pr*, 23 November 1982, 14 October 1983, and 3 August 1984. Cf. Gertraud Seidenstecher, *Berichte des BIOst*, Nos. 59 and 60 (1984), as well as "Economic Growth and Transportation: Stop at the Performance Limit," in this volume, Chapter 15.
11. *Pr*, 7 May 1983 and 21 January 1984.
12. Cf. Eberhard Schneider, *Berichte des BIOst*, No. 11 (1983).
13. On this cf. Oskar Anweiler and Friedrich Kuebart, "The New School Reform," in this volume, Chapter 8.
14. *Pr*, 5 November 1983 and 20 April 1984; *FAZ*, 28 May 1984. On this cf. Astrid von Borcke, "The Role of the Secret Service," in this volume, Chapter 5.
15. *Pr*, 16 June 1983.
16. *Pr*, 14 February 1984.
17. *Pr*, 18 March 1984.
18. K, No. 15 (1984), pp. 26ff.
19. *Partiynyi kontrol' deyatel' nosti administratsii* (Moscow 1983), pp. 283–300.
20. *Pr*, 14 October 1983.
21. *Pr*, 14 February 1984.
22. *Pr*, 27 May 1984.
23. *Sovetskoe gosudarstvo i pravo*, No. 4 (1984), pp. 27–34.

4
Military and Political Decisionmaking Processes

Peter Kruschin

In the closing months of the Brezhnev era, and even more so in the period following it, the Western press speculated more and more frequently about a growing role of the military in the Soviet leadership's decisionmaking processes. For the most part this thesis rested on rather weak arguments; nevertheless it has found its adherents.

Is it really true that the USSR's military (that is to say, not individuals from the ranks of the military, but the military as a sector of society) has begun to exert an ever-increasing influence on domestic and foreign policy? And if so, what does this influence consist of, and where does it lead to? Justifiably, these questions continue to occupy the experts. For it seems to many that, in the long run, the answer implies even more threatening perspectives on the problems of peace and a viable way to approach detente. In an attempt to clarify this question, an authentic anecdote from the days of Stalin is recounted here.

In 1933, the Ukraine was struck by famine. It was brought on because the state collected the farmers' grain—seed and all—as a levy. The republic's entire Party leadership was assembled in Kharkov, then capital of the Ukraine, to discuss the resulting situation. In view of the catastrophic food shortages and the increasingly critical famine, the secretary of the Regional Committee, N.N. Demchenko; the secretary of the Regional Committee Dnepropetrovsk, M.M. Khatayevich; and the commander in chief of the troops of the Ukrainian military district (who was also a member of the Politburo of the CC), I.E. Yakir, proposed at this forum that the Kremlin be asked to take countermeasures. Further grain collections by the state were to be discontinued and the stores of seed to be returned to the regions from which they had been removed. Moreover, aid was to be extended to the people in the areas worst hit by the famine. The Party's supreme leadership in the Ukraine, however, did not approve this proposal. Consequently, a troika convened after the session together with the secretary of the Regional Committee, Veger, and Yakir's adjutant in the Ukrainian military district, Ivan N. Dubovoy, dispatched an appropriate letter to Moscow. This letter was not without a certain effect. However, Voroshilov later told Yakir that Stalin had been most dissatisfied by the participation of the military and had allegedly remarked: "They are not part of the cooperation; the military should take care of its own tasks and not pass judgement on matters of no concern to it."[1]

In 1937 Yakir and Dubovoy were swept away by the very first wave of repression Stalin unleashed on the military, and who is to say that the main reason was not that they had once dared to "pass judgement on matters of no concern to them." Circumstances have certainly changed since Stalin's time, but it still seems that to this very day the apparatus adheres rigidly to the principle of not sharing political power with anyone. The military is permitted to participate in politics only within the bounds of "their own affairs."

The Military and the Economy

The assumption of growing military influence on the central power's decisionmaking is frequently derived from the fact that the army seems to play an ever more important part in the country's economic life. Reference is made, for instance, to railroad troops participating in the construction of the BAM, to military personnel transporting grain in summer and fall, and to construction soldiers assisting in civilian home building and the erection of industrial projects.

On the other hand, it can be argued that there is nothing new about the use of the army in the country's economic life. Throughout Soviet history railroad troops, for example, have been mobilized for the reconstruction of destroyed rail lines and the laying of new lines, as well as for the erection of large bridges. Red Army soldiers took part in the construction of the first big hydroelectric plant near Dnepropetrovsk. The soldiers of the Red Army and the sailors of the Red Fleet participated in the building of a new town in the Far East—Komsomolsk-na-Amure. Many such examples can be cited. To be sure, the massive use of construction soldiers in the civilian sector only dates back to Khrushchev, and that of military equipment operators in harvesting the crops only to Brezhnev; still, neither example can be presented as innovative. It is generally fair to assume that the participation of the army in the country's economic life has not brought on an automatic increase of its influence on central politics. All it does is characterize the economic weakness of the system as a whole. In return, the army has received only moral recognition (awards, praise in the press) as well as material pay (contractually stipulated), but no political returns.

A particularly important part of the problem—a problem recently of growing significance—concerns the course of the whole nation "towards further strengthening of the economic and defensive might" of the Soviet Union. For the time being this course has not been clearly articulated in published resolutions, but is the focal point of numerous speeches by ranking Party functionaries. And it has also found expression in declarations by Party leader M.S. Gorbachev and in the measures he has announced.

It is difficult to say which side has taken the more vigorous initiative towards this end: The exigencies of political strategy and of military as well as of economic strategy converge on this issue. Presumably, then, the political leadership as a whole is involved. Still, an urgent military interest in these matters is obvious.

Given such military interests and initiatives, then Minister of Defense D.F. Ustinov, who died in December 1984, evidently played an important part for a long time. In charge of the armaments industry for many years, he was considered very knowledgeable on the economic situation in general. The same applies to Marshal N.V. Ogarkov, who is a determined opponent of the routine and a shrewd reorganizer of the armed forces. As yet, little can be said with any accuracy about the attitude of the new chief of staff, Marshal S.F. Akhromeyev. He has had no opportunity to openly express his personal views since Ogarkov's dismissal in September 1984. Nor do we know of any important decisions he has made. But it is fair to assume that he shares Ogarkov's views after five years as his first deputy. Following Ustinov's death, Marshal S.L. Sokolov assumed the office of minister of defense. However, he does not command Ustinov's authority by far, and at seventy-three he is apt to be an interim solution.

Influence on Decrees

One way of examining the military's role here is by questioning the extent of its influence on state decrees. But this approach is not overly productive. The majority of these decisions remains a well-kept secret with only some repercussions in practical politics. Such was the case, for example, with the purge of the MVD apparatus where corruption was uncovered throughout the ministry. Published decisions proffer no unequivocal answer to the question at hand. For instance, the decree passed on 23 October 1984 by the CC of the CPSU on a long-term program of agricultural melioration scarcely points to specific military interests. In this case, the interest is the state's in general: Will this measure really bring on a consistent increase in food production, or will it all end with futile expenditures and additional damages to the environment?

The passage of the new decree on school reform of April 1984 is a different matter.[2] Though this was also aimed at solving a nation-wide problem, namely more adequate preparation of adolescents to meet the needs of the economy, military interests undeniably also found their way into this reform. The Ministry of Defense is undoubtedly interested in the largest possible number of young draftees who are well prepared in technical matters and have participated in military games. Finally, there are a number of decrees in which the Ministry of Defense likely played an influential role. Most important among these is the supplement to the USSR's law "on universal compulsory military service" that took effect on 1 January 1982 and deprived students at most universities and technical schools of the opportunity to be exempted from military service for the duration of their studies.[3] This measure, it seems, had to be taken in reaction to the demographic trend of declining numbers of adolescents subject to the draft. In 1984, the number of institutes of higher learning whose students could defer their military service was further curtailed. Even such privileged institutions as the University of Moscow and, it seems, the state universities of the Union republics are affected.

Of the other decrees which, in all likelihood, were initiated by the Ministry of Defense, let us single out the ordinance by the Presidium of the Supreme Soviet of 13 August 1984 (in force as of 1 May 1985). According to this ordinance, "Heroes of the Soviet Union" and holders of the medal of honor in all three grades are exempt from all taxes. Let us also point to the official proclamation of the same date which provided for increases in the pensions of temporary soldiers and their families.[4] Neither decree is of great significance, though, since direct taxes in the Soviet Union are relatively low and increases of pensions for members of the military are not considerable.

Generally, one gains the impression that the decrees of a military character passed over the past two to three years are drowned quantitatively by the large number of resolutions passed at the same time to solve the agricultural crisis, and—in the context of the disciplinary campaign—to fight speculation, corruption, and abuse of office. It ought to be mentioned here that many of the last-mentioned resolutions also involve the armed forces, where many of the same grievances exist as in the civilian sector. These also affect senior officers (commander in chief of the air force of the forces' northern group, Lieutenant General of the Air Force B.P. Barmin, and commander in chief of logistics of the Baltic fleet, Vice-Admiral P.B. Belous).[5] On the other hand, the relative paucity of resolutions from the military sector can by no means be interpreted as an indication of declining military influence on politics. The more appropriate conclusion seems to be that its influence has remained constant and becomes noticeable only to the extent to which certain problems demand that the country's military potential be kept at a certain level or be increased.

The Military's Internal Problems

As can be learned from A. Gurov's comprehensive article, "The Economic Thinking of the Officer" published in *Krasnaya zvezda* 5 December 1984, the material and financial resources directly employed by the military are about to be cut. This cut signals that in all areas of the armed forces, "the conditions for a genuine thrift regime" must be created. The number of exercises committing military technology will be reduced, and measures are being taken to stretch the lifespan of weapons and equipment.[6] This last circumstance suggests that the modernization of current models of combat and military technology will drag along, thus causing this problem: Decisions designed to enhance military power as a whole will prove detrimental to specific current interests in the military sector.

In this context it is necessary to analyze somewhat more closely the term "military," with regards to interests and influence. Take Ustinov, for example: Initially he pleaded the military interests of his portfolio to the political powers; but as a long-term member of the Politburo of the CPSU and thus simultaneously as a representative of this power, he was involved in the solution of problems concerning the whole nation. In this case his contribution to certain decisions cannot be regarded as participation "by the military." By contrast, not being a Politburo member, Sokolov could represent the specific interests of the military more singlemindedly. The chief of the general staff plays a different role. It is his job to thoroughly analyze the respective military-political situation, to observe developmental tendencies in military technology, and to work for their translation into practice. Furthermore, he organizes the preparation of the armed forces for war and their assured combat readiness. He coordinates the major staffs of the armed forces, the staff of the communications zone, the civil defense staff, the main and central administrations of the Ministry of Defense, the staffs of the military districts, the groups of the armed forces, and the districts of aerial defense and fleets.[7] In this sense the general staff is the primary link of the armed forces and as such can be viewed as expressing the will of the entire "military."

Naturally, by way of qualification one ought to note that within the military sector conflicts probably are far from absent. It is a fair assumption that the individual components of the military apparatus harbor special interests, and the general staff probably does not always succeed in satisfying them. For instance, it is common knowledge that as a young and modern branch, the missile forces are best provided for in terms of living conditions. By contrasts, the land forces still have to make do with their old barracks funds (*kazarmennyi fond*), and the construction troops and the civil defense troops are likely less privileged yet. But matters apparently do not come to open disputes between service types and branches; at least there is no evidence to that effect. However, there are various indications that armed forces personnel treat members of the militia with a certain contempt. Despite an ordinance by the Ministry of Defense requiring all army and navy men to salute superior and ordinary members of the militia, as well as the troops and organs of the MVD, army and navy officers try "not to notice" militia officers, a fact also pointed out by the military press.[8]

How does the military assess the overall situation of the country? Extensive speculation is hardly required to reach the conclusion that shortages of consumer goods, food, fuels, spare parts, and building materials meet with its disapproval. And this applies not only to the personal arena, but to the official one, too. This is exemplified by the so-called "food program" adopted by the CC in May 1982, that is, when Brezhnev was still alive. In principle, the military should have welcomed this program for it promised to supplement the strategic food reserves as well as a good lunch for the soldiers. In practice, however, it meant that the armed forces found they were compelled to supply themselves with 50 percent of their meat and vegetables. These were to come from second economies to be set up by each unit and each military institution. Some individual commanders may have discovered this as a source of personal gain. But the majority of the commanders responded to the ordinance with a boycott for it assigned them an additional responsibility for the effectiveness of the second economies. The central administration for combat training also balked at the second economies. Working for agricultural output keeps a significant portion of personnel from fulfilling their immediate military duties. Compared to 1982 and 1983, the second economies are barely mentioned in the military press today. They obviously failed the test. Quite possibly, the currently proclaimed objective of strict thrift in the armed forces will provoke a similar counterreaction.

There are other issues which do not exactly contribute to the military's satisfaction. For instance, commanders are expected to assume responsibility for the living conditions of their subordinates, for well-furnished little military towns and barracks. Yet additional funds and building materials are not supplied toward this end. At the same time, however, qualifications of the officers are judged by their ability to manage carefully and thriftily. Thus, commanders feel compelled to send their soldiers and sergeants off to "itinerant trades," to work in civilian institutions and enterprises, as a way of procuring building materials, tools, and even funds. But if this becomes too obvious, such a commander may be tried, expelled from the army, and demoted.

Another problem is of a demographic nature. Nowadays, more and more youths from the border republics are joining the army. Many recruits have no command of Russian at all, or only an insufficient command, causing great difficulties for group, platoon, and company leaders who are forced to organize unscheduled Russian classes. Instructions to improve Russian classes prior to military service are apparently also given to the leadership in the republics. However, due to a growing influx of Central Asians and North Kaukasians into the officer corps, new problems are to be expected. As pointed out earlier, sergeants from Central Asia overlook disciplinary violations by soldiers who are compatriots.

The Military and the Political Leadership

The developments described here, however, do not justify the conclusion that the foreseeable future will witness a conflict between the country's political and military leadership. This would not apply either, even if the measures currently undertaken by the leadership to overcome acute crises failed to produce the desired results. Two reasons in particular lead to this conclusion: In case of a conflict, there must be arrangements for horizontal and vertical connections among military leaders, with which the regime cannot interfere. And such connections simply do not exist. The armed forces are riddled with the regime's multi-layered control mechanisms: with the political mechanisms of the army and navy, with the so-called special departments (of the KGB), with supervision by the state prosector's office, and not least with voluntary informers. In an army devoid of specific traditions and of a sense of belonging to a caste, these controls function flawlessly. The second reason is even more prosaic: Like the overwhelming majority of Soviet citizens, the military is downright hypnotized by the notion that "Soviet power is stable. It will outlast us, our grandchildren, and our great-grandchildren. One must co-exist with it." Perhaps this attitude is caused by fatigue, perhaps also by a lack of political consciousness.

One last question: Is the political leadership, or are individual members, seeking the support of the military? Of course they are. This applies less to the leadership in its entirety (which is sure of the military's loyalty) than to some individual members. For such a case two instances of military men playing a decisive part are still fresh in memory: the deposition of Beriya in 1953, and the elimination of the so-called "anti-Party group" (Malenkov, Bulganin, Molotov, Kaganovich, et al.) in 1957 by Khrushchev. Whether and in what way the new secretary general will seek the personal support of the military cannot yet be determined.

Notes

1. Komandarm Yakir. *Vospominaniya druzey i soratnikov* (Moscow 1963), pp. 111–112.
2. On this cf. Oskar Anweiler and Friedrich Kuebart, "The New School Reform," in this volume, Chapter 8.
3. *VVSSSR*, No. 52, 24 December 1980, Art. 1121.
4. *VVSSSR*, No. 45, 7 November 1984, Art. 790 and 791.
5. *KZ*, 10 June 1980; 25 September 1984.
6. *KZ*, 5 December 1984; cf. also Franz Walter, "Trends in Soviet Defense Expenditures: Facts and Speculation," in this volume, Chapter 16.
7. *Sovetskaya voyennaya entsiklopediya*, Vol. 2 (1976), p. 513.
8. *KZ*, 4 November 1984.

5
The Role of the Secret Service

Astrid von Borcke

"It is impossible to understand the Soviet Union without understanding the KGB," J. Barron has justifiably observed.[1] The KGB, the "Committee for State Security," the political police, is a key instrument for securing the Soviet communist form of Party rule at home. Even today, the "Chekists"[2] still quote Lenin when they say, "Without such an institution, the power of the workers cannot exist."[3]

Naturally the KGB's organization, methods, resources, and personnel policy are a state secret, and at best open Soviet sources allude to them highly selectively. Nevertheless there is more information than commonly assumed. The KGB—today composed of four main administrative sections and five (simple) administrative sections—is a giant bureaucracy said to employ between 500,000 and 1,750,000 people.[4] Such an apparatus cannot operate entirely in the dark—nor is it always supposed to. What is more, its basic functions and structures have proven to have great continuity, rendering a historical review particularly revealing.

Development to the End of the Khrushchev Era

Lenin (who was never a completely consistent theoretition of dictatorship) never emphasized the political police as a key instrument of the new "proletariat" regime. Nevertheless, these police were among the first state institutions to emerge from the Bolshevik revolution. Under various names—"Cheka" (1917–1921), GPU (February to December 1922), OGPU (1922–1934), NKVD (after 1934), NKGB during the war, MGB as of March 1946, MVD as of March 1953, and finally KGB as of March 1954—it accompanied the entire development of the Soviet regime and, beyond that, each of its expansions.[5]

Characteristically, the institution owed its creation to a mere resolution by the Council of People's Commissars (*Sovnarkom*) and not to legislation. The original name—"Extraordinary Commission to Fight Counterrevolution and Sabotage"—said it all: The political police had been conceived as an organ of the state of emergency, as a new kind of "*Comité du salut public*" (Stalin), and as such stood outside the bounds of any constitution. Its functions unfolded with "spontaneous" pragmatism, or historically.

In the course of the "Red Terror" of 1918–1921 the Cheka, with its growing drive for "autonomy," which led it to reject any demand for supervision by the ministry of justice, threatened to turn into a state within the state. With the introduction of the NEP[6] a certain regularization was attempted—a regularization that was also the model for post-Stalinist reforms. Still, the police apparatus continued to wax in secret. When F. Dzierzynski died in 1926, Stalin, the Politburo's police expert, also became de facto master of this machinery. In 1935 a "special sector" for the direction of the political police was established in his private secretariat.

A last attempt to tame the OGPU's power was apparently undertaken by the Seventeenth Party Congress in early 1934. But then, in December of that year, the Leningrad Party leader S.M. Kirov, Stalin's potential new antagonist, was murdered, with the secret knowledge of the Leningrad NKVD at the least. Now, Stalin launched the great purge, the victims of which numbered in the millions.[7] This war of the regime against society was directed not least against the Party *qua* institution and finally also against the military leadership. Indeed, in the course of the "Yezhovshchina" in 1937, the purgers themselves were purged: Some 3,000 ranking functionaries of the NKVD were "liquidated."[8] The terror already threatened to endanger the political and social order. L. Beriya was called to Moscow in July 1938. Bringing the infernal machine back under control was his achievement. At the Eighteenth Party Congress in 1939, the new NKVD chief was promoted to candidate member of the Politburo.

In the Second World War, too, the political police played a key part:

- Supervising the evacuation of industry to the Eastern regions and assuming supreme control over strategic armament (Beria operated so successfully that in 1946 Stalin also entrusted him with the new priority program—building an atomic bomb).
- "Purging" the territories to be evacuated (and eventually the newly conquered ones as well): Thousands upon thousands were summarily liquidated; the most prominent victims included the elite of the Polish army (Katyn).[9]
- Organizing the partisan movement.
- Surveilling the armed forces (in 1946 "Smersh"[10] was founded to this end, an organization which was also to direct repatriations after the war).
- Deporting a host of ethnic groups, beginning in early 1944.

The "organs" were again a decisive instrument for the Sovietization of Eastern Europe.[11] Furthermore, after the war they enabled Stalin once more to "tame" an officer corps roused to unprecedented self-confidence. They also helped Stalin enforce "re-Sovietization" in the country after hopes of better times had been deliberately cultivated during the war. However, the old dictator was growing suspicious of Beriya's power. The new "great purge" initiated in 1953 with the publicizing of the "doctors' plot" was evidently directed first and foremost against the security apparatus and its chief.

Then, in March 1953, death caught up with Stalin—possibly not entirely a natural death.[12] Beriya now took the bull by the horns with a "liberal" program: reforms of the nationalities and agricultural policy, a new policy toward Germany, indeed, possibly even the vision of coexistence with the West.[13] On 26 June 1953, shortly after the revolt in the GDR, Beriya was overthrown by a conspiracy of the Politburo, in which Khrushchev was in league with several military leaders and played the key role.

In 1953–1954, the state security apparatus was again subjected to a radical purge: Party control was reactivated; the former Ministry of Internal Affairs was converted into a state committee "in the Council of Ministers" and subordinated to a collegium; the economic empire of the police—at war's end amounting to about one sixth of the state budget[14] (thanks to forced labor in camps where at one point 12–15 million people were wasting away[15]) was largely dismantled; the so-called Kirov legislation, foundation of the police terror, was repealed; steps were taken better to secure "socialist legality," and that by means of a new supervisory function by the state prosecutor's office (as during NEP period). But most of all, any individual was henceforth to be prevented from using the police as a personal weapon in the power struggle.

Even Khrushchev was cautious enough, though, to leave the intermediate levels and infrastructure of the KGB intact.[16] For this he paid a price. From 1963 to 1964 the KGB mounted a series of attacks, evidently aimed at subverting the novel policy of coexistence. Indeed, A. Shelepin, KGB chief from 1958 to 1961, who, as CC secretary also superintended the security apparatus, apparently played a key role in Khrushchev's overthrow in October 1964, as did the new chief of the KGB, Shelepin's protegé V. Semichastny (1961–1967).

The KGB's Comeback Under Brezhnev

Immediately following the overthrow of Khrushchev, the exceedingly energetic head of the CC Department for Administrative Authorities (which supervises the personnel policies of the security apparatus), KGB-Major-General N.R. Mironov, died in a mysterious plane crash.[17] Not until 1966 did N. Savinkin become his successor. Control of the "authorities" evidently was a ticklish question. In the new collective leadership, this responsibility was no longer the *domaine reservé* of the Party leader: It was Suslov, the "second" secretary, who saw to the effective supervision of the KGB.

But Party leader Brezhnev, who was master over cadre politics until 1966, managed to fill the positions of deputy chairmen responsible for domestic security with his men: The new First Deputy Chairman, S.K. Tsvigun, was even supposedly his brother-in-law. The head of the central administration of the armed forces, G.N. Tsinev, was a fellow student from the days at the Dnepropetrovsk Institute of Metallurgy with whom the Party leader had also worked during the war. The cadre chief (since 1967) and current chief of the KGB, V.M. Chebrikov, was formerly second secretary in Brezhnev's "fief," the Dnepropetrovsk-region.

But then, former chief of the KGB Yu. Andropov (May 1967–May 1982), previously head of the CC department for the ruling parties in Eastern Europe and "ideologue," was initially closer to Suslov than Brezhnev. In September 1967 he was appointed candidate member of the Politburo. This was possibly the "compensation" for the post of secretary he had given up, but it was also an upward reevaluation of the KGB *qua* institution. Then, at the plenary session of April 1973, the KGB chief, together with the ministers of foreign affairs and defense, was elected full member of the Politburo—a sign of the incipient fusion of the supreme Party, police, and military leadership. In 1968, the KGB was promoted from state committee "in the Council of Ministers" to "state committee of the USSR," thereby further emphasizing its de facto (functional) autonomy.

A new kind of dissident movement appeared in the mid-1960s. Initially it was only in the cultural, religious, and national areas. But following the Helsinki Conference (1975), it also took the form of a political human and civil rights movement. The new movement alerted a leadership that was either unwilling or unable to undertake far-reaching reforms to the fact that it would also require the political police in the future. At the Twenty-third Party Congress in 1966, Brezhnev called for a strengthening of the KGB. The Twenty-fourth Party Congress in 1971, which had to rubber stamp the revived course of coexistence, also appointed Andropov's three most important deputies to the CC. This meant that representation of the KGB in this (albeit expanded) body was quadrupled at one stroke.

The KGB also made a comeback in the Party bureaus of the Union republics. Khrushchev had put an end to the universal representation these bodies had enjoyed under Stalin. But by the close of the Brezhnev era, the KGB chiefs were generally represented again (Estonia being the exception) in seven of 14 bureaus (the RSFSR is directly subordinate to the center), even as full members. Indeed, in Azerbaijan, First Party Secretary G. Aliyev (up to 1982)—a professional "Chekist," formerly the republic's KGB chief from 1967 to 1969—took advantage of a radical purge of the Party apparatus and installed 2,000 of his KGB functionaries in positions thus vacated.[18] With the appointment of B.K. Pugo in Lithuania, this republic's KGB chief since 1976, another "Gebist"[19] turned Party leader, apparently not without resistance: This is indicated by the unprecedented anomaly that he was not immediately promoted from candidate member to full member of the Party-buro.

The KGB took advantage of the transition to the Khrushchev regime and launched a massive public relations campaign to improve its traditionally hateful image in society. This campaign continues to this very day. Under Brezhnev it was given new resources, new positions, and new assignments. Andropov strove for high professional competence while stressing correctness and legality. He sought to recruit an intellectual elite rather than figures from the fringes of society.

The consequence: When towards the close of the Brezhnev era the Party was in danger of losing more and more of its luster, indeed even its very capacity to lead, the KGB was left looking like the sole efficient, modern, and non-corrupt institution. (The "Chekists" in any event enjoy a considerable number of special provileges.) Undoubtedly this was a significant element that played a part in Andropov's election as the new Party leader in November 1982.

Andropov's successor as interim Party leader, K.U. Chernenko probably also entertained special relations with the "authorities." As he himself emphasized, he had started his career in the NKVD border troops. His official biography leaves a remarkable gap for the period of the Great Terror. Rumor even has it that he had been involved in purges in Dnepropetrovsk back then. Be that as it may, his position as head of the "General Department" in 1965–1983 at least entailed certain KGB connections, if only because this department organizes the "circulation" of dossiers in the Politburo and transmits the leaderships' communications from the KGB. Indeed, his responsibility for the security of the central apparatus may have implied that Chernenko was also responsible for Party supervision of the KGB and its respective "Special Department."

Nothing is known of special relations of the new Party leader Gorbachev to the police, save that he benefits from past patronage by Andropov and Suslov. He also benefits from the responsibility for cadre politics which he had already exercised prior to his appointment as secretary general. It remains to be seen how his relations with the KGB will develop. His emphasis on discipline will meet with approval in the KGB; but the specialists on internal "security" could take a dim view of his modernizing efforts—which, after all, cannot but amount to cuts in excessive bureaucratic tutelage and a greater display of initiative.

The KGB's Role in Politics

The KGB commands the most comprehensive and most objective information in the regime. An essential source of its political knowledge is the "index." In terms of volume and detail, this is probably a unique documentation kept for nearly seven decades on persons, at home or abroad, of potential significance to Soviet politics (and espionage).[20] The KGB probably commands the best historical "memory" of all the apparatuses. After all, it also serves as *ersatz* "social feedback," which is largely absent in the "monistic," anti-pluralist system. This is a consequence of the suppression of an autonomous public and of a tendency peculiar to bureaucratic empires to monopolize all information of relevance to them. Every month, the chiefs of the KGB's regional departments have to dispatch their comprehensive situation reports to the center. The leadership and especially the Party leader, who is the first to receive intelligence reports on the "state of the nation," habitually attach the greatest importance to these reports.

But the influence of secret service intelligence is apt to be particularly limited in the Soviet regime. With their conspiratorial "compartmentalized" view of the world, secret services in general are ill-suited to produce well-founded political generalizations. What is more, in the Soviet regime, the Party apparatus, whose political monopoly in the final analysis is based on a monopoly of information, has always resisted the development of autonomous centers of information and analysis. Thus, there are reports that the CC has forbidden the KGB to establish its own group of professional analysts.[21]

Of course the KGB also has analysts, required as it is to submit daily and weekly reports. But such topical analyses are rather episodic and unlikely to touch on basic questions of political strategy, that is, the monopoly of the Party leadership. Traditionally, the secret services—KGB and GRU—were to supply primarily "raw," that is, uninterpreted, information. Certain evaluations and analyses in the form of sighting and selection of the material are, of course, indispensable lest the leadership suffocate in the mass of its intelligence. (By way of comparison: During the 1960s, the CIA, for instance, received some 200,000 "pieces" of such messages, books, maps etc.!)

But in the Soviet Union the actual decisionmaking process remains "Party-centered": the KGB can affect it only through the Party apparatus. The strategic political submissions to the Politburo are supplied by the Secretariat, based on information from the expert bureaucracies as well as, in foreign policy matters, by the International Department of the CC, which is said to maintain a special division for the evaluation of intelligence material. The most explosive information, however, is put before the Politburo by the KGB chief himself.

The fact remains that the institution par excellence that has to see to the maintenance and "security" of the system is the KGB. As a consequence it has ultimate control over all other institutions. This places it in a political position well beyond that of an "ordinary" state bureaucracy. Viewed from the perspective of information theory, it is the regime's second most powerful apparatus.

The world view of the "Chekists" does not fit neatly into that of the Party apparatus. The men from state security are possessed of a marked sense of elitism. Technocrats of power, they lean more towards nationalism than towards "socialism" and ideology. For all that and from experience, the "Chekists" are well aware that any far-reaching reform movement, not to mention a revolution, would very rapidly and primarily turn against them.

Small wonder, then, that in their writings Andropov's deputies for the domestic realm have displayed pronounced neo-Stalinist nostalgia: xenophobia, chiefly towards all Western influences, anti-liberalism, authoritarianism, antisemitism. Word has it that a new right has found its main following among the police (and the military).[22]

Characteristically enough, the closing phase of the Brezhnev era in particular was marked by a whole series of restrictive measures, primarily in the cultural area, and in religious and information policy.[23] Andropov's disciplinary campaign in fact proved an attempt at extending police measures to additional sectors of society and the economy. The new border law introduced by Minister of the Interior Fedorchuk in December 1982 aroused suspicions that the "iron curtain" was to be dropped again. Especially in 1983–1984, various measures were introduced to prevent as far as possible the people's contacts with foreigners; breaches of "official secrecy" were to be punished more severely.

The Party's Two-Edged Sword: Services and Costs of the KGB

The Soviet political police is the most powerful organization of its kind in history, comparable perhaps only to the Nazi regime's *Reichssicherheitshauptamt*. It has proven an effective instrument to safeguard internal power. Without it, the one-party regime might well have been shorter lived.

Relative to the cost of, say, armaments, a secret service is a cheap, politically flexible and powerful weapon at the hands of the executive. But it has its price, too. According to I. Gouzenko, one of the most prominent defectors from Stalin's Russia, no enemy agents could have done as much harm to Soviet society as did the "authorities" with their "healthy suspicion."[24] "Civilized" (and refined) though police methods may have become in the meantime, one basic fact remains: The political police, product of revolution and civil war, have, in a manner of speaking, an institutional "interest" in maintaining the psychology and governing techniques of a "regime of the beleaguered fortress," which was its raison d'être.

For this very reason the Soviet leadership ought to be reminded of the internal costs of its secret service. As a general rule, a secret service with its conspiratorial methods is the institution most difficult to subject to political control.[25] The Soviet regime has tried to take a whole series of precautionary measures: Party membership of those functionaries; Party organizations and a sort of special division even inside the KGB; control of cadre policies and especially the creation of a series of competing "police" and control bodies. Yet, the KGB is the largest and most powerful organization of its kind, in the final analysis keeping all others under surveillance (under Stalin even the Party all the way up to the Politburo), without letting itself be subjected to full counter-control. With the appointment of V. Fedorchuk, the interim-chief of the KGB in 1982 and former Smersh functionary, as the new minister of the interior, the separation of KGB and MVD wisely re-introduced under Beriya may again gradually be undone: V. Ya. Lezhepekov, so far deputy chief of the KGB, was appointed deputy MVD minister, and V.I. Gladyshev assumed direction of the newly created political administration inside the MVD.

The regime has traditionally taken pains not to allow the rise of "Chekists" to top political office. But meanwhile there is the example of Beriya, who foundered; of Shelepin, reputedly among Brezhnev's chief rivals; and, finally, of the successful Andropov. Indeed, even the new KGB chief Chebrikov, originally a candidate member and since 23 April 1985 full member of the

Politburo, is evidently in the process of acquiring for himself an image as all-round leader, by means of political journalism and uncommonly public travel-diplomacy.

The KGB is the regime's most powerful institution second only to the Party.[26] It even keeps its own armed forces: The elite divisions of some 300,000 border troops and the internal troops of the KGB are as a rule placed under its operational command. Hence, it constitutes a traditional counterweight to the military, whose weapons depots and nuclear warheads are also in KGB keeping. But at the same time, this power also makes it the institution most likely to endanger the Party regime.

Fears of a potential "Fouché" are not unknown to the communist Party leadership: This was demonstrated by the sacking of Beriya in 1953, of W. Zaisser that same year by Ulbricht, of R. Barak in 1982 in Czechoslovakia, and of A. Ranković in 1966 in Yugoslavia. Brezhnev met his colleague A. Shelepin, whom he thought a potential rival, with utmost caution. The fact that at the Twenty-Second Party Congress in 1961 he had brought into play KGB documents against Khrushchev's old opponents from the "anti-Party group" may well have convinced the other oligarchs that Shelepin was a dangerous man.

Whether there really will be a "Fouché" some day at the end of Soviet communist development, should the Party fail, remains an open question. Any neo-Stalinist "glaciation" is bound to strengthen the police factor, just as any genuine liberalization and reconciliation of the regime with society should reduce the need for the instruments of secret internal war. In any event, the continuing "competition of the systems" under the conditions of nuclear stalemate in world politics should still guarantee that in the future as well, the KGB is unlikely to decrease.

Notes

1. J. Barron, *KGB heute* (Bern/Munich, 1984), p. 12. See also contributions of this author in *Die politische Meinung*, 220 (1985), pp. 42–48, and Herder-Korrespondenz, No. 4 (1985), pp. 161–165.

2. "Cheka" was the first name of the Soviet political police, short for Vserossiyskaya Chrezvychaynaya Komissiya (All-Russian Extraordinary Commission).

3. Pr, 20 December 1977.

4. The main administrations are: Foreign operations, internal security, combatting opponents (combatting all "dissidents"), border troops; the five (simple) administrations: armed forces, surveillance, communications, body guards, an administrative-technical "General Administration" (cf. the organizational chart, *Sp*, No. 27 (1984), p. 128). The KGB is said to employ 25,000 staff officers in Moscow, some 40,000 administrative staff, 50,000 to 100,000 functionaries in the provinces, furthermore some 300,000 to 350,000 border troops as well as a vast network of informers that reputedly made up some 8 percent of the total population at the end of the Stalin era. In addition, the nearly 100,000 personnel of the "allied" services in Eastern Europe (except Romania today) as well as Cuba and Vietnam must be included in the KGB empire. The number of agents abroad has been placed as high as 300,000. Naturally such figures must be taken with a grain of salt. By way of comparison: The CIA

is reputed to have 16,500 personnel. Cf. *General-Anzeiger*, 13 November 1982; C. Dobson and R. Payne, *The Dictionary of Espionage* (London, 1984), p. 212; *Newsweek*, 23 November 1981, p. 29; M, 7 September 1983, p. 37; B. Freemantle, *KGB* (New York, 1982), P. Deriabin and F. Gibney, *The Secret World* (London, 1959), p. 75.

5. The standard work is S. Wolin and R.M. Slusser, *The Soviet Secret Police* (New York, 1957).

6. Short for Novaya Ekonomicheskaya Politika (New Economic Policy), 1921–1929.

7. Cf. the figures in J.R. Adelman (ed.), *Terror and Communist Politics* (Boulder, London: 1984), p. 107. R. Conquest, *The Great Terror* (London, 1968), p. 533 placed the victims specifically of the Great Purge at 15 million; A. Myagkov speaks of some 20 million Cheka victims, *Inside the KGB* (Richmond, Surrey, 1977), p. 21; cf. also *Sp* No. 27 (1984), p. 120; US-Congress, *The Human Costs of Communism* (Washington, 1976), p. 125. According to A. Solzhenitsyn's estimate a total of 60 million people died due to the "internal war," *Die Eiche und das Kalb* (Darmstadt/Neuwied, 1957), p. 533. By way of comparison: The total number of casualties in World War II was 50 million (A. Gribkov, *TASS*, 18 June 1981).

8. A. Orlow, *Kreml-Geheimnisse* (Würzburg, 1953), p. 259.

9. Cf. "A.I. Romanov," (Boris Bakhlanov's pseudonym; the author had worked as head of the information department of "Smersh"; in 1984 his body was found in a pond in Wimbledon Common), *Nights Are Longest There* (London, 1972), pp. 136ff.

10. Short for *Smert' shpionam* (Death to the Spies), a special detachment with the troops, summer of 1942 to 1945.

11. Cf. the essays in Adelman, *op. cit.*

12. A. Avtorkhanov, *Zagadka smerti Stalina* (Frankfurt/M., 1976).

13. M. Gardner, *Esope*, 386, 15 September 1977, p. 14.

14. R. Pethybridge, *A Key to Soviet Politics* (London, 1962), p. 21.

15. Cf. the statements by an MVD Major, in G. Klimow, *Berliner Kreml* (Cologne/Berlin, 1953), p. 273; R. Bernstein, *IHT*, 17 November 1982.

16. A. W. Knight, in *Survey*, No. 3 (1980), pp. 138–155.

17. M. Voslensky, *Nomenklatura* (Vienna etc., 1980), p. 178.

18. W, 26 March 1983.

19. Derived from "GB," Gosurdarstvennaya Bezopasnost' (State Security).

20. Cf. R. Seth, *Forty Years of Soviet Spying* (London, 1965), pp. 19–20; P. de Villemarest, *Sowjetspionage in Frankreich* (Mainz, 1969), pp. 15, 266–267.

21. J. Barron, *KGB* (Munich/Zurich, 1978), p. 105.

22. Myagkov, *op. cit.*, pp. 48, 84; K.W. Fricke, *Die DDR-Staatssicherheit* (Cologne, 1982), p. 191; A. Yanov, *The Russian New Right* (Berkeley, Calif., 1978).

23. Cf. P. Hübner, "Cultural Policy, Culture, Opposition," in this volume, Chapter 12.

24. I. Gouzenko, *The Iron Curtain* (New York, 1948), p. 90.

25. H.H. Ransom, *The Intelligence Establishment* (Cambridge, Mass., 1971), p. 247.

26. Cf. F. Baghoorn, in H.G. Skilling and F. Griffiths (eds.), *Interest Groups in Soviet Politics* (Princeton, N.J., 1971), p. 96.

6
Ideology as a Key to Politics

Helmut Dahm

All substantial questions about Soviet politics must be classified in ideological terms. This is done with concepts and categories that suggest abstract and purely theoretical expositions. But in reality the most explosive political questions involving the very foundations of the entire Soviet socialist system or existing conditions are frequently discussed in ideological code. One such discussion has been going on since 1981 and concerns the peculiarity and quality of contradictions in the socialist system as it actually exists. The reader less conversant with Marxist-Leninist ideology ought to know in advance that a distinction is made between "antagonistic" and "nonantagonistic" contradictions. Antagonistic contradictions are attributed to the capitalist system as motor forces of revolutionary change. Nonantagonistic contradictions contain, as it were, the kinetic energy of socioeconomic progress and as such are to be encouraged methodically in socialist society.

The Difference Between Andropov and Chernenko

The discussion of the possibility of antagonistic contradictions in socialism, originally encouraged and covered by Chernenko, has been going on since September 1981. By early 1984, the course of this dispute had demonstrated unequivocally that it was Andropov who had managed to prevail all along. He prevailed with his apparent rejection of a potential danger of antagonism in the sense of crisis-like social conflict in the Soviet Union and its developed socialist society. This rejection was apparent insofar as the hieroglyph of "serious collisions," employed by Andropov and incorporated into the prescribed vocabulary of his team of theoreticians, merely veiled social antagonism without, however, convincingly disproving or denying it. In *German Ideology*, Marx and Engels considered "serious collisions" congruent with the contradictions that invariably touched off a revolution, i.e., congruent with genuine "antagonism." In Andropov's terminology, "serious collisions" can result from contradictions whose nature is supposedly not antagonistic.

And yet there was a very important and quite discernible difference between the views Chernenko and Andropov championed in a controversial way until late 1982. This difference was connected with the question of the basic origins of social conflict in socialist countries. In February 1984, H.A. Butenko made this difference clearly visible to all. At that time, the situation on the ideological front changed just as abruptly as it had in December 1982, following Brezhnev's death on 10 November.

In December 1982, supporters of Andropov's concept of socialist non-antagonism also believed in the remnants of the capitalist past in other socialist countries. With their determined criticism of the spokesmen of the antagonism debate, these supporters had become the authoritative representatives of the political ideology. But in February 1984, the authors of the Chernenko-group, formerly censored as heretics, were again allowed to express their views openly about the possibility of antagonistic contradictions developing in socialism. They were also allowed to talk about the self-engendered political negligence responsible for the development of such contradictions.

The Struggle Between the Two Schools of Thought

The theoreticians of the Chernenko group had already learned from the unprecedented "lesson" of Poland during Brezhnev's lifetime. From February 1984 on, it appeared that that lesson about the ideology of Scientific Communism and Political Economy was true once again: The unmistakable writing on the wall of social revolution in a socialist country, erupting against real existing socialism (reactionary as it actually is), could not be explained as system-stabilizing by the social criteria of a socialist society liberated from antagonistic contradictions. These criteria were cautiously developed by Suslov beginning in Stalin's reign and appropriated by Andropov against Brezhnev.

In February 1984, Butenko elaborated on this key and pivotal point of the political controversy as follows:

> The one position is far from new, clad though it is in novel argot. Adherents of this view underscore the non-antagonistic nature of contradictions in socialism. They see the root cause of all negative phenomena (the crises, serious collisions, sharp conflicts, and open clashes occurring in Socialist countries) in the existence of 'remnants' of capitalism. Or, as they say now, it is in a social antagonism inherited from the past, in its residues or 'residual antagonism,' in old morals that have still not disappeared, etc. Such a view raises the question of whether sole consideration of merely objective causes of antagonistic contradications, whether the identification of a 'residual' social antagonism from 'remnants of capitalism' suffices to explain the origins of the crisis in Poland.[1]

Butenko answered this question with a determined and well-reasoned no. Then his analysis continued: "The adherents of the other position . . . see the fundamental cause of the negative phenomena (the crises, collisions, and conflicts in the socialist world) in a bungling resolution of contradictions which (says even H.D.) are characteristic of socialism."[2]

Butenko's analysis proved that the origins of the crisis in Poland were by no means attributable to objective conditions like the incomplete transitional period and the existence of objective causes for antagonistic contradictions. In Butenko's view the effects of these objective conditions certainly had to be considered in connection with the question of the essential cause of socio-economic conflict situations. Nonetheless the

> main focus had to be on those causes responsible for the widespread discontent among the working population, and they were errors in the policy of the former leadership of the Polish United Workers Party. It lacked a scientific concept for the resolution of the contradictions (facing it—H.D.) and was therefore unable to work out proper strategy and tactics. Instead it pursued a policy contrary to the requirements of the objective laws of socialism's structure, prescribed weak medicine for social ills, and thus deprived itself of support from the working class and the working population.[3]

Following Chernenko's assumption of office as head of the Party (on 13 February 1984) and state (on 11 April 1984) the spokesmen of his original political-ideological line (including P. Fedoseyev, V. Semyonov, and A. Butenko) vigorously stressed the possibility of a rise in antagonistic contradictions in socialism, such as between collectivism and individualism, between internationalism and nationalism, between a scientific (communist) and a religious world view, between socialist society and antisocial elements, or between the development of productive forces and the real totality of productive relations, between societal and personal needs and consumption, between centralism and democracy. Those advocating such views were obviously convinced that the chances of a rise in antagonistic contradictions (i.e., those that are system-threatening because they are system-dependent contradictions), with all their dangerous effects on the fate of socialism in one country or another, were to be sought in the errors—Butenko even thought the inability and incompetency—of party leadership. They were also convinced that the risk of social antagonisms that would actually arise could be checked effectively by a consistent pursuit of the building of the socialist-communist society of the future.

As for the analysis of socio-political crisis and conflict situations, there is surely no denying that there is a certain amount of realism among the adherents of such views and arguments. Moreover, their concept of crisis management made clear the political determination to improve the Soviet economy's ideological parameters. They would thus achieve a long-term stabilization of the dynamic reference system of productive forces on the one hand and production relations on the other. This was to be accomplished by eliminating the theory deficit that had persisted for dogmatic reasons. This elimination would necessarily lead to momentous changes in the fundamental tenets of scientific communism.

Following Andropov's assumption of office (as Party leader in November 1982 and as head of state in June 1983), the ideological views inherited from Suslov (who died on 25 January 1982) became fully binding again. At the Plenary session of June 1983, Chernenko had to clearly submit to Andropov's power of setting the ideological guidelines. This power had already been foreshadowed in his memorial address on the 112th anniversary of Lenin's birthday on 22 April 1982, but then it was unmistakably confirmed, especially in his essay "Marx and Some Questions of Socialist Construction in the USSR," published in *Kommunist* in February 1983. Two of the three conferences on ideology were held by the appropriate CC secretaries of the sister parties in the socialist countries after Chernenko's election as general secretary of the CPSU. They took place in Sofia on 29 and 30 May 1984 and in Prague on 11 and 12 July 1984. (The third was from 4–7 December 1984, again in Prague, and had a different, council-like dimension and objective.) The catalogue of questions addressed indicates that it was evidently not possible for Chernenko to return consistently to the political-ideological position he had maintained in 1981/82 under Brezhnev. That had been a position that could easily be termed progressive in that he had seemed prepared to break with traditional ideological taboos. Now he was forced to accept the facts added by Andropov and his men after Brezhnev's death (10 November 1982).

Counteroffensive by the Ideological Traditionalists

In February 1984, A. Butenko, section-head in the Academy-Institute for the Economics of the World Socialist System, had again confirmed[4] the existence in the Soviet Union's ideologically based political science of two schools of thought. That is, there are two contradictory political-ideological views at cross-purposes with each other. The *Pravda*-article of 20 July 1984 entitled "Socialism and Contradictions"[5] by R. Kosolapov, editor-in-chief of the CC periodical *Kommunist* and a spokesman of the Andropov group, rendered this remarkably transparent and manifest—and in decided contradiction of the original Chernenko group's theoretical progressivists.

As he had done more than a year before in the 4 March 1983 *Pravda* article, "Socialism: Organic Wholeness of the Socialist System," Kosolapov tenaciously elaborated his views on the same topic in the core third paragraph of his *Pravda* article of 20 July 1984:

> Unlike the social contradictions in capitalism and other societies based on private property, the social contradictions in socialism are nonantagonistic in character. Until recently, this principle—a commonplace of Marxism-Leninism—was a truth commonly acknowledged by all social scientists. They adhered to Lenin's well-known thesis: 'Antagonism' and 'contradiction' are by no means one and the same. The former will disappear, the latter continue to exist in socialism.[6]

Consequently—according to Kosolapov—in socialism, which has already answered the question "who beats whom?" in its favor, and even more so in developed socialism,

> an antagonistic contrast of interests of large social groups (i.e., the case of Poland—H.D.) has been and continues to be completely out of the question. . . . To maintain the opposite amounts to demonstrating that science (more properly, individual scientists) has (have) removed itself (themselves) from life. . . . Thus, some authors began to mention the possibility that nonantagonistic contradictions may grow into antagonistic ones, without, however, providing valid proof. . . . this gave rise to polemics, in the course of which some aspects of the problem became better understood. In particular, this applies to the clarification of the meaning of the category, 'antagonism.'[7]

As Kosolapov remarked himself in this context,

> according to Marx there is an antagonism emanating from the societal condition of individuals' lives. This antagonism is of social character and is eliminated jointly with the productive relations based on private property and on exploitation; consequently, it is not characteristic of socialism. Those who (nevertheless—H.D.) attribute it to the new order either confuse later phases of socialist construction with the transitional period or fail to distinguish between social and individual antagonism. . . . But if the determination of local conflicts is coming to be presented as a 'discovery,' . . . then this must be regarded as a peculiar retrogression of thought. It calls forth natural and sound objections which are corroborated by the whole experience of building socialism and communism.[8]

Decoding Political Texts

Thus, it hardly made sense to say that the guidelines of political ideology had been laid down by Chernenko. On the contrary, throughout 1983 Andropov had commanded sufficient strength and authority either to urge the spokesmen of the Chernenko-inspired discussion on contradictions (spokesmen such as Fedoseyev, Semyonov, Gott, Butenko, et al.) to retract their views, or to be silent. Those discussions were aimed at showing the possibility of socio-economic conflict and crisis growing into antagonism during the last year and a half of Brezhnev's government. Among his various other actions, Andropov installed B. Stukalin as new CC secretary for propaganda in no time at all (December 1982; his predecessor, Y. Tyazhelnikov, had held this office since May 1977). After the June 1983 plenary session, Andropov removed B. Ukraintsev from the office of director of the Academy Institute of Philosophy (which he had held since 1974) and T. Ryabushkin from the office of director of the Academy Institute of Sociological Research (which he had occupied since 1977). They were replaced by G. Smirnov, a pupil of Suslov's Grail castle, the Academy of Social Sciences at the CC of the CPSU, and by V. Ivanov, who had also looked upon Suslov as the authority pure and simple.

At the time few took note of these events. At the June 1983 plenary session on ideology, even Chernenko himself was not spared subjugation to Andropov's deceptive formula of nonantagonism, despite the possibility of "serious collisions." In his address of 14 June on current questions of ideological, mass-political work by the Party, Chernenko addressed only those contradictions which for ever and always have been referred to as the driving forces of social development in socialism: "What is required today is the general study of the nonantagonistic contradictions befitting mature socialism, the particularities of their resolution under the conditions of growing socio-political and ideological unity of Soviet society."[9] The detailed resolution by the Central Committee of the CPSU of 15 June 1983 on the subject of Chernenko's address did not even deem that particularly worthy of mention. The accent was unmistakably on an energetic revival of the resolution of 26 April 1979. This resolution on the ideological reeducation of the entire Soviet population had been effected by Suslov. Chernenko, too, had intimated such a plan in his speech.

What is more, Andropov cleverly appropriated Chernenko's old arguments in his great speech the following day, on 15 June 1983. By simply comparing them,[10] this can readily be established. At the memorable plenary session in June 1983 Andropov said: "Mistakes in politics must be paid for. When the leading role of the communist Party is weakened, then the danger arises of sliding down into the Bourgeois-reformist path of development."[11] According to Chernenko in February 1982 (after Suslov's death), the experience of history taught "that any attempt to weaken . . . the leading role of the Party, even loosening its ties to the masses, will result in unleashing natural forces inimical to socialism, and that all such attempts create the danger of a restoration of capitalism."[12] Undoubtedly this was analogous, only much clearer and, more important, much more insiduous. On the other hand, though, Andropov emphasized: realistic politicians on the capitalist side were capable of "grasping that *irreversible* processes have already taken place in the world."[13]

Thus, one can't help but gain the impression that because of the plenary session of June 1983 and his capitulation there on the question of antagonistic contradictions, Chernenko had become the prisoner of an ideological perspective. This perspective departed rather far from the progressive views Chernenko had advanced in the last two years of Brezhnev's reign. Spokesmen for the original debate about the possible rise of socio-economic disputes had suddenly been reappearing since February. (Such disputes were to be understood in the sense of social antagonism, which is a revolutionary situation, according to Marx.) Although Andropov had temporarily suppressed the debate, spokesmen resumed it after his death, and Kosolapov's objection to the spokesmen was repeated in July 1984 in *Pravda*. This undoubtedly had to be considered a resounding slap in the face to the man who (even under Brezhnev) had obviously been their patron: Konstantin Chernenko.

The Conservative Power in the Wings

Throughout 1984, the Academy's periodical, *Voprosy filosofii,* sought to decide the struggle between the two political-ideological schools of thought on the admissibility or inadmissibility of antagonistic contradictions in socialism. It was in favor of the progessivists affirming it.[14] For they had recognized that theoretical allowance for social antagonism within a socialist society, even a developed socialist society, was the unalterably necessary political-ideological precondition for a thorough improvement of the economic mechanism as a whole, i.e., of socialist productive relations.[15]

However, strengthened by Andropov, the group of conservative traditionalists evidently proved superior enough to thwart such efforts. As late as April 1984, Ye. Ambartsumov, a political economist and representative of the progressive counter-group, had published a much noted article in the Academy periodical *Voprosy istorii* on the controversial "antagonism" question.[16] (Like the group's political science representative A. Butenko, Ambartsumov was head of a section of the Academy Institute of Economics of the World Socialist System.) This article used Lenin's causal analysis of the 1921 system-threatening crisis and of the methods for overcoming it, to support Tatyana Zaslavskaya's line of argument on the necessity of recognizing genuine social conflicts within the developed socialist Soviet society. His article appeared in the April 1983 *Novosibirsk Study* and used political ideology.[17]

Then *Kommunist,* the most important theoretical periodical of the Central Committee of the CPSU, lashed out fiercely against Ambartsumov and Butenko as the spokesmen of all those who, from the vantage of the political ideology of Scientific Communism, might be considered adherents of an "Away-from-Stalin-and-Suslov-Movement."[18] In June 1984, the Scientific Council of the Institute of Philosophy of the Academy of Sciences of the USSR met at the institute. At this session the publishing activities of the periodical *Voprosy filosofii* since 1982 were critically reviewed. In October 1984, this periodical, until then publishing organ of those theoreticians who endorsed progressive development in the area of political ideology, printed the review report of the Scientific Council of the Academy-Institute of Philosophy as the lead article by the editorial staff.[19] According to this article,

> the collegium of editors and the editorial board have recently committed several serious mistakes in their work. In the course of the discussions on contradictions in socialism, some researchers made the point that in socialism there actually are antagonistic contradictions. However, that is inconsistent with the well-known sentence by Lenin pursuant to which 'antagonism and contradiction are by no means one and the same. The former will disappear, the latter continue to exist in socialism.'[20]

This criticism of the Academy's periodical *Voprosy filosofii* appeared in its October 1984 lead article. That article also contained a clear hint, but nothing that was new to careful observers of ideological processes. It hinted at when the binding resolution of political science's aforementioned core question of contradictions was passed and by whom. It said in the third major section on the chief problems of developed socialist society:

> It is no coincidence that the June plenary session (1983) of the CC of the CPSU calls the problem of nonantagonistic contradictions under conditions of developed socialist society the cardinal question for all social sciences and for the practice of perfecting social relations. Essential today, is the universal study of the nonantagonistic contradictions befitting mature socialism as well as the peculiarities of their solution under conditions of the growing sociopolitical and ideological unity of Soviet society.
>
> Historical experience has demonstrated convincingly that in those countries of the socialist community where the tasks of the transitional period (from capitalism to socialism—H.D.) have been fully solved and where socialist achievements have been secured, reliable guarantees exist which preclude the appearance of social antagonisms. Social antagonisms involving a clash of irreconcilable interests of social groups flow from the irreconcilability of the interests of conflicting classes which is alien to the nature of socialism. The base-line in the work of the periodical *Voprosy filosofii* has been and is determined by these fundamental methodological and theoretical guiding principles of Marxism. . . . Both the editorial board and the collegium of editors must pay special attention to this question, far removed as it is under current conditions from merely academic significance.[21]

Anyone acquainted with the contemporary history of Soviet political ideology knows that this view, inherited from Stalin, was laid down by Suslov's followers, during a phase of comparatively liberal "evolution *nolens volens*," at the Union conference on current problems of dialectical materialism in April 1965. This can be gleaned from the third volume of the conference materials, edited in 1966 by F. Konstantinov et al.: Its contributors had treated the question of contradictions fundamentally and thoroughly.[22] Andropov was the one who, at the plenary session of June 1983, had restored this well known opinion to respect and universally binding applicability—against Chernenko and the ideologically adventurous experiments of the progressive theorists of "antagonism." And Gorbachev (a former favorite of Suslov and, like his sponsor (1939–1944), formerly First Secretary of the Northern Kaukasian region of Stavropol (1970–1978) was the one who, already in his memorial address on the 113th anniversary of Lenin's birth, on 22 April 1983, declared himself for it, and thus for Andropov.[23]

Gorbachev has been able to remain true to his beliefs to this very day. Chernenko, however, was forced to bow to Andropov's "nonantagonism" views at the June 1983 plenary session. And therefore the conservative power in the wings—the apparatus supporting the traditional Lenin-Stalin-Suslov line of political ideology in a formation-theoretical context—succeeded in preventing him from returning to his original view regarding "the danger of social tension, of political and socioeconomic crisis" to socialism proper,[24] and this even after his own election as secretary general.

Notes

1. See A.P. Butenko, *VF*, No. 2 (1984), p. 127.
2. *Loc. cit.*
3. *Loc. cit.*
4. Beforehand, see Butenko, in *Novoe vremya*, No. 6 (1982), pp. 5–7.
5. See R. Kosolapov, *Pr*, 20 July 1984.
6. *Loc. cit.* Lenin's thesis is found in *Leninskiy sobrnik* XI[2] (Moscow/Leningrad, 1931), p. 357.
7. Kosolapov, *op. cit.*
8. *Loc. cit.*
9. See *K*, No. 9 (1983), p. 20.
10. See H. Dahm, *Berichte des BIOst*, No. 32 (1983).
11. *K*, No. 9 (1983), p. 13.
12. *VIKPSS*, No. 2 (1982), p. 15.
13. *K*, No. 9 (1983), p. 15.
14. See *VF* (1984), No. 2, pp. 116–140 (discussion report by four authors as well as contributions by Butenko and Semnov); No. 3, pp. 39–45 (Dzumadurdyev); No. 6, pp. 3–50 (contributions by Fedosesyev with Ilyichev, Burlatsky, and Sulimov); No. 8, pp. 3–31 (contributions by Medvedev, Kozlovsky, and Stolyarov).
15. See "The Study of Novosibirsk," *OE*, No. 1 (1984), pp. A1–A29, and *Obshchestvennye nauki*, No. 6 (1983), pp. 202–212 (conference report).
16. See E.A. Ambartsumov, *VI*, No. 4 (1984), pp. 15–29; cf. B. Knabe, *Gelesen, kommentiert . . . des BIOst*, No. 7 (1984).
17. Cf. also H.-H. Höhmann, "The Soviet Economy at the End of the Eleventh Five-Year Plan: Counting on Gorbachev," in this volume, Chapter 13.
18. See *K*, No. 11 (1984), pp. 112–117 (violent criticism of Butenko's views by V. Kuzmenko), and *K*, No. 14 (1984), pp. 119–126 (violent criticism of E. Ambartsumov's views by E. Bugayev).
19. See the unsigned lead article in *VF*, No. 10 (1984), pp. 13–19.
20. *Ibid*, p. 5. Cf. the round-table discussion on literature and literary artistic criticism in the context of philosophy and social science of April 1983, *VF*, No. 11 (1983), pp. 94–107; *VF*, No. 1 (1984), pp. 88–95; *VF*, No. 2 (1984), pp. 98–115.
21. *VF*, No. 10 (1984), p. 10.
22. See F.V. Konstantinov (ed.), *Dialektika sovremennogo obshchestvennogo razvitiya. Materialy Soveshchaniya po sovremennym problemam materialisticheskoy dialektiki 7–9 aprelya 1965* (Moscow, 1966); esp. V.P. Rozhin, "Dva tipa protivorechiy obshchestvennogo razvitiya," pp. 149–159.
23. See *Pr*, 23 April 1983.
24. K.U. Chernenko, *K*, No. 13 (1981), pp. 6–12; esp. p. 11 (Leninskaya strategiya rukovodstva).

7
How to Mobilize the Soviet Working World: Discipline or Participation?

Bernd Knabe

When, following Gorbachev's election as secretary general of the CPSU, the Soviet mass media reported on country-wide "peak work output to further strengthen the might of the homeland," they likely pursued at least two aims. On the one hand, they meant to suggest broad approval of the new Party leader and on the other to convey the impression that many employees could be mobilized to work harder and selflessly.

What methods have been tried during the past few years to counter various negative tendencies in the working world? In particular, what has been done to achieve a "cardinal increase of labor productivity," which, since Andropov has been regarded as the "paramount element . . . for the victory of the new social order?"[1] Under Gorbachev, too, the unsatisfactory condition of work discipline is among those negative tendencies impugned. Even in places where the prerequisites for productive work are objectively present, work often proceeds only at half speed, if at all. Many do not at all consider salaries and gratifications as the main path to maintain, much less improve, their standard of living. Second jobs, and networks to barter for and secure agricultural products are often deemed much more important. In early 1985 the central press quoted one worker who said in an almost melancholy way that he had observed a continual decline in "innovationalism." The degree of immobility and lack of willingness to perform, even among younger employees and especially graduates of universities and technical colleges, seems to have risen to a point where planning authorities encounter increasing difficulties.

These system-specific tendencies had emerged by the mid-seventies and were exacerbated by additional adverse factors, primarily related to difficulties in the domestic economy. What is more, in the US, President Reagan returned to the concept of a "policy of strength" and successfully held his own both in foreign and in domestic politics. Since 1982, the Soviet leadership has wanted to respond to this new challenge with a partially renewed material and personnel program; this attempt to do an "about-face" was most clearly manifest in the decision at the CC plenary session of November 1982. These did not just represent the prelude to a "law-and-order" campaign, but also aimed at an accelerated intensification of the economy. These two elements have been and continue to be complemented by

- a strong emphasis on "Soviet patriotism," visible as early as 1980 in the context of the Olympic games and the celebration of the 600th anniversary of the battle on the "Kulikovo polye";
- "populistically" accented attempts at blending current political practice with certain traditions from Russian history considered potentially useful by the leadership (e.g. popular meetings and activities "all together");
- the attempt at re-ideologizing all sectors of Soviet society, beginning with the CC plenary session of June 1983 and continuing with the Union conference of December 1984.

The leadership believes it can already point to preliminary successes. Since Chernenko's speech to the expanded Politburo on 15 November 1984, the four years before have almost invariably been put into the same period as the late 1970s. This is an attempt to pass off 1981–1982 as a part of the phase of decline (carried over from the late seventies.) The following two years by contrast were put into the period marking the beginning of the recovery. Of course, since mid-1983 and throughout 1984, voices have been raised time and again, deploring the campaign of order or the merely "formal character" of its implementation. Occasionally those voices have even advocated stepping up the pace. In October 1984, Chernenko had to admit to damages in the billions due to difficulties in delivery and losses in production time.[2] In his inaugural address on 11 March 1985, Gorbachev reiterated the goal of achieving the five-year plan by year's end; "Arrears in some sectors of the economy," he merely attributed to the harsh winter.[3]

In his speech before ideology specialists in December 1984, Gorbachev had stressed that the "significant results" of 1983 and 1984 had been achieved through intensified political, organizational, and ideological work. Remarkably, oil production in western Siberia, which had fallen short of its planned output in 1984, was singled out as a negative example. After this had resulted in some personnel changes, a conference was held in Tyumen in mid-February, though it was less concerned with the description of objective difficulties and possibilities of surmounting them than with the mobilization of the employees. The "human factor" had gotten short shrift, they said: "Informational, educational, and organizational work in the collectives tapered off. Often people are unaware of what they do and to what end."[4]

Unions and Komsomol: Suitable Instruments of Mobilization?

There is little doubt that the decline in the standing of the unions over the past few decades (in early 1985: 135 million members) and of Komsomol

(42 million) has not been just in the eyes of the population, but in the eyes of the leadership as well. Now as much as ever, though, union membership is practically indispensable for almost everyone, unless one is prepared to accept considerable disadvantages. The leadership evidently sees the marked increase in the percentage of farmers and laborers among the elected representatives since late 1984 as one way of raising union prestige.

Matters are a bit different with the Komsomol which is estimated to comprise "only" some 60 percent of the age groups in question (14 to 28 years). Especially in early 1985, the Komsomol leadership repeatedly pointed out that the quantitative aspect was not decisive, that the widespread practice of automatically accepting pupils in grades seven and eight into the Komsomol should be dispensed with. In the summer, after the endeavor to transfer larger tasks to social organizations had even become discernible at the CC plenary session of April 1984, definite attempts were made to raise union and Komsomol "efficiency." In late June, the Politburo devoted almost an entire session to problems of the young and to the condition of the Komsomol. Growing passivity, religiosity, detachment from the high points of Soviet history, and other forms of "deviant behavior" were criticized. Proposals were requested on how to improve under the guidance of the Party organizations and with the support of other elements of the political system.

In July 1984, the Politburo discussed possibilities for strengthening the role of the unions. More than in the past, Moscow's Central Council has, meanwhile, been seeing to it that elected union representatives and functionaries from organizations acting on the periphery become more knowledgeable; in addition, it encourages such efforts by regional and branch organizations. Experts, individually or in groups, are dispatched across the land to hurry along an improvement in the work by union representatives. Since 1984, even medium-echelon tenured union functionaries have apparently been dismissed for incompetence or other offenses in greater numbers than before. At the various levels, the "union activists' collective" is convened more frequently, for the purpose of receiving new instructions and exchanging experiences. After some 50,000 such "schools of the union activists' collective" were already in existence by November 1984, the Central Council demanded that they be set up in all committees employing full-time functionaries. The intention may well be to stop the misuse of elected representatives as mere extras and to stop the establishment from belittling them as laymen devoid of opportunities. Incidentally, the "union activists' collectives of the whole country," occasionally convened in Moscow, might well serve the function of enforcing the Party line against conceivable resistance within the established union bureaucracy.

Since late 1984, there have been repeated reports of deliberations in which the collegium of a branch ministry consulted with the top leaders of the respective union on joint efforts to improve economic indices as well as other problems in its domain. Occasionally ranking representatives of the CC Secretariat of the CPSU have been in attendance, presumably to monitor observance of the course that has been determined. The forms of cooperation between union and Party at the regional level are also to be raised to "a new level." The immediate future will tell whether the Kemerovo-case becomes exemplary. With this case, a larger number of union functionaries in the regional Party committee and of Party functionaries in the regional union committee is considered ideal. There, the "schools of the union activists' collectives" have been attached to Party headquarters and are open to plant managers as well; Upon their initiative, a "council of union functionaries" has also constituted itself. On the one hand, these efforts are likely to add to the weight of the union representatives' vote; on the other, this will be at the expense of the remnant of union autonomy, which is modest anyway.

Since more than two thirds of those employed in industry have been organized into brigades, a large part of union work is also to be shifted to this lowest level. By March 1985, related organizational efforts (which were pushed particularly hard in 1984), had resulted in the existence of such groups in over 80 percent of brigades; the union leadership's declared goal is to be able to point to at least one union group per brigade.

The real extent of the contribution by unions and Komsomol to the "Andropov effect" of 1983 and 1984 (in a weaker way) must remain speculative. It goes without saying that the Soviet media as well as the management of these organizations tend to inflate the respective contribution as much as possible so as to prove the "social maturity" of the population or the "efficiency" of these organizations. At any rate, in a closing commentary to accountability and electoral assemblies of the union organizations held between the Fall of 1984 and January 1985, V. Provotorov, a secretary of the Central Council, claimed "broad approval everywhere for the measures designed to strengthen further the socialist work discipline, the level of organization, and order."[5] Nor was there a lack of verbal affirmations of this kind following Gorbachev's election. One of the top union functionaries declared: "The struggle for the greatest possible strengthening of discipline and order in production must be carried on constantly and vigorously."[6]

An Alternative: "Grassroots" Initiatives

In a manner of speaking, the Soviet social order is characterized by frequent attempts to produce the impression that the trigger for certain measures was the "voice of the people." Such was the case again in 1983 and 1984, when various campaigns seemed to originate at the grassroots level.

One example of this is the campaign started by *Pravda* in early September 1984 in which an "open letter" was authored by five brigadiers from different parts of the country.[7] They intended to show the reasons for the numerous deficiencies in the construction industry and submit proposals for an improvement of the situation. Remarkably, they argued that the particular urgency to introduce changes for the better was the result of an increase in the defense budget. This in turn was a consequence of "aggressive acts by the powers in the West hostile to us." The publication's primary objective was undoubtedly to propagate the performance-oriented and autonomous large-scale brigade. So far these had not been nearly as prevalent as envisaged in the plan documents for 1981 through 1985. Barely three weeks later, *Pravda* published a decision by the CC of the CPSU, registering construction workers' approval of the letter and requiring every brigade in the country to consider the letter.

A whole series of approving letters and editorial contributions were printed in the months that followed. One of the more interesting contributions, a conversation between *Pravda*'s economics editor A. Chekalin and the construction worker V. Serikov, who had been on the road for years to promote "brigade organization of work." It contained, for example, the ensuing two statements, and these are almost revolutionary by Soviet standards: (1) Only he who works in a brigade, which receives its payroll funds in return for filling actual orders, can consider himself "a true master of societal wealth." That is, he is an owner of a means of production; and (2) Genuine co-determination by the workers is desirable in the form of an "economic council," enabling "subordinates" to maintain effective control over plant managers by periodically changing composition. This would amount to a kind of rotational principle.[8] In late January 1985, the Politburo approved a catalogue of measures "for the perfection of organization, the wage system, and stimulation of work in construction," which the Council of Ministers of the USSR and the Central Council of the unions had passed shortly before. After L. Kostin, a deputy chairman of the State Committee of the USSR for Labor and Social Questions, had sketched out the major innovations in the press. The text of the resolution—with an unusual delay of five weeks—was also published in early March.[9] Suffice it here to list few key words: brigade system, piece-rate-wages, a system of bonuses tied to deadlines and oriented to quality, and firmer control of wage funds with concomitant acceptance of the essential elements of the so-called Shchokino experiment. Before long, no doubt, these elements will be made mandatory for other branches of the economy as well.

Mobilizing for What and Against What?

Unlike the campaigns of earlier decades, usually designed to achieve a specific objective within a surveyable time frame, the Soviet media have been emphasizing time and again since late 1982 that the campaign for order does not amount to one of the usual temporary phenomena. Instead, it is a long-term move towards a new state of normalcy—specifically, to a reconstitution of the prevailing social mentality or, differently put, to an alteration of certain facets of the national character. This formulation has been chosen here deliberately to clarify the dimensions of the program, and also to hint at the remote chances of lasting success. Of course, as long as the so-called "antipodes of society"—and especially the "antipodes of social progress" (as defined by the Party)—stand in the forefront of state efforts, it is probably reasonable to deduce the lack of a reform concept, as indeed Andropov admitted when he took office.

If sufficiently effective positive stimuli could be brought to bear within the framework of a reform a good many negative phenomena would presumably be at least noticeably reduced. (1) The institution of the merit system, (2) work organized in the form of brigades, as well as (3) a more discerning system of distribution are to be propagated. The first objective implies a wide-ranging reordering of the wage and salary system, of the norms and bonus structure, as well as a comprehensive expansion of the system of competition. The latter is to be achieved in such a way as to let every single employee feel the effects of competition's results, as had been demanded by a leading union functionary in March 1985.[10] To the majority of employees who had gotten somewhat used to the old humdrum ways and manage passably with them, such declarations of intent by the leadership make at least for great insecurity, if they are not taken as an open challenge. Norms would, after all, have to be set so that their fulfillment would ensure the full daily output. The means of production, energy supplies, etc. would also have to be assured. However, since even Soviet media admit that to date the average plant is incapable of this, the skepticism of the employees becomes readily understandable. Lest the generation of such worries block new economic approaches from the outset, the norms have been frozen. For instance, in some plants in Novosibirsk, sites of a special experiment, for the duration of that experiment norms remain the same. It is also emphasized that the change in the norms was to be effected from the bottom up, in cooperation with experts on norm-setting and union representatives, and in an atmosphere of mutual trust. (The latter was not the case as late as mid-1982, according to one tell-tale report.) The Presidium of the Union Central Council considered the question of "measures to improve the setting of labor norms in the economy"[11] in late February 1985 and was then already able to point to considerable "successes" in some sectors of the economy.

The second case, that of implementing the brigade principle, also entails a rather momentous step. Aside from the vast autonomy in terms of labor organization and finances which the brigades strive for, employees this means first of all that they cannot insist on a particular position and a particular kind of work, corresponding to their profession or qualifications acquired through many years,' experience. Instead they must perform different tasks at work as specific exigencies demand. Thus far, a skilled laborer has not, as a rule, been prepared to do work he considered "inferior"—the sole exception being assignments to agriculture or other projects sponsored by a plant. In connection with the third set of endeavors dealing with modifications of the system of distribution, it must be noted that since 1984 categories of "socialist justice" have increasingly been propagated. In March 1985, A. Zdravomyslov began singing hymns of praise, in the union paper *Trud*, about the old ideal of socialist justice: "He who does not work shall not eat."[12] In his speech before ideology experts in late 1984, Gorbachev had also expressly declared himself for "social principles of distribution." By all appearances, more intensive experiments have been launched since February/March 1985 to acquaint the population with the new course of imminent incisive measures; levelling and welfare state principles are to be shelved for some time to come.

One could object that since 1983/84 the media have referred to "social bottlenecks" with greater frequency than before and that the CC of the CPSU has repeatedly called upon all official and social agencies to pay greater attention to social questions. One could further point out that—at least under Chernenko—"the barometer of public opinion" gained a certain measure of importance. But all this is likely attributable primarily to the fact that by 1980/81 at the latest—as a result of developments in Poland—a group within the Party leadership had become aware that certain needs of the people actually had to be taken seriously, or social unrest would be risked. There is another group, to be sure, which cannot conceive of such eruptions in the Soviet Union. This group is convinced potential acts of this sort could be nipped in the bud by the traditional elements of repression. Hence, such statements or measures should not be taken as "social policy" in the good or neutral sense; rather, their character as instruments of crisis-prevention should be emphasized.

Further Levers of Mobilization: Control and Education

Currently, the political leadership is not satisfied simply to decree and administer but seeks the support of "the people" and would like to make credible their greater regard for the "human factor." Party organizations in particular appear eager to trigger "grassroots pressure" to make sure that mobilization takes the direction intended as much as possible. Thus instruments of control are created, the actions of which are parallel to those of state organs of control. In this context, there are reminders of Lenin's "principle of the unity of legislation, management, and control." For the past few years, it even seems to be possible to define periods of stricter control, and this places the concerns emphasized by the media in the foreground: activation of "popular control" in 1981/82; shift to the enterprises, the "collective," and the individual departments/brigades in December 1982 to mid-1983.

Indubitably, the "Law on the Work Collectives and the Increase of their Role in the Management of Enterprises, Institutions, and Organizations," passed in June 1983, must be taken as an outward sign of this last shift of emphasis. This law was highly praised in parts of the Western press in the first months following its adoption as a "Soviet-type right of codetermination." However, the Soviet media then, and again in 1984, never ceased to point out that the tasks of the collectives—and particularly of their management, which, by official version, means first and foremost union committees—

involve primarily the disciplining of the employees. Though other possibilities envisaged by the law are also occasionally mentioned, it is evident that as a rule they are "future dreams." (These other possibilities include participation in the development of projects for the five-year plan, in the appointment or dismissal of executives, and in the distribution of material and social privileges.) Interesting, in this context, is the result of a poll, apparently taken among industrial workers in 1983/84. This poll was brought to the attention of the public in mid-1984 by G. Shakhnazarov. From a list given them, the workers had to rank by priority certain domestic political measures. If the demand to "establish order" clearly came in first place, the desire for participation in business decisions was last. Ostensibly it was also determined that only one in five was dissatisfied with his immediate superiors.[13]

This renewed focus on business often leads to the principle (which is apparently being pursued more vigorously again) that "production . . . is the working man's second home."[14] Hence, reports made particularly positive mention of the fact that in some places union committees, in cooperation with plant management, had succeeded in satisfying all the needs of employees in regard to organized vacations, day care facilities, medical care, and certain services.

Both in terms of importance and membership, the "Committee for Popular Control" with some ten million members ranks first, ahead of the Komsomol control group with five, and the unions' "Social Control group" in the trade and service sector with four million. The organs for popular control are occasionally labelled the "benevolent mentors" of the last two. In his address to the delegates of the "Popular Control group" (October 1984), Chernenko used one of Lenin's phrases, according to which, "accounting and control" is "the main economic task"; he promised the organization more support by the Party committees and the proper Soviet organizations—more support, that is for everything undertaken "courageously and determinedly . . . to protect the interests of society." As he presented the case, the leadership at that point was eager to expand considerably the rights to and opportunities for popular control.

The current situation is marked chiefly by the fact that the Soviet social and economic system has reached the limits of its capacity. In this situation the leadership is searching for new ways to secure Party rule in the medium and long term, to maintain approximately its military might, relative to the US, and to provide for domestic political stability. A rationalization of the centralist system of a planned economy—at the expense of the intermediate level, and for the benefit of the central administration and the plant level—seems the main way to pursue these aims. Simultaneously, the experience gained from solving previous major tasks, or from crisis situations, should be put to more use—and here the industrialization that started in the late 1920s, and in the years 1941 through 1945, come to mind as models. The system of the command economy aside, the focus with regards to the "great Patriotic War" is on the ideological mobilization and the morale probably of the better part of the population. In 1984, attempts were made time and again to give the domestic and foreign public the impression that even today "the people" were still prepared for significantly greater sacrifices. But then Chernenko and others appeasingly expressed their view that this was not necessary yet; but the message could not be missed. Nor should it be forgotten that Andropov *expressis verbis* gave the external threat as justification for the necessity of introducing regulations that entail stiffer penalties.

There is little evidence so far that under Gorbachev the switches will be set differently in the foreseeable future. Thus, the report on the first session of the Politburo after the election of the new secretary general says: "The need to increase labor, state, and Party discipline, to struggle determinedly . . . against everything contrary to socialist norms of life, was particularly stressed."[15] In any event, this is a declaration of intent by the majority of the Politburo. This is also the context in which we must understand Gorbachev's wish to pick up on the alleged popular enthusiasm for the forced industrialization campaign launched in the late twenties. But this also requires an emphatic reminder that at that time peasantry and artisans were all but liquidated as an "incidental phenomenon" of this policy.

In the next few years, the individual Soviet citizen (and especially the individual employee) is most likely to be affected by the manner in which the demand for "control of the rate of work and consumption" advanced at the Twenty-sixth Party Congress of the CPSU (1981) and increasingly translated into daily politics since Andropov, is realized. In the coming decades, it will hardly be possible to retain many of the liberties in various areas of society and of the economy, obtained through the pertinacity of the population or granted to them between 1955 and 1975.

Notes

1. *Iz*, 12 July 1983.
2. *Pr*, 6 October 1984.
3. *Iz*, 21 April 1984; *Pr*, 12 March 1985.
4. *Iz*, 16 and 20 February 1985.
5. *Trud*, 15 March 1985.
6. *Loc. cit.*
7. *Pr*, 8 September 1984.
8. *Pr*, 7 October 1985.
9. *Trud*, 5 March 1985.
10. *Trud*, 15 March 1985.
11. *Trud*, 28 February 1985.
12. *Trud*, 10 March 1985.
13. *Iz*, 31 July 1984; *Sovetskaya Rossiya*, 6.2.1985.
14. *Trud*, 15 March 1985.
15. *Iz*, 22 March 1985.

8
The New School Reform

Oskar Anweiler and Friedrich Kuebart

Following the failure of the rashly implemented "polytechnical school reform" of 1958/59 under Khrushchev, Soviet education policy after 1966 was characterized for about a decade by the "stability and continuity" demanded by the Party leadership: Long-term and more comprehensive reform objectives took a back seat to the expansion of the existing school system, to the demands for increases in instruction quality and performance, in vocational training, and to efforts towards an increasingly political-ideological education. The sweeping effectuation of compulsory education for at least ten years for juveniles, which can be acquired in the existing general and vocational schools ("full secondary education"), was considered the main achievement of the seventies: In the ten grades of secondary school, in the part-time general evening or shift-secondary school, in the secondary vocational-technical training institutions, or in the secondary technical schools. The two last types of schools also provide "general secondary education" together with their main objective of a professional qualification.

The formal rise in the level of education achieved in the seventies and the general extention of schooling for most juveniles, however, exacerbated the discrepancies between the educational and the occupational system. This is because numerous so-called "mass occupations" suffer from a shortage of recruits. At the same time, there is a run on universities. The number of university applicants has been reduced overall, but still, averaged nationwide and by discipline, it is more than double the number of available openings. As early as 1977, polytechnical job instruction in grades 9 and 10 of secondary schools was doubled to four hours per week in order to effect a reorientation of adolescents' training and occupational preferences. The course was charted in the direction of enhanced occupational relevance and training for work as well as guidance towards critical occupations in "material production." However, the about-face in school policy initiated here has not shown as yet whether these innovations will lead to a more comprehensive reform of the school and training system. Up to 1983 contradictory opinions on the function and character of the vocational polytechnical job instruction were put forth, and the relationship of the general to the vocational sector was left undefined.

The "Reform Package" of 1984

Such plans were announced at the June 1983 plenary session of the CC of the CPSU, and there was no hint of intended educational reform. A special commission of the Politburo was set up to prepare the reform.[1] In early January 1984, a draft reform document appeared, entitled "Main Directions for Reforms of General Schools and Vocational Schools."[2] Ever since the autumn of 1983, it has been possible to find numerous position papers and letters to the editor in the general and the specialized press on various aspects of the reform, reflecting a broad spectrum of views. The reform plans were formally adopted at the sessions of the CC of the CPSU on 10 April 1984 and of the Supreme Soviet of the USSR on 12 April 1984; compared to the draft, the final version of the "Main Directions" contained several rather insignificant alterations or additions. In a parallel move, a total of six further Party and government decrees were issued, comprising implementing statutes and numerous details of the projected measures.[3] The substitution in December 1984 of M.A. Prokofyev, who had been Minister of People's Education since 1966, for S.G. Shcherbakov marked the turning-point in school policy even at the very top.

In content, the reform projects extend to pre-school education and starting school a year earlier, to the new structure of "general and vocational secondary school," to work instruction and the pupils' productive labor, to the system of occupational training, and, finally, to teacher training and pay. The area of university education is also autonomous in terms of ministerial responsibility, and it is not initially affected by the reform. Secondary-level vocational training, subject to the same ministry, is touched only to the extent that the reform aims at greater unification of the general educational content of all curricula in senior high school.

The timetable envisages a step-by-step implementation between 1985 and 1990 even and beyond. Particular attention will be paid to regional and local pecularities so that certain differences in practical solutions (e.g. regarding children's starting school earlier), may also occur. Phased implementation of the reform, the possibility of regional deviation in details, as well as firm emphasis on continuity with previous school policy are meant to prevent the errors of Khrushchev's 1958 reform, to which reference was occasionally made during the reform debate.

Structural Alterations and Content Changes in the General Education System

The alterations to the school system envisaged by the reform concentrate on the entrance phase and the senior level. In part this takes up and puts into practice goals and innovative approaches already contemplated in the past few years. This holds especially for the younger age at which children now start school. The Twenty-sixth Party Congress of the CPSU decided to lower the age from seven to six. Now, elementary school is extended by the extra year to comprise four years again after it had been reduced to three years in around 1970. This way the general secondary school—as was the case between 1958 and 1964–again has an eleventh grade. However, this will not delay the availability of graduates to the labor market by a year.

The centerpiece of the Soviet unified school system, the "incomplete secondary school," will henceforth comprise nine grades. The reform brings no changes to the duration and organizational-administrative structure of educational careers on the senior high school level following grade 9, i.e., senior level of the secondary school (grades 10 and 11, and in the Baltic republics, 10–12), secondary vocational-technical school and secondary trade school. The consolidation of the three school types at the senior level into the new designation of "general and vocational secondary school" indicates a long-term integration-intent; still, it retains but a somewhat symbolic character for the foreseeable future, intended to signal the common tasks of these curricula and their equivalence in principle.

According to the reform plans, the number of graduates from the mandatory ninth grade who transfer to a vocational school is to double approximately in the long run. This would require some 50 percent of a class to be channelled into this type of school. The secondary school's senior level, which on a nation-wide average currently absorbs some 60 percent of those leaving grade 9, would be considerably reduced in quantitative terms. The redirection in the flow of pupils is to be achieved as a supplement to rigid educational planning at the regional and central level and chiefly through intensified occupational orientation and by means of job instruction.

The principle of a uniform basic education, mandatory for all pupils, remains applicable to the general secondary school. Yet at the same time, the reform continues along the path of limited differentiation in the content of the curricula in the senior grades. This is a path taken in the sixties in the form of optional courses aimed at giving greater consideration to the development of individual penchants and talents. The reform documents sidestepped the question of special schools because then as now it is ticklish in terms of social policy. It is also controversial, as debate of the draft reform shows. These special schools have expanded course offerings in certain subjects and partially selective character. The Party leadership, in any case, indicated that it considers a demonstrative expansion of this form of talent selection and promotion uncalled for.[4]

Structural adjustments aside, the reform also aims at changing the shape of the content of school-education and at improving the quality of instruction. This means another review of the "model time-table" and of syllabi. After the curricula had been subjected to repeated revisions since the mid-sixties, the new time-table and the reformed syllabi are to take effect in 1986. Since the number of hours devoted to the subject of "vocation" has been greatly expanded—in grades 10 and 11, it has doubled from four to eight hours per week, six hours each for grades 8 and 9. This must be compensated for by reducing the number of periods devoted to other subjects. Moreover, the subject of "Ethics and Psychology of Family Life," combining elements of biology, pedagogy, and sex education, has been added since 1985, though it is granted only one hour per week in grade 10. Shifts in the number of periods are also projected for foreign languages and geography. However, on a whole the new revision of the time-table is not supposed to alter significantly its traditional basic structure.[5] The reform of the syllabi, especially in the major science-oriented subjects (*osnovy nauk*), involves a structure of content which would "clear out" redundancies in the curriculum, do away with mere "memorization," and avoid an excessive degree of scientific abstraction. This is to diminish inordinate demands on pupils, which is increasingly a subject of public criticism. This problem was particularly acute in connection with the introduction of mandatory secondary education in the seventies.

The key position in the reforms of syllabi and time-tables is undoubtedly held by vocational instruction, which entails the acquisition of preliminary occupational qualifications. Thus, the secondary school is included in the new educational policy concept of "occupational training for all adolescents" which ties into a solution that provides a "secondary education for all." While since 1977, vocational instruction in secondary schools has set chiefly pre-professional objectives, the new school reform requires that from now on schools generally supply training for "mass occupations." Up to grade 7, vocational instruction is to be "polytechnical," but from grade 8 onwards the aspect of productive labor and occupational specialization will move to the fore. The first level, in grades 8 and 9, will still concentrate mainly on a broad orientation regarding occupational areas and preparation for choosing one's further course of study. In grades 10 and 11 (and sometimes 12), students will receive regular on-the-job training during the time that had previously been reserved for vacations. The focus will be on specialized occupational training, leading up to a qualifying examination.

Occupational training as part of the school curriculum requires close cooperation between school and business, but the necessity of providing the requisite training and jobs causes considerable economic and organizational problems. Already on 30 August 1984, the Council of Ministers of the USSR had enacted a "Regulation for the Base-Enterprise of General Schools" which governs relations between the two institutions and their respective tasks.[6] The inter-school teaching and production combines which have been expanded over the past decade as training and work places for pupils from several schools and which also handle part of the occupational orientation, will henceforth be increasingly available to pupils in grades 8 and 9. As occupational orientation in schools and combines has not so far proven sufficiently effective, a separate system of local occupational counselling centers is currently being tried out. These are subordinated to the State Committee for Labor and Social Questions as the central state labor authority. But of course, the multitude of measures aimed at intensifying occupational training in schools does not guarantee that the frequently deplored aversion of many adolescents towards unskilled physical labor can be overcome.

Above all, clashes are to be expected between the mandate of the secondary school to take on training for jobs that require few qualifications and its traditional function of providing college-preparatory education. There is reason to doubt that this is the way the majority of pupils will form a lasting identification with the occupation learned in school.

The projected introduction of computer courses to contribute to the "elimination of computer illiteracy"[7] in Soviet society must also be viewed in the context of the reform's desired modernization of educational contents and adaptation to the needs of the economy. Initial plans started at first with the premise that these classes would essentially be concentrated in schools with enhanced emphasis on math classes, until the requisite personnel and material infrastructure has been created and the didactic experience has been gained. They can then be offered at the "mass school." However, in early January 1985, the USSR's Ministry for Popular Education passed a "priority plan" providing for an autonomous subject called "Basics of Computer Science and Electronic Computer Technology," to be taught in all schools starting with the 1985/86 academic year.[8] Because computers are not available to schools in sufficient quantities for the time being, syllabi for this subject are prepared in two variants for instruction with or without machines. The forced "computerization" of schools is accompanied by extensive training and continuing education for teachers, though qualitatively speaking these measures can be no more than stop-gaps for the time being. This computerization is, incidentally, connected to the program to foster production and application of computer technology to the year 2000, which was adopted by the Politburo at the turn of 1984/85.[9]

For some time, the Soviet public and experts have been criticizing not only the content, but also the forms and results of school instruction. Only a few of the problems involved can be pointed out here. Improvement in the quality of instruction is to be achieved above all through the modernization of forms and methods of instruction. This means teachers should be granted more leeway for autonomous, flexible action. However, that would presuppose dismantling bureaucratic hindrances and control mechanisms that often stand in the way of pedagogical innovation "in the field" and time and again stifle the initiative demanded of the teachers. An improvement in the quality of instruction is also expected from a reduction of class sizes. Here specific standards are provided: In grades 1 to 9 the number of students is to be lowered to thirty in grades 10 and 11 to a maximum of twenty-five, whereas the currently applicable limits are forty and thirty-five, respectively. These limits, however, have frequently been exceeded in practice. Often overcrowded classes are combined with instruction in shifts, to boot. Given its financial implications, this innovation, in any event, can be realized only in the long run—in the next decade.

Public criticism of the work done by schools often culminates in the problem of assessing performance of the pupils primarily, but beyond that of the teachers and the school itself. Also, this problem was brought to its current head by the increase in school attendance in the seventies and the official call upon teachers to take even less motivated and capable pupils to successful completion of their program. Since teacher performance is evaluated predominantly on the basis of the percentage of successful pupils, they tend to produce a more advantageous picture of their performance than warranted by grading accordingly. This is a practice frequently denounced as "percentomania." Now, the reform is to blaze a trail for more objective criteria to control the work of teachers and schools as well as for a more discerning assessment of pupil performance. Taking the judgements advanced during the reform debates as a yardstick, that practice has cost schools a considerable loss of trust and public respect, damage the reform seeks to repair.

Expansion and Restructuring of Vocational Training

As indicated by the projected changes on the senior secondary level, a significant emphasis of the reform focuses on raising the standing of vocational training. The guiding objective of "vocational training for all adolescents" means that at least in the long run every adolescent is to receive qualified vocational training upon graduating from grade 9.

Notwithstanding considerable expansion during the past decades, the system of vocational-technical schools will be unable to solve this problem in the foreseeable future on its own: Nearly two thirds—the precise data vary here—of those starting out in an occupation still receive only short-term and narrowly specialized training on the job or—in more propitious cases—at educational facilities in the company. Since, in the course of the reform, the secondary school is assigned the training for industrial "mass jobs," it assumes in a way the function of on-the-job-training, which had long been criticized as ineffective from the perspective of educational economy and the contents and quality of on-the-job training can hardly be regulated.

The new comprehensive system of vocational training as conceived by the reform, then, concentrates on forms of vocational training in schools, and the secondary vocational school retains its function of training lower and middle-echelon management personnel ("sergeants of industry"). At the same time, a division of labor between the senior level of the secondary school and the vocational-technical school system is projected for the training of blue collar workers. Here, the secondary school takes responsibility for less skilled "mass occupations" that require a shorter investment of time to learn. Training for occupations demanding higher qualifications, particularly in the area of modern technology, is restricted to the vocational school sector. Bringing about this division of labor in vocational training creates new problems of planning and coordination. Since the prevailing practice has proven unsatisfactory, adequate planning instruments remain to be devised for directing the transition to the various types of training after grade 9 and setting the appropriate quotas of pupils. These quotas are to be handled flexibly, according to regional and sectoral needs for qualified manpower. An essential point of departure rests with the business and its planning needs. The insufficient planning discipline of business, due to a lack of adequately stringent guidelines, is widely criticized.[10] Beyond that, however, coordination among vocational training institutions is required with regard to the respective qualifications and occupations they are to impart. The compilation of a list of training occupations and their assignment to the various forms of training was initiated under the auspices of the State Committee for Vocational-Technical Training of the USSR, and completion is slated for 1985.

The distribution of tasks in vocational training as well as the projected quantitative redirection of the flow of pupils underscores the significance of the vocational-technical schools as a core component in the overall system of vocational training. To enhance its attractiveness as the main road to the working world and to give it greater flexibility in the satisfaction of local and regional manpower requirements, it is to be reorganized, though without fundamental adjustments to its existing individual components: Various departments are being subsumed under the label "secondary vocational-technical school." Depending on the educational background of the pupils, this (a) follows grade 9 of the secondary school and, in conjunction with vocational training, offers graduation with "completed secondary education" (up to now the secondary vocational-technical schools); or (b) following graduation from secondary school, imparts an occupational qualification in no more than one year of training (up to now technical training institutions). For the time being, (c) the remaining "ordinary" vocational-technical schools, too, will survive under one roof and offer training for less demanding occupations. The reassignment of the individual school types is already scheduled for 1985. To prevent it from happening on paper only considerable investments are necessary, and these will certainly require ample time.

Vocational-technical schools also face another revision of their syllabi. For one, the new canon of general education, mandatory for all types of secondary schools, must be integrated; for another, the modernization of subject contents is to be promoted. Thus, the "Basics of Programming and Computer Technology" is to appear as a new subject. Finally, there is the matter of establishing direct links to the preparatory activities of the general school. But the educational tasks set for the vocational-technical school are apt to be even more difficult, not just regarding such objectives as "high working morale" and "civic-mindedness," but even more in the sense of overcoming everyday educational difficulties. These difficulties result from the fact that in the past these schools often had to accept the less motivated and capable pupils. This has enduringly tarnished their public image; only when this has been changed will it be possible to talk about a success of the reforms.

The Ideological Component in Education

Soviet education theory has always followed the principle of "unity of instruction and education," and since the seventies it has placed particular emphasis upon the task of "complex educational action."[11] This was both to take into account the increasingly complex tasks of teaching juveniles and to achieve a planned coordination of the prime educational institutions: home and family, school, children's and juvenile groups, and business. The guidelines for school reform call for intensified educational efforts, especially in the area of political-ideological, ethical and vocational education. The most important measure envisaged is the elaboration of a compulsory central "Program for Educational Work" which is to replace the existing "model schedule" of education and to guarantee unified and controllable educational work in schools. For the task of ideological consciousness raising, notable emphasis is placed upon the need for a "pugnacious atheist education" to counterbalance widespread "neutral" attitudes towards religion or existing religious practices and tendencies among the young.[12] The task of "immunizing" Soviet youth "against bourgeois ideology" is just as striking, and it is now openly referred to as such.[13] This defensive component of ideological education, designed to shelter adolescents from all uncontrollable influences, is also at the bottom of the projected content-review of syllabi and textbooks for history and social studies classes in the new general and vocational secondary schools.

The first year of the school reform coincides with the 40th anniversary of the "victory over fascism." The large-scale propaganda actions covered all schools and institutions of higher learning from the beginning of the academic year 1984/85 to May 1985.[14] This is also the outward culmination of efforts at patriotic defense training, considerably stepped up since the early eighties. In addition, schools are to be involved to a greater extent and more effectively in the overall "system of military-patriotic education" through the establishment (already under way) of a network of "base and supply depot schools for premilitary training."[15] Reports by draft boards and district command headquarters of inadequate premilitary knowledge and skills on the part of young male draftees seems to have been as alarming here as the frequently deplored lack of ideological "firmness." Though it is probably incorrect to speak of a direct "militarization" of Soviet schooling, the intensified measures in this area, planned in the school reform, are undoubtedly meant to contribute to tightening political control over the young and thereby indirectly to discipline Soviet society.

Notes

1. For details on the course of events from June 1983 to April 1984 see O. Anweiler, "Die sowjetische Schul- und Berufsbildungsreform von 1984," in: *OE*, No. 34 (1984), pp. 838–860.

2. *Pr*, 4 January 1984.

3. Individually listed with sources in Anweiler, *op. cit.*, p. 841. These documents and other materials are collected in O *reform obshcheobrazovatelnoy i professionalnoy shkoly. Sbornik dokumentov i materialov* (Moscow, 1984).

4. On this see M. Zimyanin, Secretary of the CC of the CPSU, in *K*, No. 7 (1984), p. 23.

5. Cf. the interview with the First Deputy Minister of Popular Education of the USSR, F.G. Panachin, in *Uchitelskaya gazeta*, 15 December 1984.

6. *Sobranie postanovleniy pravitelstva SSSR 1984*, 29, Pos. 160, pp. 531–537.

7. Thus M.A. Prokofyev, Minister of Popular Education of the USSR, in *Narodnoe obrazovanie*, N. 9 (1984), p. 3. Cf. also Arnold Buchholz, "Science and Technology," in this volume, Chapter 10.

8. *Uchitelskaya gazeta*, 15 January 1985; cf. also the report on the session of the Politburo in *Pr*, 29 March 1985.

9. *Pr*, 4 January 1985.

10. Cf. *Iz*, 31 October 1984.

11. Cf. on this Anweiler, in OE, No. 7 (1978), pp. 573–585.

12. Cf. Prokofyev, *op. cit.*, p. 4.

13. Prokofyev, in *Narodnoe obrazovanie*, No. 11 (1984), p. 25.

14. Cf. the action-program for the preparation and implementation of the celebrations on the occasions of the victory anniversary enacted by the Ministry of Popular Education of the USSR, in *Byulleten normativnykh aktov Ministerstva prosveshcheniya SSSR*, No. 11 (1984), pp. 3–7.

15. *Byulleten normativnykh aktov Ministerstva prosveshcheniya SSSR*, No. 6 (1984), pp. 17–19.

9
Why Does the Party Need Sociologists and Psychologists?

Thomas Kussmann

The Party would like to utilize the expertise of specialists and at the same time protect itself from codetermination by experts.

On the one hand, the social and behavioral sciences are to supply empirical foundations for measures involving family policy, education, manpower, health policy, social security for the elderly, and other areas with political aims and state regulatory functions; i.e., to place socio-economic planning on a rational footing and promote its translation into practice.[1]

On the other hand, Party leadership does not want to become dependent on experts. The Party wants to make its own decisions. Only the Party is supposed to assign priorities to goals and still retain the option to decree the timing and nature of any given measure down to the last detail. It legitimizes this claim with the ideology of historical materialism.

Ideology and Empirical Social Sciences

When the Party began soliciting advice from scientists in the late fifties, scientific analysis took aim at ideology proper.[2] Since the late sixties the Party has signalled time and again: Advice on practical politics is welcome, but it must not touch on ideology. Such signals are broadcast and received on many channels; basic Party organizations in institutes and in administration assume a special role.[3]

In 1983 and 1984, members of the Politburo of the CPSU left no doubt about the fact that the basic values of the political system of the USSR must not be assailed (Andropov in February 1983, Andropov and Chernenko in June 1983, Gorbachev in December 1984).

Various discussions were tangent to ideology. In 1982, academic circles began leaking them to the public. Party organizations have either ignored or blocked these outward discussions. In 1984, the editors of the periodical *Voprosy filosofii* had to engage in public self-criticism for assigning space to a controversial discussion of the ideologically "correct" explanation of political crises of confidence and conflicts in communist-ruled countries.[4]

Similarly drastic calls for unity on the ideological front during Stalin's times caused the prevention of whole sciences, such as sociology and psychology, not only from dealing with "ideologically sensitive" questions, but some were prohibited altogether. What is apparently at issue today is not the prohibition of individual social and behavioral sciences, but their mobilization to further the Party's influence in all areas of state and society. Through "practical recommendations," sociologists are to assist the Party in maintaining the political system as it is.

The resolution of the June 1983 CC plenary session concerned with ideological and mass political work by the Party said: "Party and state expect economists, philosophers, historians, sociologists, psychologists, and jurists to work out reliable ways to raise productivity and to research the laws of the development of the classless structure of society, the internationalization of social life, the development of socialist popular rule, social conscience, and problems in communist education."[5] The subjects listed are the social sciences, and each of these subjects is represented at the Academy of Sciences with an institute of its own.

Control by Coordination

Through "coordination," the CC in Moscow would like to take a firmer hold on the results of research at the Party, Academy, and state institutes. Each discipline is to get a center of coordination. To be sure, all important posts at the institutes are already subject to the "Nomenklatura," i.e., the Party has final say in filling them. Depending on type and location of the institutes, however, they fall under the jurisdiction of different CC departments in several Union-republics, where "interesting" research institutes have meanwhile come into being, e.g., the Institute for Research and Formation of Public Opinion at the CC of the Georgian CP in Tbilisi.[6]

At the Twenty-fifth Party Congress, Brezhnev had demanded that the Party put to use those research findings that skirt the borderline between natural and social sciences (those are the behavioral sciences) and that it pay more attention to public opinion research (this applies to sociologists). The entire "Party work" must be better coordinated by means of a "complex approach."[7] The first step in this direction consisted in assigning central responsibility for all Party colleges throughout the Soviet Union to the Party College for Social Sciences at the CC in Moscow (*Akademiya obshchestvennykh nauk pri Tsk KPSS*, abbreviated: AON). This highest educational establishment of the CC of the CPSU has been the leading teaching, science, and scientific-methodological center for Party, state, and ideological cadres since the spring of 1978.[8]

In 1978, an unsuccessful suggestion was advanced to establish an institute for scientific communism in the Academy of Sciences. This would have raised the standing of this science, provided it with an academic center of coordination, and faciliated direct control by the Party College for Social Sciences of the CC. During an inspection of the social science section in the Academy of Sciences by the Presidium of the Academy, various members of the Academy went on record as believing the establishment of an institute of scientific communism to be superfluous because this science already had a coordinating center in the Party College for Social Sciences at the CC in Moscow. The philosopher B.S. Ukraintsev (director of the Institute of Philosophy of the Academy of Sciences from 1974 to 1983) declared that scientific communism was inseparable from the rest of philosophy; if this were done anyway, the result would only be "scholastic theorizing" (a formulation employed by Brezhnev in 1976).[9] In 1978, the Presidium of the Academy was apparently unwilling to impose such an institute of ideology and Party politics on the section.

Following the CC's 1983 plenary session on ideology, "coordination" gathered momentum again. Chernenko had endorsed the foundation of a central institute for research and the formation of public opinion.[10] From 20 to 21 November 1984, a so-called scientific-practical conference on questions of the development of sociological research was held in Kiev. It brought together functionaries from Party, state, and the Academy of Sciences, among them the ideology secretaries of the Georgian (G.N. Enukidze) and Ukrainian (O.S. Kapto) central committees, the head of the Department of Ideological Work of the Academy of Social Sciences at the CC (S.T. Toshchenko), the Vice-President of the Academy of Sciences (P.N. Fedoseyev), and the director of the Sociological Academy Institute (Vilen Ivanov). Possibly, this conference was preparatory to the establishment of the institute Chernenko had called for.[11]

Stepping Up Social Research

In June 1983, Chernenko had demanded a restructuring of the Sociological Academy Institute. It was to offer more practically applicable recommendations. On 16 October 1984, V. Ivanov, head of the institute since mid-1983, communicated the results of the restructuring in *Pravda*. According to him the institute now has two main projects: "the social sphere and its development up to the year 2005" as well as "sociological problems in research on, and formation of public opinion."[12]

Microcensus. A microcensus covering 5 percent of the population (14 million citizens) was taken from 2 to 11 January 1985. It is expected to yield insights into prospects for manpower reproduction. Presumably, measures will be implemented to stimulate population growth in the European parts of the USSR and to establish a trend towards smaller families in the Asian (Islamic) parts of the Soviet Union. This could be done by readjusting state child support payments for instance.[13] It would certainly be useful to use opinion polls to find out how the affected population groups would react to conceivable measures and alternatives.

Opinion Research. Opinion polls have been taken in the USSR since the sixties and even published in part. Prior to the death of Suslov there seem to have been differing opinions in the Politburo regarding the extent to which such information was to be collected and used. In 1983, E. Teague concluded in an analysis of the revival of opinion research in the USSR that Suslov was always more concerned with influencing public opinion than with researching it. Time and again Suslov warned emphatically against "slipping" into "pragmatism" and "empiricism." Chernenko, in contrast, declared in 1979 that opinion research was important to "fathom the moods in the masses," for it enabled the Party "to understand the masses and express correctly what they have on their minds."[14] From this perspective, the function of opinion surveys is to determine conflict potentials and receive crisis signals. There were crisis situations in 1953 in the GDR, in 1956 in Hungary and Poland, in 1968/69 in Czechoslovakia, and in 1970 and the early eighties in Poland. As stated earlier, there have been increasing signs since late 1984 that opinion research is being put on a broader base.

Counterpropaganda. A great deal of importance is attached to scientific corroboration of propaganda. If Brezhnev had spoken of information policy having to "follow the hot trail of events," Chernenko was more outspoken yet: "Let us not deceive ourselves: If we explain any given event superficially or report it belatedly, we no longer merely have to convince, but we must alter convictions, and that is considerably more difficult."[15]

A renunciation of "ideology by the ton" is emerging in Soviet propaganda. If the question so far has been, "How many posters do we need," it is now: "Who selects what from the information available and why? Where do we pick up the threads?" This is a commonplace in the West generally and in the Soviet Union among a handful of experts. It is news to ideology and propaganda functionaries.[16]

Propaganda should be attuned to national, cultural, educational, age, and other differences. For instance, social scientists have established that in Estonia, eighteen-year-olds with an eighth grade diploma are more likely to tune in Finnish television than other population groups.[17] Now sociologists are supposed to tell the Estonian CC why this is so and what can be done about it; tearing down aerials from roofs and jamming the signals are out of the question.

The Tasks of Psychology

Psychology's catalogue of duties has been expanded. In 1983, the Presidium of the Academy of Sciences confirmed the Academy Institute of Psychology's coordinating role in experimental and applied psychology. (The Academy Institute of Psychology has been in existence since 1971.)[18] This institute has been particularly successful in its work on labor-psychological and ergonomic questions, i.e., subjects of inquiry that can be operationalized and studied in a comparatively clear way using mathematical and natural science methods and experimental scrutiny.

Now the institute has been assigned additional tasks in "ideologically sensitive" fields. For example, it is to establish a department of experimental social psychology that will be devoted to the study of relations between group and performance in business and other organizations. But it might also concern itself with research into national prejudices and possibilities of fighting them.

The "human factor." The decisive tasks of psychology are perceived as being investigation of the "human factor" and means of influence. Even in a factory crammed with robots, man remains the decisive "factor," as Chernenko, like many before him, said in an election speech in 1984.[19] The achievements of Soviet engineer-psychologists in optimizing the operation of machines and the design of workshops are undisputed. The training center for cosmonauts in Baykonur is headed by a psychologist who holds the rank of general.

In the summer of 1982, the director of the Psychological Academy Institute cautioned against expecting lasting improvements from crude campaigns for "work discipline." In 1983, he was placed in charge of research on the fundamentals that would make such a campaign effective.[20] In 1982 he stated:

> The findings from psychological studies can be used to improve social and productive processes. But it must be said that this task is not an easy one. For instance, it is naïve to assume that a significant and lasting rise in work productivity can be achieved by direct influence upon the psyche of the working people. That is a complex task.[21]

This would necessitate synchronization with contributions by technicians, organizational sociologists, physicians, and other experts. While there are no pat solutions, practice reports from psychologists' workshops, like those published time and again in Soviet dailies, indicate that any psychological cure for an organization and its working conditions starts with the improvement of communication and mutual information through the creation of new working groups and changed reporting procedures.[22]

In 1979, the Institute for General and Pedagogical Psychology of the Academy of Pedagogical Sciences founded a counselling center for family psychological assistance. This center has been expanded, and it now counsels on educational and marital problems. It is under the leadership of the Counsel for Family Problems, established by the local Party Committee in Moscow's Lenin district.[23]

Political socialization. There is a working group on political psychology in the Psychological Institute of the Academy of Sciences that holds fully to the line of the CC's Party Academy in denouncing the abuse of psychology to indoctrinate people. This abuse is allegedly observable in the West.[24]

In 1977, other high-ranking psychologists proposed to make political socialization a long term focus of investigation; in other words, of research on how political opinions and values are learned. Soviet psychologists envisage this learning as a life-long process. They believe that before one can try to influence it, one has to study its uninfluenced course first. How, then, do people learn any given set of opinions and values, including political ones?[25] Like developmental and social psychologists in the West, they led off with research into the acquisition of moral concepts such as honesty in children.

Hence, today, as indeed ever since the renewed acceptance of psychology and sociology in the late fifties, one finds criticism by Soviet experts that conforms to the ideology of "bourgeois science," along with methodologically acceptable empirical work on the same questions. There are publications by adherents to each school of thought. The really important problem is how politically motivated interpretations of basic assumptions in archetype-ideology result in expert scientists excluding "ideologically sensitive" questions because they do not want to be accused of "slipping into pragmatism and empiricism."

This problem is caused by the fact that all branches of science are obligated to adhere to the ideology. For there are three prongs for each individual science: ideology, ideological foundations for the scientific subject, and working methods for the scientific subject. If they correctly use the tools of their trade (the methodology of their particular branches of science), social and behavioral scientists working empirically time and again come upon research findings which fail to confirm the ideology's claim to cover everything. Areas of research are "ideologically sensitive" if they produce results at variance with basic ideological principles. Empirical psychological research that has practical applicability must augment revision of "ideologically sensitive" subjects (and in the process comes up against the ideological objections added in parentheses): differential psychology ("but psychologists are not supposed to classify people"); individual motivation ("but, after all, the motives supplied by the collective are the guiding ones"); individual and group performance ("but there isn't a problem that the individual can solve better on his own; as a general principle, the collective is superior to the individual"); personality ("after all, we see personality in the sense of an improvement. Only he who accepts the values of our social order and lives by them is recognized as a personality"); individual ("but we have overcome bourgeois individualism"); political socialization ("Beware of making historical materialism psychological!").

Open Questions

Sociology's peculiar academic status and the absence of a professional classification for psychologists are questions that are left open in discussions about a "mobilization" of sociology and psychology.

Sociology is a secondary course of study. The relevant knowledge and skills are acquired during the candidacy of philosopher, historian, jurist, or economist who is interested in sociology and academic degrees are bestowed in those disciplines. Among the 6,000 sociologists, one finds many experts on historical materialism and few on empirical social research, but among them are several who have been held in high esteem since the sixties.[26] Since the early seventies the directors and staff at the Sociological Academy Institute have been replaced repeatedly.

In contrast, more natural science-oriented psychology succeeded in the sixties and seventies to establish itself as a field of instruction with its own faculties and institutes at eleven universities. Since the late sixties, psychologists have been granted psychology degrees (and no longer teaching degrees as before).[27]

Since 1978, when it was charged to do so by the Presidium of the Academy of Sciences, the Soviet Psychological Society (with 5,000 members) has attempted to set up a central administration for "psychological service" in the USSR.[28] This central administration might be attached to the State Committee for Science and Technology and assume tasks similar to those of a ministry of health dealing with the employment and training of physicians, or a ministry of justice dealing with the employment of lawyers. There is no ministry of psychology in any Western country, only more or less specific regulations for the professional activities of psychologists. However, under the circumstances in the USSR, a central administration for the employment of a university-trained professional group is apparently indispensable. Nonetheless, the establishment of a "state committee for psychology" is treated with reluctance, though it is not being blocked. Against all expectations, the topic was not central in reports on the Society's convention in August 1983; still, in 1983 the Presidium of the Academy urged the Institute to take on the coordination of all facilities providing psychological services in the USSR.[29]

In mid-1984, a "long-expected" meeting of all heads of psychological services took place. The psychologists in the training institutes and practicing psychologists are forming "four sections for psychological services" (industry, health, school, university). They are joining together in an all-Union center for the coordination of psychological services, under the auspices of the executive board of the Soviet Psychological Society. It is to coordinate working out scientific, legal, organizational, and methodological fundamentals for service in the USSR as well as the supply of technical and computer-mathematical resources. Above all, a methodology center must also be established to control the selection and approbation of working methods and instruments (e.g. testing procedures).[30] Perhaps the Soviet Psychological Society is intent on integrating its all-Union center with the State Committee for Science and Technology.

The institutionalization of sociology as a teaching subject at universities, which is possibly to be expected, and the steps towards a professional classification for psychologists are simple indicators that there is a genuine political will to procure rational bases for political planning decisions. It also indicates that will is growing. Be that as it may, in that special area of tension between politicization and professionalization, the mobilization of these sciences will remain an adventure to be mastered only by means of a certain pragmatism.[31] And, paradoxically enough, that seems intentional: Experts are to concern themselves with questions for specialist, and ideologists are to see to the "maintenance of the purity of doctrine."

In February 1985, the Academy of Sciences published a resolution on the Sociological Institute's scientific activity. This resolution confirmed the well-known areas of emphasis (public opinion research, social structure, problems of manpower), holding out the prospect of the institutionalization of sociology as a subject of instruction at universities, and urging the Institute to cooperate more closely with the central statistical office, with Gosplan, and with the State Committee for Labor. Like the Psychological Institute a year earlier, the Sociological Institute was not also charged with the coordination of all pertinent specialized institutes.[32]

Notes

1. V. Ivanov, in *SIss*, No. 4 (1983), pp. 3-8, and No. 4 (1984), pp. 3-9.
2. Dmitri N. Shalin, in *Annual Review of Sociology* (1978), pp. 171-191.
3. Robert F. Miller, in *Soviet Studies*, Vol. 37, No. 4 (1985), pp. 31-59.
4. Cf. Helmut Dahm, "Ideology as a Key to Politics," in this volume, Chapter 6.
5. Quoted in: *Psikhologicheskiy zhurnal*, No. 5 (1983), p. 3.
6. E.A. Shevardnadze, in *SIss*, No. 3 (1984), pp. 7-12.
7. Cf. T. Kussmann, in *The Soviet Union 1978/79*, pp. 21.
8. *K*, No. 5 (1978), p. 3.
9. *Vestnik Akademii Nauk SSSR*, No. 9 (1978), pp. 35-47.
10. *Materialy Plenuma Tsentralnogo Komiteta KPSS 14–15 iyunya 1983 goda*, Politizdat (Moscow, 1983), pp. 32, 63, 79.
11. *RL*, No. 460 (1984).
12. For more detail see notes 1 and 32.
13. *KZ*, 3 January 1985, and *RL*, No. 491 (1984).
14. *RL*, No. 109 (1983); *K*, No. 4 (1980), p. 26; *World Marxist Review*, No. 5 (1979), p. 9 (cit. in E. Teague).
15. *ND*, 15 June 1983.
16. A.A. Bodalev, Yu.A. Sherkovin, in *Voprosy psikhologii*, No. 3 (1977), pp. 3-11; T. Kussmann, *Berichte des BIOst*, No. 38 (1978).
17. *RL*, No. 461 (1983), p. 3; V. Ivanov, *SIss*, No. 3 (1983), pp. 36-43.
18. *Vestnik Akademii Nauk SSSR*, No. 2 (1984), pp. 10-21, p. 21.
19. *Sotsialisticheskaya industriya*, 28 July 1984.
20. *Vestnik Akademii Nauk SSSR*, No. 2 (1984), p. 20; cf. also Bernd Knabe, "How to Mobilize the Soviet Working World: Discipline or Participation?" in this volume, Chapter 7.
21. *Psikhologicheskiy zhurnal*, No. 6 (1982), p. 8.
22. *Sovetskaya Rossiya*, 10 October 1984; cf. *Trud*, 27 June 1984.
23. *Iz*, 26 March 1980; T. Kussmann, *Berichte des BIOst*, No. 21 (1980); B.F. Lomov. in *Psikhologicheskiy zhurnal*, No. 6 (1982), p. 9.
24. S. Roshchin, in *K*, No. 12 (1983), pp. 102-112.
25. Cf. note 16.
26. W. Teckenberg, in *Beiträge zur Konfliktforschung*, No. 4 (1984), pp. 35-58, and *Gegenwartsgesellschaften: UdSSR* (Stuttgart, 1983). Cf. *SIss*, No. 2 (1983), pp. 207-212, and see note 2.
27. T. Kussmann, *Berichte des BIOst*, No. 31 (1983).
28. See note 9.
29. *Psikhologicheskiy zhurnal*, No. 1 (1984), pp. 3-8 and pp. 145-151; see note 8.
30. *Psikhologicheskiy zhurnal*, No. 6 (1984), pp. 145-149.
31. Cf. C.A. Kern Smirinenko (ed.), *Professionalization of Soviet Society* (New Brunswick, 1982).
32. *Vestnik Akademii Nauk SSSR*, No. 2 (1985), pp. 12-22.

10
Science and Technology

Arnold Buchholz

In his inaugural address before the extraordinary plenary session of the CC of the CPSU, convened after Chernenko's death on 11 March 1985, secretary general Gorbachev declared: "We must achieve a decisive turnabout in shifting the economy onto the path of intensive development. We must, indeed we are obligated to reach the foremost scientific-technological positions and the world's highest level of social labor productivity in a short time."[1] Demands of this kind are not new, as they have been advanced in similar formulations for some twenty years at Party congresses, in speeches by leading personages, as well as in expositions by scientists and practitioners. Nevertheless, it is quite evident that the problems of intensifying the economy are increasingly moving to the center of all discussions and all tasks set. Numerous appeals and resolutions for the acceleration of scientific-technological progress point to the urgency of this objective.[2]

The decisive bottleneck in the intensification of the Soviet economy lies in the so-called "transfer of scientific findings into practice." This represents a continuous theme of Soviet self-criticism. The problem can be overcome by constant efforts at improving the economic mechanisms. One must bear in mind here that there is a fundamental difference in the interplay between science and practice in a market economy and a planned economy: In market economies, business practically pulls research findings from science in order to beat the competition to their application and thus profit. The planned economy is largely dependent on pumping research findings into the economy.[3] Practice has shown sufficiently that the mechanisms of the market economy are more flexible and effective in this transfer so that, all efforts notwithstanding, Soviet technology and economics cannot keep up with the Western industrialized countries in regard to a wide-ranging degree of modernity. Proceeding from this general statement, the following pages are to direct attention to the narrow sector of science and technology, the more so since this sector produces the primary factors of developmental progress that determine decisively the level and direction of the transfers.

General Assessments of Soviet Science and Technology

To pose the question of the innovative capacity of Soviet science and technology and its level compared to the forefront of world scientific progress meets with extraordinary difficulties. These start with the fact that a fair portion of Soviet basic research is closely tied to the military-industrial complex, and relevant publications are thus not available for scientific discussion. Though Soviet representations of their own work in various scientific fields are the most important source, they also largely leave out information necessary for a discerning and especially for a comparative assessment. The evaluation of Soviet primary sources on natural science and technology is possible only in narrowly restricted sectors. To obtain a general view in this fashion proves extraordinarily difficult so that only a few studies of this kind exist.[4] Reports on experiences put together under the aegis of scientific exchanges are revealing in many ways, yet publications with the requisite assessments are rare. In the US, following the "third wave of emigration" in the seventies, systematic questioning began, including "intensive interviews" with former Soviet scientists (which have already produced some preliminary results).[5] Systematic evaluations, however, are yet to come.

These comments should make it clear that a multitude of different sources must be tapped to assess the level of Soviet science and technology. The way to a summary assessment is still paved with many uncertainties. Based on longstanding experience, however, the following guidelines can serve as an approximate guide.

Soviet science boasts its greatest achievements in the sector of basic theoretical research, and work in this area is reviewed internationally. Difficulties increase along the various steps to translate these insights into practice, and the international standard declines.[6] To be sure, there are important exceptions and considerations to be taken into consideration here (which will be explored briefly in different contexts). Still, numerous reasons for this general trend can be cited: Theoretical sciences require a minimum of material supplies ("blackboard sciences"), while the equipment and administrative requirements grow with the translation from theory into practice. Here, in turn, there are persistent bottlenecks since tremendous efforts notwithstanding, the connection between science and industry remains underdeveloped, and discords in the Soviet economy generally have a greater impact on the applied sciences than on the theoretical disciplines. The trend is towards a downward differential, from peak performances in the mathematical-physical, chemical, and geological sciences to the biological, medical, pharmaceutical, and psychological sciences. In the latter case, again, aftereffects of Lyssenkoism, secondary priorities or ideological constraints play a significant part.

Overall, the level of performance in Soviet science is most unbalanced, which in turn is due largely to the priorities set by scientific funding. All uncertainties apart, conservative estimates assume (J. Cooper) that at least 60 percent of all qualified Soviet scientists and engineers are working in the armaments sector.[7] Here, it must be borne in mind that nuclear physics, missile technology, satellite technology as well as many classic armaments sectors are extraordinarily capital and manpower intensive so that the absorption by these sectors of a large portion of scientific potential cannot but cause deficits in other sectors.

If one proceeds from this analysis to a concrete assessment of Soviet science, one must first acknowledge the fact that regardless of how much one tries, one's judgment will be highly uncertain. No uniform appraisal is possible because the picture is very uneven. Still the general impression is that in the West—apart from specific military aspects—there are generally no great fears that today the Soviet Union might take the lead in major scientific-technological sectors or even be on its way to doing so. On the contrary: Reports from Western scientists who travelled to the Soviet Union in droves in the sixties and early seventies show that they were lastingly impressed by Soviet achievements; but since then the assessments have become ever more modest. In 1977, a large survey of US scientists who had been to the Soviet Union contributed decisively to a more skeptical appraisal of Soviet science and, at the same time, because of the imbalance, cast doubt on the usefulness to the US of scientific exchanges.[8] Citations of Soviet works by US scientists, even those who had been to the Soviet Union, have remained few and far between. Stipends for long-term sabbaticals in the Soviet Union are not fully used. All these criteria are only partial evidence since, to some extent at least, other reasons (linguistic barriers, lack of interest, etc.) than those pointing to the relative backwardness of Soviet science could also be advanced. Moreover, time and again reports are appearing on remarkable Soviet feats of catching up or of peak performances.[9] Nevertheless, it must also be borne in mind that even in its powerful sectors, Soviet science is hampered by the Soviet economy's inadequate advances in efficiency, information deficits, bureaucratic impediments, and the lagging modernization of the system as a whole.

The Role of Computer Technology

From a scientific-technological perspective, the broad sector of data processing and modern communications systems assumes a central role in the Soviet economy's modernization process. But especially in these sectors, all observations—ranging from on-sight inspections during visits, to Soviet self-criticism—show the unmistakable backwardness of the Soviet Union. To be sure, the numerical data are uncertain and classifications continue to render comparisons problematic. Still, the figures in Table 10.1 serve as indicators. More important yet is the production and distribution of minicomputers of various kinds, peripheries, and highly differentiated software programs that have proliferated by leaps and bounds in Western industrialized countries. Hence, quantitative comparisons with the Soviet Union are even

TABLE 10.1
Installed Computers by Country

	Amann 1978 numbers	Diebold 1982 in billion DM
USSR	22,000	-
Eastern Bloc	-	32
USA	200,000	155
Japan	45,000	38
Western Europe	110,000	103
Others	-	32

Sources: E. Amann, Report at the "Symposium on Soviet Science and Technology," Center for Russian and East European Studies, Birmingham, Sept. 1984; Diebold Statistik, FAZ, 1 Sept. 1983.

more difficult, but experts take it for granted that the distance is even greater in these sectors than in that of large machines. For instance, a Soviet source divulged the remarkable information that the indigenous production of personal computers (PCs) is only a few dozen per year.[10] By contrast, on a world-wide scale (according to a Soviet source) 62,000 PCs (1982) and 350,000 computers for teaching purposes (1983) were produced. The latter number is to be raised to 2.5 million by 1990. In the Soviet Union, it is said regarding the PC, that "there is little interest in them, save for a small group of biologists, chemists, and other specialists who are using equipment . . . purchased abroad."[11] Reading the most recent Soviet reports and discussions on the situation in computer technology, and references to advances in the US and Japan,[12] one gets the impression that the Soviet side was literally steam-rolled by the explosive burst of developments in the Western countries and is now duly alarmed.

Conscious of the newly emerging situation, the Soviets established a separate department of computer science, computer technology, and automation at the Academy of Sciences of the USSR in 1983, together with the former basic institutes of computer technology and applied mathematics, as well as with the newly founded institutes of cybernetics, computer science, and microelectronics.[13] Considering the role played by computers of all sizes in science everywhere in Western countries, it is a reasonable assumption that from this aspect alone there are lasting repercussions for the level of Soviet science.

Strategies of Following Suit

Given the higher degree of technological and economic modernity in Western industrialized countries and the closely connected tremendous total potential of the US, Japan, and Western Europe, the Soviet Union cannot realistically expect to keep up with these developments on a broad front in the vanguard of progress. Necessarily, it has to follow behind in the second rank, as it were, on many world scientific advances and their applications. To this end, a series of specific strategies is pursued, of which the following objectives are especially relevant to the scientific-technological sector:

1. By means of a comprehensive promotion of education, scientific personnel, and research establishments, the Soviet Union is striving for large-scale autarchy in the area of science and technology. Soviet descriptions of their own science often begin with the statement that the Soviet Union boasts the most scientists of all industrialized countries (1983: 1.4 million), and relative to the national income devotes the most money to this sector (4.8 percent). All these figures, however, must be scaled down in comparison with other countries—especially the US—because of different categories, and also in terms of quality.[14] Still, it is fair to assume that Soviet science commands a sufficiently large number of qualified specialists to produce indigenously anything achieved elsewhere in world science, contingent upon an appropriate concentration of forces. The total spectrum of modern science is so broad, however, that the Soviet Union can keep up steadily with but a fraction of it (the Soviet share of the total number of scientists in the world at best amounts to a quarter). Furthermore, there are grave problems on account of bottlenecks in the supplies of equipment, and they are exacerbated the more science becomes dependent upon the sluggish mechanisms of planned economy.

2. Given limited means, the determination of priorities is the decisive strategy for overcoming backwardness and, if need be, achieving pioneering feats. Such a concentration of forces enabled the Soviet Union to develop in a short time a nuclear and missile potential all but equal to that of the US, build a modern aeronautical industry, and make often unexpectedly great progress in the areas of chemistry, automobile construction, digitally controlled machine tools, and in other sectors. As for the armaments industry, the Soviet time-lag in individual technologies was best illustrated as a curve paralleling American developments, but at a distance of several years.[15]

3. Probably the most important catch-up strategy is the Soviet Union's selection of specific models from the cornucopia of leading international scientific technologies in order to subject them constructively to a "Sovietization" (J. Cooper), rendering them suitable for long-term mass production and adjusting them operationally to its own needs. Propitious conditions, in turn, are created by advancing automation. For some time this has been a priority program in the Soviet Union and an area where remarkable feats have apparently been accomplished. Following suit in this fashion is in many ways a rational strategy for science because it saves expensive, wide-ranging experiments of uncertain success and, by contrast, guarantees concentration on promising research avenues on short notice.[16]

4. Next to the acquisition of scientific-technological prototypes. The selective importation of technology is, of course, of prime importance, and this is a timely and much debated subject to which we can only allude here.

5. A further strategy of following suit is directed at the analysis and application of world scientific research findings. As early as 1952, a Central Institute of Documentation for Science and Technology (VINITI) was established. It caters to these needs with hundreds of information bulletins, including so-called "express information." All other Soviet efforts to legally or illegally acquire information are a part of this—which is relatively simple given the openness of Western societies.

6. For some sectors, the division of labor inside the CMEA is also of special importance. In computer production, for example, the Soviet Union benefits from the comparatively highly developed technologies in the GDR and in Hungary.[17]

7. Propagandistically, these catch-up strategies are sheltered by a purposeful information policy that brushes aside the Soviet Union's own deficiencies as mere peripheral phenomena and spotlights selected pioneering accomplishments in grand propaganda style. Viewed from this angle, then, it would hardly be surprising for the Soviet Union one day to launch a spectacular mammoth enterprise, such as a manned landing on Mars, in order to counteract the current loss of face in the scientific-technological sector.

Based on this large total potential and aided by system-specific strategies, the Soviet Union apparently manages to follow the degree of modernity in advanced industrialized countries at a distance (varying in size depending on the sector) as if in their wake. In the process both adequate military potential and economic stability are assured. However, in the long run, the decisive question is whether the Soviet Union can afford a strategy of following suit in its competition with the industrialized Western countries, and what consequences this entails.[18]

Aspects of the Scientific-Technological Revolution

It is of fundamental significance for all deliberations about the future that so far no "limits of growth" are discernible in the scientific-technological sector. Suffice it to think of nuclear physics, where large expenditures are devoted to generating energy for industry from nuclear fusion (practically from water); of the exploration of space, where the construction of stations on planets close to Earth must be regarded as no more than a question of time; of chemistry and solid-state physics, where new materials with previously unknown qualities are constantly being produced; of biotechnology, where prospects are as yet unfathomable due to the possibilities of creating new organisms; or of full automation, robot-technology, and miniaturized high performance computers. Whereas the "second industrial revolution" was still marked by comparatively classical technologies, rapid developments since the late seventies are already frequently being termed the "third industrial revolution."

In this context it must be realized that there are powerful determinist forces inherent in scientific-technological development. Research projects build cumulatively on one another, are mutually interwoven, and to a certain extent at least follow an inner logic that causes many identical or similar results to be produced independently of one another. Furthermore, due to their "model character," phenomena discovered exude strong attractive forces for their application, the more so since technological abstinence would rather quickly lead to economic backwardness in international competition.

Marxism-Leninism proceeds from the theorem that the rationality of technological development and the rationality of the socialist planning system correspond to each other and thus produce an economic order structurally superior to "anarchic capitalism." Because of this theorem, the conviction prevailed for some time following the establishment of the Soviet state that in this configuration "catching up with and passing" the advanced capitalist countries would be possible in a historically short period. These expectations found their expression above all in the Party program of 1961, with exceedingly optimistic predictions. In the second half of the sixties, when it was recognized that these goals were not attainable, the Siberian section of the Academy of Sciences developed the motto of "passing without catching up." This slogan was then highlighted propagandistically for some time in the GDR under Ulbricht. Finally, in 1971, Brezhnev coined the phrase that said the important thing was to combine "the achievements of the scientific-technological revolution with the advantages of socialist society," the purpose of which was to shift the focus away from the objective of technological superiority towards the "socialist way of life." What matters today is whether the Soviet Union is pushed even further into a defensive position in the competition with Western industrialized countries.

The decisive problem is that the most recent stage of the scientific-technological revolution since the late seventies is characterized by a sudden proliferation of communication structures and complex interdependencies of all kinds. This raises the question of whether in this case the Soviet Union will also be able to follow suit on developments in a relatively brief time, or whether the barrier thrown up by the "information society" will lead to a drastic technological-economic lag vis-à-vis the advanced industrialized societies. Today, considerations along these lines form the focus of certain military-political considerations in the West and are simultaneously an alarm signal for the Soviet Union.

Had socialism succeeded in creating superior social structures as a counterweight to the trend of technological development and allowed for an attractive unfolding of man's intellect, the backwardness in the material-technological sector might be accepted more calmly. But since the humanitarian-ideological sector, if anything, displays even greater weaknesses than the technological-innovational, Soviet development toward the future is subject to mounting pressure from two sides. In Marxist terminology these sides are labeled as "productive forces" and "superstructure" and substantial reforms would touch the system's very core structures.

Notes

1. *ND*, 12 March 1985.

2. Most recently in *Pr*, 12 June 1985.

3. A. Buchholz, *OE*, No. 5, 1972, pp. 329ff.

4. R. Amann, J. Cooper, R.W. Davies, *The Technological Level of Soviet Industry* (New Haven and London, 1977), as well as proceedings of the annual conferences of the Center for Russian and East European Studies (CREES) of the University of Birmingham. Additional comments in the collective review, D.R. Herspring, in *Problems of Communism*, No. 1 (1985), pp. 73–76. The most recent surveys are found in North Atlantic Treaty Organization, *Adaptability to New Technologies of the USSR and East European Countries*, colloquium held in Brussels, 17–19 April 1985.

5. L.R. Graham, in E. Hoffman (ed.), *The Soviet Union in the 1980s* (New York, 1984), pp. 124 ff.

6. Schematic representations of the "barriers to innovation" in S. Kassel/C. Campbell, *The Soviet Academy of Sciences and Technological Development*, The Rand Corporation (1980), p. 12; on this also Ph. Hanson, *RL*, Munich, 14 February 1985.

7. *SIPRI Yearbook 1983*, pp. 213–243, and J.M. Cooper, *CREES Discussion Papers* (Birmingham, 1981 and 1983), p. 17.

8. National Science Foundation, *Review of the US/USSR Agreement on Cooperation in the Fields of Science and Technology* (Washington, May 1977).

9. J. Cooper, *CREES Discussion Papers* (Birmingham-Conferences 1981) *passim*.

10. E.P. Velikhov, in *Vestnik Akademii nauk SSSR*, No. 8 (1984), pp. 3–9.

11. *Ibid*, p. 6.

12. Supplementary to the Soviet sources mentioned above attention shall be drawn to A.A. Samarsky, in *Vestnik Akademii nauk SSSR*, 11, 1984, p. 17 ff.

13. *Cf.* note 11.

14. L.E. Nolting/M. Feshbach, in *Soviet Economy in a Time of Change*, vol. 1 (Washington, D.C., 1979), pp. 710–758.

15. *Militärwesen in der Sowjetunion* (Stuttgart/Munich, 1977), p. 67; F. Walter, *Berichte des BIOst*, No. 1 (1985); C.W. Weinberger, *The Technology Transfer Program, A Report to the 98th Congress* (Washington, D.C., 1984).

16. Graham, *op. cit.*

17. S.E. Goodman, "Socialist Technological Integration: The Case of the East European Computer Industries," in J. Becker (ed.), *The Information Society* (New York, 1984), pp. 39–83.

18. Cf. on this, H. Vogel, *Aktuelle Analyse des BIOst*, No. 22 (1984).

11
Churches in the Soviet Union

Gerd Stricker

The Legal Situation of the Churches

Making the development of religious life possible in a society depends on the constitution and legislation. Therefore, religion must arouse particular interest if both are rewritten—as they were in the Soviet Union in 1975 and in 1977 respectively. Article 52 of the new constitution, promulgated on 7 October 1977, though, merely paraphrases previous formulations in the Decree on the Separation of State and Church (1918) and in Article 142 of the 1936 constitution. Only the prohibition to incite religious hatred is new. According to official interpretations, this clause is directed against believers and others who allegedly reject socialist society and, under the cover of religion, slander the social order in the USSR and consciously disregard Soviet laws.[1]

Religious legislation in the RSFSR had already undergone revision in 1975 (subsequently adopted by other republics) with the decree "On Religious Congregations," which is more repressive than earlier decrees. But, to be sure, many of the guidelines laid down in the new law have been in practice since the sixties, some even longer: Ordinances previously secret, or published in remote locations, instructions (1961, 1968), and amendments all went into the decree of 1975. All exacerbations notwithstanding, its publication constitutes an improvement in the situation of the religious communities to the extent that for the time being their *Lebensraum*—although it is very much restricted—has at least been officially circumscribed. Formerly, official arbitrariness had ruled supreme in this field due to ignorance of the legal situation on the part of the believers and due to legal uncertainty in general.

Now, it is law (§ 13) that the clergyman, who may assume office only subsequent to registration (i.e., approbation) with the State Church Authority, can neither be the head of his congregation (as was the case until 1960), nor even join the parish council (*ispolnitelnyi* organ). This greatly facilitates control and direction of the "cult communities" by the administration authority and its subordinate organizations (the "authorized representatives"). It no longer needs to fear the authority of the clergyman, to whom the law only leaves the position of "cult servant," in the parish administration. The influence of the "authorized representative" is further enhanced by the fact that he can reject every one of the three parish council members proposed by the "cult community" (§ 14) and thus in the final analysis is able to force the election to the parish council of those parishioners willing to cooperate with the State Church Authority.

All former prohibitions remain in force: "cult activities" outside the "cult building" (e.g., baptisms, §§ 59, 58, 19), any social or charitable activity, religious education and youth groups, bible study, women's and other religious circles, and support of the needy in the parish (§ 17). Moreover, practice has shown that believers have no legal claim to what little the decree grants them. Thus, applications for registration of Russian-Orthodox and also Catholic parishes in Lithuania are rejected time and again despite the fact that they name hundreds of applicants rather than the twenty stipulated. Or, though a clergyman may minister to the seriously ill and dying in a hospital (§ 58), so far this legal claim has apparently never been successfully effectuated. But on the other hand, it must be emphasized that "cult communities" and the institutions above them (e.g., consistories) are now recognized as "limited-restricted legal entities."[2]

The "Order by the Council for Matters of Religions at the Council of Ministers of the USSR" of 1966 transformed this office from an organization of coordination into one of control. Not just the *Samizdat*-news but also official documents that have reached the West from the USSR, however, bear witness to how inadequately the activity of the State Church Authority is circumscribed by the term "control": This authority completely determines the framework of a parish's activities or usually limits them well beyond the legally possible. A secret account by the State Church Authority to the CC of the CPSU of 1975 lays out in great detail and with cynical candor the practices of the authority and its subordinate organizations towards the Russian-Orthodox church,[3] for instance, how sessions of the Sacred Synod and their minutes are set ahead of time in the "Council of Matters of Religious" or how installations and transfers of bishops are regulated by the "Council."

The "Religious Revival"

If a phenomenon characterized as a "religious revival" or a "religious renaissance" can be observed in the USSR, it is indicative of a "pervasive process of fermentation"[4] that Soviet society is experiencing at a time for which Khrushchev had already predicted the end of all religions in the Soviet state. Understandably, Soviet media are silent about this development. But it is also characteristic of the situation for churches that even they make only surreptitious reference—if at all—to the vast circles of Soviet society turning to matters religious; and it also must not be overlooked that the new trend occasionally confronts the registered (i.e., officially permitted) churches with considerable problems.

For some time, an agonizing disgust with ideology, with its all-pervasive lie—propaganda, indeed the whole system—has been felt among vast parts of the Soviet intelligentsia. The lack of a convincing ethical canon comes to light in general moral decline, expressed by corruption, fraud against the system by means of the system, lies and opportunism. Many intellectuals no longer feel up to coping with the Soviet citizen's schizophrenic day-to-day situation (caught between the morals postulated by the Party and the generally practiced immorality). They want to return to decency and self-respect, the first precondition of which, they feel, is liberation from the lie.[5] Consequently, escape into individualism, into privacy, is a widespread phenomenon.

The quest for new value standards, the "departure for new shores," has led many Soviet intellectuals to turn towards the metaphysical. As is the case in the West, there is much interest in astrology, parapsychology, occultism, and even alchemy. A whole set of additional groups can be subsumed under the label of "God seekers." Here, Eastern religions especially appear to find many adherents (Hinduism, Buddhism, Chinese and Japanese religions, and others). "God seekers" seem to turn to Christian religions, especially Orthodoxy, only as a second choice. The absorption into an Eastern religion (e.g. Yoga) often constitutes the initial stage of an ultimate conversion to Orthodoxy. To many intellectual newly converted, Orthodoxy is the bearer and emblem of the national culture, symbolizing the future of a new, a believing Russia. Almost the same thing can be said about the Lithuanian intelligentsia, though its majority has recognized the Catholic church as the bearer of the national identity since the sixties. There are priests in both churches, also teachers at ecclesiastical seminaries, who found their way to the faith through disappointment in atheism.

Many "God seekers" take exception to the registered churches' conformity with the system, others seek nothing but their individual salvation. These latter, although they do attend services and participate in public worship and holy communion, otherwise retain their place in socialist society. The former, by contrast, select a spiritual father from the priests within their reach, and he guides them; beyond that, they often engage in activities unacceptable within the framework of the registered churches. Recent converts in particular form centers of religious dissidence, e.g. the "religious-philosophical youth seminaries" (in Leningrad, Moscow, and Smolensk) and edit religious underground papers (e.g. *Congregation*, *Nr 37*, *Twenties*, *Light of Ecstasy*, *Mary*, *Hope*). Groups more strongly committed to civil rights objectives were also formed. In complaints to government offices and members of the political leadership, they charged transgressions and violations of religious laws by the State Church Authority. "Committees for the defense of the faithful" were founded by Orthodox priests and laypeople in 1976, by Catholic Lithuanian clergymen and laypeople in 1978.

While the Lithuanian Catholic Church can easily integrate phenomena such as a "religious revival," the more so since it takes a less spectacular course among a people of which no less than 50 percent is deeply religious and 60 to 80 percent of whose priests are in opposition to state religious policy, the Russian-Orthodox church officially dissociates itself from Orthodox dissidents and condemns their actions. When the leading personalities of the individual groupings (youth seminaries, underground papers, committees) were indicted between 1979 and 1982, there were no reports of the Russian-Orthodox church officially siding with them.

Unlike intellectual "God seekers" who find their individual salvation or their spiritual, intellectual, and cultural home in the national churches, the non-intellectuals tend to be converted more by denominations of a protestant ilk (Evangelical Christians, Baptists, Adventists, Pentecostals, etc.). These offer a spiritual-intellectual home in a very tightly-knit community of faith to those disappointed by life in Soviet society, a community that supports the individual as a social group, helps him in daily life, and, within the bounds of the possible, seeks to shelter him from the grip of the state.

This very complex process of a remarkable turn to Christianity (among other things) in Soviet society, which also finds expression in an ever more frequent appearance of religious motifs in literature, music, and the creative arts signals a general rethinking of everything religious in the USSR. People are tired of the primitive anti-religious propaganda. The churches and their representatives (especially the "popes") are no longer the ones to be blamed for grievances (as was the case decades ago); rather, the direct object of popular ire today are those state and social institutions that, in the eyes of many, are responsible for the hopeless situation. The so-called "religious revival" must thus also be considered a partial aspect of a process that reaches far beyond the specifically religious realm and indicates a fundamental crisis in the official ideology.

Christianity in the USSR, even the "loyal," registered churches, derives many an inner boost from this process, but the attempt at an evalution requires caution. Those involved do not close their eyes to the fact that some things about the so-called "religious revival" in the USSR are also intellectually fashionable "because in our circles it is already considered backward and parochial not to believe."[6] It seems premature, then, to deduce from all this that there is a definitive "spiritual revival" in Russia or even a comprehensive "religious renaissance" in the USSR as is often done far too euphorically in the West.

From Brezhnev to Chernenko

The Brezhnev era brought the religious communities in the USSR a time of stabilization, which they needed badly following Khrushchev's persecutions: The Russian-Orthodox church alone lost nearly two thirds of all their facilities between 1959 and 1964 (churches: in 1959, 22,000; in 1964, 7500; Monasteries: in 1959, 69; in 1964, 17; ecclesiastical seminaries: in 1959, 8; in 1964, 3). Brezhnev did not repeal the repressive measures of his predecessor. Nor is it exactly fair to say that his religious policy was determined by principles of the rule of law; still, a certain security did emerge.

In retrospect, even the non-registered congregations look upon the time up to the mid-seventies (as compared with today) as a period of relative security, in spite of inhuman actions by the authorities in many instances; but since about 1979, persecution of these congregations has been stepped up (for example, up to 1979 there were about thirty to forty non-registered Evangelical Christians-Baptists in penal camps, but in mid-1984 there were some 200). Now the situation of the registered churches is coming to be characterized by a juxtaposition of repression and concession: Congregations are fighting the almighty State Church Authority's restrictions and harassment. At the same time, concessions are being made to church leadership and churches as institutions. These concessions are effective as propaganda but hardly improve the situation of the individual congregations. Thus, church representatives are frequently permitted to travel to the West (to praise the peace and liberal church policies of the Soviet government), occasionally spiritual literature may be printed or imported in minute numbers, existing institutions of religious teaching may raise their entrance quotas (without, however, seriously abating the shortage of clergymen), and the Russian-Orthodox church was allowed to dedicate a factory for church paraphernalia in 1981, a new publishing house in 1982, and a new administrative center in 1983. Also in 1983, a run-down monastery complex was turned over to the church with the permission—a first in Moscow—to restore it as a monastery.

Statistics recently submitted by V. A. Kuroyedov, who was chairman of the State Church Authority until 1984, cast a different light on the situation of religious communities from the one that the West is used to from the accounts of church dignitaries: from 1977 to 1982, 810 new parishes were registered, but 1,035 were closed during the same period. Furthermore, there are tell-tale details: Thirty-three Orthodox churches were newly licensed in this period, and there are some fifty million believers and 7,500 to 8,000 parishes. The approximately seven million Catholics with some 1,050 parishes (650 in Lithuania) were able to secure licences for forty parishes (fewer than ten of them in Lithuania); Evangelical Christian-Baptists, Adventists, Pentecostals, and other "sects," on the other hand, procured registration of some 300, usually smaller, parishes; German-Russian Lutherans, finally, were allowed to register 129 parishes.[7] These figures illustrate what is at issue: on the one hand, to reduce the number of national churches, and on the other hand to bring non-registered congregations of the "sects" under the control of the authorities. Unlike before, the German-Russian parishes have encountered less trouble with their registration requests snce 1977; it is hoped that the "emigration psychosis" among German-Russians will be countered by giving at least some of them a spiritual home in a legal parish.

The Russian Orthodox Church is the Russian national church pure and simple. Under Brezhnev it finally grew into its role as the Soviet state church in a (thus far) Russian-dominated empire. At a time when the Russian predominance in the USSR—from an ethnic point of view—is seriously imperilled, it is especially conspicuous that the overwhelming majority of the few churches that the Russian-Orthodox Church was allowed to register are located in national fringe and mixed areas outside Russia: A Russifying function is obviously intended for them.

All registered churches in the USSR make an effort to fill and exceed their quota of Soviet patriotism. This is the sole level at which they can cooperate with the atheist state without incurring dogmatic difficulties. In recent years, "Soviet patriotism" has been largely identical with the "peace-making activities" of the churches. Essentially, this consists in the churches "voluntarily" having to pay a fair part of the donations by the faithful (up to 40 percent) into the state peace funds and in their having to support and champion Soviet foreign policy, presented to the outside world as a priori peace policy. It ought to be remembered that the Russian-Orthodox Church, for instance, justified the invasion of Afghanistan by Soviet troops[8] or that Patriarch Pimen in an open letter accused Reagan[9] of war propaganda and "in slavish servility,"[10] praised "the illustrious peace-making policies of the Soviet state," as well as the freedom of conscience and the non-interference of the state in church affairs. In all these activities the Russian-Orthodox Church again occupies the leading role: It coordinates the "peace-making" actions of all religions in the Soviet Union. Thus, in 1982 for instance, it organized the "World Conference of Representatives of Religions to Save the Holy Gift of Life from Nuclear Catastrophy." The Patriarchate's journal spells out the purpose of this and various follow-up conferences as well as further initiatives: "We will make the supreme effort for the bulk of believers abroad to become acquainted with, understand, and support [Andropov's] proposals."[11]

The deterioration of the climate of religious policy in the late seventies is certainly related to the reawakened interest in matters religious and the emergence of Christian dissidents. The non-registered congregations were the first to feel the more stringent actions against church non-conformists, which started in 1979. The individual parish has not always been affected by the increasing number of sentences to lengthy imprisonment in camps, but rather by the rapidly increasing short-term administrative jail sentences (two weeks as a rule) or fines (fifty rubles as a rule). Time and again, the "Council of Female Relatives of Imprisoned Evangelical Christian-Baptists," petitions important people in the USSR and has been organizing help for families of imprisoned brothers since 1964. The council reports on actions by the authorities against non-registered Evangelical-Baptists (*Initsiativniki*). Its newsletter, *Bulletin of the Council of Relatives*, as well as the periodicals *Messenger of Truth* and *Brothers' Newspaper*, are published by the secret publishing house of the *Initsiativniki*, *The Christian*, which lost four of its printing shops, various binderies, and laboratories due to arrests and seizures by the authorities. The capacity—and thus significance, incidentally, also for other denominations—of this secret publishing house is highlighted by the fact that between 1973 and 1983 it was able to print more Bibles and New Testaments (over 500,000) than the Patriarchate in over twenty years (450,000).

The publishers of the *Chronicles of the Catholic Church of Lithuania* are subject to similar persecutions: Since 1972, 65 issues of the *Chronicle* have appeared, and ever since they have reported on violations of the law by the authorities and on other harrassments. Here, where the majority of priests and the bulk of laypeople actively resist governmental repression, the *Chronicle* performs a function beyond that of merely supplying information: It shows believers in the far corners of Lithuania that they are not alone in their struggle. Time and again the *Chronicle* also reports on complaints launched at the State Church Office by the "Committee for the Defense of Believers' Rights," for instance after desecrations of churches, unjustified repressive measures, and often muggings or murders of priests who were members of the "Committee" (1981: B. Laurinavicius, L. Mazeika, L. Sapoka; though alleged murderers were also put on trial, much has remained in the dark).

Following the 1983 sentencing of two further "Committee" members, the priests A. Svarinskas and S. Tamkevicius, to seven and six years in a camp and to subsequent exile, there were numerous protests that culminated in a petition to Andropov bearing 123,000 signatures. It pointed out that these priests had done no more than obey the laws of the Church by preparing the children for communion, spreading religious writings, organizing pilgrimages, and supporting the needy. Since 1981 (cf. Poland) the State Church Authority has been galvanizing loyal priests into more stringent action against their oppositional brothers-in-office and trying to widen the chasm. Between 1979 and 1982, charges were also brought against orthodox nonconformists—usually younger people who must be classified as part of the "religious revival," and who had become involved with Christian youth seminaries and underground papers, or with the "Committee for the Defense of Believers' Rights."

The sentences were harsh: five or six years in a camp and subsequent exile for the leaders (the priest G. Yakunin who had been hampered in the execution of his office, V. Poresh, V. Kapitanchuk, L. Regelson, A. Ogorodnikov); others got three to four years in a camp (T. Shchipkova, S. Yermolayev, I. Polyakov, T. Velikanova, N. Maltseva, and others; Zoya Krakhmalnikova, publisher of *The Hope*: one year) with subsequent exile. However, not all of them had to serve their sentences. Some followed the example of the hapless priest Dr. Dudko who had been cautioned many times and also transferred, indeed suspended temporarily, and finally arrested in early 1980 for his rousing sermons, his discussion groups after services as well as his Samizdat activities. He "repented" his actions before Muscovite television cameras in mid-June 1980 and referred to his "anti-Soviet activities as directed from imperialist foreign countries."

Chernenko's address at the plenary session of the CC of the CPSU in June 1983 must be interpreted as a signal for a more stringent church policy, even though prior measures had given reason to fear such a development. He accused the Party of total failure in regard to ideology and announced the slogan, "Ideological work is the entire Party's affair!" He expressly mentioned the "not small number" of Soviet citizens with religious affiliations and threatened them with befitting punishment in case of "breaches of socialist law" and "subversive activities under the cloak of religion." Antireligious articles have frequently appeared in Pravda and Izvestiya since then, calling for intensified atheist education and for well-aimed ideological work. The transition would have to be made from the traditionally antireligious propaganda to atheist propaganda proper; now there is even talk of "aggressive atheism" (*atakuyushchiy ateizm*). The antireligious struggle itself, however, takes place at the level of regional papers, where local parishes and individuals are derided and defamed, and names and addresses were supplied.

Lately people have again been strongly encouraged to inform on each other—even anonymously. In the Ukraine, in Lithuania, and in Western Siberia questionnaires were handed out. Citizens were asked to enter their neighbor's behavior or habits that seemed illegal or suspicious. One column on this questionnaire seems nothing short of tailor-made for believers and for secret meetings: "Violations of public order and the laws of socialist life." One hears of ever more cases of children in kindergartens, schools, and other educational institutions being sounded out about the religious habits of their parents.

In such times, personnel changes in important offices assume an even greater importance than usual, the more so if they become much more frequent (as they have since mid-1984): The exarchs of the Russian-Orthodox Church for Western and Central Europe as well as this Church's permanent representative at the World Council of Churches in Geneva were recalled on short notice and quite suprisingly. The chairman of the "All-Union Council of Evangelical Christian-Baptists," V.I. Klimenko (December 1984), also had to tender his resignation. Just as unexpectedly, the chairman of the "Council of Matters of Religions at the Council of Ministers of the USSR," V.A. Kuroyedov, was dismissed on 28 November 1984. He was succeeded by the former Soviet ambassador to Guyana, K.M. Kharchev (50).

A statement made by a member of a registered, and therefore loyal, parish in Moscow in late 1984 is characteristic of the mood among the believers: "We are all afraid! for the time being, we can not discern whether the current arrests even among us represent a threatening posture by Chernenko or else mark the beginning of a new ice-age."

Notes

1. V.A. Kuroyedov, *Religiya i tserkov v sovetskom obshchestve* (Moscow, 1984), p. 6.

2. O. Luchterhand, "Die Religionsgesetzgebung der Sowjetunion" (Berlin, 1978), p. 41; cf. G. Simon, *Berichte des BIOst*, No. 14 (1976).

3. "Iz otcheta Soveta po delam religii—chlenam TsK KPSS," in *Vestnik russkogo khristianskogo dvizheniya*, No. 130 (1979), pp. 275–344, and No. 131 (1980), pp. 362–372.

4. O. Luchterhand, *Herder Korrespondenz*, No. 36 (1982), p. 235.

5. T. Goritschewa [T. Goricheva], *Von Gott zu reden ist gefährlich: Meine Erfahrungen im Osten und im Westen* (Freiburg/Basel/Vienna, 1984), p. 57.

6. *Ibid.*, pp. 119, 61.

7. In late 1984 there was a total of 200 registered (and some 200 non-registered) Lutheran German parishes in the USSR. Statistical data according to Kuroyedov, *op. cit.*, p. 144.

8. *Zhurnal Moskovskoy Patriarkhii*, No. 5 (1980), pp. 3–6.

9. NYT, 3 April 1983.

10. *The Orthodox Church*, No. 5 (1983), p. 8 (Patriarch Pimen Assails Pres. Reagan's Speech). On the entire address of G. Stricker, *Kirche im Osten*, No. 27 (1984), p. 170f.

11. *Zhurnal Moskovskoy Patriarkhii*, No. 4 (1983), p. 5.

12
Cultural Policy, Culture, Opposition

Peter Hübner

The Opposition's Origins in the Spirit of Cultural Policy

Perhaps the spirit of Soviet politics is most visible where it has to deal with the mind—in cultural policy. The treatment of culture will also continue to be a reliable indicator in the Gorbachev era that is just dawning. A retrospective of the past twenty to thirty years of Soviet cultural policy indicates that there have been and continue to be many parallels developing between the treatment of culture and the treatment of the opposition in the post-Stalin period: Some cultural areas are treated like opposition. Overall, there is an emerging trend towards firmer, more effective, more discerning control and restrictions. On the other hand, though, this is matched by a trend towards freer cultural activity and political forms of opposition: It is fair to speak of a reciprocal escalation of emerging trends (in culture and opposition) and control. There is no end in sight to this process, even though the end of non-conformism and of opposition and the ultimate triumph of repression have been prophesied repeatedly.

For all that, the parallelism in the treatment of culture and opposition is less of a temporal than a systematic nature: Here as there the issue is to cut off tendencies that seem to depart from a predetermined system of political rules and interests—from a system that, due to the regime's ideologically disguised claim to total control, knows no political vacuum, no political neutrality, but only the pro and con, the position of the "*tertium non datur.*" This has been unalterably so since the late twenties when the criteria of prosocialist/anti-socialist, pro-Soviet/anti-Soviet came to determine Stalinist cultural policy.

One instance of this dualistic thinking was the question posed by Gorki in 1934, "Whose side are you on, masters of culture?" He sought to urge the cultural intelligentsia all over the world to make a choice for the Soviet Union and against fascism. High-ranking functionaries to this day like to quote this question and do so often. Most recently Chernenko used it on the occasion of the 50th anniversary of the Soviet writers' association with a timely reference to Soviet-American differences: "There is no such thing as a 'golden mean': either with those who prepare for war, or with those who reject the adventurous policy of imperialism and fight for peaceful co-existence, for disarmament."[1] The either-or, devoid of a golden mean, adds the menacing undertone of a "potentially anti-Soviet attitude" to the reproach that is frequently levelled against artists and literati: They have an "apolitical attitude" (*apolitichnost'*). The Marxist-Leninist view of culture is not as a sphere of autonomous intellectual activity, but as a phenomenon of the ideological superstructure mirroring contesting progressive and retrogressive political interests. Lenin's division of all cultures into two cultures—into a progressive and a retrogressive one—was transposed from pre-revolutionary times beyond the revolution to the USSR's culture and is used even today as justification for the practical culture-policy.

This politicization of culture from above (through the ideology of those in power) has had an effect that was able to come to the fore only in the post-Stalin period, namely a non-conformist counter-culture next to the politically conformist pro-culture that has always been desired: The parts of the culture defined and labelled from above either a priori (e.g., religion) or ad hoc (e.g., abstract painting) as "retrogressive" and that are therefore discriminated against immediately started resisting discrimination when this became feasible under the liberalized conditions of the post-Stalin period. Only then did those who were discriminated against even find the courage to resist and to criticize the political system. This system practically furthers such discrimination in a programmatic way with its dualistic cultural policy: Cultural policy remained unchanged due to the principally dualistic attitude prevalent during the post-Stalin era. Because of this, cultural (intellectual, artistic, religious, and national) discrimination also persisted and actually split and politicized the cultural situation when the conditions of repression became milder. All this made the subjects of discrimination into the focal point of political opposition.[2] The origin of current Soviet oppositions can be traced rather easily from the fact that to this day scientists, artists and literati, believers, and nationally-oriented personalities are dominant in them. By contrast, social, economic, and political discrimination have thus far remained the exception as a primary motive for opposition: To date the USSR has experienced few strikes and little worker or agricultural protest.[3]

Because their roots are predominantly in the cultural area Soviet oppositions have been seen as something elitist or at least—also potentially—just for a minority, having little prospect of resonance in broad strata, though this is a dubious criterion by which to judge the weight of the oppositions. The idea of human rights, after all, served as a common denominator that has brought together the various parts of the opposition, gained it sympathies among other parts of the intelligentsia, and also among other strata of the population (though this sympathy has for the most part remained passive). At the same time it has internationalized this opposition, i.e., brought it up to the level of the internationally recognized principle of human rights and obtained international support for it.[4]

The rise in oppositions has, in turn, affected culture itself and cultural policy in various ways: On the one hand, these oppositions stimulated culture by setting new intellectual and moral standards that the cultural intelligentsia could not bypass.[5] This process fostered the split of culture into an enlightened component and a more closed, dogmatically oriented one—a split clearly visible in literature, art, and the humanities. It evidently also put the more dogmatic components on the defensive with regards to their intellectual substance, even though the clamour of their attacks on the more open part of culture may distract attention from this fact.[6]

The effect of the oppositions on cultural policy is conflicting: On the one hand they have drawn the fire to themselves and reduced cultural policy proper to a secondary battleground in the ideological struggle. On the other hand they have reinforced the regime's suspicion of culture as a potential and actual bulwark of opposition. Both processes have transpired together. However, out of sheer alarm, the struggle gainst oppositions appears to have occupied the authorities' attention for some time to a disproportionate extent. Only the events in Poland in 1980 conclusively drove home to the Soviet authorities the realization that even strong non-conformist currents in culture could shake the political system, not only in the other socialist countries (CSSR in 1968) but possibly in the USSR as well. The very hard line—and it is growing harder—prevalent against the oppositions since 1979 was followed, starting in about 1981, by a clearly hardening line in cultural policy as well. That the Soviet regime has been and continues to be very serious about snuffing out opposition and consequently also about eliminating non-conformist tendencies in culture, as the incubator of future opposition, is illustrated by the hard line against oppositions prevalent since 1979 which boded ill for cultural policy as well.

Repression of Opposition

The hardening line against oppositions has been a continuous process, observable since the late sixties through the changes at the top from Brezhnev to Andropov, Chernenko, Gorbachev, a process which, however, has been exposed to various braking and accelerating factors. A certain increasingly hardened automatism took hold when the initial, as yet tentative stirrings of opposition in the sixties, far from being snuffed out by the repressive measures of the regime, instead became ever more unequivocal resistance. This, in turn, called forth new, harder phases of repression. The reciprocal escalation has continued into the present. On the opposition side, the escalation consisted of a position increasingly conscious of content and meaning, more political, and more determinedly advanced. It also consisted of novel forms of communications and organization (Samizdat, and formal and informal formation of groups); on the side of repression it was made up of an extension, sophistication, increase in efficiency, and brutalization of methods of persecution—a line of such continuity, no doubt, because since 1961, the KGB had been uninterruptedly in the hands of one man—Andropov.

Beginning in the mid-seventies, something was added to this (to some extent necessarily) hardening line, something that might be termed the internationalization of the opposition. Though it did temper the hardening for a while, it did not stop it altogether. Nevertheless, the outcome of this process remains completely uncertain. Be that as it may, nearly all dissidents make a positive assessment of the internationalization since otherwise repression would have struck sooner and with even greater abandon. A retarding element resulted from a certain Soviet consideration—with regards to better known members of the opposition, at least—for Western detente partners. But, to be sure, from the Soviet perspective, the enhanced ideological defense, including the struggle against the opposition, was a correlate of the detente policy. In Soviet opinion, the "peaceful co-existence of states with differing social orders" excluded all ideological co-existence; indeed it meant increased ideological struggle. Out of the same consideration there were concessions by the Eastern side on "humanitarian questions" ("humanitarian relief"), but not in matters of principle.

The internationalization of opposition originally came about on its own: Since 1968, it has loudly stressed *inter alia* the International Declaration of Human Rights. Thanks to the policy of detente, the Soviets had begun to offer "pragmatic" concessions in the area of human rights which, thereafter, were the oppositions in the USSR, mainly the democratic opposition, the human rights movement, and in particular by the "Helsinki groups," used consciously and actively. These Helsinki groups began their activities in May 1976 in the wake of the signing of the Helsinki Final Act. Their objective was to supervise USSR adherence to the Helsinki human rights resolutions. This unequivocal step towards the internationalization of the opposition from within certainly contributed to the gradual abandonment of the minimal consideration the Soviet side had previously given to the West. The self-integration by the major Soviet opposition—the human rights movement—into the policy of detente, i.e., into an officially endorsed policy line, did cause the opposition to practice restraint by preventing radicalization. Yet it did not, on the other hand, result in restraint, but rather in more stringent action on the regime's side. The deeper reason was that the center of the human rights movement, the Helsinki groups, adopted the human rights issue, which was a focal point in the East-West conflict. This was recognized as fundamentally dangerous to regime and system in the long run: For tactical reasons, the Soviets made concessions on certain human rights questions, but these proved insincere when put to the test by the demand for tolerance of oppositions.

In addition to the internationalization from within, there was an internationalization from without that was also finally answered by more stringent persecutions. With the inauguration of President Carter in 1976, a lively interest in internal Soviet oppositions sprung up in the US when Mr. Carter replied to a letter from A. Sakharov, and Vice-President Mondale received the exiled civil rights activist V. Bukovsky. In the US, this was accompanied by a growing disinterest in the policy of detente. This development provided the persecuting authorities in the Soviet Union with a welcome pretext for even less consideration of detente than in the past and for even more stringent persecution of opponents. This, in turn, made the public in the West and Western governments support victims of persecution and the Soviet opposition as a whole even more unconditionally. While the USSR had hardly ever shown consideration for Western sensitivities regarding human rights violations, consideration in the West for Soviet sensitivities now atrophied visibly: The internal Soviet escalation of opposition and repression was further entrenched and stabilized by an escalation of antagonisms between the Soviets and the West. The CSCE follow-up meeting in Belgrade in 1977/78, just as the Madrid follow-up meeting in 1980/83, witnessed sharp confrontations chiefly between the US and the USSR over Soviet disregard for human rights. The human rights question was cast into sharp relief as a focal point of East-West tensions; in the aftermath, the USSR took ever fewer pains to keep up the impression that human rights were held in greater respect there than anywhere else.

Following the Belgrade meeting, a noticeable exacerbation of the persecution of opposition members began; in 1979/80 there was another ceasura in the hardening line, not, however, its termination. Most better-known dissidents were not eliminated in one way or another until after 1979.

The deportation of A. Sakharov in January 1980 was overshadowed by the Soviet intervention in Afghanistan. It was also tantamount to crossing another border in light of the fact that it had previously been taken for granted that the scholar was sacrosanct. It was a signal to the whole world that henceforth neither the scientific and moral authority of a dissident nor international protests would have any effect whatsoever on Soviet opposition policy. The oppressive uncertainty as to Sakharov's fate, the Soviet authorities' deafness to international appeals, the defamation of Sakharov and his wife, the sheer breach of law (namely his deportation without court sentence) that remained uncorrected for five years—all this, in a manner of speaking, has been the mark of a ruthless opposition policy since 1979. It can be proved that some 1,000 dissidents were arrested between 1979 and 1983.[7] By now this figure exceeds 1,500. Aside from the Helsinki groups (which eventually disbanded under pressure) and their subsidiary organizations, it was the free union movement SMOT (Russian abbreviation for "Free Inter-Occupational Association of Workers") that was formed in 1978, the independent peace initiative "Group for the Establishment of Confidence Between the USSR and the US," founded in June 1982, and also nationally motivated dissidents who were the main victims of persecution. For the persecution of members of the various religious communities 1979 was also a benchmark. Apart from numerous laypeople, some 350 leading personalities from various, mostly Christian religious communities are currently under arrest.[8]

The fact that Jewish and German emigration was all but throttled in the same period also fits this context: While 51,320 Jews emigrated in 1979 (this was the largest number ever), there was a decline of 95 percent to

2,688 in 1982, 1,314 in 1983, and 1984 brought the absolute low point to date of eighty emigrants on a monthly average; while in January 1985 it was even a mere sixty-one.[9] Jews willing to emigrate are increasingly harassed, and an anti-semitic propaganda campaign is afoot, camouflaged as anti-Zionist (cf., the formation of the "Anti-Zionist Committee of the Soviet Public" in April 1983). The emigration of Soviet-Germans has also been cut down radically from the record year 1976 (9,626 emigrants): to 1,958 in 1982, to about 1,000 in 1983, 474 in the first six months of 1984, and a mere 244 emigrants in the first six months of 1985.[10]

The legal position and the treatment under criminal law of opposition members has deteriorated: Charges of "crimes against the state" have multiplied. Maximum penalties are often imposed so that in just one year, the average prison term grew from three years and eight months (1983) to six years and nine months (1984).[11]

Causes for arrest have become pettier and marginal figures on the opposition scene are arrested and tried more frequently.[12] Since 1983, thanks to new regulations similar to those in existence in the Stalin period, in a simplified procedure, convicts can be sentenced while serving time to further imprisonment from one to five years for "malicious insubordination" to the camp administration, i.e., at the whim of its authorities.[13] This regulation has already been applied repeatedly. The conditions in prisons and penal camps have deteriorated. Torture is frequently used on prisoners awaiting trial to extort confessions in so-called "press chambers";[14] poor medical services for political prisoners, together with poor nutrition and working conditions caused at least six deaths between July 1983 and late 1984;[15] many political prisoners are in poor to grave physical condition;[16] prisoners ever more frequently enter unlimited hunger strikes to protest the conditions of their imprisonment and are ready to die; and the suicide by the Ukrainian civil rights activist Yu. Lytvyn is on record.[17] Moreover, the situation of opposition members released from detention has taken a turn for the worse due to more stringent compulsory registration laws for them. (These were passed in 1981 and 1983).[18]

An amendment (February 1984) to the "Political Crimes Law" further impeded the activities of members of the opposition, limited their support from abroad, and restricted their connections to the outside.[19] The "economic war" against opposition members was further exacerbated by the Soviet Union's cancellation of contracts with companies organizing shipments to private persons in the USSR.[20] According to an amendment to the regulations governing the registration and residence of foreigners in the Soviet Union (1984), in addition to the foreigners themselves, Soviet officials and private individuals can now be held responsible for non-compliance of a foreigner with the relevant regulations and laws. These regulations are also intended to impede contacts with foreigners.[21] The fact that in 1984 for the first time representatives of the Western press were publicly threatened with prosecution for anti-Soviet propaganda points in the same direction (hindering contacts by the population with foreigners and vice-versa). Several Western correspondents were temporarily arrested, questioned, reprimanded, and denounced in 1983 and 1984.[22]

Soviet representatives and authorities met remonstrances regarding the numerous documented violations of human rights with arrogance and impudence (as did for example A. Gromyko with inquiries about Sakharov, miscellaneous official interpreters of Moscow's policies, as well as the Soviet delegation before the UN-human rights commission on the occasion of the report delivered by the USSR in 1984 on the realization of civil and political rights, provided for in the 1966 Civil Rights Pact). Here the cheeky tenor always was that human rights violations allegedly were nonexistent in the Soviet Union, that in any event these questions as internal matters did not concern foreign countries (e.g., the case of Sakharov), and that human rights were honored in the USSR better than anywhere else.[23]

Restrictive Cultural Policy

The regime's dispute with deviant tendencies concentrated throughout the seventies on the emerging oppositions, so culture was allowed to develop relatively freely within the country, even before the law. Cultural activity was like a secondary theatre of war, even well into Brezhnev's final years and after 1979, that fatal year for oppositions. This can often be ascertained in belles-lettres, creative arts, theatre, and music. Works that blaze new, previously unthinkable trails in terms of content and form managed time and again to slip through the censorship net. Though they usually had problems before or after their début, they managed to reach at least a small audience. At the same time—so to speak in the shadow of the dissidents—a multi-faceted, non-standardized "second culture" was able to blossom.[24] But on the other hand, as always, many literati and artists were discriminated against because of their works. These people found themselves drawn into the circle of opposition, either in a direct way due to their sympathies for members of the opposition, or in an indirect way. They were also repressed.

Traditionally, the quality of trends in the USSR's cultural policy is most evident in literary policy, especially in the treatment of the fashion-setting "thick" literary magazines. While, prior to 1982, the Party had issued only rather insignificant statements on literary policy, a CC decree of July 1982 assailed these magazines and the bodies responsible for them[25] (the writers' association at various levels, and Party organizations all the way up to the Republic level). This decree is a reaction to the trends toward autonomy that have been mentioned and have so far not been reprimanded sharply enough. With this CC decree, probably inspired by Andropov, the Party expected to bring about better and more enthusiastic conformity to the Party's policy on the part of the literature and art scenes. Socialist realism was already believed dead and was no longer even mentioned by Brezhnev in his late phase, but it and the equally unfashionable notion of the "positive hero," experienced a renaissance.

In diction and prose, the decree is reminiscent of literary decrees in the Stalin era, though it is far more equivocal. Events in Poland proved the politically explosive power of cultural non-conformism. Against this background, the new decree showed the Party's awareness that there was indeed an urgent need for action. On the other hand, it also realized it was unable to offer any substantial alternatives or positive ideas except for slogans like "partisanship." Strictly speaking, its demands amounted to committing literature and art totally to the Party and to renouncing any ideological (liberal, national, dogmatic) independence. This was an unenforceable demand that amounted to ignoring literary and cultural reality and led to the re-creation of a course that would be dominant and persuasive. This course was based on conformity to the Party. The June 1983 CC plenary session on ideology[26] confirmed the impossibility of such a re-adjustment, for it raised the same demands and levelled the same criticism as the CC decree of 1982. However in 1983, prompted by the Polish crisis and Reagan's course, literature and art were put on the ideological defensive in the "psychological war" during a general assessment of the entire ideological arsenal: ideological independence virtually assumed the menacing connotation of criminal high treason. A CC decree on movies (1984)[27] and miscellaneous semi-official articles on the theatre followed the same line as the literary decree of 1982.[28] Chernenko's speech on the 50th anniversary of the Soviet Writers' Association (September 1984)[29] added nothing new to previous criticism and earlier claims; only threats against ideological switches to the opponent's camp were even more clearly articulated.

Nonetheless, in practical cultural policy the edicts of the past few years have had little substantial effect beyond a profusion of politically obedient, conformist cultural products (among other things, a great range of light literature with anti-American themes): Latent arguments between "liberals," "Russian-nationals," and "neo-Stalinists" continue (with many overlapping trends). This is because the Party line itself is not chemically pure, containing as it does liberal, nationalist, and neo-Stalinist impurities. Also, these arguments persist because the existing cultural landscape with its strong factions cannot be replaced by a design that is really only rudimentary at best. The Party must reconcile itself to a cultural reality that includes pluralistic tendencies and meets with great resonance from the audience as well. It cannot replace the present reality with another. In this situation, all it can do is to make administrative cuts and enforce prohibition censorship. These methods have been used more and more in recent years (e.g., the de facto prohibition to work for directors Yu. Lyubimov and A. Tarkovsky, which caused both not to return to the USSR from Western countries), but can only be sporadically and temporarily effective. They do occasion the continuous emergence of oppositions due to cultural discrimination, unless the latter is prevented temporarily—as it was in Stalin's times—by radical methods. However, these are methods that satisfy the wishes of the "neoStalinists," who miss no opportunity to come forward to celebrate their idol, Stalin, in literature and film.

The treatment of culture as having a potential for opposition and the attempt to bring its deviant, non-conformist parts back into line only spawned opposition in the USSR. A repetition of this process is predictable so long as culture is divided into good and evil from above. Official regimentation is not conducive to cultural development, which always relies on the creative powers of the individual. Time and again the fact that it is impossible to plan talent confronts the Soviet cultural bureaucracy with the problems of spontaneity and of non-conformism. Other unplanable and unpredictable developments that encompass broad strata (such as religiosity among youth and nationalisms, but also novel forms of communication, like video-technology that together with other things has already produced a vast black market for Western video tapes) also bring Soviet cultural policy face to face with difficult problems. Thus, there can be no Soviet master-plan for culture that could actually be realized. Opposition policy and a cultural policy resembling it are treating the symptoms of the terminal disease of spontaneity.

Notes

1. *Pr*, 26 September 1984.
2. Cf. P. Hübner, in: *Opposition in der Sowjetunion* (Düsseldorf, 1972), pp. 52–90.
3. Cf. K. Schlögel, *Der renitente Held* (Hamburg, 1984).
4. *The Soviet Union 1978/79*, pp. 83–88.
5. *The Soviet Union 1980/81*, pp. 78–89.
6. *Loc. cit.*
7. IHT, 2 December 1983.
8. *RL*, 297/84; cf. also Gerd Stricker, "The Churches in the Soviet Union," in this volume, Chapter 11.
9. *RL*, 25/84, 208/84, 391/84; *FAZ*, 10 November 1984; *Vesti iz SSSR*, 3/4, (1985).
10. *dpa*, *UPI*, 17 January 1985; *RS*, 193/83; *Vesti iz SSSR*, 3/4 (1985); *FAZ*, 3 July 1985. Cf. also Fred Oldenburg, "Relations Between the USSR and the Federal Republic of Germany," Chapter 23.
11. *W*, 2 March 1985.
12. *NZZ*, 8 March 1985.
13. *VVS RSFSR*, No. 37 (1983), *st.* 1334; *NZZ*, 19 January 1984; *RS*, 218/83, 21/84.
14. *IHT*, 2 December 1983; *RS*, 184/83; *WSJ*, 29 December 1984; *ddp*, 11 January 1985.
15. *NZZ*, 27 April, 31 May, 11 October, 18 October, and 12 November 1984; *FAZ*, 30 May, 10 October, and 11 October 1984; *WSJ*, 7 November 1984; *dpa*, 27 October 1984.
16. *W*, 22 October 1984; *NZZ*, 22 October 1984.
17. *Arkhiv Samizdata* (Munich), 5335, 5322; *dpa*, 26 and 27 October 1984; *AFP*, 22 October 1984; *WSJ*, 7 November 1984; *FAZ*, 9 May 1984, 2 January 1985; *W*, 22 and 23 October 1984; *NZZ*, 22 October 1984.
18. *VSS SSSR*, No. 10 (1981), *st.*, No. 32, 39 (1983), *st.* 584; *RS*, 228/83.
19. *VVS SSSR*, No. 3 (1984), *st.* 581.
20. *AFP*, 17 May 1984.
21. *VVS SSSR*, No. 22 (1984), *st.* 380; K. Schmid, *Aktuelle Analysen des BIOst*, No. 41 (1984).

22. *Sovetskaya Rossiya*, 26 September 1984; *General-Anzeiger*, 7 April 1984; FAZ, 27 September 1984; *SN*, 14 April 1984.

23. FAZ, 3 and 10 November 1984; *AP*, 6 November 1984; NZZ, 10 December 1984; *Pr*, 9 December 1984.

24. Cf. P. Hübner, in *The Soviet Union 1980/81*, pp. 78–89.

25. *Pr*, 30 July 1982.

26. LG, 16 June 1983.

27. *Pr*, 26 May 1984.

28. For instance, *Pr*, 11 July 1984.

29. *Pr*, 26 September 1984.

Part Two

The Economy

13 The Soviet Economy at the End of the Eleventh Five-Year Plan: Counting on Gorbachev

Hans-Hermann Höhmann

The Economic Situation Demands a Change of Course

At the end of the eleventh five-year plan (1981–1985) Soviet economists are in a dilemma. On the one hand, some of the greatest difficulties of the initial phase of the plan have been overcome. In particular, after a series of bad years, which reached a low point in 1982, industrial growth rates picked up again in 1983 and 1984 and even productivity growth accelerated in this sector. On the other hand the bad harvest in 1984 caused agricultural output to stagnate at the previous year's level, construction and transport showed renewed weakness, and in the energy sector crude oil extraction declined for the first time. Taken together, this brought a renewed decline in the overall rate of economic growth. The Soviet gross national product, measured by Western standards, probably increased by 2–2.5 percent in 1984 compared with about 3 percent in the preceding year. True, this figure is above the level to which the growth rate dropped at the turn of the decade, but it shows clearly that the breakthrough to steady, long-term economic recovery that the Soviet authorities had hoped for has not yet been achieved. With the annual plan for 1985, which envisages an overall growth rate of 2.5–3 percent again (by Western standards), Soviet planners are trying to secure a satisfactory conclusion to the current medium-term plan. However, many of its targets are unattainable. Even if the planned growth acceleration is successful (something which is far from certain in view of the renewed slackening of pace in industry during the early months of 1985), the scope for maneuver within the "magic triangle" of Soviet economic policy—consumption, capital formation and armaments[1]—remains extremely circumscribed. Disagreements over priorities in resource allocation are likely to persist. The central bottleneck sectors continue to be investment and transportation. Furthermore, it is an open question whether Siberia represents a reserve or a burden for future economic development. The problems of these sectors are discussed in the respective essays in this volume.[2]

The Soviet Union's only partly satisfactory economic situation shows some positive tendencies and displays stubborn areas of weakness. In past years, these have led to continuing discussions about the future direction of Soviet economic policy. These were graphically disclosed in both the specialized and the daily press, and the participants included leading politicians as well as economic practitioners and academics. Increasingly, the view came to prevail that the desired intensification of the Soviet economy could not be achieved without major changes in the system of planning and management. Moreover, politicians and academics alike are agreed that a fundamental intensification of the economy cannot be postponed, and the new secretary general, Gorbachev, has equated the scale and urgency of the forthcoming intensification tasks with those of industrialization in the 1930s.[3]

Frequent demands to improve, perfect, or transform the existing system of planning and management must not be taken to imply imminent, far-reaching reform. Despite intensive efforts to improve the efficiency of both management and production, an overall change in the basic institutions and performance mechanisms of the Soviet Union's economic system is not among the options for Soviet economic policy at this time. What can be expected from Gorbachev, however, is a revised and tightened economic policy, a package of course corrections in many economic policy areas, and a policy of economic reform, which seeks to reverse the present adverse development trends. At the end of this chapter we shall discuss the outlines of Gorbachev's policy that are beginning to emerge at the time this is being written. The problems of reform in the narrower sense are reserved for a separate essay.[4]

Economic Growth 1983–1985

In 1979 the Soviet economy's growth rate had fallen markedly. This lasted until 1981 for agriculture and 1982 for industry.[5] In most branches of the economy there was a recovery in 1983, which continued into 1984 for industry, while other sectors contributing to the national product registered a renewed decline. As a result, the rate of increase in national income produced dropped from 4.2 percent in 1983 to 3.5 percent in 1984. For domestic consumption, the corresponding figures are 3.5 percent and 2.6 percent. The growth of the Soviet gross national product according to the Western definition is likely to have been around 3 percent in 1983 and between 2 percent and 2.5 percent in 1984. For 1985 planners are counting on an acceleration in the growth rate again to 3.5 percent for domestic utilization and around 4 percent for aggregate economic output, which should correspond to an increase in gross national product of 2.5–3 percent. With taut growth targets for industrial production (planned increase 3.9 percent), which can scarcely be reached after the unsatisfactory start of the year, achievement of this goal depends above all on whether agricultural output can indeed be raised by the 6 percent envisaged. This is by no

FIGURE 13.1
Growth of the Soviet Economy, 1976-1985
(annual percentage changes)

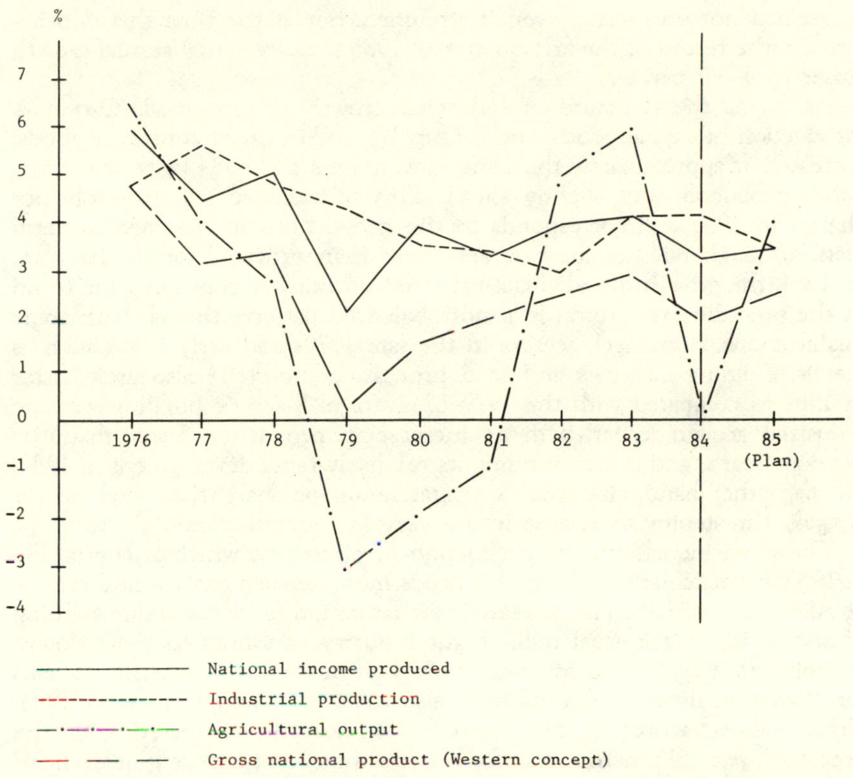

means certain, but in view of the previous year's stagnation it is nevertheless quite possible, assuming a distinctly better grain harvest.

Assuming plan fulfillment in 1985, Soviet economic growth during the eleventh five-year plan as a whole has not fallen far below the goal set in the plan (see Table 13.1). This is surprising, in view of the numerous concerns given prominence in the Soviet press, and it casts doubt on the reliability of official data. In particular, the figures for total economic volume in rubles are likely to be inflated. The extent of underfulfillment of the eleventh five-year plan is thus presumably larger than the published data show.

Industry: The Leader in Production Growth

The economic growth of 1983 and 1984 was founded on a distinct acceleration in the expansion of industrial production. The increase in gross production amounted to 4.2 percent in both years, which was clearly above the 1979–82 average. But the growth rates achieved up to 1978 were not reached. The growth rate targets of the eleventh five-year plan also remain unattainable. At first, the annual plan for 1985, with projections of 3.9 percent for industry as a whole and for Group A, and 4 percent for Group B, seemed not unrealistic, even if stretched; but at the time this is being written, the results of the first quarter of 1985 indicate actual annual growth closer to 3–3.5 percent.

As far as the structure of industrial growth is concerned, Group A (production of capital goods) and Group B (production of consumer goods) increased at approximately the same rate in 1983 and 1984, with consumer goods production but slightly ahead. This relationship will probably not change in 1985 and corresponds to the proportions in the medium-term plan, although rates of increase are lower than provided for in the plan. In 1984, the growth of individual branches of industry continued the trend of the preceding year towards a more balanced pattern, though with some qualifications. Bottleneck sectors in the late 1970s and early 1980s such as metals, building materials and food processing industries also grew faster in 1984 as compared with the 1979–82 average. Machine building was the industrial growth leader, with an increase in production faster than the previous year's, and it is continuing its relatively rapid development in 1985. On the other hand, after two comparatively good years, the metals sector is again threatening to relapse into a very low growth rate.

The rapid increase in the production of electricity, which is continuing in 1985, is particularly striking; this needs more detailed analysis and cannot be adequately explained by increased mechanization or by the commissioning of additional electric steel mills. Light industry continues to grow slowly, though here the demand for quantity has given way more recently to calls for higher quality. Output of fuels also grew at a slower pace in 1984. Crude oil extraction, at 613 metric tons, dropped compared with the preceding year (616 metric tons) for the first time, and coal output declined slightly as well. This stagnation in output of the "classical" sources of energy could not be completely offset by the continued rapid and indeed accelerating expansion of natural gas extraction. We shall have to wait to see whether the drop in oil production will lead to major bottlenecks. Export adjustments could conceivably become necessary.

Productivity Improvements: Breakthrough to Greater Efficiency or "Slenderizing Effect"?

As mentioned above, recent trends in industrial labor productivity have been highly satisfactory for Soviet planners. For industry as a whole an increase in productivity of 3.6 percent was recorded in 1983, followed by an increase of 3.8 percent in 1984. This means that in 1984 fully 90 percent of production growth was attributable to productivity increases (86 percent the previous year) and that even compared with the last normal years, 1976–

TABLE 13.1
The Soviet Economy's Growth Rates for 1981-1985
(annual increase in percent)

	1981	1982	1983	1984	1985 (plan)	1981-5 (actual[1])	1981-5 (11th FYP)
National income produced	3.3	3.4	4.2	3.4[a]	(4.0)	3.7	(4.0)
Employment in the state sector	1.3	1.0	0.8	0.6	0.4	0.8	-
Aggregate labor productivity	2.6	3.2	3.7	3.0	(3.5)	3.2	(3.5)
Industry, gross production	3.4	2.8	4.2	4.2	3.9	3.7	4.7
Group A	3.3	2.8	4.2	4.2	3.9	3.7	4.7
Group B	3.5	2.9	4.3	4.3	4.0	3.9	4.8
Labor productivity	2.7	2.1	3.6	3.8	3.7	3.2	4.2
Construction and installation	1.9	2.0	3.0	3.0	(3.3)	2.7	(3.0)
Labor productivity	2.2	2.0	3.1	3.1	3.5	2.8	2.8
Agriculture, gross output	-1.0	4.0	6.0	0.0	6.7	3.4	(4.5-5.0)
Labor productivity[b]	-2.0	6.0	7.0	1.0	(7.0)	3.7	-
Transport, freight	2.3	1.2	4.8	2.9	4.4	3.2	3.5
Labor productivity[c]	0.8	-1.5	3.7	2.0	2.8	1.4	2.0
National income consumed	3.2	2.6	3.5	2.6	3.5	3.4	3.4
Retail trade turnover[d]	4.3	0.0	2.7	4.2	5.2	3.2	4.2
Social consumption fund	4.2	4.8	4.6	3.5	5.0	4.6	4.2
Gross capital investment	3.8	2.0	5.7	2.0	3.4	3.7	(1.5)
Distribution							
Average monthly income of state-employed labor force	2.1	2.8	2.4	2.5	3.0	2.5	2.8
Average monthly pay of collective farm members[b]	4.0	4.0	9.0	3.0	3.5	4.9	3.8
Social consumption fund per head	3.4	4.3	3.8	2.6	3.9	3.6	-

Notes: [a]Assuming fulfilment of the 1985 annual plan.
[b]Socialized production.
[c]Rail transport.
[d]State and cooperative trade.

Sources: USSR statistical yearbooks and plan fulfillment reports.

TABLE 13.2
Growth of Soviet Industrial Production by Branches
(annual increase in percent)

	1979	1980	1981	1982	1983	1984	1985[a]
Industrial production	3.4	3.6	3.4	2.9	4.2	4.2	3.9
Group A	3.4	3.6	3.3	2.9	4.2	4.1	3.9
Group B	3.3	3.5	3.5	2.9	4.3	5.3	4.0
Electricity	3	5	2	3	3	6	-
Fuels	2	2	1	2	2	0.9	-
Ferrous and non-ferrous metals	0.2	0.6	0.5	0.9	4	3	-
Chemicals and petro-chemicals	3	6	5	3	6	5	5
Machine building and metalworking	8	6	5	5	6	7	6.5
Timber, wood processing and paper	-2	2	3	3	3	3	-
Building materials	-1	0.9	2	0.9	4	2	-
Light industry	2	3	3	0.2	0.9	1	3.5
Food processing industry	2	0.3	2	4	4	3	-
Household wares and consumer durables	5	8	7	2	3	4	6

Note: [a]Annual plan 1985.

Sources: USSR statistical yearbooks, plan fulfillment reports, and plan documents.

TABLE 13.3
Growth of Mechanical Engineering Production and Productivity

	1978	1981	1983	1984
Number of ministries	11	11	11	11
Growth of production > growth of productivity	9	3	3	0
Growth of production = growth of productivity	2	5	6	2
Growth of production < growth of productivity	0	3	2	9

Sources: USSR plan fulfillment reports.

78, a distinct advance in intensification has been recorded. Then 70 percent of production growth was achieved by means of productivity increases.

The improvement in productivity in Soviet industry shows itself both on the regional and sectoral levels. Regionally, it is noteworthy that in 1984 the entire increase in production in the parts of the USSR particularly affected by labor shortages (the RSFSR, which includes Siberia, Estonia, Latvia) was achieved by means of productivity increases. Sectorally, Soviet mechanical engineering emerges as the leading branch. Table 13.3 shows that more and more of the eleven ministries attached to the mechanical engineering sector for which statistics have been published are achieving their production growth through increased productivity, in most cases with a declining labor force (data of this kind are not published for the ministries of the armaments industry).

In 1978, in nine of the eleven mechanical engineering ministries for which we have statistics, production increased faster than labor productivity, so that the number of workers employed grew more or less sharply; but in 1984 the relationship was reversed: In nine of the eleven ministries the growth of productivity exceeded the increase in production, which means that compared with preceding years, accelerated growth was usually combined with a decline in the labor force employed.

What are the reasons for the improvements in productivity shown by these statistics? Do they indicate the breakthrough to more "efficiency and quality" demanded under Brezhnev—and indeed before?[6] There are undoubtedly several different factors working together. First, the better balance of production achieved in 1983, though partially lost again in 1984, led to a reduction of bottlenecks, to improved supply of materials and components, to better use of capacity and, through rising production combined with a slower increase in the supply of production factors, and to improved productivity. Similar effects could be attributed to the commissioning of new capacity, which proceeded rapidly during 1983, but slowed down again in 1984. Undoubtedly there has also been a continuing "Andropov effect" at work (which evidently should merge into a "Gorbachev effect"): More discipline at all levels of the production process had favorable effects on productivity trends. Still, it is questionable whether and how long this effect will last. More important, probably, is another effect that should be seen as a "slenderizing effect." At present the rate of growth of the labor force is falling sharply; at the same time the number of employees ceasing work on account of their age is rising at an accelerating rate. This trend must lead to a situation where the overemployment existing in Soviet industrial enterprises diminishes, where the enterprises' labor reserves are "slenderized." Since productivity growth is calculated as the ratio of the rate of increase in production to the change in the number employed in the workforce, a decrease in overemployment has a productivity-enhancing effect—even if the efficiency of the work process itself undergoes little or no improvement.

Resorting to trimming labor reserves allows the Soviet economy to achieve productivity improvements for a time without far-reaching changes in the planning system. Yet the "slenderizing effect" cannot work in the long run and is one of the "superficial effects," that are occasionally mentioned in Soviet economic publicity and that need to be strengthened and reinforced. Without thorough economic reform, however, there is little prospect of this being achieved.

Other Sectors of the Economy: Agriculture, Construction, Transportation

In contrast to industry, the situation in Soviet agriculture must once again be regarded with skepticism. Nevertheless, there are positive as well as negative features, and there has not (yet?) been a relapse into the thoroughly unsatisfactory situation of 1979–81.[7] On the one hand, the expansion of the livestock sector continued in 1984, albeit at a slower pace than in the preceding year. The production of animal products, and above all meat, rose further. Total cattle holdings increased. The number of cows was not held at quite the level of the year before, although in light of the need to economize on feed supplies, this was certainly a rational development, and the productivity of milk cows increased. The numbers of pigs, sheep and goats also declined slightly in 1984.

On the other hand, the USSR's grain harvest turned out very badly again. According to American estimates it was probably around 170 metric tons in 1984—distinctly below the preceding year's figure of around 190 metric tons, which itself was not exactly impressive.

As the shortfall in domestically produced feed grain has so far evidently been partly compensated by imports, livestock production was successfully maintained. On balance, despite the adverse trend in the crop production sector, total agricultural output was at least stabilized at the level reached in 1983. Nevertheless this did not prevent the decline in the overall rate of the economy's growth. For 1985 a rapid increase in agricultural output is envisaged—6.7 percent—which, given a distinctly better grain harvest, does not seem unattainable following the low 1984 base from which it is measured.

Construction and transportation also made smaller contributions to the growth of the economy in 1984 than the year before. Yet, both sectors recorded a growth rate above the average for 1979–82. Actual output of state construction and installation organizations (value of completed projects) amounted to around 75 billion rubles, and the volume of construction and installation work done increased by 3 percent. Freight carried by all means of transportation grew by 2.9 percent in 1984. This is distinctly slower than in 1983 (4.8 percent) but is likewise above the 1979–82 average and thus indicates a limited degree of consolidation. Pipeline shipments of natural gas continued to expand at the fastest rate. Railways, on the other hand, with a 1 percent increase in freight carried in 1984, scarcely contributed to the stabilization. All together, the Soviet transportation sector will probably exhibit the flexibility to deal with future bottlenecks in the expansion of the economy for the medium term only if the overall rate of growth remains around 2.5 percent. However, the fact that the share of rail transportation in total investment rose somewhat at the beginning of the 1980s should have a beneficial effect. In 1985 freight transportation is planned to increase by 3.3 percent.

Factors of Production

As regards trends in the supply of production factors, the number of blue-collar and white-collar workers employed in the state sector of the economy increased smewhat more slowly again in 1984, i.e., by only 0.6 percent (after a 0.8 percent rise in 1983). For 1985 planners are expecting a further drop in expansion to 0.4 percent. The overall trend in labor productivity, was not unfavorable, though less balanced than in the previous year. The improved trend in industry has already been noted. Increases in labor productivity anticipated in the 1985 plan, 3.7 percent in industry, 3.5 percent in construction and 2.1 percent in rail transportation are in accordance with the current trend.

The trend in capital input in 1984 was marked by a decline in the rate of growth of commissioning new capacity, compared with the previous year. Commissioning of fixed capital assets increased by 3 percent (6 percent in 1983). Nevertheless, the capital formation process maintained a rapid tempo—despite a renewed cut in the growth of investment that will be discussed below. As in the preceding years, the increase in capital stock in 1984 is likely to have been around 6.5 percent. In the long run, however, it cannot remain at this level.

Utilization: Faster Consumption and Reduced Investment Growth

As regards the utilization of national income, consumption increased more rapidly than capital formation in 1984—the opposite of what the relationship had been in 1982 and 1983. The growth of gross capital investment, at 2 percent, was distinctly below the figure for the year before. The annual plan was thus not fulfilled. In the three preceding years gross capital investment had increased at the following rates: 3.8 percent in 1981, 3.6 percent in 1982 and 5.7 percent in 1983.

TABLE 13.4
Production of Animal Products

		1981	1982	1983	1984
Meat and poultry (live weight)	(metric tons)	15.2	15.4	16.4	16.7
Milk	(metric tons)	88.8	91.0	96.4	97.0
Eggs	(billion)	70.9	72.4	75.1	76.0
Wool	(000 tons)	460.0	452.0	462.0	463.0

Sources: USSR statistical yearbooks and plan fulfillment reports.

TABLE 13.5
Livestock Numbers in Soviet Agriculture
(excluding privately owned livestock, as of 1 January, in millions)

	1981	1982	1983	1984	1985
Cattle	115.1	115.9	117.2	119.6	120.8
of which cows	43.4	43.7	43.8	43.9	43.5
Pigs	73.4	73.3	76.7	78.2	77.8
Sheep and goats	147.5	148.5	148.5	151.8	148.8
Poultry	1032.4	1067.5	1104.5	1126.1	-

Sources: USSR statistical yearbooks and plan fulfillment reports.

TABLE 13.6
Growth of Freight Transportation
(billion ton/kilometers and change in percent)

	1982		1983		1984	
Rail	3464.5	-1.1	3600.1	3.9	3641.0	1.1
River	262.4	3.0	273.2	9.0	265.0	-3.0
Road	143.0	2.0	142.0	-0.4	138.0	-3.0
Oil pipeline	1306.8	3.5	1353.1	3.5	1370.0	1.2
Gas pipeline	771.5	13.3	863.4	11.9	997.0	15.5

Sources: USSR statistical yearbooks and plan fulfillment reports.

TABLE 13.7
Growth of the Labor Force and Labor Productivity
(annual change in percent)

	1976-80	1981	1982	1983	1984
Labor force employed in the state sector of the economy	1.9	1.3	1.1	0.8	0.6
Labor productivity					
Industry	3.2	2.7	2.1	3.6	3.8
Construction	2.1	2.2	2.0	3.1	3.1
Rail transportation	0.2	0.8	-1.5	3.9	2.0

Sources: USSR statistical yearbooks and plan fulfillment reports.

TABLE 13.8
Indicators of National Income Utilization
(annual growth in percent)

	1976-80	1981	1982	1983	1984
National income utilized	3.8	3.2	3.6	3.5	2.6
Consumption	-	4.0	1.2	2.9	3.2[b]
Accumulation	-	0.9	11.0	5.8	1.0[b]
Retail trade turnover[a]	4.4	4.3	0.1	2.7	4.2
Gross capital investment	3.3	3.8	3.6	5.7	2.0

Notes: [a]State and cooperative trade.
[b]Estimated.

Sources: USSR statistical yearbooks and plan fulfillment reports.

Compared with capital formation, consumption (measured by indicators like retail trade turnover, household services turnover and the "social consumption fund") expanded relatively rapidly in 1984. Above all, turnover in state and cooperative trade, the volume of which stagnated in 1982 and rose by only 2.7 percent in 1983, grew considerably faster again at 4.2 percent, though even this rate was below the plan's target figure. How far the growth of turnover shown is actually "real," in other words, how far price increases have been taken into account, cannot be ascertained. The rise in retail trade turnover is attributable, for one thing, to the marked increase in sales of meat and meat products (7 percent) and animal fats (8 percent) and, secondly, to the significant rise in turnover and clothing, underwear, and footwear (averaging 4–5 percent compared with no increase the previous year). Since production of these goods did not rise to the same extent as sales turnover (and the gaps were presumably not met by imports), price increases can be assumed here, and only the Soviet consumer can judge whether these were justified by improvements in quality.[8]

It is not possible at this time to say whether the shift from capital formation to consumption, as compared with the previous year and the 1984 annual plan, was a deliberate economic policy move or a result of the spontaneous processes that occur even in a planned economy of the Soviet type. For economic and domestic policy reasons, a marked rise in the standard of living was certainly overdue after the stagnation of consumption in recent years. A cutback on the investment side may also have seemed quite acceptable to the planners because growth in commissioning of new capacity continued in 1984, and the increase in capital stock itself is still around the 6.5 percent level. Since, furthermore, investment targets of the eleventh five-year plan—in contrast to most of the plan's other targets—have been reached, curbing the investment pace may perhaps have seemed advisable, even from the perspective of a middle-term plan. Planned growth of investment by 3.4 percent and of retail trade turnover by 5.2 percent in 1985 basically maintain the utilization proportions of 1984 (with a higher rate of growth for the whole economy).

As far as distribution is concerned, the cash income of the population also showed a marked rise in 1984. The average monthly income of the state-employed labor force increased more quickly (plus 2.5 percent) than envisaged in the annual plan. The growth of collective farm members' income from "socialised activity," that is to say excluding income from the cultivation of private plots, reached the annual plan target of 3 percent. Despite the speed-up of turnover in state and cooperative trade that we have noted, there was also another strong rise in savings bank deposits, which increased by around 15 billion rubles—a full 19 percent more than in the previous year. Even Soviet specialists occasionally regard this as an indicator of repressed inflation. The 1985 plan anticipates an increase of 3 percent in wages and salaries and 3–5 percent in collective farm members' earnings from work on the farms.

Foreign Trade

As an important sector in the Soviet economy, foreign trade is also the subject of a separate essay in this volume.[9] A review of the basic trends and prospects will therefore suffice here. The USSR's foreign trade, measured by nominal turnover, expanded at rates of 6.6 percent and 9.6 percent in 1983 and 1984 respectively, faster than any other sector of the economy. Yet, compared with the trend up to the start of the 1980s, this was a clear deceleration. The shares of the principal groups of trading partners (socialist countries, Western industrialized countries and developing countries) shifted in both years (again in current prices) in favor of the socialist countries, yet because of the differing price trends in its trade with East and West, the USSR's real level of trade with the West, measured in quantity of goods, actually increased in 1983. This however continued only to a limited degree in 1984. In particular, imports from Western industrialized countries probably declined in that year, primarily because of a marked reduction in imports of machinery and equipment. The USSR's trade balance with the West improved distinctly, its net indebtedness was further reduced, and Soviet foreign trade as a whole (with all areas of the world) registered a record surplus in 1984.

The reasons for the present trends in the growth and pattern of Soviet foreign trade by regions and commodity groups must be sought at various different levels. They are a combination of the effects of:

- Fundamental decisions concerning trade policy such as stronger demands on CMEA partners for delivery of larger quantities of higher quality goods in order to reduce their large accumulated trade deficits with the USSR;
- Uncertainties about future foreign trade policy of the Western industrialized countries, especially the USA, which, combined with growing doubts about the value of equipment and technology imports, led to caution in placing such orders;
- Continuing weakness in Western European demand (Western Europe is the most important Soviet trading partner in the field of equipment

and technology), with imparied prospects for increasing hard currency earnings by additional exports of energy and other products;

- The conclusion of projects in the final stage of the eleventh five-year plan (1981–85) and uncertainties in respect to Soviet foreign trade policy in the twelfth five-year plan (1986–90);
- Restriction of imports of technology, machinery and equipment because of the necessity for massive grain imports due to the 1984 harvest failure, thus changing the structure of imports more towards greater concentration on the food sector.

All the same, the current trend in Soviet foreign trade relations cannot be interpreted as a general return to autarchy within the Eastern bloc. It is only the extent of trade links with the West at any particular time that can be the subject of economic policy decisions. In principle, continued cooperation with Western countries is unavoidable owing to the present economic situation and development goals of the USSR.

Soviet Economic Policy from Andropov to Gorbachev

At the end of the Brezhnev era the Soviet economy had entered a crisis phase in its development, marked by the coincidence of chronic systemic dysfunctions affecting the coordination of the economic process and the efficiency of production, adverse trends in the supply of production factors, counterproductive structural changes, and acute disproportions. The massive imbalances that arose at the end of the 1970s above all led to a major decline in economic growth, which can thus also be described as a "crisis of disproportions."

When Andropov succeeded Brezhnev in November 1982, he left no doubt of his conviction that there was a need for comprehensive action on economic policy. But his introductory measures were subject to three basic restrictions, which will also continue to limit Soviet leadership's scope of action in the future: the shortage of resources for far-reaching sectoral and regional redistribution, the impossibility of effectively changing the basic institutions and mode of operation of the administratively planned economy within the foreseeable future—in other words, of tackling reforms that would really change the system—and the necessity of grappling with the limited competence and vested interests of the established administrative apparatus even to introduce minor revisions in economic policy.

What was left, in view of these restrictions, was (and is) a package of less wide-ranging, goal-, resource-, and productivity-oriented measures. Andropov had little time to implement an economic policy course of his own. For some months before his death, he was scarcely able to take an active part in the management of the economy. Yet his first speeches and measures showed a series of efforts that can be summed up as an attempt to "turn muddling through into a plan of action." Andropov was well aware that precisely when far-reaching alternatives with the impact necessary to change system and structure were not available, a well-coordinated, tightly managed and diversified package of measures was required.

Andropov's Program: Watered Down by Chernenko

Under Andropov it was possible to distinguish four areas concerning such a concept:

- In the field of economic policy, consolidation at a less demanding level (reduction of plan targets) and shifting the emphasis within the use or input structure (raising the rate of investment growth) were the major key words.
- In the field of labor policy, there were the attempts to strengthen labor discipline, to introduce better coordination between performance and pay and to move against corruption and other economic crimes.[10]
- In the area of economic reform policy a number of measures of a general or locally limited nature were introduced in 1983 to promote technical progress, save energy and materials, relate remuneration more closely to performance, etc. Above all, however, an experiment was started on 1 January 1984 in five industrial ministries, and extended to major parts of Soviet industry in 1985.[11]
- Finally, in foreign trade policy, cooperation with socialist trading partners in the CMEA was intensified, but trade with Western industrialized countries was also continued, which indicated an effort to divorce foreign trade policy somewhat from foreign policy, an attitude that corresponded to that of most of the Western trading partners.

The economic policy of reorientation and tightening up, by which Andropov sought to tackle the visible weaknesses of the Soviet economy from various directions, and which contributed to its temporary revival, was basically accepted by Chernenko and initially continued by and large. But it soon lost any clear shape. Many of Andropov's initiatives faded away—among other things, the emphasis originally placed on the discipline campaign was soon dropped. There appeared an unmistakable tendency to relapse into the "muddling through" of the last phase of the Brezhnev era.

Gorbachev: Back to Andropov and Beyond?

The renewed slowdown in economic growth in 1984 and 1985, the persistent bottlenecks in the supply of production factors, which show tendencies of becoming more serious, and the still unsatisfactory prospects for intensification during the twelfth five-year plan (1986–90) and beyond place considerable pressure on Soviet leadership under the new secretary general. Action is required and expectations are high. Gorbachev himself has repeatedly declared that economics deserves priority in the whole field of Soviet policy and that thorough modernization of the Soviet economy, (a change from the previous type of resource-based development to growth based on productivity) and better satisfaction of the consumer and other social requirements of the population can no longer be postponed.[12] In economic policy this calls for nothing less than a definite "about-face."

Under the conditions of the present political, economic and social system of the USSR such an about-face cannot, however, mean a far-reaching, liberalizing reform directed towards a transition to a market-type (even if it is a socialist market) control system. If the change that Gorbachev seeks is successful, it can only—but "only" could still mean a lot here—be a matter of revision and tightening of traditional elements of Soviet economic policy, none of which would in themselves be new. What would be new, though, would be their being lumped together in a diversified overall concept, which—if it could be conceived with expertise and implemented with firm leadership—could prove an effective instrument for securing the desired and necessary improvement in efficiency.

If we take Gorbachev's past statements, together with his first economic policy pronouncements after taking office and in particular his program speech at the April 1985 plenum of the Central Committee,[13] and assess them against the background of the present economic situation and the political and social structure of the USSR, the following picture emerges of a tightened and revised economic policy, which is clearly reminiscent of Andropov's intentions, and yet is starting to go beyond them in its concern for reforms in planning, management and the economic mechanism:

- In the field of labor policy: persistent pressure for improved labor discipline, tougher action against economic crime of all kinds, changes in the wage and bonus system designed to establish a closer linkage between wage scales and economic policy priorities and between wages and performance, and extension of elements of participation to strengthen responsibility and initiative in production associations and enterprises.
- In the field of structural policy: development of consumption-oriented branches, emphasis on those sectors of the economy that are especially important for modernization, and raising the level of technology (such as parts of the mechanical engineering industry), continuation of the high-priority development in agriculture and the energy sector.
- In the field of reform policy: partly decentralizing, partly tightening up the reform of the system of industrial planning and management on the basis of the experiment currently under way (that is to say, retaining the basic structure of the traditional system while simultaneously revising its concrete forms so as to concentrate central control on strategically fundamental sectors, and broadening the decision-making scope of subordinate levels of management, particularly the economic units themselves). Changes in the organizational structure of planning and management (for example, dissolution of industrial associations), stronger emphasis on regional aspects of planning and management, possibly

more far-reaching reforms in agriculture and sectors of the economy which, from the point of view of central priorities, are more peripheral in nature (handicrafts, services), limited expansion of private economic activity (partial development of NEP-elements on the basis of the scope created for this in the 1977 Constitution), elaboration of special planning methods and incentives to promote rapid technological progress (an extraordinary Central Committee plenum on technology was announced for June 1985).

- In the field of foreign trade policy: development of economic relations with Western industrialized countries (but also with CMEA countries) in order to enrich the USSR's own technology and expand the equipment base for the approaching twelfth five-year plan.

Provided that it was well coordinated and consistently implemented, such a "revised economic policy" could have the effect of raising performance and stabilizing the rate of economic growth, even with real systemic reform. The following arguments can be put forward in support of this view:

- The seriousness of the situation ultimately requires decisive action; yet, on the other hand, the trend is (still) economically and politically stable enough for a consolidation (and not a crisis) program to be tackled without excessive haste.
- The strategy outlined could be comprehensive and thus really mean a new quality of economic policy without arousing too many conflicting interests within established social groups in the USSR; it affects individuals rather than whole strata and is thus compatible with a "circulation of elites," directed from above. This, like the tightening of economic policy, is urgently needed and has already been put into effect by the new secretary general.
- Gorbachev may be a promising exponent of reorientation; by appearances more of a "doer" than a charismatic leader, he is the bearer of the hopes of many Soviet citizens; these hopes can be used to make policies successful, especially if there should be an early "Gorbachev effect" (perhaps on the basis of a good harvest in 1985).

On the other hand, of course, persistent policy disputes, resistance by the apparatus, and failures in the initial period could turn the bearer of hopes back into one who merely muddles through. In that case a further decline in Soviet economic performance, with all its domestic and foreign policy implications, would be unavoidable.

Notes

1. On the problems of the armaments burden see Franz Walter, "Trends in Soviet Defense Expenditures: Facts and Speculation," Chapter 16.

2. Boris Rumer, "Problems of Soviet Investment Policy," in this volume, Chapter 14; Gertraud Seidenstecher "Economic Growth and Transportation: Stop at the

Performance Limit?" in this volume, Chapter 15, Hermann Clement, "Siberia: Resource or Burden?," in this volume, Chapter 17.

3. *Pr*, 11 December 1984.

4. H.-H. Höhmann, "Soviet Economic Reforms: Higher Achievement as a Result of New Premises?" in this volume, Chapter 18.

5. H.-H. Höhmann, "Die sowjetische Wirtschaft nach dem Wachstumstief: Stagnation, Zwischenhoch oder anhaltender Aufschwung?" in H.-H. Höhmann and H. Vogel (eds.) *Osteuropas Wirtschaftsprobleme und die Ost-West-Beziehungen* (Baden-Baden, 1984), pp. 13 ff.

6. H.-H. Höhmann, in *Sowjetunion 1982/83*, pp. 113 ff.

7. G. Pospelowa and E. Schinke, *Aktuelle Analysen des BIOst*, No. 37 (1984).

8. H.-H. Höhmann, *Aktuelle Analysen des BIOst*, No. 28 (1984).

9. Christian Meier, "Soviet Foreign Trade Restricted by Foreign Policy?" in this volume, Chapter 19.

10. On the new labor law restrictions see *Pr*, 7 August 1983.

11. Features and principles of the experiment were published in *Pr*, 26 July 1983.

12. *Pr*, 11 December 1984 and 12 March 1985.

13. *Pr*, 24 April 1985.

14
Problems of Soviet Investment Policy

Boris Rumer

The development of the USSR at the beginning of the 1980s was marked by an unparalleled decline in the growth of economic resources, namely labor, raw materials, fuels, and capital investment. The figures produced for the first half of the 1980s by the leading Soviet economist A. Aganbegyan show only a 3 percent increase in the labor force, a 5 percent growth in the output of the raw material extracting industries and a 17 percent rise in productive capital investment. The corresponding figures for the preceding five years come to 6 percent, 10 percent, and 23 percent respectively, and for the first half of the 1970s they are 6 percent, 26 percent, and 44 percent.[1]

Intensification: A Problem of the Scale of Industrialization

Opportunities for economic growth became scarcer in the 1970s and the process continued and became more pronounced in the 1980s. The reason for this was a decline in the supply of basic resources. As a result of this decline, Soviet economists felt compelled to revise their basic model of economic planning. Economic policy and practice had to be designed so that the planned results were achieved with a minimum expenditure of resources. Thus, more economical use of resources became the central theme of an "intensification campaign." In fact the word "intensification" today denotes as comprehensive and all-embracing a concept as did two other words in Soviet history: "electrification" and "industrialization." The parallel with industrialization was explicitly stressed by new secretary general Gorbachev.

How successful has this intensification campaign been? So far, not very. According to D. Chernikov, deputy director of a Gosplan research institute, the role played by intensive factors in Soviet economic growth is not increasing, but has actually been diminishing. The share of productivity in the rise in national income dropped from 40 percent in 1966–70 to 25 percent in 1981–82.[2] It follows that, despite all their vows to pursue a more intensive form of economic development, Soviet authorities have not succeeded in putting a stop to the increasing expenditure of resources and abandonment of the extensive form of economic development. Unless this changes, given smaller growth rates of resources, it will severely restrict the economic development of the country in the future.

This is the real situation in which Soviet planners have to formulate their economic strategy and tactics for the second half of the 1980s and work out their next five-year plan, the twelfth.

Investment: The Focus of the Decisionmakers

In both theory and practice the Soviet leadership focuses particular attention on its investment policy. The problems of labor and natural resources, in contrast, have always been of secondary importance to Soviet decisionmakers. This becomes evident from sources such as technical Soviet economics books and Gosplan methodological instructions on the preparation of five-year plans. Even now, in spite of the increasing severity of the labor shortage and the growing difficulties in securing supplies of raw materials, the earlier attitude towards economic resources has hardly changed. The scarcity of labor and natural resources is accepted as something unavoidable, as something that has objective causes and is simply impossible to combat. The labor shortage is attributed to a reduction in the population's growth rate, which in turn is supposedly nothing more than a consequence of the Second World War. The scarcity of natural resources is ascribed to the exhaustion of old deposits in the western parts of the country (oil in Azerbaijan and the Volga region, coal in the Don basin, iron ore in the Urals, etc.) and the consequent shift in the country's fuel and raw material basis to the eastern regions, where the expansion of production involves difficulties in opening up new territories under harsh climatic conditions.[3]

In fact, however, underlying the difficulties with labor and resource supplies, there are some fundamental factors that have long been present in the Soviet economy. There is no reason to regard them as purely a manifestation of objective tendencies that are independent of the Soviet leaders and would not be affected by their policies. The main reason for the increasing labor shortage is the fact that about half the industrial workers and 70 percent of the agricultural workers are performing non-mechanized manual labor. The increasing appetite for fuels and raw materials cannot be satisfied either until the development of advanced industries is successfully speeded up.

A basic feature of Soviet industry is the preponderance of raw-material extracting and primary industries, which account for around one-half of total industrial production and absorb about two-thirds of all industrial investment. The dominance of raw material extracting and primary industries is continually increasing and gives Soviet industrial production a distinctly primitive profile. Thus a vicious cycle has begun to manifest itself: The more resources are used to maintain and step up production of fuels and raw materials, the less there are available for the development of advanced industries; and the more the advanced industries fall behind modern standards, the more fuels and raw materials are needed per unit of output and the greater is the need to extract fuels and raw materials.

The theorists and practitioners of Soviet economic planning are seeking a way out of this situation through optimization of investment policy. On this subject, however, serious differences of opinion have arisen among the leading experts in the USSR. The crucial question is whether, with diminishing investment, a further decline in economic growth can be avoided. In the following paragraphs we shall briefly examine the two principal schools of thought.

One side,[4] whose views are very convenient for the leadership, represents the notion that in essence the slower rate of investment growth is justified. Their argument runs as follows: the USSR has created an enormous stock of capital and productive capacity, and, even if the investment curve flattens out, there are still significant reserves in the form of more efficient utilization of available productive capacity. Furthermore, to tap these reserves requires no great expenditure on new investment. In practice this school of thought wants to direct investment into the modernization of existing enterprises and reduce investment in the expansion of fixed capital stock that would be accomplished by the building of new enterprises. This policy prescribes faster writing off of old equipment and acquisition of new, more modern replacements. From the point of view of this theory a flattening out of the investment curve is completely justified. In addition, such a policy would induce Soviet economic managers to use the investment allocated by the state more efficiently.

The opposite school of thought[5] argues that the limits of maximum exploitation of the existing production potential were already reached in the middle of the 1970s. Proof of this is the decline in utilization of productive capacity in the late 1970s and early 1980s: Simply, no more juice can be squeezed out of this lemon. Therefore, if the negative investment trend is not reversed, a further decline in growth rates for industrial production and national income—with all the resulting consequences—cannot possibly be prevented.

In this connection an important comment needs to be made: While the first school of thought represents the orthodox party position (as articulated in various official pronouncements and decisions), the director of the Gosplan research institute, V. Kirichenko, represents the opposite school. This school appears to support the heretical view of Gosplan and its chairman, N. Baibakov. If this were not the case, Kirichenko would scarcely keep his post as director of a Gosplan agency. In his speech at the XXVI party congress in March 1981, the prime minister, Tikhonov, declared that the planned rise in national income would have to be achieved with an absolute reduction in the increment in capital investment.[6] But in September 1982, citing research done by his institute, Kirichenko wrote in the Gosplan organ, *Planovoe Khozyaistvo*, that a declining pace of capital investment, even accepting the possibility of higher yields, would lead to a declining rate of growth of national income.[7] Therefore it seems justified to conclude that, for the first time since the 1920s, we are witnessing a dispute among the Soviet elite concerning a fundamental economic question: investment policy.

Investment Growth and Capital Intensity

What is the real rate of investment growth in the present period? According to official statements it is currently increasing more rapidly than planned. In 1981–84 the average annual rate of growth was around 3–4 percent, and for 1985 the plan envisages an increase of 5 percent.[8] But do these figures take inflation into account? Inflation is, after all, a striking fact of the Soviet economy. It can be observed in both the production and the consumption sectors. One leading economist at the Institute of Industrial Economics in Novosibirsk (Aganbegyan's institute), Professor K. Val'tukh, concluded on the basis of his calculations that "*in real terms* there was an absolute decrease in productive capital investment" in the period 1976–80, as compared with 1971–75 (author's emphasis).[9] We can thus assume that, taking inflation into account, investment has declined.

In order to answer the question of whether the planned development of the economy can be achieved with the existing investment possibilities, we must try to estimate the present and expected trends in capital intensity that will result from current and planned investments. The trend towards increasing capital intensity has been a characteristic feature of Soviet industrial development for at least twenty-five years. In the 1960s the capital intensity of newly installed capacity rose sharply. The annual rates of capital intensity increase for the main branches of industry (ferrous metals, mechanical engineering, chemicals, coal, building materials, etc.) rose from 5 percent in 1971–75 to 7.4 percent in 1976–80.[10] Since the rate of capital intensity growth exceeds that of capital investment, it follows logically that the development of new enterprises and of productive capacity in volume terms is being reduced.

A study by a leading Soviet expert in the field of investment, V. Fal'tsman, of the Central Institute of Mathematical Economics in Moscow, concludes that the capital intensity of new productive capacity is rising.[11] Even if one applies quality standards of comparison to the output, an increase in capital intensity can be observed.

The increase in the capital intensity of new productive capacity is to a certain extent the result of objective phenomena in the economic development of the USSR, such as the mechanization of manual labor and the automation of technological processes (which leads to the replacement of labor by capital), the shifting of the raw material extracting industries to new regions in the east and north-east (and the consequent necessity to open up new areas under adverse climatic conditions), higher costs for environmental protection, and so on. But a large part of the increase in capital intensity is explained by the ever more rapidly growing costs per unit of production for new machines. Between 1971–75 and 1976–80 the costs of equipment purchases (per unit of production capacity, e.g. per ton of steel, per kilowatt of electric power capacity, per cubic meter of ferro-concrete, etc.) rose by 72 percent, while construction costs increased by only 23 percent.[12]

One of the principal reasons for rising equipment costs, according to Fal'tsman, is the higher expenditure per unit of productivity. According to his calculations, costs for domestically produced machinery rose by 15 percent between 1971–75 and 1976–80, whereas between 1966–70 and 1971–75 they had risen by only 7 percent.[13]

The rise in equipment costs per unit of productivity is a complicated process, in which both inflation and objective factors play a part: These include the costs of raising labor productivity, of improving the quality of products, of economizing on fuel and raw materials, etc. Technological progress in Soviet mechanical engineering is directed less towards labor productivity than towards reduction in the consumption of fuel, raw materials and components.

The theory and practice of accounting for expenditures on Soviet industrial production does not make it possible to calculate the degree to which a price increase for machinery is justified by an increase in productive capacity or qualitative improvement. The absence of established methods to determine production costs, which would correspond to changes in their real economic utility (in terms of their consumption characteristics), enables mechanical engineering enterprises to make unjustified increases in the price of their machinery.

As is well known, the prices of machines produced in the USSR are set by the State Price Committee and published in official price lists. Improvements in the products of mechanical engineering enterprises are followed by adjustments (i.e. increases) in their prices. In practice these adjustments require approval via numerous technical and bureaucratic procedures and consequently lag substantially (one to two years and more) behind production of the improved equipment. In the period before the new prices are announced in official price lists "temporary prices" apply, which to a large extent are set completely arbitrarily. In many cases these prices contain a considerable measure of pure inflation.

An even better opportunity to make unjustified price increases exists when prices for the production of non-standardized machines and special designs are set as single unit or small series prices, for these products are not included in the official price lists. The proportion of such machines in total Soviet machinery output comes to 42–50 percent.[14] In actual practice the prices of these kinds of machines are set by agreement between producer and customer. These unjustified, arbitrary price increases for types of equipment that are not included in the price lists are one of the basic reasons for inflation in the investment sector.

There is no way of estimating the extent of this inflation. But we have good reason to assume that the figures on the growth of capital stock, which are given in Soviet statistical sources (in "comparable" prices), in no way reflect correctly real growth in investment. If these figures were corrected to allow for inflation, they could well confirm Val'tukh's claim that investment has been at a standstill in the USSR.

Possible Changes in Investment Policy

The leading Gosplan functionaries, like the experts in academic circles, are quite clear that there is no hope of overcoming the negative trend in investment, at least not before the end of the current decade. There is no basis for expecting an increase in the growth rate for national income, nor a rise in the share of accumulation in it—the chief source of investment. In the first half of the 1970s, the share of capital accumulation amounted to 28 percent; it then dropped to 26 percent and has since remained stagnant at this level. It is highly improbable that Soviet leadership will try to raise the share of accumulation at the expense of the share allocated for consumption. Such a step would have serious political consequences. Even though the boiling point for the Soviet population is substantially higher than in Poland, the events there could hardly have failed to make an impression on those with political responsibility.

Aganbegyan assumes that the rate of capital investment growth in the production sector of the economy will fall during the twelfth five-year plan (1986–90) to half the rate of the present plan period.[15] Under these circumstances Soviet investment policy strategists are looking for possibilities of raising the effectiveness of the available investment. Naturally they will make efforts to restructure investment, with emphasis on two main courses: (1) concentration on renovation of existing enterprises, and (2) raising the share of investment in mechanical engineering. We shall examine both these courses more closely.

The switching of investment from the construction of new enterprises to the reconstruction and modernization of existing ones has been widely advocated in the Soviet press for the past decade and a half. It is the principal measure meant to bring about an increase in the effectiveness of capital investment and, more generally, intensification of the economy. At first glance the effectiveness of this course seems completely convincing: The period in which results are yielded is shortened and capital turnover is thus accelerated; the costs of increasing capacity per unit of production are lowered; and old technologies are more rapidly written off and replaced by new machines. All these advantages, however, are only short-term ones.

From the point of view of long-term returns, such a policy has a number of serious negative consequences. As always when a campaign of this kind is conducted in the USSR, the limits of what makes economic sense are ignored. In relation to the overall economic development of the country, the priority allocation of investment into the development of existing enterprises, of which by far the greatest proportion is situated in the western parts of the USSR (with their exhausted natural resources, overloaded infrastructure and ecological capacity limits), has harmed regional interests that are so vital for Soviet industry. This policy is in fact contributing to the increasing territorial polarization of branches of the economy with manufacturing industries in the west of the country and raw material extracting industries in the east. The enormous distances and difficult transportation situation must be taken into consideration here, also. As a result of this policy of renewal and modernization, the development of new branches and production sites and the introduction of fundamentally new technologies has in some sectors of industry become impossible or uneconomical.

If we leave the theoretical pros and cons aside and turn instead to the practical possibilities of putting the policy so widely advocated into effect, we find that the planners' ideal scheme runs into trouble when faced with reality. It turns out that the existing industrial structure, communications patterns, technological networks, energy systems, raw material supply arrangements, and repair and other auxiliary services are in such a run-down state that in most factories it is impossible to modernize the overall technological level without a fundamental renovation of the buildings and other structures. In practice, measures of this kind also swallow up the lion's share of modernization funds.

It must, moreover, be added that the investment sector of the Soviet economy is totally unprepared for this renovation policy. The essential basic institutions for science, designing, planning, and mechanical engineering are not geared to the new situation. The design organizations have traditionally concentrated on designing new enterprises—on standardized series of projects, which are easier to execute and more profitable. The construction industry was not reorganized or re-equipped for renovation work. Soviet construction firms still try to avoid modernization projects because they are 20–35 percent more labor intensive (according to Soviet sources) and offer 75 percent lower profit than new buildings.[16] The enterprises in the mechanical engineering industry, in turn, greatly prefer production of series of standard types of equipment to that of machines that would be suited to the particular conditions and dimensions of an enterprise undergoing renovation. Finally, nowhere have the material incentives been created to reward enterprise managers for the risk that during the renovation period they may be unable to meet their production plans.

The consequence of this situation is that directors and managers in Soviet industry are not interested in spending money on rebuilding and modernization of plants but try to secure state investment for the construction of new plants. The Soviet leadership has no means of counteracting their resistance. The result of this has been that efforts to shift the emphasis in industrial investment from construction of new production capacity to renovation of the old have been unsuccessful. Thus, for 1981–1982, for instance, planners intended to increase the share of investment going to reconstruction and modernization by 5.4 percent, but only a 0.5 percent increase was actually achieved.[17] At the same time the share going for construction of new plants rose slightly. The share of rebuilding and modernization in the total investment in the production sector of the economy amounts currently to no more than 3 percent, and it does not look as though any significant increase will take place in the foreseeable future.

Mechanical Engineering Problems

The principal obstacle in the way of effective renovation is the inability of the Soviet mechanical engineering sector to deliver the necessary machinery and equipment, and, in particular, highly complicated and advanced technologies. The inadequate investment, and industry's consequent inability to satisfy the requirements of the country's economy, have become a central theme of the Soviet technocratic elite's written and verbal comments. The most crucial question is undoubtedly the lag in the field of advanced technology.[18] As the president of the Soviet Academy of Sciences, A. P. Aleksandrov, admits, domestic producers can satisfy only one-third of the demand for the most modern technological apparatus and equipment. The increasingly acute shortage of machines and equipment, as well the failure to fulfil the requirements of modern standards, are a direct cause of the extremely low depreciation rate of worn out, obsolete capital goods. The 1975 reform of depreciation, which reduced the normal utilization periods for fixed capital assets, did not have the desired results. The average utilization period for machines rose by 13 percent in the 1970s.[19] All attempts to speed up the renewal of fixed assets and modernize industrial plants are thwarted by the inability of the mechanical engineering sector to meet the demands placed on it.

The inadequate level of investment in the mechanical engineering sector became especially noticeable in the second half of the 1970s, when investment in the oil and gas industries increased sharply. In the period from 1976 to 82, the share of these latter branches in investment jumped by 7.5 percent, while that of mechanical engineering rose only by 0.2 percent.[20] The widening gap between output and demand for machinery had damaging effects, delaying the development of the fuel industries and slowing down the growth of all other sectors of the economy.

If the output of the mechanical engineering industry is to satisfy real demand in quantitative and qualitative terms, investment in the sector must be increased sharply. Under the present circumstances of a de facto decline in investment, the funds needed for this can only be made available at the expense of other sectors of the economy. Kirichenko (along with several prominent experts) has argued that the priorities in investment policy must be altered in favor of the mechanical engineering sector and that for this purpose even short-run losses must be accepted. He did not, of course, specify which sectors of the economy would have to bear the burden of this sacrifice. In fact there are scarcely any reserves for redistribution visible anywhere.

As prominent Soviet economists admit, restructuring investment for the purpose of stepping up mechanical engineering requires a "far-reaching economic maneuver." But any such "maneuver" causes, at least in the short run, a further slow-down in economic growth. Even if such setbacks can eventually be compensated for, there are still many limits on effective reallocation—even for a leadership that (as Gorbachev claims) is aiming to achieve a major turnabout in economic policy.

Conclusion

Let us return to the main question: Is there any possibility that, under present investment conditions in the USSR, an economic decline can be checked in the future? The opinion of those Soviet experts who regard this as a very real possibility seems well-founded.

The rise in industrial production in 1983, during the time of Andropov's discipline campaign (a rise generally not foreseen by Western observers) showed clearly that there are significant reserves of productive capacity and that these reserves can be tapped quickly should an extraordinary situation arise. There are good grounds for assuming that a similar effect would be derived from modernization of the administration, planning and organization of the economy. It seems even more obvious that, in case of war, mobilization of the reserves of production potential in Soviet industry would permit a substantial rise in output without any additional investment whatsoever.

Even under normal circumstances, however, an increase in investment is by no means an indispensable condition for the economy to emerge from stagnation. Much more important would be to optimize the structure of investment, both at the macroeconomic (intersectoral) and the microeconomic (intrasectoral) levels. However, to approach such fundamental structural changes in the economy, the Soviet leadership must above all show flexibility and willingness to maneuver and compromise in domestic and foreign policy. It remains to be seen whether the prospects for this improve under Gorbachev.

Notes

1. A. Aganbegyan, *EKO*, No. 6 (1984), p. 9.
2. D. Chernikov, *Ekonomika i matematicheskie metody*, No. 4 (1984), p. 593.
3. See also Hermann Clement, "Siberia: Resource or Burden?" in this volume, Chapter 17.
4. See, for example, A. Buzhinsky and S. Kheinman, *EKO*, No. 10 (1983), pp. 144–8.
5. See, for example, K. Val'tukh, *EKO*, No. 3 (1982).
6. N. Tikhonov, in *XXVI s"ezd KPSS. Stenograficheskii otchet* (Moscow, 1981), p. 17.
7. V. Kirichenko, *Planovoe Khozyaistvo*, No. 9 (1982), p. 62.
8. *Narodnoe Khozyaistvo SSSR v 1983 g.*, p. 355; *Pr*, 28 November 1984.
9. F. K. Val'tukh, *op. cit.*, p. 5.
10. V. Fal'tsman and A. Kornev, *Voprosy ekonomiki*, no. 6 (1984), p. 38.
11. V. Fal'tsman, *EKO*, No. 3 (1982), p. 5.

12. V. Fal'tsman and A. Konev, *op. cit.*, p. 38.
13. V. Fal'tsman, *EKO*, No. 2 (1982), p. 130.
14. L. Rozenova, *Voprosy ekonomiki*, No. 2 (1984), p. 30.
15. V. Danilov, *Pr*, 17 December 1980; T. Bakaeva and V. Zadorozhnyi, *Vestnik statistiki*, No. 10 (1977), p. 18.
16. M. Zotov, *Voprosy ekonomiki*, No. 2 (1984), p. 21.
17. Chernikov, *op. cit.*, p. 594.
18. On this see Arnold Buchholz, "Science and Technology," in this volume, Chapter 10.
19. *Narodnoe Khozyaistvo SSSR v 1982 g.*, p. 341.
20. *Narodnoe Khozyaistvo SSSR v 1970 g.*, p. 483; *Narodnoe Khozyaistvo SSSR v 1982 g.*, p. 339.

15
Economic Growth and Transportation: Stop at the Performance Limit?

Gertraud Seidenstecher

One of the essential conditions for the integration of an economic area, as well as for smooth development and steady economic growth, is adequate infrastructure capacity, that is to say, the provision of structures and installations that are not included in commodity production in the narrow sense but are prerequisites for economic life, such as roads and other transportation facilities, postal and telephone services, water and electricity supply, etc. Among Soviet academics, as well as practical experts and economic policymakers, there is wide agreement these days that the country's infrastructure has increasingly become bottleneck.

The sector of the infrastructure that is most conspicuously inadequate at present is transport. In a country that is almost two and a half times the size of the USA, and some ninety times larger than the Federal Republic of Germany, transportation naturally takes on particular importance. However, it also presents particular problems, not only because of the extent of the country's territory, but also because of geographical conditions that are unfavorable for transportation (the rivers run in the wrong direction for development), the very uneven territorial distribution of raw material deposits and industrial plant location, and the very adverse nature of the terrain and climate in large parts of the country for the construction and maintenance of roads and railroads. In spite of these difficult natural conditions, Soviet transportation has in the main operated satisfactorily for much of the post-war period, although of course there have been periodic complaints about the bad work of transportation enterprises. Since the beginning of the 1970s, the demands placed on the transportation system have increased considerably, however, and from around the middle of the decade growing difficulties appeared in this sector. Transportation became a bottleneck, acting as a brake on overall economic growth, so that a kind of "stop at the limit of performance" was reached.

TABLE 15.1
Structure of Soviet Freight Transport
(share of each mode in percent)

	Total	Rail	Sea	River	Road	Air	Oil Pipeline	Gas Pipeline
1960	100	79.2	7.0	5.3	5.2	0.05	2.7	0.7
1970	100	62.7	16.6	4.4	5.6	0.05	7.2	3.3
1975	100	58.9	13.5	4.0	6.2	0.05	12.2	5.1
1980	100	50.6	12.5	3.6	6.4	0.04	17.9	8.8
1983	100	48.2	11.9	3.6	6.4	0.04	18.1	11.6

Source: Narodnoe Khozyaistvo SSSR v 1983 g. Moscow, 1984, p. 314.

The Structure of Transportation: Dominance of Railroads

The first clues to the problems in Soviet transportation are to be found in its divisional structure: As Table 15.1 shows, land transportation is predominant. This fact alone places a substantially higher burden of transportation costs on the Soviet economy, in comparison with West European countries, which can make extensive use of internal waterways and coastal sea routes. The principal mode of freight transportation continues to be the railroads. Their predominance was established in the pre-war period, when investment in the transportation sector was essentially concentrated on the railroad network. In the post-war period road building and air transport were developed more strongly, but it was above all pipeline construction that received higher priority in investment allocation. This can be seen from the change in pattern of the shares of these forms in total freight turnover. The major function of the railroads is long-distance transportation of bulk goods, which account at present for over 80 percent of the turnover in ton-kilometers and almost 74 percent of the tonnage of freight moved by the railroads. Still, they also have to carry a considerable portion of short-haul traffic. In the RSFSR, 10 percent of the freight transported distances of less than 50 kilometers, and 20 percent of that transported up to 100 kilometers, is carried by railroads.[1] In 1983 the average haul was, for example, 1,740 km. for timber, 1,500 km. for ferrous metals, 1,023 km. for mineral fertilizers and 1,000 km. for grain.

Freight transport by truck still plays a minor role, with a share fluctuating around 8 percent of the total. In all modern market economies trucking is far more heavily used. In the Federal Republic of Germany, for instance, its share of total freight transportation was 52 percent in 1983. In the Soviet Union trucks are used predominantly for short distances in factory transportation, agriculture, and construction work. The average shipping distance of goods, per ton, came to 21.5 km. in 1983. More rapid development of truck transport would not only be to the benefit of the railroads, which could be relieved of some of their load in this way; it would also favor more extensive cooperative relations within smaller economic areas and permit closer linkage of town and country, though this would also require the expansion of bus services and private transportation.

In passenger transportation the share of automobile travel has risen steeply in the last fifteen years. Today, according to Soviet estimates, it is up to 19 percent.[2] The share of railroads (26.5 percent in 1983) has declined at around the same pace. The shares of the other modes of transportation changed little during this period. The performance of the railroads in passenger transportation has in recent years been frequently subjected to strong criticism by both Party and government, but (in contrast to other subdivisions) no noteworthy improvements have been achieved so far in this field.

Pipeline transportation has developed at an extremely rapid rate in the last twenty-five years. The total length of long-distance oil pipelines grew by 59,000 km. between 1960 and 1983, when it reached 76,000 km.; the performance of the transportation system rose by 26.5 times and amounted to 1,370 billion ton/km. in 1984. Yet even this performance "did not lead to balanced development of production and transportation."[3] Crude oil production rose more rapidly than the capacity of the pipelines, so that the railroads could not be relieved sufficiently but in fact had to move a growing quantity of oil. In 1960, 8 percent of oil shipments was by rail, whereas in the 1980s the figure has been over 11 percent (as a proportion of total rail freight, figures for oil shipment were 13.7 percent and 13 percent respectively). Natural gas transportation by pipeline registered even faster growth than oil; the total length of gas pipelines increased by 143,000 km. between 1960 and 1983, reaching 155,000 km., and the amount of gas conveyed rose by almost seventy times to 863 billion ton/km. (and 997 billion ton/km. in 1984).

Sea transportation is more significant for saving than for actually earning foreign currency. It has however been a cause of some anxiety in Western markets because of its undercutting of rates. Since the beginning of the 1970s, it has expanded very much more slowly than in the preceding decade. Whereas the freight it transported (in ton/km.) in 1970 was almost five times the 1960 figure, the increase between 1970 and 1980 amounted to only 30 percent. In 1982 there was an absolute decline and in 1983 the figure was only 5 percent above the 1980 level. The small share of coastal shipping in internal transportation, estimated at 2–2.5 percent, is partly explainable by the short navigation period for the northern sea routes.

The share of inland waterways in domestic freight transportation has been falling slightly since 1960, and came to 4.7 percent in 1983. "Where it is expedient, the movement of freight should as far as possible be shifted from the railways to inland waterways"[4]; nevertheless river and canal transportation have not expanded at the desired rate. This is due among other things to the short navigation period of only 170–210 days per year, the inadequate turnover capacity of river ports, and the unwillingness of many enterprises to make more use of inland water transportation since this would require that they bear the costs of necessary improvements to their sections of the bank.

Air transportation has for twenty years been responsible for only about 0.05 percent of freight transportation. In 1983, 3.1 m. tons (including mail) were carried. In spite of the comparatively small quantity, the importance of air transportation for shipment of urgently needed high-value goods to remote areas with inadequate infrastructure should probably not be underestimated even today. Presumably, air transportation will play a larger role in the future, especially for the development of Siberia and the Soviet Far East, not only in freight but also in public passenger transportation. Its share of the latter has risen sharply, from 10.4 percent in 1965 to over 18 percent in 1984, when 112 million passengers were carried on domestic routes. Because of the high energy consumption of air transportation, efforts are currently under way to shift more hauls of less than 1,200–1,500 km. back to the railroads.[5]

Transportation Problems: Quantity and Quality Bottlenecks

As mentioned above, the unbalanced structure of Soviet transportation is itself a source of many transportation problems—not to say that other countries do not experience them also, even though they are mostly of a different kind. The Soviet Union's No. 1 transportation problem, at present, is the sheer quantitative inadequacy of the transportation system. For a number of years now, the Soviet press has been full of complaints about bad transportation. Although it is possible to observe problems in other sectors too, the railroads were at the center of the criticism since, because of their high share of total transportation turnover, their shortcomings have a particularly detrimental effect on the entire economy. In 1976–80 the freight turnover for all modes of transportation rose by only 18.5 percent compared with a plan target of 32 percent, and for the railroad, the figure was 6 percent instead of a planned 22 percent. While it is true that production of material goods also grew more slowly than planned, this was not the cause but, at least partly, the consequence of inadequate transportation services, even if in particular cases there may actually have been fewer goods to transport than originally anticipated.

The second transportation problem is the low quality of freight transportation service. The economy suffers, in particular, from frequent disruptions and unreliability of transportation, lack of flexibility to accommodate variations in the times and places when and where goods need to be moved, inadequate regard for the requirements of consignors and consignees, neglect of freight not classified as of special economic importance, and use of unsuitable or defective rolling stock. In addition, there are serious deficiencies in passenger transportation, such as failure to stick to timetables, insufficient numbers of seats, long travel times because there are too few express trains, and bad service.

Another important problem is high transportation costs. High costs are inevitably incurred because of the great distances between new material deposits and production locations, in addition to the transportation structure we have described (i.e., the proportion of low-cost modes of transportation is too small), but they are also caused by the fact that the transportation sector itself frequently operates very inefficiently. "We can no longer carry on in the old way and meet production goals by means of excessive expenditure of labor, capital, and material resources, without the slightest concern for the economic consequences."[6]

The negative effects of the quantitative and qualitative deficiencies of the transportation system represent a heavy burden on the Soviet economy as a whole. Considerable economic losses are incurred because the normal course of operations in many enterprises is disrupted. Inadequate transportation services frequently compel enterprises to stop production temporarily and cause shortfalls in output that often cannot be made up even by "storming" and working special shifts; changes in production technology and/or the planned assortment of output become unavoidable; this makes it harder to keep delivery contracts, and it obstructs technical progress (to the extent that it involves use of special materials or output of a special range of products, or requires a particular technology). Substantial direct losses of goods already produced also occur because freight is damaged, spoiled, or lost in the course of transportation and because perishable goods are not moved and delivered promptly.[7] All this is a brake on the growth of the economy and delays the transition to a more intensive type of economy operating with greater efficiency.

Causal Factors I: Resource Problems

Underlying the difficulties with the performance of the transportation system are both resource and productivity problems. We shall consider the resource problems first. The technical basis of the various modes of transportation is no longer fully appropriate to modern requirements. The Soviet Union produces 21 percent of the world's industrial output but its rail and road networks make up less than 7 percent of the world network.[8] The relationship between transportation performance and the USSR's technical basis is illustrated in the diagram below using the example of the railroads. It shows that initially there was a certain flexibility about the infrastructure that production could "grow into," that is to say, transportation performance could be increased rapidly by higher utilization of network (and rolling stock) capacity.

Towards the end of the 1970s, however, a "kink" appeared in performance curves. As criticism of the transportation system by Party and government shows, this cannot be attributed to a reduction in the demand for transportation, but is predominantly due to the exhaustion of capacity reserves (and to a certain extent to shortcomings in operational organization).

The failure to expand the capacity of the railroads and other modes of transportation sufficiently is a consequence of the shortage of investment resources. From 1929 until the beginning of the Second World War, between 18 percent and 21.5 percent of total state investment was put into transportation and communication (and the railroads received over 10 percent).

FIGURE 15.1
Trends in Transportation Turnover (billion ton=kilometers), Length of Rail Network (kilometers), and Average Utilization of the Railroads (ton=kilometers per kilometer) (1960=100)

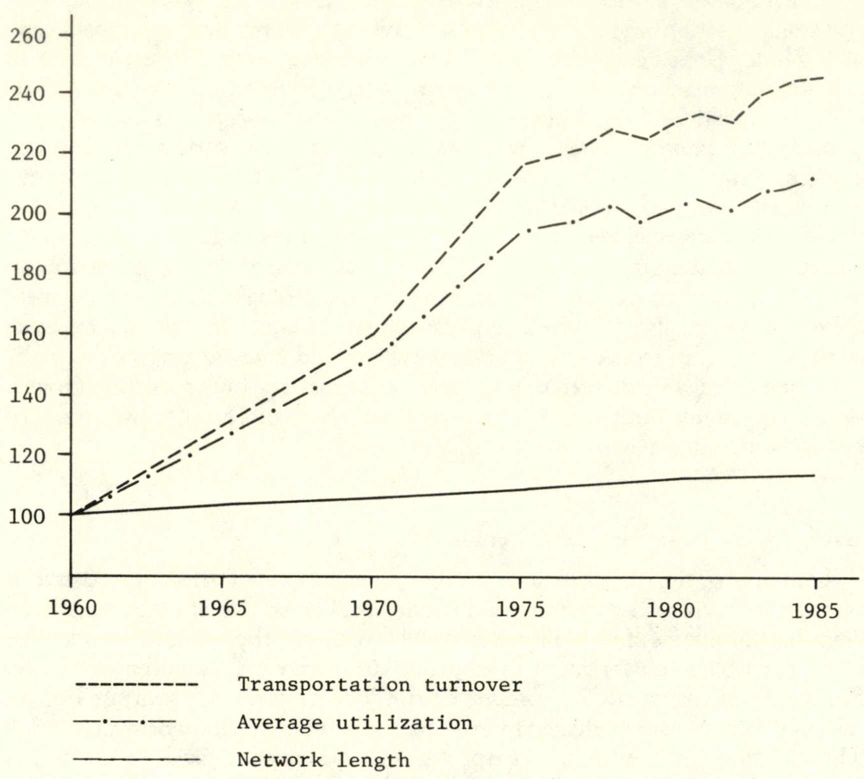

In the post-war period, however, the share of transportation and communication steadily declined and from the beginning of the 1950s to the end of the 1960s was around 9–10 percent. The share of the railroads, was also very severely reduced. In the first five post-war years, it was 7.7 percent, but thereafter it diminished steadily, oscillated around 2.6–2.7 percent from the middle of the 1960s on, and even in the first half of the 1980s was only 2.7–3 percent, because by then pipeline construction, air transportation, and road haulage were being expanded much faster than in the pre-war period. The shift in the scale of priorities of investment policy led, in the judgement of one Soviet specialist, to a "disproportionality in the develoment of the production and transportation sectors" that caused a "substantial lag in the pace of development of transportation in comparison with other sectors of the economy."[9]

As a consequence of this, the extension and modernization of the railroad network (and of factory connecting lines)[10] has not kept pace with its increasing utilization. Investment funds, which were scarce overall, were allocated predominantly for the construction of new lines, but even so not enough new lines could be built. Nor could as much as was necessary be done to modernize the existing network. The "project of the century," the building of the Baikal-Amur Mainline, has swallowed up an enormous amount of resources. At the end of 1984 it was announced, amid a great amount of propaganda, that the laying of the track had been completed, but it will still be some time before a normal heavy traffic load can be carried on this line because an important tunnel is not yet ready. Very large sums will also be necessary for electrification, the building of engineering and technical installations and facilities like locomotive and railroad car depots, and for social and cultural construction (housing etc.) for the railway men employed there. Whether after the completion of the BAM (and other new lines) more resources will be made available for the improvement of the existing network and other equipment, or whether they will be directed to other sectors of the transportation system or of the economy, remains to be seen. The capacity of the network is currently circumscribed by the inadequacy of many stations and by other bottlenecks. According to Soviet specialists' calculations, about 40,000 kilometers of additional track would be necessary for normal functioning of the network and full satisfaction of transportation requirements.

The development of road haulage is obstructed more by the restricted length of the road network than by the level of truck production. Road building is a costly undertaking everywhere, but especially in the Soviet Union, where in large parts of the country there is a lack of gravel. Because of this, in earlier times in the countryside, often only carriage roads were constructed. Because these are not hard surfaced, these are scarcely usable during "muddy times," i.e., during the rainy season and the spring thaw. In 1983, the country's total length of "public roads" was around 973,000 kilometers according to Soviet statistics. Over 20 percent of these are not hard surfaced roads, and by Western standards these would not be counted as roads at all. Basically, only those described as having improved surfacing (i.e asphalt, concrete or tar) are roads according to our terminology. They constitute only 43 percent of all public roads. The remaining hard surfaced roads (about 36 percent) are roads with a water-bound gravel surface, paved roads, etc.[11]

Although a great deal of road building has been done in the last 20–25 years, there is still a very large unsatisfied need for hard surfaced roads. According to Soviet specialists' calculations, the present network of public hard surfaced roads in the RSFSR, for example, which was extended by 2.8 times between 1960 and 1983, would have to be increased by a further 1.5 times in order to create connections between all administrative centers and all collective farm and state farm centers. In addition, some 200,000 kilometers of intra-enterprise roads would have to be built.[12]

A further resource problem is the low degree of specialization of the railroad rolling stock and of trucks and ships. There is a shortage of refrigerator cars and trucks, tank cars of all kinds, flat cars and trucks, trailers and other specialized means of transportation. Although this shortcoming is becoming ever more discernible, and the necessity for more rapid growth of specialization has long been officially recognized, industry is tackling the problem only with very great reluctance.[13]

Further extension of the transportation network is difficult because of the enormous costs involved. In the second half of the 1970s the specific costs for capital investment in transportation facilities were 30–60 percent higher than in the first half of the decade.[14] The increase in costs is primarily attributable to the extremely difficult conditions in the new regions to be opened up and to the higher technical standard of construction demanded in view of the rising utilization level of transportation facilities.

Causal Factors II: Productivity Problems

As already mentioned, the problems with the performance of the transportation system are in large part productivity problems. Capital productivity has declined since the second half of the 1970s both in the economy as a whole and throughout the transportation sector (with the exception of pipeline transport).[15] One factor that played a role in this was the steep rise in investment costs already cited. Another reason for the drop in productivity was the obsolescence of a large part of the fixed installations and rolling stock, which is a consequence of inadequate replacement of the transportation sector's technical equipment. In the case of the railroads, for example, at the beginning of 1982 the total length of track on which the rails had exceeded their normal service life (which depends on the level of utilization) amounted to over 40,000 kilometers.[16] The age structure of a large proportion of the vehicle stock of freight carriers is also highly unsatisfactory. Obsolete technical equipment swallows up large expenditures on repairs but is far less productive and works far less reliably than new, modern equipment. This contributed to the fact that the rolling stock could no longer be used so productively. Its technical condition also deteriorated as a result of the excessive demands placed on it because of the bad condition of many stretches of railroad lines and roads—a truck used on unsurfaced roads consumes substantially more fuel and is worn out after four to five years at the longest—and as a result of the shortage of repair facilities and the inadequate availability of spare parts. Moreover, around the middle of the 1970s, the optimal level of capital utilization, at which production costs are minimized, was frequently exceeded, not only in transportation but also in industry. This not only brought about a rise in unit costs but, because of overloading, frequently led to stoppages, so that technical utilization figures worsened.

This brings us to the second group of productivity problems, for the worsening of utilization of available technical resources (and thus the decline in performance) was in large measure the result of labor and organizational problems. The increasing gravity of the situation in the transportation sector was not attributable solely to inadequacies in the technical basis, but also to "bad organization of the transportation process, neglect of production and labor discipline, weak supervision of adherence to timetables, and late work by all parts of the overall system."[17] This quotation refers to the situation on railroads, but things were not very different on the internal waterways and in road haulage.

Solving the transportation system's problems was (and is) made more difficult by the fact that cooperation between different carriers frequently functions badly, whether as a result of planning mistakes, organizational incompetence, or failure to regard partners' interests. When hauls are broken up, freight often lies for long periods at the interstices between different carriers, which causes substantial losses of time, material resources and labor expenditure.

Is the Transportation System a Bottleneck for the Twelfth Five-Year Plan?

The problems that we have described will affect the performance of the transportation system in the future also, for they are predominantly problems which cannot be solved overnight. In the political leadership's view, raising the efficiency of the transportation sector (and of the entire economy) depends crucially on fundamental improvements in working style, labor discipline and motivation. "Without further tightening of discipline and strengthening of order and organization, the successful fulfillment of the growing tasks of the transportation system and assurance of the stability and regularity of transportation operations are inconceivable."[18] Whether the new secretary general of the CPSU, Gorbachev, will have any more success in this than did Andropov and Chernenko, cannot be foreseen at this moment. Since he is decades younger than his predecessors, he has the opportunity to plan a longer-term policy and implement it more energetically and systematically than they did. If he were to be successful in this respect, however, this would provide but one essential precondition for a thorough and lasting improvement of the transport sector's performance. So far this has not been achieved. After the marked improvement in railroad freight movement in 1983 (which was probably partly attributable to the discipline campaigns under Andropov), which must, however, be seen in relation to the drop in 1982, only 1 percent growth was achieved in 1984. At the same time, turnover for internal waterways and road haulage declined absolutely (−3 percent), and in the opening months of 1985, the railways did not reach their plan target.

With more discipline and better motivation worthwhile improvements could certainly be achieved. If at the same time the available investment resources are concentrated on eliminating bottlenecks in the technical basis, the transportation system should be in a position to improve the service it provides to the economy sufficiently to allow the attainment of an annual rate of growth of gross national product of around 2 percent (or 3–3.5 percent growth in national income), as envisaged in the twelfth five-year plan.

In the long run, however, one of the highest investment policy priorities will unavoidably have to be reserved for the transportation system and the whole infrastructure,[19] so as to modernize it fundamentally and supply it with more efficient technical equipment. The longer this is postponed, the more real costs the transportation bottleneck will impose on the economy and the more the investment funds that will be needed, for today the transport system is living off its capital in many places.

Notes

1. V. Shishkin, *Ekonomicheskaya gazeta*, No. 24 (1981), p. 12.
2. V. Biryukov, *Gesellschaftswissenschaften*, No. 1 (1985), p. 89.
3. A. Mitaishvili, *VE*, No. 3 (1980), p. 7.
4. *Pr*, 5 March 1981.
5. V. Biryukov, *Planovoe Khozyaistvo*, no. 12 (1983), p. 8.
6. *Gudok*, 3 February 1985.
7. For details see Gertraud Seidenstecher, *Berichte des BIOst*, No. 60 (1984), pp. 43 ff.
8. A. Mitaishvili, *op.cit.* p. 9.
9. *Ibid.*, p. 7.
10. The main railway network has a length of around 143,000 kilometers and is supplemented by almost 100,000 kilometers of individual factory-connecting lines.
11. In addition to the public road network there are around 506,000 kilometers of roads owned by individual enterprises, of which around 286,000 kilometers (57 percent) are surfaced roads.
12. I. Evgenev, *KZ*, 28 August 1984.
13. *Iz*, 13 February 1982.
14. For details see A. Mitaishvili, *VE*, No. 3 (1982), p. 51.
15. *Ibid.*
16. *Gudok*, 19 February 1982.
17. A. Mitaishvili, *VE*, No. 3 (1980), p. 6.
18. *Gudok*, 24 March 1984.
19. Cf., Boris Rumer, "Problems of Soviet Investment of Policy," in this volume, Chapter 14.

16
Trends in Soviet Defense Expenditures: Facts and Speculation

Franz Walter

Official Soviet Data and Western Estimates

If a fact is something that scarcely anyone disputes, then, as far as the USSR's defense expenditures are concerned, it is above all a fact among observers outside of the Soviet power bloc that the figure given in the Soviet state budget for "expenditures for defense" in no way reflects either the volume or the growth of what the USSR really spends on the equipment, operation, and maintenance of its armed forces. In Table 16.1 official Soviet data are compared with a variety of estimates. They are intended first of all to illustrate just how unreliable the Soviet figures are considered to be.

The estimates by SIPRI, the CIA, and Lee are all relatively close for 1970. They amount to 2.3–2.8 times the Soviet figure. As far as the trend in the following years is concerned, the USSR would have us believe that its defense expenditure diminished slightly year by year. According to the estimates cited, on the other hand, it increased during the period 1970–80: by 105 percent per annum according to SIPRI, by around 4 percent according to the CIA, and by almost 10 percent according to Lee. Corresponding to the differences in growth rates, there are also substantial disagreements among the estimates for the beginning of the 1980s. Even the SIPRI estimate, however, is about three times as high as the official Soviet figure.

For 1985, the Soviet Finance Minister, V. F. Garbuzov, announced a sharp increase in "expenditures for defense": up 12 percent compared with 1984 (see Table 16.1). Even if the budget item hitherto was more than a purely arbitrary number, that is to say, if it represented particular parts of overall defense expenditures, this recent announcement cannot tell us much. Types of expenditures that had previously been concealed in civilian items, or had not been published at all, could have been included in the "expenditures for defense." Some such practice was assumed once before, in 1961, when, according to official statements, expenditures rose by 25 percent.[1] The problem is that the USSR does not define or provide any breakdown of what it calls its defense expenditure, and that no types of

TABLE 16.1
USSR Defense Expenditure
(billion rubles)[a]

	Official Soviet Figures (plan data)	Stockholm Peace Research Institute (SIPRI)	Central Intelligence Agency (CIA)	W. T. Lee
1970	17,900	42.0	43 - 47	43 - 50
1975	17,854	45.5	53 - 59	71 - 83
1980	17,100	48.7	62 - 67	108 -126
1981	17,054	49.5	64 - 69	
1982	17,050	50.2		
1983	17,050			
1984	17,050			
1985	19,063			

Note: [a]The figures in the first two columns are in current prices, those in the last two are in 1970 prices.

Sources: Official Soviet figures from the Finance Minister's budget speeches; other figures from F. Walter, Berichte des Biost, No. 1, 1985.

expenditure can be identified that allegedly have been at a level of 17 billion rubles annually for the last fifteen years, without any increase whatever.

Many Western observers regard the officially published defense expenditure figure as significant only as a political signal: By claiming stable or diminishing expenditure, the USSR wanted to underline its desire for peace and readiness for détente, both at home and abroad. Now it would like to make clear to the USA that it is willing and able to react in a corresponding manner to the sharp rise in American military expenditure since 1981. This is supported by the justification given by Garbuzov for the defense item in the 1985 state budget, in which he mentioned the increase in the US defense vote and estimated it at 10–12 percent per annum.[2] The Soviet leadership could have seen a special motive, which we shall discuss below, for making clear its willingness and (even more) its ability to step up its defense expenditures greatly. As far as the purpose of this increase as a political signal is concerned, it should not be overlooked that at the same time, after a phase of refusing to talk with the USA, the USSR has shown renewed readiness to enter into arms control talks. To the Soviet consumer the increase can only indicate that he must postpone his expectations of a rise in standard of living.

The widely differing rates of growth shown by the estimates in Table 16.1 cannot be regarded as having an equally sound base. As this author has spelled out in detail elsewhere, Lee's method of calculation includes many speculative assumptions.[3] As a result, it leads to excessively high figures. SIPRI's figures have no methodological foundation. SIPRI and Lee both view their much-quoted estimates as alternatives to those of the CIA, which they criticize as substantially too high or low respectively. There has also been criticism of CIA estimates from other authors in past years. F. Holzman has performed a valuable service in illustrating the statistical problems of the CIA method of estimating. But in this author's opinion,

Holzman was unable to justify serious objections to the use of the results achieved with the method. Thus, there are really no alternatives to the CIA estimates available. One may well regret that the CIA has this monopoly position—the Soviet Union could easily change that.[4] One may also regret the impossibility of checking or replicating the CIA estimates—but then the data in the statistical yearbooks of both Eastern and Western countries cannot be checked either.

The Slowdown in the Growth of Soviet Defense Expenditures After 1976

In the autumn of 1983, the CIA and NATO announced a reassessment of the trend of estimated Soviet defense expenditures. According to this, in the years 1977–1982, they increased less than half as quickly as in the period 1971–1976, or by only about 2 percent per annum on average instead of 4–5 percent as previously. Thus, the year 1976 marks a kink in the trend right in the middle of the twelve-year period 1971–1982.

One can speak of a reassessment insofar as up to the end of 1982, the CIA took the view that, in spite of the slowdown in overall economic growth, Soviet defense expenditures had risen at a more or less constant "historical" rate of 4 percent annually from the end of the 1960s to the beginning of the 1980s. This picture, however, was to a certain extent contradicted by the ruble figures for estimated Soviet defense expenditures published at the same time by the CIA itself. They clearly indicated a slackening in growth in the way described above. The reassessment at the end of 1983 therefore applied less to the actual estimated figures than to their interpretation, or to the underlying trend. Hence, the fact of the reassessment cannot be taken as an indication of unreliability of the CIA's estimating method.

Why the CIA continued for several years to adhere to a view of the trend that was apparently increasingly at odds with actual developments can perhaps be explained as follows: What it is interested in assessing is the medium and long-term trend. There can thus only be talk of a "new trend" when a divergence from the previous course has been observable for several years. Moreover, the estimates are beset by uncertainties. They cannot claim to capture annual fluctuations precisely. For this reason, estimates are presented as ranges of rounded numbers (see table 16.1). Above all, however, the knowledge that since the end of the 1960s the USSR had been pressing forward with the development of numerous new weapons systems and expanding considerably the production capacity of its armaments factories is likely to have played a significant role in the CIA's assessment. Seen against this background, an acceleration of the growth of procurement expenditures, a new arms boom, could be expected and the slowdown actually observed could be regarded as a temporary phenomenon presaging the coming upswing.

Finally, one can easily imagine that the declared intention of the new Reagan administration to increase drastically the USA defense budget may have somewhat delayed the announcement that a contrary trend was observable in the USSR. That the announcement was nevertheless made at a time when the American programs were first getting under way is a fact that deserves to be noted: To many people it seems to be a foregone conclusion that CIA estimates of Soviet defense expenditures are produced for the purpose of supporting the budget demands of the President and the Pentagon. The 1983 reassessment certainly did not perform this function, and the Pentagon accepted it only with visible reluctance.

When the new estimate of the trend of Soviet defense spending was announced, it was emphasized at the same time that the slowdown in the growth of total expenditures was attributable to a standstill (zero growth) in the level of spending for the procurement of weapons and equipment. The remaining types of expenditures (research and development and operating costs) had continued to rise at an undiminished rate. This zero growth of procurement expenditures, arms expenditures in the narrow sense, on the one hand, should not allow us to lose sight of the fact that the volume of these expenditures has remained enormous—in 1980, calculated in dollars, it exceeded US expenditures by not less than 75 percent (CIA estimate).[5] With this level of spending, the USSR was still able to bring an impressive quantity of new weapons into service after 1976, including the SS-20. (It can be assumed that this program, which has dominated the European Security discussion of recent years, has not absorbed any very great percentage of the total procurement expenditures.) In the future too the USSR would be able, with no further increase in its procurement budget, to carry out a number of major programs. On the other hand, against the background of the freeze in relations between the USA and the USSR since the Soviet invasion of Afghanistan, this static level of expenditure seems a fact worthy of note.

At the time of writing (January 1985), no definite US estimates of the course of Soviet procurement or total defense expenditures in 1983 and 1984 are available. In the summer of 1984, the Pentagon information service (DIA) informed the press that according to preliminary calculations Soviet procurement expenditure had risen by 5–10 percent in 1983. We have already noted that, first, it is difficult to establish short-term fluctuations precisely, and that second, such changes do not initially tell us much anyway. The CIA has issued no confirmation of this information. Even if in fact a larger rise in 1983 were to be assured, we should still have to wait to see if this was the commencement of the long-expected "arms boom."

Possible Reasons for the Slower Growth of Soviet Defense Expenditures

As to the reasons for the stagnation of procurement expenditures, we can unfortunately only speculate. The CIA has cited economic and technological problems as causes, without specifying them more precisely, but it has not completely ruled out political decisions on the part of the Soviet leadership, either.

The first kind of explanation—economic problems—appears entirely plausible. It corresponds to a course of events that has been predictable for several years. If we cast our minds back to the situation in 1979, we recall that until then the rate of growth of the aggregate output of the economy had been as high as that of defense expenditures. The latter's share of the social product, at 11–13 percent, usually regarded as a measure of the arms burden on the economy, had thus at least not increased any further. In other words, the growth of consumption and investment did not have to be unduly curtailed. This was no longer going to be true for the first half of the 1980s, at which time a further slowdown in the general rate of economic growth was forecast, if defense expenditures were to continue to rise at their "historical rate." It was easy to figure out that in this case the growth of civilian utilization of the gross national product would inevitably have to be reduced to an extent that the Soviet leadership would possibly not consider advisable any longer.[6]

This scenario related to a "normal" course of economic development. This would in all probability be marked by a distinct decline in the growth of the labor supply, only a slow rise in raw material production (energy, metals) and an unpropitious productivity trend. If unforeseen difficulties such as a series of bad harvests occurred in addition, the Soviet leadership would be faced with the guns or butter dilemma in all its vehemence. In such a case, information regarding a number of new weapon developments and persistent expansion of arms factories could only serve as an indication that a build-up in arms production had indeed been planned, but there would have to be doubts as to whether these plans could be implemented.

This dilemma was in fact posed in the years 1979–1982, when the course of economic development turned out to be anything but "normal," even in the above-mentioned sense. Four years in succession, the grain harvest was very bad, making extensive imports of grain necessary. The distribution of these imports meant an additional job for the already overloaded transportation system, and one which could not be postponed. One can imagine that in such a situation, delivery of supplies fell behind schedule throughout the industrial sector, including the armament industry. Another important factor that must be mentioned is the crisis in the growth in the metal-producing branches, which has had a distinct effect on the mechanical engineering sector, in which armaments are produced. Table 16.2 shows how the growth rate of the gross national product declined in the second half of the 1970s, in comparison with the first half. The corresponding slowdown in defense expenditures avoided an increase in the burden on the economy.

The Soviet Union cannot be expected to admit any economic difficulties in the armaments sector. It may be that the former chief of the general staff, Ogarkov, was alluding to such difficulties when he referred several times in recent years to the necessity of "continually seeking to improve the system of production relations in enterprises that produce the major kinds of weapons, . . . to guarantee that they receive the necessary supplies

TABLE 16.2
Annual Growth of Output
(Western estimates,[a] in percent)

	1971-75	1976-80	1981	1982
Iron and steel industry	4.0	0.9	-0.2	-0.4
Non-ferrous metals	5.9	2.3	1.3	1.5
Mechanical engineering (civilian and military)	7.8	5.0	3.2	3.8
Gross national product	3.7	2.6	2.1	2.6

Note: [a]The figures are lower than the corresponding Soviet data, which, in addition to double counting, also include price increases and to that extent do not indicate real growth.

Source: CIA, Handbook of Economic Statistics, 1984, Washington, D.C., 1984, p. 69.

and to create a reserve of equipment and materials."[7] He also referred to the "mobilization deployment" of the entire economy to be undertaken in the case of war, which however made "planned measures and coordinated action necessary in peace time as well." Other statements by Ogarkov, which, although hedged with safeguards, were too self-assertive for Soviet conditions, can be interpreted as criticisms of the political leadership's arms policy.[8] All together he appears to have advocated even more far-reaching subordination of the economy to the objective of the country's defense than seemed necessary or tolerable to the government.

The second kind of possible reasons for the stagnation of weapons procurement expenditures in the years 1977–1982 relates to technological difficulties. It is not hard to imagine that the USSR, like the West, is always faced with such difficulties, both during the development and after the introduction of new weapons. But this is not what we have in mind here. If technical problems are supposed to have led to six years of stagnation of procurement expenditures as a whole, this would have to be due to a general crisis in technology, which applied not just to particular systems. It would have to relate predominantly to the sphere of industrial production, not actual research and development. For in the latter, the USSR has stepped up its efforts substantially and has achieved considerable successes: According to the CIA, the dollar value of Soviet military research expenditures at the beginning of the 1970s was at the same level as the US, while at the end of the 1970s it was twice that of America.[9] The Soviet armaments sector was also said to suffer from the problem, familiar in civilian sectors, that new technologies can only be incorporated into production with difficulty and delays. Increased efforts to catch up technologically would thus have led precisely to overtaxing of industry—exacerbated by the familiar economic problems.

If we look for Soviet statements that could refer to these technical difficulties, we find the speech that Brezhnev made to the assembled military leadership thirteen days before his death.[10] He said that there must not be any lag in the field of military technology, and that the engineers would have to do all it takes to solve the impending problems. The sentences can be found in the section of the speech clearly devoted to domestic policy, which makes it unlikely that he had in mind a lag vis-à-vis the West. On the other hand, the military leadership was told that there were difficulties in the economy and that they had sufficient weapons, which had to be mastered better, just as leadership and training had to be improved. There was no suggestion from Brezhnev that "the international situation demanded new additional efforts," even though that was what the military were arguing in the same year.[11]

This brings us to the third kind of possible reason: a conscious political decision to "freeze" procurement expenditures. If there has been such a decision, the economic and possible technical problems that we have discussed will have played a part in it. At the same time zero growth in procurement expenditures must have been regarded as militarily justifiable by the political leadership. This seems quite possible, if they took the same view of their own armaments efforts in relation to the USA as did the CIA. In that case, the USSR would still be able to bring more new weapons into service than the USA, and this with a clear quantitative capacity advantage in most weapons families. This then would not be reduced so quickly even if the USA increased its budget substantially in the future.

The Magic Triangle: Consumption, Capital Formation, Defense

That there was in fact a decision against a further increase in procurement expenditures is best attested, in this writer's opinion, by the appreciable continuing rise in production after 1976 of both capital equipment goods and consumer durables. Like weapons and other military equipment, both of these kinds of goods are produced by the mechanical engineering sector. Thus, the CIA gives a growth figure for 1976–1980 of 5.8 percent annually for output of means of production in the mechanical engineering sector, and 6.6 percent for production of consumer goods.[12]

Furthermore, from the middle of the 1970s on, weapons were exported in rising quantities (even though not all these came out of current production): In 1978–1980 the value of net exports was around 24 billion US dollars, compared with less than 18 billion in 1975–1977 and 1972–1974.[13] It is also worth taking note of a RAND study in which the "empire costs" of the USSR (economic favors for Soviet allies and countries being courted by the USSR) are estimated. According to this study, the growth rate of these costs accelerated substantially, precisely at the time when the growth of defense expenditures was slowing down.[14]

Thus we have a situation where, during a period of economic difficulty, investors, consumers, and allies enjoyed a greater share of the benefits of growth than did the armed forces. In the West an impression has gained wide acceptance that during the Brezhnev period, party and military leadership had developed a strong common interest in continually rising defense expenditures. The economy is seen ultimately to be important only as an instrument. Consumption is regarded only as a means to an end: maintenance of labor motivation and avoidance of unrest.

It apparently hasn't been quite like that. There is no doubt that Soviet leadership assigns the utmost importance to military strength. Still, there can be many places on a scale of priorities, and the relative position of the items occupying them can change, depending on the situation. Even military strength is ultimately important only as an instrument, as a means for policy. Soviet military writers have long defined the role of the army in just such a way. This understanding, agreed upon in quite a different sense between the politicians and the military, certainly does not mean that they are always in accord about the resources to be allocated to the armed forces. Yet military leadership too must know that a flourishing economy is a prerequisite for the satisfaction of their demands. However, it is not they, but economic leadership, and ultimately political leadership, who are responsible for drafting this prerequisite. The political leadership made a decision about the trend of defense expenditures on the basis of the available evidence in accordance with its overall responsibility. If we look at Brezhnev's "farewell address" from this point of view, we find in it a clear enough expression of the primacy of politics.

To speak of the military and political leadership, incidentally, seems to simplify reality too much. As far as the former is concerned, it may be more than chance that the growth of defense expenditures slowed down after the year D. Ustinov—who was not a professional soldier—became Minister of Defense. In 1979 he wrote that, in its concern for the security of the country, the party operated on the principle that "defense capacity depends directly on the level of development in the economy. A characteristic of present conditions is that further expansion of the capacity of defense industries, and procurement of the material and technical basis of the armed forces, are becoming more dependent on the country's economy and its rate of development."[15] At this point, one can even recognize an increasing linkage between growth of resources available for military purposes and overall economic growth. This, if you will, is primacy of economics.

Whatever the actual details of the slowdown in the growth of Soviet defense expenditures may have been, the fact that it was made public by the CIA, combined with terse references to economic and technical problems, at a time when the US was pursuing a policy of rebuilding its military strength, can explain why the Soviet leadership thought it necessary to demonstrate its capacity to make an equally significant increase in defense expenditures. Finally, the CIA announcement was widely reported in the Western press.

Prospects for Future Development

The actual future course of Soviet defense expenditures is difficult to predict because, for the most part, we can do no more than construct hypotheses about the reasons for the post-1976 change in the trend of expenditures. We cannot even rank the three factors we have considered (economics, technology, and politics) in order of importance. It seems least questionable that the economic situation has had some influence. This means that the arms sector, however much priority it may enjoy in the allocation of resources, is in no way an island within the economy.

This raises the question of the prospects for the development of the Soviet economy as a whole. The annual rate of growth for the Soviet gross national product up to the end of the present decade is likely to amount to "only" about 2 percent. In view of the experience of previous years, it appears unlikely that this will be attainable without an increase in investment growth to a rate distinctly higher than this figure, say to about 2.5–3 percent. It is difficult to estimate what Soviet leadership would regard as the minimum necessary growth in consumption. In the late 1970s, when annual per capita consumption increased on average by 1.5–2 percent across the entire country, local supply difficulties ensued. These gave rise to a certain amount of discontent among the population. It has to be assumed that (in light, for example, of increased "militaristic" activities on the part of the US) an even lower rate of consumption growth will be considered tolerable, say 1 percent per capita, i.e., 1.5 percent in total volume.

With these rates of investment and consumption growth, the major competing items in the allocation of the gross national product, there is room for an annual average increase in defense expenditures of 1.5–2.5 percent up to the end of this decade. This prediction is tantamount to an extrapolation of the trend in expenditures that has been observed since 1976.

A British author[16] also dealt with the future trend of Soviet defense spending, after information concerning its lower growth since 1976 first became available. In his opinion, it would soon be increasing again at 4–5 percent annually, as it did in the first half of the 1970s. He bases this view on the large number of newly developed weapons systems, which we have mentioned, and which are ready for production and introduction into the armed forces. But here we must once again ask in what numbers, or better, at what pace the new systems will be delivered. Should it be deemed necessary or desirable to adapt the arms program to the economic situation, this could be done precisely by reduction or expansion of planned programs.

In any case, the information regarding these weapons systems should be taken seriously. The prediction of a possible increase in total expenditures of 1.5–2.5 percent is quite consistent with a disproportionately large rise in procurement expenditures (at least for some years). Neither may we overlook the fact that the type of analysis that operates only with the aggregate categories of gross national product, investment, consumption, and military expenditures is very crude: With 2 percent future growth in the gross national product, the rate of production increase in the mechanical engineering sector can be higher, as it has been till now. This too would permit an appreciable increase in the already high level of arms production. This is all the more so should our assumption concerning the future growth of the economy prove too pessimistic and the favorable trend in 1983 and 1984 turn out to be more than a temporary revival.

Notes

1. A. S. Becker, *Soviet Military Outlays since 1955*, RAND RM-3886-PR, Santa Monica (1964), pp. 50 ff. Becker, however, admitted that he failed to find any clear statistical confirmation of his assumption.

2. *Pr*, 29 November 1984.

3. On this and other statements in this chapter that are not further documented or supported see F. Walter, *Berichte des BIOst*, No. 1 (1985).

4. The UNO project for the reduction of defense expenditure, which the USSR initiated over ten years ago, ran into the ground because it had not taken any part in the pertinent experts' work on the creation of a uniform scheme for calculation and publication of militry expenditures.

5. At the alliance level (Warsaw Pact/NATO), the situation is probably considerably more favorable for the West; on this, however, no figures are available. On the limited meaningfulness of such comparisons see Franz Walter in *The Soviet Union 1978–79*, pp. 141 ff.

6. For discussion of this subject, see F. Walter, *op. cit.* There a slowdown in the growth of defense expenditures to 3 percent per year was deemed probable, on the assumption, which today seems very optimistic, that in the years 1981–85 the social product would increase at an average annual rate of 2.5–3 percent.

7. N. Ogarkov, *K*, No. 10 (1981), N. Ogarkov, *Vsegda v gotovnosti k zashchite otechestva* (Moscow, 1982).

8. See his interview in *K*, 9 May 1984, in which he accordingly called for greater attention to be devoted to conventional armanents and downgraded the importance of the strategic nuclear program.

9. On Soviet military technological successes see the booklets published by the Pentagon, *Soviet Military Power*, September 1981, March 1983 and April 1984.

10. *Pr*, 28 October 1982.

11. Col.-Gen. Beletsky, *Voennyi Vestnik*, No. 10 (1982).

12. CIA, *Handbook of Economic Statistics 1984* (Washington, D.C., 1984).

13. Arms Control and Disarmament Agency (ACDA), *World Military Expenditures and Arms Transfers 1971–1980* (Washington, 1983). For world-wide statistics on defense expenditures in dollars, ACDA uses the CIA estimates for the USSR.

14. C. Wolf et al. *The Cost of the Soviet Empire*, R-3073/1-NA (Santa Monica, 1983).

15. D. F. Ustinov, *Ausgewählte Reden und Aufsätze* (Berlin [East] 1981), p. 525; VIKPSS, No. 2 (1979).

16. D. Fewtrell, *The Soviet Economic Crisis: Prospects for the Military and the Consumer, Adelphi Paper*, No. 186 (1983).

17
Siberia: Resource or Burden?

Hermann Clement

The question of whether Siberia represents a resource or a burden for the USSR would meet with blank incomprehension from most Soviet citizens. The enormous land area, the wealth of water power, the gigantic forests, the immense reserves of energy, the innumerable deposits of raw materials and the ever-fascinating gold, platinum, and diamond deposits seem to provide an unequivocal answer. Long ago, Lomonosov saw "the future of Russia's power" in Siberia. And to the present day the riches of Siberia are a source of pride in their homeland for almost all Soviet citizens. The men and women who are opening up these riches are the new generation of heroes in the Soviet Union. This positive image has replaced the terrors with which the name of Siberia used to be associated; Siberia is no longer a synonym for an inhospitable land to which people are banished.

Siberia[1] occupies an area of 12.8 million square kilometers[2]—unimaginably large by Western European standards. It is equivalent to some fifty times the territory of the Federal Republic of Germany. From north to south this vast land measures more than 4,000 kilometers and from east to west more then 6,000. The continental land mass is marked by enormous contrasts. Although West Siberia encompasses the largest lowland area in the world, 2.7 million square kilometers, three-quarters of Siberia consists of mountain massifs and high plateaus, rising to an altitude of 4,500 meters. While in some regions natural levelling processes are under way, the eastern blocks, which are tectonically extremely active, are still rising. The climate is distinguished by extreme seasonal and daily variations in temperature, and the average is low. In some places in Siberia, the maximum range of absolute temperatures amounts to 100 degrees.[3] As a consequence of the continental climate and low temperatures, there are extensive areas of permanently frozen ground, which stretch over more than 8 million square kilometers and thus cover nearly two-thirds of the total area of Siberia. Precipitation, with low average figures of 300 mm, varies from 150 mm to 600 mm per year in the agriculturally important forest steppe zones of West Siberia.

Because of these hostile natural geographical conditions, Siberia has little arable land. Large parts consist of tundra or are covered with taiga. The latter represents the great forest wealth of Siberia. The agriculturally useful area is at present about 160 million acres, some 11.7 percent of the total arable land in the USSR. Siberia has a slightly larger area of agricultural land per head of population (5.7 acres) than does the USSR as a whole. It is hardly possible to extend this area much further: "At present the reserves of new and fallow land that do not require large investments are practically exhausted."[4]

The relatively favorable per capita supply of agricultural land simultaneously points to the second major deficiency in Siberia's resource endowment: the shortage of labor. There are only 28 million people living in this vast area, half the number of inhabitants of Great Britain or the Federal Republic of Germany. The distribution of the population is uneven. In the southwest, which is comparatively developed, the population density is relatively high; in the north, northeast, and east it is extremely low.

Raw Material Deposits

Siberia is poor in people but rich in many raw materials.[5] The varying age and diversified geological structure of Siberia mean that practically all kinds of rock and their concomitant raw materials of different origins and ages are found in the region. Not known for very long, but economically most important, are the reserves of hydrocarbons. The center of the deposits is the province of Tyumen in the north of West Siberia. Although development did not start until the 1960s, more than half of Soviet oil and gas production, which is the largest in the world, comes from this region today.

Soviet coal reserves are even more heavily concentrated in Siberia: 90 percent of Soviet and 50 percent of world reserves are to be found in the region. The principal mining centers are the Kuznetsk basin (Kuzbas), the Kansk-Achinsk district (KATEK) and southern Yakutia. In addition to these enormous reserves of fossil fuels, there is the large hydro-electric potential of Siberian rivers. A great part of the total usable resources of hydro-electric energy in the USSR is provided by the powerful river systems of Siberia.[6]

If Siberia holds the dominant position in Soviet energy reserves, its advantage is not nearly so salient in non-energy raw materials. It is true that practically every element in the periodic table can be found in Siberia, but economically exploitable mineral deposits are not so heavily concentrated there as is the case with energy raw materials. All the same, the fact that the territory has yet to be fully explored means that further finds can be expected.

In the case of precious metals and diamonds, a very large proportion of deposits and of mining operations can be found in Siberia. The largest part of Soviet gold production comes from East Siberia and the Far East. Over 90 percent of the platinum group metals are obtained as a by-product of the nickel sulphide ores in the Norilsk area, and diamonds are found predominantly in Yakutia. As far as the steel-hardening group of metals is concerned, Siberia actually does not occupy as significant a place as it is often credited with, either in regard to deposits or production. The ores in the Norilsk area are the most important. The nickel-copper ores there form the largest deposits of nickel and cobalt in the Soviet Union. They also contain substantial quantities of copper, platinum, gold and silver, which are obtained as by-products.[7]

More important for the Soviet economy are the cobalt deposits in the Tuvin ASSR and the molybdenum deposits near Sorks in the Krasnoyarsk region. Less significant so far are the production and deposits of wolfram ores. Siberia's share of other major steel hardeners is negligible. It has only 2 percent of the Soviet Union's large reserves of manganese, in deposits that so far have not been worked. Chrome reserves are so small that they are not even mentioned by Soviet geologists; and vanadium, which occurs mostly as a by-product in the Soviet Union, is not procured in Siberia either.

Even in the case of the USSR's enormous iron ore reserves of 111 billion tons, Siberia's share, as far as is known at this time, is only 10 percent.[8] The southern Kuzbas and East Siberia are the main areas where deposits are found. The present production level is not sufficient to supply Siberia's comparatively small iron and steel industry.[9] Gigantic deposits are supposed to exist in the West Siberian lowlands, but for the foreseeable future it is not possible to exploit them economically, and they are therefore not included in the estimates of reserves.

Non-ferrous metals are better represented in the Asiatic part of the Soviet Union; all the same, the known deposits and active mines are located primarily in Kazakhstan and Central Asia, and Siberia's share is smaller. Copper is obtained mainly as a by-product at Norilsk; but Siberia accounts for scarcely over 10 percent of total Soviet production. Siberia's share of lead and zinc production is only slightly higher. On the other hand, it is known that there are some deposits of these ores in Siberia, and they are said to be particularly rich and high-grade. Udokan is supposed to have 700 million tons of copper ore with a copper content of 1.15 percent. There is allegedly an important deposit of high-grade lead ore at the mouth of the Angara (Gorevsky). In addition there are various, and in some cases extensive, deposits of polymetallic ores. However, development and processing problems have so far been a major obstacle to their utilization. The Soviet Union has been looking for a Western partner for Udokan for over ten years. Even the building of the BAM (Baikal Amur railway) has not succeeded in accelerating the opening up of Udokan very much, and it is likely to become a project for the 1990s, if not for the next century. Work at Gorevsky, on the other hand, is supposed to be started during the next five-year plan period. On the other hand, in the case of tin mining and tin deposits, Siberia is of central importance in the Soviet Union. Many of these deposits, however, are worked only because the USSR has not yet achieved self-sufficiency in tin supplies.

In view of the exceptionally cheap electric power in Siberia, the lack of light metal ores is extremely unfortunate. So far, no workable deposits of bauxite have been found. While there are deposits of nephelin and alunite, smelting them presents technical and economic problems. By far the largest part of the aluminum oxide smelted in Siberia must therefore be brought in over long distances. Soviet bauxite production is insufficient overall, and rising quantities are imported. As with aluminium ores, Siberia at present has no titanium ores of economic significance either.

Principal Products: Energy and Timber

Energy and timber are thus the principal products in the development of Siberia. Only in a few localities have metals been able to take over this position. The Kuzubas have been developed as the most important industrial region based on coal. In the South Yakutia territorial production complex (TPK) coal is also the leading product. The current center of development in Tyumen is based on hydrocarbons. Many localities in Siberia such as Bratsk and Sayansk owe their growth to cheap water power. Timber is the major product in the development of the region around the middle Yenisei. One of the most important exceptions is the Norilsk area. It owes its growth to the rich nonferrous metal ores there, with their larger admixture of precious metals. Still, no secondary industries can be established in this area of extreme natural conditions. The gold and diamond mines similarly do not lead to any more comprehensive development in their region. In the future, Gorevsky and Udokan might possibly become examples of development areas based on metals. Yet, they are also saying here that only enrichment of the ore is to be carried out on site: Smelting would be undertaken at a location with more favorable natural conditions.

The goal to be achieved has long been the comprehensive development of Siberia; but with the exception of southwest Siberia the development strategy actually pursued has concentrated on a few raw materials. The territorial production complex approach accentuates this tendency, because it places exploitation of a major raw material deposit at the center of the development model. The investment policy of the past fiften years illustrates this clearly.

During this period, Soviet economic leadership has redirected a substantial part of investment into the "northern regions." The latter are almost exclusively in Siberia. Between 1965 and the beginning of the 1980s investment in northern Siberia rose 7–8 times. It has recently reached 8.4 billion rubles per year, over 6 percent of the investment in the entire Soviet economy.[10] Within Siberia, the share of the northern regions in investment doubled between 1966–1970 and in 1976–1980 reached 36%.[11] Using Soviet data, Leslie Dienes has shown that both investment and construction capacity have been concentrated in the Tyumen region with its oil and gas fields, the building of the Baikal-Amur railway, and the South Yakutian coalfield.[12] Growth in the remaining areas of Siberia was below average. Furthermore, both investment and construction were heavily concentrated directly in mining and, especially, oil and gas extraction. Infrastructural investment was neglected. This is consistent with complaints about Siberia's inadequate infrastructure.

The expansion of the oil and gas industry in West Siberia proved extremely profitable. Between 1966 and 1975, for example, net output grew faster than gross output; the proportion of material costs in total output dropped; labor productivity increased faster than the national average; and profits after deduction of usage costs rose considerably. The trend in East Siberia was just the opposite. While West Siberia gained from the commissioning of highly productive oil and gas fields, the economic structure in East Siberia is more heavily weighted towards material and energy-intensive branches (ore extraction, coal mining, the timber and aluminium industries), in which in some cases natural conditions deteriorated substantially.[13]

Since 1978, however, conditions in the oil industry have also worsened in west Siberia. While investment expenditure and operating costs have continued to rise rapidly, the growth in production has steadily fallen. The productiveness of individual fields has declined, and costs per unit of output have increased rapidly. According to Dienes, not even the diminishing cost of gas production, which was itself affected by rising transportation costs, was enough to counterbalance this trend.[14]

Siberia as a Growth Region

The investment strategy pursued has resulted in a faster rate of growth of gross industrial production in Siberia than in the Soviet Union as a whole since the middle of the 1960s.[15] During the decade of the 1970s, industrial production in East and West Siberia rose by 87 percent compared with 72 percent for the entire USSR. However, the gap diminished during the 1970s. By the tenth five-year plan, east Siberian industry was growing at a below average pace: The same was true of southwestern Siberia.

Siberian industry, which has produced more per capita than the national average during the last ten years, has thus become more heavily concentrated on mining and extraction. In 1976–1980, the average annual growth rate, for example, of the extractive industries in Siberia was 5.8 percent, while manufacturing industry achieved only 4.4 percent.[16] The latter was thus below the national average. Excluding the oil and gas industry, the growth of industrial production in Siberia dropped to 3.8 percent.[17]

The above-average growth of Siberia was thus attained solely on the strength of the rapid expansion of oil and gas production[18] in northwestern Siberia, where the average annual growth of gross industrial production reached 46 percent in 1971–1975 and 31.6 percent in 1976–1980. The economic center of gravity in Siberia thus shifted in the course of the 1970s to northwestern Siberia, which is now responsible for 16.1 percent of west Siberia's industrial production. In east Siberia, the northern regions'

TABLE 17.1
Siberia's Share of Total Production and of the Increment in Gross Production of Industrial Branches of the USSR (in percent)

	Share of Gross Production		Share of Increment in Gross Production
	1975	1980	1976-1980
All industry	9.0	9.2	10.4
Electric power	15.3	15.8	13.9
Fuels	21.1	26.7	59.3
Chemicals and petrochemicals	9.4	9.2	8.6
Mechanical engineering	7.7	7.4	6.6
Timber, wood-processing, cellulose, and paper	16.0	16.0	15.3
Building materials	9.0	9.5	15.9
Light industry	5.4	5.9	8.7
Food industry	6.3	6.0	1.9

Source: T. B. Baranova, Izvestiya Sibirskogo otdeleniya AN SSSR, Seriya obshchestvennykh nauk, no. 11 (1982), p. 73, table 2.

share of total production amounted to 17.7 percent in 1980, though this represented a fall of 1.5 percentage points compared with 1970. This reflects the slow initial expansion of Norilsk: With the development of timber projects on the Angara and the middle Yenisei and the commissioning of the smelter at Nadezhda, near Norilsk, the proportion is likely to have risen again during the 1980s.[19] Dienes comments as follows: "Without oil and gas, Siberian industrial growth noticeably lagged behind the average for the country. Not only did other processing industries perform poorly but evidently so did other extractive branches."[20] The statistics in Table 17.1 confirm this trend.

Besides the fuel industries, only the building materials industry, which is essential for the development of oil and gas complexes, raised its share in total Soviet production. The proportion declined in all other branches, except light industry. This applies even to the branches whose raw material base is in Siberia, like chemicals and petrochemicals and wood-processing, cellulose, and paper. In spite of the improvement in the position of light industry, its output per capita of population in east and west Siberia is still below the national average.

Astonishingly, in calculations based on actual prices, the northern parts of west and east Siberia are said to have been responsible for only about 1.5 percent of total Soviet industrial production in 1980. A. Granberg points out, however, that prevailing prices seriously undervalue Siberia's real share. He submits that the contribution of Siberia's industrial production (with its high proportion of mining) to the national economy as a whole exceeds its measured share of industrial production by 1.5–3 times. For the northern regions the appropriate multiplier would be somewhat higher still.[21]

Costs and Benefits

This calculation, which can hardly be replicated, illustrates the problem of trying to make even an approximate estimate, on the basis of published figures, of the costs and benefits for the Soviet economy of developing Siberia. Still, Dienes has attempted to calculate the net effect of the development of Siberia on the basis of the latest usable data.[22] He reached the conclusion that in 1975, 17 percent of national income used in Siberia represented unrequited inflows from the regions west of the Urals. Calculated in 1973 prices, the net inflow amounted to 9.2 billion rubles or 2.5 percent of the national income produced by the USSR. According to his estimates, 83 percent of this went into the area east of the Yenisei, and 59 percent to the far east alone.

Yet this calculation can at most provide a starting point, since, as noted above, the administration pricing policy probably substantially undervalues the contribution of Siberia to the USSR's economy. Even Dienes comes to the conclusion that, for example, West Siberia's small "need for subsidy" disappears completely if world market prices are applied just to the part of its oil and gas output that is exported. The net inflow is then confined exclusively to east Siberia and the far east and is reduced to 7.5 billion rubles, which would still be 2 percent of the USSR's national income.

This correction shows once again how problematic the Soviet pricing system makes the calculation of the net transfer. Why, for example, should not the whole of oil and gas production be valued at world market prices? How are other raw materials, such as gold, platinum, copper, and coal, valued? Should the prices of investment goods then be altered? Dienes' calculations show, however, that very probably east Siberia and the far east are regions that have to be subsidized by the other regions of the Soviet Union. For west Siberia this is not clear. The wealth of hydrocarbons in the north and the relatively well-developed zone in the south appear to make a sufficient contribution to the national income utilized (once a more scarcity-oriented pricing system is applied), to render a net inflow unnecessary. A. Aganbegyan even works on the basis of a 40 percent higher productivity of social labor in Siberia with an equivalent proportion of fixed capital. "The shifting of productive forces to Siberia does not lower their economic effectiveness but raises it."[23] In the far east the high net inflow has to be set against the strategic significance of this area, which is certainly not underestimated by the Soviet leadership.

The development of Siberia, as it has proceeded over the past fifteen years, must thus be assessed as a positive factor for the Soviet economy as a whole. While certainly enormous investment funds had to be found, the contribution they enabled Siberia to make to the provision of supplies of low-cost energy for the Soviet Union is immense. The central position of major products of Siberian extractive industries in Soviet foreign trade reinforces this importance.

Oil and gas, the entire production increment of which has come from Siberia in recent years, earn over 50 percent of the Soviet Union's total export revenue. In exports to the OECD countries, these items accounted for as much as 78.3 percent in 1983.[24] The positive contribution of gold and platinum to the Soviet balance of payments is unmistakable, quite apart from its psychological effect. Timber likewise is a product with a promising export potential. The developments of recent years show, however, that raw material extraction in Siberia can be an extremely expensive business. Profitable projects like the oilfields of west Siberia are not to be discovered every decade. Even gas extraction, according to the general estimate, is not yielding the profit that oil production has earned. The use of Siberian raw materials will therefore become less advantageous again in the future.

Restricted Branch Structure

Looking at the development of Siberia from the point of view of the Soviet economy as a whole, the region must thus be seen as a resource. This applies both to the provision of raw materials for the central region and from the point of view of the strategic hinterland. The necessarily capital-intensive development of the region, which for the most part suffers from unfavorable natural geographical conditions, leads, however, to high investment and current costs, which are becoming unpleasantly evident for the Soviet economy, with its prospects of declining investment growth. Concentration on the development of extremely valuable and profitable energy and raw material deposits is the consequence. The other sectors receive too little investment, and the branch structure in Siberia is restricted. In this manner, for example, Siberia has lost its advantage as a region with significant reserves of electric power, which obstructs the overall development of the region. Soviet scholars consider this at least a medium-term concern.[25] The major delays besetting the opening up of the BAM zone are also an eloquent example of this.[26] In the energy sector, however, Siberia will retain its central importance for the Soviet economy. Still, the choice of variants in the exploitation of coal deposits will present Soviet leadership with further major problems.

From the point of view of the development of Siberia itself, it must be said that concentration on the exploitation of west Siberian hydrocarbon reserves has given little impetus to the development of this area. The same holds true of the working of non-ferrous metal deposits in Norilsk (East Siberia) and of gold mining in the far east. The products are processed very largely on site and then dispatched to consumer regions, which are mostly outside Siberia, or are designated for export. Oil and gas yield the smallest downstream effect of all. They are transported away out of the region without major processing.[27] Only a small portion remains in the region, and even development of the large petro-chemical complexes in Tomsk and Tobolsk has fallen far behind the planned schedule. In 1981–1985, the structure of Siberia's economy will worsen further in this respect, as practically the entire growth in investment envisaged for west Siberia is going into the oil and gas complex.[28]

Many scholars are warning against this development strategy. In their view, optimal growth of the entire Soviet economy can only be ensured if Siberia grows more quickly than the Soviet economy as a whole,[29] and the processing industry also participates adequately. This would enable overall development costs to be reduced. B.P. Orlov starts by considering three possible development strategies for the 1980s:

- Further concentration of development on energy and raw material extraction, transporting them away to supply the economy as a whole, with correspondingly low growth in other branches.
- Closer incorporation of Siberia into the overall economy by exploitation of regional advantages, with a higher degree of processing of the available raw materials, which would reduce total transportation expenditures.
- More comprehensive development of the Siberian economy, which would, however, require the allocation of significantly more capital and labor than the second variant.

Under the conditions currently prevailing, Orlov's view is that in the present, initial stage of development, the first variant will predominate. Not until a second stage, in which economic constraints (capital and labor shortage) have diminished, could the second variant be implemented.

For the foreseeable future, therefore, the greatest part of Siberia will hardly advance beyond the status of a raw material store for the developed western part of the country. In this way, production can be directed so that Siberia remains a resource without becoming a burden, even if the faster growth sought by the Siberian lobby is not achieved. Only Soviet planners, who have the necessary information at their disposal, could decide where the economic optimum lies in development strategy for Siberia.

Notes

1. In this chapter, Siberia means the region of the RSFSR east of the Ural mountains. This comprises the administrative units of west Siberia, east Siberia, and the far east.

2. West and East Siberia 9.7 million square km., far east 3.1 million square km.

3. A.A. Trofimuk and S.M. Nikolaev, *Siberia. Geographische Gegensätze, Mineral ressourcen und Probleme, deren Erschließung* (Novosibirsk, 1982), p. 6.

4. *Ibid.* p. 9.

5. On raw materials see J. Bethkenhagen and H. Clement, *Möglichkeiten der deutsch-sowjetischen Energie-und Rohstoff-kooperation vor dem Hintergrund der sowjetischen Produktions-und Verbrauchsentwicklung* (Berlin and Munich, 1984).

6. The economically still viable potential of the USSR amounts to 900–950 billion kwh and is predominantly concentrated in Siberia. A.A. Trofimuk and S.M. Nikolaev, *op. cit.*, p. 19.

7. Practically all the rare metals, of which Siberia accounts for over 50 percent of production, are found in Norilsk. These include selenium and tellurium. Th.

Shabad, "Siberia and the Soviet Far East. Exploitation Policies in Energy and Raw Materials Sectors: A Commercial Assessment," in NATO, *Regional Development in the USSR. Trends and Prospects* (Brussels, 1979), p. 155.

8. USBM, *Minerals Yearbook*, Vol. III, *Area Report International, Centennial Edition, 1981* (Washington, D.C., 1983), p. 1056.

9. F. Th. Shabad, *op. cit.*, p. 157.

10. L. Dienes, "The Development of Siberia." Regional Priorities and Economic Strategy." Manuscript for international colloquium, "La Sibérie: colonisation, développment et perspectives, 1582–1982" (Paris, 1983), p. 1.

11. These regions' share of the population of Siberia is only one-eighth.

12. Thus, for example, the Tyumen province's share of Siberia's construction work rose from under 10 percent in 1970 to over 18.3 percent in 1980. L. Dienes, *op. cit.*, p. 2.

13. In addition, the prices of the products of this branch of industry allow for only a small profit margin and may include a turnover tax, which makes their net contribution appear relatively small in comparison with differently structured regions.

14. L. Dienes, *op. cit.*, p. 5.

15. Cf., *Sibir' v edinom narodnokhozyaistvennom komplekse*, (collective authorship) (Novosibirsk, 1980), p. 27.

16. The share of extractive industries in all industries is 2.3 times higher in Siberia than in the USSR as a whole. B. Rumer, *Berichte des BIost*, No. 48 (1984), p. 6.

17. T.B. Baranova, *Izvestiya Sibirskogo otdeleniya AN SSSR*, Seriya obshchestvennykh nauk, No. 11 (1982), p. 75.

18. A.G. Granberg, *Izvestiya Sibirskogo otdeleniya AN SSSR*, Seriya obshchestvennykh nauk, No. 11 (1983), p. 64.

19. F.A.G. Granberg, *op. cit.*, p. 65.

20. L. Dienes, *op. cit.*, p. 11.

21. F.A.G. Granberg, *op. cit.*, p. 66. Aganbegyan claims a similar variation in Siberia's share of national income, 10–30 percent according to price basis. A.G. Aganbegyan, *Sowjetwissenschaft*, No. 3 (1982), pp. 410 ff.

22. L. Dienes, *Soviet Geography* (April 1982), pp. 214 ff., Table 2.

23. F.A.G. Aganbegyan, *op. cit.*, p. 415.

24. J. Bethkenhagen and H. Clement, *op. cit.*, p. 185.

25. T.B. Baranova, *op. cit.*, p. 73.

26. The development of the South Yakutian TPK was, for instance, delayed so much that the delivery of coal to Japan at the time agreed on was endangered. The development of the copper deposits at Udokan was postponed almost to the next millennium.

27. B.P. Orlov, *Izvestiya Sibirskogo otdeleniya AN SSSR*, Seriya obshchestvennykh nauk, No. 11 (1982), pp. 65, 68.

28. *Ibid.* p. 69.

29. Most regard a 30 percent faster growth rate as optimal. *Sibir' v edinom . . . op. cit.*, Chapter 3.

18
Soviet Economic Reforms: Higher Achievement as a Result of New Premises?

Hans-Hermann Höhmann

Reasons for Reform: Growth and Efficiency Problems

There is no doubt that during the past two years, interest in reform has revived on the Soviet economic scene. True, since the last major package of measures in the summer of 1979, no comprehensive reform project has been adopted, yet all signs indicate that one is in preparation. This year or next, therefore, revisions in planning, management, and the economic mechanism are likely to be decided on—modelled on the experiment currently under way in Soviet industry—and we can expect them to be continued during the twelfth five-year plan. The new secretary general, Gorbachev, outlined the importance of such measures: "Whatever question we examine, from whatever direction we approach the economy, it always ultimately boils down to the necessity of serious improvement in management and the overall economic mechanism."[1] At the same time the intensity of the reform discussion has increased and it has reached a breadth not seen for a long time.

The reasons for renewed reform efforts are clear for all to see. At the end of the 1970s, the Soviet economy entered a crisis phase in its development. Growth rates in the USSR's gross national product (calculated according to the Western concepts) fell to an annual average of 1.3 percent between 1979 and 1981; and from 1982 to 1984, when they averaged around 2.5 percent, they were also clearly below the level reached prior to 1978.[2] The targets of the tenth five-year plan were missed by a large margin. Above all, productivity progressed extremely unauspiciously.

The shortfall in growth was caused by a variety of reasons and was by no means entirely attributable to systemic factors.[3] Exogenous influences like bad weather, which affected the performance of the whole economy through a succession of harvest failures; effects of changes in economic structure such as the eastward shift of the economy; aging of capital stock and the marked slowdown in the growth of the labor force; consequences of serious bottlenecks that developed at the end of the 1970s, with their negative multiplier effects (in addition to agriculture these included the metals sector, investment, and transportation); and troubles with labor motivation and labor discipline all played a crucial part. Yet the shortfall in growth also underlined the deficiencies of present-day Soviet planning in relation to the principal tasks it has to perform: guiding the economy in accordance with the leadership's objectives, coordinating the operations of the economy, and ensuring the most efficient possible production processes. Thus, doubts were reinforced about the ability of the current set of economic planning instruments to cope with the structural problems of transition to an intensive type of economic development. Such transition is urgently needed.

From Andropov via Chernenko to Gorbachev

After his accession to power Andropov criticized the delaying policy of his predecessor and hastened to introduce a variety of different measures.[4] Chernenko followed his predecessor at any rate in his readiness to act (even if not in his ability to do so), and the new secretary general of the CPSU, Gorbachev, is also under considerable pressure to take action on economic policy. The question, however, is what to do.

Andropov initially surprised observers by admitting to a certain helplessness. He declared that he had no patent remedies at his disposal, and he thus revealed one of the principal barriers in the way of successful economic policy in the USSR: The frequently inadequate economic competence of top leadership. Distinguished economic specialists are not in fact very numerous at the top levels of political decisionmaking in the USSR, especially in the party leadership. None of the recent secretaries general could be described as such. Although circumscribed by the condition that as a matter of principle the economic system be kept stable, successful economic policy in the Soviet Union must consist of conceptualizing, introducing, implementing, and supervising a plethora of measures within the framework of a mosaic-like strategy, and it therefore depends crucially on a central leadership that is both decisive and economically competent. Possibly, Gorbachev has an advantage here, compared with his predecessors.

Andropov also criticized the state of the political economy of socialism, which offered no guidance for action in the matter of economic policy. This was closely followed by the Central Committee's criticism, directed at the economic research institute of the Academy of Sciences (the Institute of Economics) in the form of a CC resolution, combined with an urgent call—allegorically speaking—for a suitable libretto for the leadership's economic-policy opera.[5]

The weakness of economic theory and the uncertainty in leadership's economic policy orientation also make up the background for a distinct revival of reform discussion, which, despite some continuing ideological constraints, is taking place remarkably openly and for the moment has reached a high point in Tatyana Zaslavskaya's Novosibirsk Conference paper.[6] Yet other authors' contributions have also brought criticisms and far-reaching reform proposals which—cautiously, but nevertheless clearly—went beyond the limits of the established system. Meanwhile, however, economic policy orthodoxy is also marshalling its forces, as will be shown more fully below.

Apart from the adverse economic situation there is also a cyclical factor working to promote reform at this time: the proximity of the start of the twelfth five-year plan in 1986. In the past, in 1965, 1973 and 1979, reform measures were adopted during the period leading up to a new five-year plan. The approach of the new plan, however, puts the reformers under time pressure, something which—as we shall see—has seldom served reforms well.

Economic Policy and Economic Reform Policy

When one asks whether reforms are a way of increasing efficiency or a blind alley, it must be noted that efficiency—quite apart from the influence of exogenous factors—depends not only on reform policy but on economic policy and on policy in general, and that these represent in a certain sense an alternative, or at least a complement, to economic reform. Andropov, at the start of his short period in office, relied more on economic policy than on economic reform. Key words, in this respect, are: reduction of plan pressure, stepping up of investment activity, tightening of investment procedures, general emphasis on discipline, stricter labor laws, adjustments to the pay system, overcoming sectoral bottlenecks, making use of international economic relations, etc.

The result of this policy—and of an improvement in exogenous factors, namely the weather—was a revival of economic growth (which, to be sure, has since slowed down again). As a consequence, the pressure for reform temporarily abated, and the priority of econoimc policy over economic reform seemed to persist. The academic elite among committed reformers immediately saw a danger here. Abel Aganbegyan hastened to warn against being misled by the temporary upswing.[7] Certainly an economic revival had been achieved in 1983 and 1984—and for this he primarily praised Andropov. However, only "superficial reserves" were uncovered. In the longer term, in view of the dramatically increasing scarcity of factor supplies, there was no way out without a reform—and a comprehensive reform at that.

After the upswing in the Soviet economy was curbed by the bad grain harvest of 1984 and also by a loss of momentum in industry at the turn of the year 1984–85, Soviet politicians—Gorbachev in particular—stressed the necessity of sustained economic policy measures. This does not, however, indicate a readiness for comprehensive reform in the sense of a change in the basic institutions and functional mechanism of the administratively planned economy, but rather an imminent revival of a "revised economic policy" of the Andropov type. As will be shown later, this is better described as "comprehensive in breadth" than "radical in depth."

Even after the recent change of power in the Kremlin, a radical reform that would alter the system is not currently on the Soviet leadership's economic policy agenda. What will be implemented or planned in the field of reform are more limited measures in the six main areas of reform familiar from the past. The most significant of these is the "economic mechanism," enterprise planning, and micro-economic steering. As far as the other areas are concerned, we shall first indicate just the major policy headings:[8]

Organization of Planning and Economic Administration. Upgrading of the functions of "staff bodies" like the CC Secretariat in the party sphere and Gosplan in the state sphere, combined with organizational changes within the economic administration (abolition of the industrial associations) and some shift of decisionmaking to the union republics and to the level of production associations and enterprises.

Planning Methods. Renewed emphasis on strengthening the five-year plan as the most important plan governing the economic activity of enterprises, expanded use of automatic plan accounting systems and the so-called target-program method, as well as revival of regional elements.

External Enterprise Organization. Continuation of the establishment and reorganization of production associations, so-called scientific and production associations, and agro-industrial associations.

Internal Enterprise Organization. Development of the brigade system into the main form of labor organization in industry and construction and into the central element in remuneration and bonuses, with limited expansion of participation.

Prices. New 1982 industrial wholesale prices, with alterations in relative prices but essentially unchanged price-setting principles and only partial extension of the functions of prices.

From Large-Scale Experiment to Reform

In the crucial area of the economic mechanism, the microeconomic steering, an experiment (ambitiously called a "large-scale experiment") was started in 1984 in five industrial ministries at all-union, republic, and local levels, and was extended in 1985 to twenty-one other ministries and to parts of the service sector. The assumption is that this will become the basis for a new round of reform in Soviet industrial planning. The need for rapid improvement in light of persistent and increasingly serious problems, and the proximity of the twelfth five-year plan starting in 1986, make it at least improbable that other proposals will be prepared, tested, and favoured. All the same, the adoption of the principles of the experiment throughout the whole of industry is likely to be more a process than a one-time measure.

Much of what is planned for the experiment is familiar from the reforms of 1965, 1973, and 1979. In particular, there is unmistakably a reorientation towards the "Kosygin-Liberman" reform of the late 1960s. Thus there is once again talk of "extending the rights and increasing the independence of enterprises" (Gorbachev).

The four principal elements of the experiment are:[9]

1. Reform of the time-frame of planning by insisting that plans are drawn up on time and that medium-term plans remain unchanged throughout the five-year period.
2. Expansion of enterprises' scope for decisionmaking by allowing production associations and enterprises to participate in drawing up plans at all stages of the planning process, by reducing the number of compulsory plan indicators, and by strengthening the role of inter-enterprise contracts.
3. Extension of the financial autonomy of production associations (enterprises) by giving them control over their production development funds and over portions of the funds for the development of science and technology allocated by ministries. This is to be accomplished by the use of depreciation allowances to finance technical re-equipment, by the expansion of credit latitude for financing investment, and by transition to the so-called normative method of deductions from profits, a system of profit taxation under which successful enterprises are supposed to have more profits left to use for the purposes of investment and bonus payment.
4. The system of material incentives is to be refined and improved. The amount of the bonus fund depends primarily on fulfillment of delivery plans based on the contracts concluded. If the delivery plan is not fulfilled, senior employees receive no bonus. According to specific conditions in particular enterprises, additional bonus indicators are used: Special bonuses can be paid to leading personnel for the development and production of particularly valuable products. Subsidies in case of losses resulting from technical innovations are supposed to mitigate the risk involved in innovation and increase willingness to innovate. The development of the enterprise wage fund is linked by a norm to the expansion of output. Savings in the wage fund from reducing employment can be used for paying performance supplements to wages and salaries.

So much for the major provisions of the experiment. Presumably, essential elements will become the basis for a general reform of all industry.

Reform Within the System

A new reform following the principles of the experiment would not mean any change in the basic institutions and functional mechanism of Soviet planning. To that extent, certain specific functional problems that are fundamentally connected with administrative planning remain unsolved: overloading of the center with tasks that it cannot solve as the complexity of the economy increases, unsatisfactory information about prices as parameters for decentralized decisionmaking, inadequate sanctions mechanisms, insufficient ability to adapt the material supply system to the expanded financial latitude granted to enterprises. Yet, the question remains whether, despite all the persistent structural problems, partial improvements are not still possible, the more so as in principle the experiment is a move in the right direction of relieving the load on the center and shifting decisionmaking (of course only to a limited degree) down to the enterprises.

Initially the Soviet press is carrying both positive and negative reports on the experiment. Not surprisingly, the positive elements predominate; the claque is in position, as it used to be once upon a time at the opera. As far as the likely effectiveness of a reform modelled on the experiment is concerned, the negative phenomena, which are visible in both the horizontal and the vertical links of production units, are of course more important. As far as horizontal lines are concerned, there is criticism of both lack of sales opportunities for increased output and, more often, lack of supplies of components and materials of all kinds, with the result that the extended financial autonomy cannot be utilized. As for vertical links, ministries are criticized for persistent interference. At this point the observer who has been following Soviet development for some time is overcome by a feeling of déja vu.

Types of reform and their effects are familiar from past experiences. During the twenty years of Soviet reform history mentioned above, particular organizational principles, planning procedures and methods of enterprise steering succeeded one another without bringing about any change in the traditional basic structure of the planning system and the fundamental pattern of interaction between the units involved in the economic process (central management organs, ministries, production associations and enterprises). All the reforms since 1965 have left the following basic elements of the traditional planning system untouched: the priority of central political decisions on production and utilization, the transmission of these decisions via administrative hierarchies, the predominance of compulsory directives over price signals and the principle of plan fulfillment as the primary criterion of success at the enterprise level. Consequently Western observers rightly continue to speak of "reforms within the system," and concepts like "improvement" and "perfecting" imply the same understanding on the Soviet side.

Krylov or Popper?

Judging by previous experience, what are the prospects for success of a new reform of similar type? In the West, as in the East, they are judged on the basis of two different paradigms, which can be referred to as the Krylov paradigm and the Popperovich paradigm.

The Krylov paradigm assesses "reforms within the system" using the parallel of the Russian poet's fable in which a quartet of animal musicians, full of hope that they will produce a more harmonious sound, keep changing places, only to produce the same unmelodious screeching over and over again.

The Popperovich paradigm[10]—piecemeal social engineering according to the formula that what is right for London's (or Vienna's) Popper is right for Moscow's Popperovich—holds that, despite all the imperfections of the present forms of planning, learning processes are, in principle, possible in socialist planned economies. According to this paradigm past experience tells us nothing about the likely success of similarly structured measures in the future. In particular, gains in efficiency are thought to be possible through "reforms within the system" by means of a combination of more consistent reform measures with better accompanying conditions.

Unfortunately neither the Krylov nor the Popperovich hypothesis can be satisfactorily tested empirically. To do this we would have to compare efficiency data for the Soviet planning system before and after the implementation of reforms. But which system: the system of the reform model, of the legal norms and administrative regulations, of the day-by-day routine, the system of the first, the second, the black economy? In short, it is scarcely possible to determine in precisely what concrete form the planning system actually works. And how would one eliminate non-systemic effects, the influence of exogenous factors, structural effects, changes in factor supply, consequences of economic policy decisions, changes in motivation and many other elements from the data relating to efficiency? The problem of empirical measurement of the effects of reform is unsolved and may well be insoluble in principle.

All the same, some reflections can be offered on the possibility of learning processes in administratively planned economies. In the first place, whatever structural weaknesses an administrative planning system may show, there can be no doubt that it is in principle possible to improve it. Improvements would only be impossible if within all its limits it were already optimally constructed, but this case would be pure chance and can be excluded. Thus, learning processes with a positive effect on efficiency within definite limits—limits that are set by the functional mode of the system—should generally be possible. They presumably can be made most successfully where the structures are simple and there are no serious conflicts of interest. This may apply, for instance, to the case of planning techniques or intra-enterprise organization, where, apart from reforms, improvements of professional standards also have the effect of raising efficiency.

In these areas, besides "reforms from above," there are also numerous "reforms from below," i.e., improvements of all kinds on the basis of individual and collective initiative. Again and again these are held up by the Soviet press as praiseworthy examples. The benign and malign forms of the second (shadow) economy also represent a particular type of "reform from below."

Problematical Learning Processes

Doubts about the possibility of successfully organizing learning processes are, however, in order in a field as complex and fraught with conflicting interests as micro-economic steering, in other words, the economic mechanism. In the first place, it is hard to determine the direction and dosage of measures intended to improve the system. The proper measure of centralization or decentralization, the appropriate concrete structure of indicator systems or incentive mechanisms can change, depending both on objective factors like resource supply and on subjective factors like the structure of the planners' goals and their level of ambition.

Further difficulties arise in the process of the formulation and implementation of reforms. Soviet leadership generally introduces reforms late, following the motto: as late as possible, not before it is absolutely necessary. Thus, from the outset, reform is caught up in an atmosphere of haste. Consequently, reform decisions are often ill-prepared, inconsistent, and wide open as to concept and time, to borrow Gert Leptin's description.[11] The institutional pluralism from which reform designs emanate, and the conflicting interests of leadership, administration, and enterprises lead as a rule to dilution, delay, or even obstruction of proposed measures. The less competent and skilled the leadership, the easier it is to dilute and delay reform. On the other hand, the worse the economic situation that leads to the reform, the more pronounced is leadership's subsequent inclination to intervene, thus undermining the reform.

What has been said above may suffice to make it clear that a number of preconditions must be fulfilled if success greater than in the past is to be expected from renewed partial reforms. Of these preconditions, the following four are of particular importance:

1. The conception of the reform would have to be more consistent than its predecessors.
2. The implementation of the concept would have to be more consistently carried out by a decisive leadership.
3. The reform policy would have to be accompanied by a more helpful plan attitude (the most important thing is a reduction of plan pressure) and a structural policy more specifically designed to eliminate disproportions than in the past.
4. The reform policy would have to be supported by "readiness to participate" on the part of the population.

Under Chernenko's weak and conceptually vague leadership, even approximate satisfaction of these distinctly "heroic" conditions could scarcely be expected. Under Gorbachev, on the other hand, the prospects for more successful "piecemeal engineering" have undoubtedly improved. To a much greater extent than did his predecessors, he combines a clear analysis of the situation with a concept of how to overcome the difficulties, the energy to tackle them and—because of his age—time to put his ideas into effect. Still, the above mentioned difficulties will probably be hard to overcome, even for a leader with a concept and with the capacity to act. In any case, at present it is still an open question whether the reforms now introduced suggest the Popperovich or the Krylov paradigm. Yet, even the latter would not necessarily mean giving up any possibility of raising efficiency. Even with persistent problems in the economic mechanism, there are a number of opportunities for measures in other policy fields, such as investment policy, which could produce improvements in efficiency.[12]

The Comprehensive Reform and Its Limits

All the same, there is an increasing number of voices in the USSR that consider improvements of this kind insufficient and also cast doubt on the prevailing idea that it is possible to improve the planning system without fundamental changes. The best known example of this view is Zaslavskaya's April 1983 conference paper, the so-called "Novosibirsk study." "Strictly speaking," the author notes,[13] "in the preceding decades attempts have been made over and over again to introduce individual progressive methods into the existing system, which subsequently have been eliminated again as being incompatible with its spirit." The analytical conclusion is that "it is not possible to improve the mechanism of economic management that originated many decades ago by exchanging its mostly obsolete components for more efficient ones, one at a time." Finally, the bottom line for reform policy is that the replacement of the existing but now obsolete system of management must be "comprehensive and fundamental."

A model for such a reform, the author concedes, is, however, not available as yet. But the direction she has in mind is clear from her remark that more active use of automatic regulators in combination with the extention of market relations is necessary to ensure a balanced production process. Zaslavskaya refers to other authors, among whom the economic jurist, B. Kurashvili, is particularly interesting. He puts forward a planning model that he himself calls "regulative planning" and that can be understood as an administratively registered, adjusted, and confirmed market process.[14]

For the foreseeable future, however, a fundamental and comprehensive reform of this kind, structured like a market economy, will encounter virtually insuperable barriers. For one thing, there are the economic difficulties of a radical reform. First, there is the substantial risk to the stability of growth, employment, and prices, not least on account of considerable repressed inflation. There are other general problems. The Soviet economy has developed for past decades under a system of administrative economic planning. Consequently, economic structures and behavior and motivation structures developed that in all probability do not fit the requirements of a market economy system.

Besides economic constraints, there are also political limits to reform. The latter have both domestic and foreign policy aspects. Domestically, the communist party's rule and supervision are based on the use of administrative economic planning, which allows for comprehensive control over society according to set economic and political objectives. A far-reaching, market-oriented reform could also mean a loss of control of nationalities policy for the center in Moscow. From the point of view of foreign policy, the administratively planned economy reinforces Soviet hegemony in Eastern Europe.

Yet it is not only the leadership that is afraid of the effects of a fundamental market-oriented economic reform; so are many other social groups that consequently exert their influence against such changes. When, finally, we add the ideological constraints on reform that derive from the present-day Soviet brand of Marxism-Leninism, the overall conclusion is well justified: Despite growing criticism, the phase of administrative socialism in the USSR is by no means at an end yet.

For this a new "revolution from above" would be needed, which is unthinkable without a revolutionary situation and a charismatic leader. What the "doer" Gorbachev could succeed in achieving is improvements in efficiency using a combination of tighter operating policy and moderate reform. Transformation of the system is not on the new secretary general's list of priorities. Nor, therefore, should the West's expectations move in this direction.

Notes

1. *Pr*, 24 April 1985.

2. These figures and the data on productivity trends are taken from CIA, *Handbook of Economic Statistics 1984*, Washington, D.C. (September 1984), p. 68.

3. For details on this see H.-H. Höhmann, *Berichte des BIOst*, no. 28, 1984.

4. H.-H. Höhmann in *Sowietunion* 1982/83 (München 1983), pp. 113 ff.

5. H.-H. Höhmann, *Berichte des BIOst*, No. 14, 1984.

6. German text in OE, No. 1, 1984.

7. A.G. Aganbegyan, *EKO*, No. 6, 1984.

8. M. Bornstein, *Soviet Studies*, Vol. XXXVII, No. 1 (January 1985).

9. *Pr*, 26 July 1983.

10. A. Nove, *The Economics of Feasible Socialism*, London, Boston (Sydney, 1983), pp. 213 ff.

11. G. Leptin, "Das 'Neue Ökonomische System' Mitteldeutschlands," in K.C. Thalheim and H.-H. Höhmann (eds.) *Wirtschaftsreformen in Osteuropa* (Cologne, 1968), p. 118.

12. See also H.-H. Höhmann, "The Soviet Economy at the End of the Eleventh Five-Year Plan: Counting on Gorbachev," in this volume, Chapter 13.

13. *OE*, No. 1, 1984, A1 ff.

14. B.P. Kurashvili, *Sovetskoe gosudarstvo i pravo*, No. 6 (1982), pp. 38 ff.

19
Soviet Foreign Trade Restricted by Foreign Policy?

Christian Meier

In his report to the XXV CPSU Congress in 1976, Secretary General Brezhnev observed that in foreign economic relations, politics and economics, diplomacy and business, and industrial production and trade, were all interwoven in a single entity, and that their direction required a comprehensive approach.[1] He thus made it clear that the Soviet Union's attitudes to foreign trade are determined by a variety of different political and economic factors, both internal and external. At the same time, therefore, he raised the fundamental question of the importance of political considerations in Soviet foreign trade activities. On this topic, as far as inter-system economic relations are concerned, the political declaration of the CMEA Summit conference of 14 June 1984 stated that political detente in the preceding decade had promoted the development of mutually advantageous relations between states and that without this precondition no lasting basis for the reinforcement of detente could be created.[2] One would thus have to assume that the relationship between politics and economics in inter-system economic relations was an automatic one, such that good political relations between states lead directly to increased economic relations and, conversely, that any deterioration in the political situation is bound to have an immediate and direct impact on economic connections.

No Automatic Link Between Economic and Foreign Policy

The course of Soviet economic relations with the West during the 1970s does not confirm the existence of any such automatic link between foreign policy and foreign trade behavior. Instead, it conveys the impression that, despite a close mutual relationship, both fields possess a considerable degree of independence. The marked upswing in Soviet economic relations with Western countries up to 1975 was indeed also influenced by a favorable East-West political climate, yet was largely attributable to the stimulating effect of economic factors. These included strong economic growth in Western industrialized countries, an advantageous international financial framework and a great Soviet need for development.[3] When the growth of the USSR's economic relations with the West subsequently levelled off, it was by no means due only to the increased tension and friction that had developed in East-West relations—though that certainly affected the atmosphere and the range of cooperation—but also principally to the disappearance of favorable economic factors and the change in both world economic conditions and internal economic circumstances which circumscribed Soviet foreign trade activities.

In cases of conflict between political and economic interests in bilateral relations with individual states, the Soviet Union has reacted in the past in various ways. It considered the Jackson-Vanik Amendment to the Act of Ratification of the 1972 Soviet-American Trade Treaty a good reason to annul this Treaty at the beginning of January 1975; but it did not take it as a reason to reduce economic relations with the US drastically. A long-term agreement concluded with the US the same year led in fact to a considerable subsequent increase in Soviet grain imports from the United States.[4]

Political and Economic Framework

When we examine the political and economic framework of Soviet foreign trade activities during the period of this survey, we find the Kremlin leadership facing a very complicated situation surrounding foreign trade policy decisions. The worsening of the foreign policy framework, noted in our analysis above, has not only persisted but has even been exacerbated in some fields. The most prominent factors have been:

- The imposition of economic sanctions against the Soviet Union by President Reagan on 29 December 1981.
- The new Western foreign trade strategy vis-à-vis the Warsaw Pact/CMEA countries announced by President Reagan on 13 November 1982.
- The NATO INF deployment, possibly leading to increased diversion of Soviet rsources from the economic to the military sector.

This negative foreign policy picture was brightened slightly by the signing of a long-term, and above all "embargo-safe" grain agreement between the USSR and the USA on 25 August 1983. Another positive element was the continuing efforts of West European countries to reconcile the essential security demands of the Western alliance and their own legitimate economic interests in trade with the East. The US, on the other hand, attempted to place additional restrictions on economic links with the Soviet Union.

At the same time, however, there were a number of economic factors that favored further growth of Soviet foreign trade relations, above all with Western industrialized countries. These included:

- The necessity of switching the Soviet economy into a path of intensive development by means of fundamental modernization of production capacity in major industrial branches.
- The development of new sources of raw materials and energy, so that increased raw material and energy exports to the West would provide the funds to finance imports.
- The 1982 food program to stabilize the supply of agricultural products to the population, in view of the static or declining agricultural output since the middle of the 1970s.

Setting the Course of Foreign Trade Policy

Under these circumstances, discussions among the top Soviet leadership about possible reactions to deterioration in the external political framework of Soviet foreign trade activities were unavoidable. There were evidently two fundamentally different views under consideration, one of which leaned toward a retreat into greater self-sufficiency and the other toward expansion of Soviet economic involvement in the world economy.[5] In this dispute the advocates of a "new economic autarky" (to use H. Machowski's phrase) lost out, at least for the time being.

At the CMEA summit conference in Moscow in June 1984, the Soviet Union together with other CMEA countries voted clearly against economic isolation, and they expressed interest in "developing commercial cooperation with the capitalist states and their enterprises and firms," in the spirit of the ECSC Final Act and the Madrid ECSC Follow-up Meetings Agreement, and in concluding an agreement between CMEA and EEC. True, these intentions were publicly linked with the demand for an improvement in the climate of East-West relations. Yet at the same time Soviet leadership carefully sought to decouple beneficial economic relations from political tensions with individual countries. Regional and sectoral differentiation among the USSR's foreign trading partners was therefore virtually obligatory.

As a result of Western economic sanctions, the Kremlin leaders' sensitivity in matters of economic security increased; consequently, the decision in favor of economic relations with the West, even under restrictive foreign policy conditions, was accompanied by measures to reinforce the economic, scientific, and technical independence of the Soviet Union and the other CMEA countries and to strengthen economic links with other socialist countries, primarily Yugoslavia and the People's Republic of China.[6] According to the "Declaration of the Principle Directions for Further Development and Intensification of Economic and Scientific and Technical cooperation between CMEA member countries,"[7] cooperation in individual sectors of the agro-industrial complex is to be stepped up. Soviet leadership is also interested in focussing intra-bloc trade even more than hitherto on the USSR, so as to clear the deficits accumulated by smaller CMEA countries and to orient the structure of this trade to meet the requirements of the Soviet market. In order to make better use of the scientific and technical potential in the CMEA for the future modernization of the USSR's economy, a "comprehensive program of scientific and technical progress for fifteen to twenty years" is to be worked out and cooperation in the field of high technology promoted.

Trade Development and the Regional Structure of Exports and Imports

As compared with the results in other sectors of the economy, and in spite of complicated political and economic conditions, the foreign trade sector was an important positive item in 1983–84. Clear evidence of this is provided by the development of foreign trade, the volume of which reached a figure of 139.7 billion TR[8] in 1984. Compared with the preceding year's figure of 127.5 billion TR this was an increase of 9.6 percent. The nominal growth of foreign trade thus accelerated somewhat again, for in 1983 it had dropped to 6.6 percent. The underlying real increase amounted to 4.1 percent.

In 1984 Soviet commodity exports came to 74.4 billion TR, which was an increase of 9.6 percent over the 1983 figure. In the very same year, exports of goods rose by only 7.5 percent from 63.2 billion to 67.9 billion TR. This figure was equivalent to a real increase of 3.7 percent, which corresponded exactly to the growth in national income produced. The value of Soviet commodity imports in 1984 amounted to 65.3 billion TR; compared with the previous year's figure of 59.6 billion TR, this meant a 9.6 percent expansion. In 1983 imports of goods rose by only 5.6 percent in nominal terms, and 4.5 percent after allowing for price changes. The figure for the real increase in imports thus exceeded the rise in national income produced by one percentage point. In this way, the Soviet economy once again opened up a little more to the outside world. When we examine the development of Soviet foreign trade as to the importance of the three groups of foreign trade partners during the period 1983–84, we find distinct and unmistakable shifts in the relative weight they carry.

The regional structure moved steadily in favor of the socialist countries. Commodity exchanges with them increased by 9.9 percent (and 11.2 percent with CMEA members) in 1983 and by 12.5 percent (and 11.5 percent with CMEA members) in 1984. Accordingly, their share of Soviet foreign trade turnover increased from 56 percent in 1983 to 57.5 percent in 1984, and that of the CMEA countries from 51.2 percent to 52.0 percent. The high nominal growth in Soviet exports to these countries of 10.5 percent (and 10.6 percent to CMEA members) in 1983 concealed stagnation of the real volume of deliveries because export prices had risen by almost the same amount, 10–11 percent.[9] If we assume, as J. Vanous does, an average increase in Soviet export prices of 7–8 percent in 1984,[10] a nominal increase in exports to the socialist countries of 11.6 percent (and 10.8 percent to CMEA members) could have represented a real increase of around 4 percent. Soviet commodity purchases from these countries grew by a nominal 9.3 percent

TABLE 19.1
Regional Structure of Soviet Foreign Trade

	Million TR		Increase over previous year		Percentage share	
	1983	1984	1983	1984	1983	1984
EXPORTS						
All countries	67,890.6	74,383.7	7.5	9.6	100.0	100.0
Socialist countries	37,714.0	42,106.3	10.5	11.6	55.6	56.6
CMEA	34,449.3	38,164.6	10.6	10.8	50.7	51.3
Other	3,264.7	3,941.7	9.3	20.7	4.8	5.3
OECD countries	19,652.9	21,349.4	4.3	8.6	28.9	28.7
EC	13,739.4	15,288.2	3.2	11.3	20.2	20.6
Developing countries	10,523.7	10,928.0	3.4	3.8	15.5	14.7
IMPORTS						
All countries	59,589.2	65,327.3	5.6	9.6	100.0	100.0
Socialist countries	33,695.7	38,220.0	9.3	13.4	56.5	58.5
CMEA	30,811.5	34,587.3	11.8	12.3	51.7	52.9
Other	2,884.2	3,632.7	-11.6	26.0	4.8	5.6
OECD countries	18,718.8	19,574.1	-0.9	4.6	31.4	30.0
EC	8,570.4	8,342.0	16.5	-2.7	14.4	12.8
Developing countries	7,174.7	7,533.2	7.0	5.0	12.0	11.5

Sources: USSR foreign trade yearbooks, *Vneshnyaya torgovlya*, No. 3, 1985, supplement.

(and 11.8 percent from CMEA members) in 1983. Estimating the increase in import prices at around 5 percent, real imports from these countries probably rose by 4–5 percent. The renewed rise in Soviet imports from the socialist countries in 1984, by 13.4 percent (and 12.3 percent from CMEA members), was due, for one thing, to increased purchases from Yugoslavia and, especially, from the People's Republic of China, with which the Soviet Union would like to improve political relations. For another, they were presumably the first effect of Soviet pressure on the smaller CMEA countries to deliver more and qualitatively better products for the Soviet market so as to halt the rise in, or even slowly reduce, their trade deficits with the USSR.

The Soviet Union's trade with the OECD countries registered only marginal growth of 1.7 percent in 1983. In 1984 the increase was somewhat larger, at 6.7 percent. However, the Western industrial countries' share in Soviet foreign trade turnover fell from 30.1 percent in 1983 to 29.3 percent in 1984. The nominal 4.3 percent rise in Soviet commodity deliveries to the OECD area in 1983 corresponded to a real increase of around 10–13 percent because the estimated decline of 11–14 percent in the dollar-denominated prices of primary energy sources, which constitute 80 percent of Soviet exports to the West, was offset by a rise in the quantities delivered. The nominal expansion of 8.6 percent in exports to the OECD area in 1984 probably meant a real growth rate at least as high because the Soviet

Union was able to increase its energy exports there thanks to the economic recovery in the Western countries. Moreover, it is also likely to have profited from the boom in the value of the dollar.[11]

The nominal 0.9 percent decline in imports from the OECD countries in 1983 corresponded to a real increase of 6 percent because prices of imported goods declined by about 7 percent. Among them, a rise of 20 percent in machinery purchases was particularly noteworthy and more than counterbalancing the drop in grain purchases in the same year.[12] The 4.6 percent rise in imports from the Western countries in 1984 is likely to have been influenced principally by a large requirement for agricultural raw materials and foodstuffs.

Just how much the Soviet Union was guided by the dictates of economic pragmatism was shown by its behavior vis-à-vis those countries on which it sought to place the chief responsibility for the worsening of the foreign policy framework for international economic activity. The repeated threat to the Federal Republic of Germany that in case of INF deployment, it would reduce economic relations was quietly withdrawn. In the expectation of good opportunities to sell energy and raw materials on the German market and earn more hard currency, Soviet leadership decided in favor of uninterrupted expansion of economic cooperation (with a 6.8 percent increase in 1984). Its economic relations with the other West European NATO countries, which likewise began with INF deployment at the end of 1983, also continued to develop in accordance with available opportunities and without spectacular initiatives. After an "embargo safe," long-term grain agreement with the US was signed, the latter was confirmed in its role as a welcome stop-gap supplier in years of bad grain harvests. The decline in economic relations with Japan (−5 percent in 1984) was attributable not to the exacerbation of already existing conflicts, but to the expiring of various major projects and to the growing attractiveness of the Chinese market for Japanese industry. Conversely, Finland discovered in 1984 that exemplary foreign policy conduct vis-à-vis the Soviet Union does not necessarily elicit an immediate response in terms of increased foreign trade activity from Moscow: Its commodity turnover with the Soviet Union declined by 8.6 percent.

Soviet trade with developing countries rose by 4.8 percent in 1983 and slightly less in 1984, 4.3 percent. Their share of total Soviet foreign trade dropped from 13.9 percent in 1983 to 13.2 percent in 1984. The boom in Soviet goods exported to the Third World in 1982 (when they rose 17.4 percent), was the result of large arms sales amounting to US $8.1 billion. This was followed by a rise of only 3.4 percent in 1983,[13] but this was so primarily because the market for weapons sales could no longer be significantly expanded.

As regards imports from Third World countries in 1983, the rise of 7.0 percent was principally attributable to increased oil purchases from the OPEC countries which were then reexported to individual OPEC states. The modest 5 percent rise in imports from the Third World in 1984 was probably caused primarily by a fall in food purchases from some developing countries such as Argentina and Brazil, and in oil purchases from Iran.[14]

Commodity Structure of Exports and Imports

On the export side, by far the most prominent item in the commodity structure is "fuels and primary energy sources." This is followed at some distance by the category "machinery, equipment and means of transportation." This latter, in turn, holds the leading position on the import side, followed by "agricultural raw materials and foodstuffs." A close interrelationship exists between these two, such that the proportion of machinery in imports rises when there is a good harvest and declines when the harvest fails.

The proportion of "fuels and primary energy sources" in exports rose in 1983 by 1.4 percent to 53.7 percent and climbed again in 1984 to 54.4 percent. The share of these items in exports to CMEA countries was 50 percent in 1983 and 51.2 percent in 1984, and to the industrialized West it reached 80 percent and 81 percent in these years. In order to fulfill its contractual obligations to deliver energy and fuels to the OECD countries, the Soviet Union had to import, according to Western estimates, 2.5 million tons of oil in 1983 and 14.1 million tons in 1984 from the Middle East, which it immediately passed on to Western markets.

The share of the product group "machinery, equipment and means of transportation" in total exports declined slightly in 1983, by 0.4 percent, to 12.5 percent and remained at this level in 1984. The socialist countries took 73 percent of Soviet mechanical engineering exports[15] (and 72 percent in 1983). Industrial consumer goods played only a marginal role in Soviet exports: The proportion dropped fractionally further in 1983, from 1.9 percent to 1.8 percent, and maintained this level in 1984. The manufacturing industry's performance and export weakness has long been striking. One significant product category always goes unmentioned in the official data on the commodity structure of Soviet exports: weapons and military equipment. Insofar as information is available, it is based on US sources. Thus J. Vanous maintains that in the years 1983 and 1984 weapons and equipment came to exactly 20 percent of exports to the non-socialist world.[16]

As far as the commodity structure of Soviet imports is concerned, the proportion of the "machinery, equipment and means of transportation" category showed a substantial rise of 3.8 percent in 1983, to 38.2 percent. The reason for this was the latitude provided by the drop in agricultural imports. The picture was somewhat different in 1984, when the category accounted for only 36.6 percent of imports.

The drop in imports of food and agricultural raw materials recorded in 1983, from 23.7 percent to 20.5 percent, did not last. In 1984 the proportion rose again to 22.5 percent. The reasons for this was the bad harvest, which, according to Western experts' estimates, made it necessary to import over 50 million tons of grain in the period from 1 July 1984 to 30 June 1985. By the end of April 1985, the Soviet Union had already imported around

50 million tons, with a value of US$6.85 billion, exceeding the 1981/82 import figure of 46 million tons. The largest supplier of grain has been the US—21.5 million tons since 1 July 1984. The USSR bought over 6 million tons from the European Community, and 6.4 million tons each from Canada and Argentina. India contributed 1.5 million tons and the People's Republic of China 1 million tons towards meeting the Soviet Union's grain requirements.[17] The proportion of industrial consumer goods in imports declined by 1.2 percent in 1983 to 11.5 percent, but rose again by 0.2 percent in 1984 to 11.7 percent.

Trade Balance

Since the USSR does not publish any figures on its balance of payments, our analysis of its exchange relations has to be confined to the visible trade balance. The Soviet Union achieved a trade surplus amounting to 8.3 billion TR in 1983, and exceeded this with a new record figure of 9.1 billion TR in 1984. Around 43 percent of this balance (and 48 percent in 1983) was earned in trade with the socialist countries. Since the transition to the Moscow price-setting formula in 1975, Soviet trade with the CMEA has shown a large surplus. In the period from 1976 to 1984 the Soviet Union delivered a total of 24 billion TR worth of goods more to the other CMEA countries than it received from them. This sum is equivalent to about two-thirds of Soviet imports from the other CMEA countries in 1984.

The condensed Soviet foreign trade statistics do not allow us to judge whether the export surplus with the Third World of 3.35 billion TR (equivalent to US $4.5 billion) in 1983 and 3.4 billion TR in 1984 represented earnings in hard currency or whether these were for the most part credit-financed deliveries, including arms.

On trade with the OECD countries, which is settled in convertible currency, the Soviet Union achieved an export surplus of 934 million TR in 1983 and raised this to 1.8 billion TR in 1984. Revenue from energy exports accounted for over 80 percent of the total foreign currency earnings. In addition to this the USSR sold 56 tons of gold in the West in 1983, receiving an estimated US $760 million for it. In 1984, according to Western sources of information, Soviet gold sales more than tripled and amounted to nearly 200 tons.[18] According to OECD and BIS statistics, the Soviet Union's gross hard currency debt as of 31 December 1983 came to US $23.1 billion. Deducting assets of 10.7 billion left a net indebtedness of US $12.4 billion.[19] There is obviously no way the level of debt could possibly be considered critical in the case of the USSR, which is deemed a sound-risk debtor in Western banking circles.

Outlook

Since the change of top leadership in the Soviet Union there have been signs that foreign trade will find much more extensive use as a growth factor in the Soviet economy. The new CPSU secretary general, Gorbachev, has declared the intensification and modernization of the Soviet economy the priority goal of his domestic policy. Following his basic foreign policy conception that detente in East-West relations has not been irreparably torpedoed,[20] he has offered the heads of state and government of the leading West European countries a political dialog parallel to the current Soviet-US negotiations and declared his interest in wide-ranging economic, scientific, and technical cooperation.

The expansion of Soviet economic relations with the West will, however, continue to depend very much on internal and world economic conditions. The key questions are whether the Soviet Union will succeed in producing larger quantities of energy and raw materials for export, whether the recovery in the Western economies will be consolidated, so that higher imports of energy and raw materials are possible, and what the trends in prices of these commodities will be in Western markets.

As regards the political framework for an extension of economic cooperation with Western countries, no perceptible relaxation of US regulations on technology transfer can be expected in the forseeable future. The USSR's access to the US market is made yet more difficult by the Reagan administration's political "linkages" policy, clearly demonstrable economic interests of US businesses notwithstanding. Hence, the regional structure of Soviet imports from the West is likely to shift even more in favor of the European OECD countries and Japan, as well as the newly industrialized countries.

As Gorbachev stated at the Central Committee plenum of the CPSU on 23 April 1985,[21] the Soviet leadership in its economic relations with the CMEA countries will press for prompt implementation of the resolutions of the CMEA summit conference.

Notes

1. *Pr,* 25 February 1976.
2. *Vneshnyaya torgovlya,* No. 7 (1984), p. 6.
3. G. Joetze, "Politische Aspekte der West-Ost-Wirtschaftsbeziehungen," in H.-H. Höhmann and H. Vogel (eds.) *Osteuropas Wirtschaftsprobleme und die Ost-West-Beziehungen* (Baden-Baden, 1984), pp. 299–305; H. Machowski, "Sowjetunion," in R. Rode and H. D. Jacobsen (eds.) *Wirtschaftskrieg oder Entspannung? Eine politische Bilanz der Ost-West-Wirtschaftsbeziehungen* (Bonn, 1984), pp. 276–81.
4. See "The Soviet Union and the United States" in *The Soviet Union 1974–75* (London, 1976), pp. 205–11; see also M. Görtemaker, "Soviet Policy Towards the United States," in this volume, Chapter 20.
5. N. Shmeljov, "The Soviet Union and World Economic Relations," *International Affairs,* No. 1 (1984), pp. 12–20.
6. H.-H. Höhmann and Christian Meier, *Berichte des BIOst,* No. 55, 1985.
7. *ND,* 16 June 1984.
8. *Ekonomicheskaya gazeta,* No. 12 (1985), pp. 20 ff.
9. J. Vanous, "Soviet Foreign Trade Performance 1983," in Wharton EFA, *Centrally Planned Economies Current Analysis,* Vol. III, No. 22–23 (1984), p. 2.

10. J. Vanous, "Soviet Foreign Trade Performance During the First Nine Months of 1984," in Wharton EFA, *Centrally Planned Economies Current Analysis*, Vol. V No. 1–2 (1985), p. 4.

11. J. Bethkenhagen, DIW, *Wochenbericht*, No. 13 (1985), p. 165.

12. See note 9.

13. See note 9.

14. See note 10.

15. *Nachrichten für Aussenhandel*, 27 March 1985.

16. J. Vanous, "Soviet Foreign Trade Performance in 1984," in Wharton EFA, *Centrally Planned Economies Current Analysis*, Vol. V, No. 31–32 (1985), p. 11.

17. *Frankfurter Allgemeine Zeitung*, 20 May 1985.

18. *East-West*, Vol. 16, No. 364 (18 June 1985).

19. K. Schröder, "Ost-West-Finanzbeziehungen nach der Krise 1981–83," in the supplement to the weekly *Das Parlament*, Vol. 5 (1985), pp. 42–45.

20. *Pr*, 28 June 1984.

21. *Pr*, 24 April 1985.

Part Three

Foreign Policy

20
Gorbachev: A New Manager for the Soviet Superpower

Wolfgang Berner

Foreign Policy Institutions and Development Trends Surveyed

Throughout the years following the end of World War Two, both Soviet involvement in foreign policy and the degree of the Soviet Union's international interdependence have been growing continuously. Besides, its top functionaries let it be known at every turn that they see themselves as a genuine world power, by no means second-rate relative to the US. Nonetheless, the bulk of the important switches in the central directing organs of the USSR continue to be thrown in accordance with the "primacy of domestic politics."

This is in part attributable to the system-imposed overburdening of the supreme leadership with economic and supply problems, and in part to the fact that the overwhelming majority of Soviet leaders rose through career-stages that confronted them with domestic tasks. The new Secretary General Gorbachev is no exception. The first time he was sent abroad was in 1972. He was forty-one, and he went as a member of a delegation.

Also, in the forefront of domestic politics there is a command doctrine that has always required the keepers of the power monopoly to concentrate a maximum of their attention on safeguarding it against internal subversion. Added to this is the pressure of specific administrative and integrational problems of a huge multinational state, and to rule over it has always entailed enormous difficulties for Moscow's central authorities. Consequently, Article 28 of the 1977 Constitution, which lists some major objectives, sets Soviet foreign policy the primary task of ensuring "international conditions favorable to building communism in the USSR."

Of Stalin's five successors in the position of CPSU leader—Khrushchev, Brezhnev, Andropov, Chernenko, Gorbachev—four had little or no foreign policy experience. The sole exception is Andropov. For seven years following the overthrow of Khrushchev, until 1970/71, Kosygin and Suslov felt mainly responsible for foreign policy. Only thereafter did Brezhnev increasingly move to the foreground. Likewise, Gorbachev will have to assert himself gradually vis-à-vis members of the Politburo as experienced in foreign policy as Gromyko and Tikhonov.

Gorbachev is a native of the Stavropol region extending north of the Caucasus. There, after completion of his studies, he worked his way up as a full-time Komsomol and CPSU functionary until he was appointed to the CC secretariat in November 1978 to assume the position of Secretary of Agriculture. In 1979, he advanced to candidate member, in 1980 to full member of the Politburo. Until February 1984, however, Gorbachev was responsible in the CC Secretariat only for the supervision of several economic sectors and the (very important) cadre policies. Wider-ranging directorial and management functions did not devolve on him until after Andropov's death, when he became "second-in-command" to Chernenko. Among these new duties was responsibility for ideology and international affairs (relations with communist "sister parties," with "liberation movements," and with front organizations as well as with the non-communist left in the "capitalist camp," and also foreign information). In this connection, his appointment to the position of Chairman of the Permanent Commission on International Affairs of the Soviet of the Union in the Supreme Soviet of the USSR followed in April 1984.

The survey below will describe briefly the chief functions of the apparatuses and institutions in the Soviet Union involved in the foreign policy and security policy decisionmaking process. Moreover, it will illustrate by way of current examples their importance and their interactions. And it will also outline the framework within which Gorbachev must work as the new, ambitious "manager" of Soviet world power.

The System of Apparatuses and Control Authorities

The Soviet Union's system of foreign and security policy decisionmaking is a component of an overall system based on single-party rule. The CPSU leadership must unequivocally be regarded as the main pillar of power in international affairs. The individual Party organs, the Foreign Ministry, the Ministry of Defense, and other departments partake in the exercise of this power to varying degrees. The institutional framework surrounding the decisionmaking process, however, guarantees as a matter of principle that relative to the state apparatus (in the narrower sense) the Party apparatus always determines the direction and retains the final say.[1]

Normally, the Politburo functions as the supreme decisionmaking body in all important cases. It is possible for the Secretary General, aided by the CC Secretariat, to circumvent the Politburo in foreign and security policy as in all other questions, but he is unlikely to consider this as long as the "collective leadership" functions. In principle, the Central Committee can also reverse or revise decisions made by the Politburo (or by a Politburo-majority without CC backing), but thus far this has happened only in rare exceptional situations. Finally, decisions by the Defense Council of the

USSR, where the Politburo is represented with six to seven or even more members, occasionally carry extraordinary weight. But even in cases where it has factually pre-empted decisions on security policy supposed to be made by the Politburo, confirmation by the Politburo as the ultimate authority remains indispensable.

In the political decisionmaking process of the Soviet system, phases of initiative, of planning, of preparation, of consultation, of decision, and of implementation of the decision and its control are discernible. The state and Party organs responsible in each case participate in a specific manner in the individual phases. In the initial phases, the state organs are more involved; in the later phases and particularly in the actual decisionmaking, the Party organs dominate.

The Ministry of Foreign Affairs

The Ministry of Foreign Affairs as the competent ministry in charge takes a decisive part in the exercise of foreign power. The Minister of Foreign Affairs belongs to the Council of Ministers of the USSR, which boast more than 100 members, and his ministry is formally subordinate to the Presidium of the Council of Ministers as well as to the chairman of the Council of Ministers. The same applies to the Ministry of Defense and to the Committee for State Security. The two ministries named and the state security service, though, maintain such a tight special relationship to the Party leadership that in all three cases it is fair to speak of an effective dual subordination to the Presidium of the Council of Ministers and also to the Politburo of the CPSU.

The Minister of Foreign Affairs, who is in charge of the general operational direction of his ministry, is the immediate superior of all diplomatic representatives and consuls of the USSR abroad. He is assisted by eight to ten deputies who, under his supervision, co-ordinate the work of the ministry's various departments. Currently, the first Deputy Ministers of Foreign Affairs are G.M. Korniyenko and V.F. Maltsev (both CC members). Within the sphere of his jurisdiction, the Minister of Foreign Affairs is authorized at all times to engage in international negotiations, to sign treaties, and to represent the Soviet state abroad.

Negotiations on treaties of a military nature as well as on arms limitations and disarmament are also carried out under the aegis of the Ministry of Foreign Affairs. In such instances the Soviet delegations as a rule include representatives of the Ministry of Defense and the KGB, as well as military experts, in addition to one or more top diplomats. Since the Soviet leadership starts out from a distinctly political, by no means simply military notion of security, security policy and foreign policy processes in the USSR are always tightly interwoven in so far as decisions do not concern military policy in the narrower sense (recruitment, structure of the armed forces, supply, training and equipment of the military units, etc.). The treaty and legal department of the Ministry of Foreign Affairs, of course, also has decisive input into the wording of agreements of a predominantly security-related nature.

In the final analysis, the Ministry of Foreign Affairs, the diplomatic service and all missions abroad, is merely an auxiliary apparatus of the Party leadership, meant to carry out the Politburo's foreign policy decisions and to shelter the Soviet Union from unwanted foreign influences by means of diplomacy, or bureaucratic exploitation of international law and international institutions (chiefly the United Nations and its subsidiaries). Thus, there were long periods in the history of the USSR during which the Minister of Foreign Affairs did not belong to the innermost circle of Party leaders. Gromyko, for example, was not even a "candidate member" (i.e., member without voting rights) of the Politburo during his first sixteen years in the office of Minister of Foreign Affairs. However, he could at all times be called in to sessions of the Politburo and other deliberations as an expert. Of his six predecessors in office[2] only two, namely Trotsky and Molotov, were members of the actual top leadership of the Party, or full members of the Politburo (created in 1919), which from 1952 to 1966 was temporarily called CC Presidium. Two others, Vyshinsky and Shepilov, had to make do with "candidate member" status.

In April 1973, Gromyko was admitted to the Politburo—immediately as a full member at that—as was Minister of Defense A.A. Grechko. At the same time, then KGB-Chief Andropov advanced from "candidate" to full member. Thereafter Gromyko found it much more possible to influence decisionmaking in the top Party leadership. Undoubtedly he has since been able to participate far more intensively, consistently, and effectively in the process of foreign and security policy decisionmaking.

The Presidium of the Council of Ministers

Pursuant to Article 29 of the Law on the Council of Ministers of 1978, the chairman of the Council of Ministers of the USSR is also entitled to act on behalf of the Soviet state in international relations, to engage in negotiations, and to conclude treaties without special authorization as well as to represent the state abroad. Both he and the Presidium of the Council of Ministers are endowed with functions relevant to foreign and security policy. This is partially due to the fact that the chairman of the Council of Ministers assumes the ceremonial position of "prime minister," partially due to the subordination of the Ministry of Foreign Affairs, the Ministry of Defense, the Ministry of Foreign Trade, the State Committee for Foreign Economic Relations as well as other ministries and agencies with foreign activities, and finally, it is partially due to particular responsibility for questions of integration within the framework of the Council for Mutual Economic Assistance (CMEA).

However, the Law on the Council of Ministers states expressly that he exercises his responsibilities in consonance with the decisions of the CPSU. In other words, the basic decisions made by the supreme Party organs, primarily the Politburo, are binding on the Council of Ministers, its Presidium and chairman not just de facto, but de jure. For the rest, joint decisions by the Politburo of the CPSU and the Presidium of the Council of Ministers occur relatively frequently, and occasionally they serve to coordinate important decisions in the area of international, security, or foreign-economic policy. Also, the chairman of the Council of Ministers, as a full member of the Politburo, can at all times intervene to coordinate the work of Party organs and government agencies preparatory to decisions. At Politburo deliberations, he can, at the same time, bring to bear the entire influence and full weight of the government apparatus, including particular interests arising from the functions of state and economic administrations.

The German-Soviet treaty of 12 August 1970 was signed by then Chancellor Brandt and Foreign Minister Scheel on the one side, and by Kosygin and Gromyko on the other. On the one hand, this corresponded to the specific responsibilities of the "Prime Minister" and the Minister of Foreign Affairs, on the other hand, to their active role in the negotiations, in which Brezhnev did not once intervene directly. For twenty-six years, Gromyko was not among the (now fourteen) deputies to the chairman of the Council of Ministers who form the Presidium of the Council of Ministers. But in March 1983, he was suddenly appointed one of Tikhonov's three first deputies (next to G.A. Aliyev and I.V. Arkhipov), which certainly further enhanced Gromyko's influence and authority in this circle.

The Presidium of the Supreme Soviet

The Presidium of the Supreme Soviet (SS) of the USSR, the Soviet Union's collective head of state, contributes to the exercise of power in the international arena. This primarily extends to the ratification and termination of international treaties of all kinds. Moreover, pursuant to Articles 121 and 122 of the 1977 Constitution, the SS Presidium is endowed with responsibilities for the creation of the Defense Council and the confirmation of its composition, for the appointment of the supreme command of the armed forces, for the appointment and removal of ambassadors and of USSR representatives at international organizations, as well as for the appointment and dismissal of individual members of the Council of Ministers. Otherwise the chairman of the SS Presidium and his sixteen deputies mainly carry out representative duties.

In addition to his responsibilities as Party leader, Brezhnev also took over the chairmanship of the SS Presidium in June 1977. His chief motive was presumably the linkage of the supreme Party office with the ceremonially significant position of supreme representative of the state. This enabled him to be in the international limelight even more. There had been no Soviet precedent for the exercise of both functions by one person, though there had been Eastern European models. Nevertheless, Andropov and Chernenko carried on the practice initiated by Brezhnev, and it may be assumed that, in the long run, Gorbachev plans to follow in their footsteps.[3]

Factually subordinate to the SS Presidium (in addition to other committees) are the Permanent Commissions of the Soviet of the Union and the Soviet of Nationalities for Foreign Affairs. In the absence of commissions for security and defense policy, the foreign policy commissions are possibly also in charge of matters in that area. Both bodies, to be sure, assume a certain limited importance only in the examination of draft treaties and the process of ratification. They deserve more attention for a wholly different reason. To wit, there are obvious connections between certain activities abroad that fall under the jurisdiction of key-figures in the CC apparatus and the system governing the appointment of the chairmen of foreign policy commissions.

Thus, the post of chairman of the Foreign Policy Commission of the Union Soviet has apparently always been reserved for the CC secretary with particular areas of responsibility for ideology and foreign relations in the CC secretariat (Suslov 1954–82, Chernenko 1982–84, Gorbachev 1984–March 1985).[4] Since mid-1966, the Foreign Policy Commission of the Soviet of Nationalities has been chaired by the influential policy maker and Party ideologist B. N. Ponomarev, candidate member of the Politburo since 1972, CC secretary since 1961, head of the International Department of the CC secretariat continuously since 1955, a Comintern functionary of long standing and a Suslov-follower for many years. On trips abroad and in encounters with prominent foreign non-communists, Suslov and Ponomarev like to pass themselves off as chairmen of "parliamentary committees" on foreign policy, while other communists they have talked with have always been aware that they were dealing with the two leading CPSU-delegates in charge of relations with the "sister parties," as well as agitation and conspiratorial work abroad. There is some evidence that both commissions were deliberately used during the Khrushchev and Brezhnev eras to create for their chairmen and members a masking function, i.e., the foundation for such a dual role.

The Ministry of Defense

Initially, the USSR's Ministry of Defense is involved only in the starting phases of security policy decisionmaking. The leading figures of the Soviet military apparatus re-appear—though at a higher level of the foreign and security policy decisionmaking process—within the framework of the deliberations of the Defense Council, or if they assume special jurisdiction as in the case of the downing of the Korean airliner on 1 September 1983 (pursuant to the Law on the state borders of the USSR). Beyond that, the minister of defense has always been able to wield considerable influence on foreign policy whenever he was also a full member of the Politburo, which was the case in the period from April 1973 to the end of 1984.

Marshal Grechko, Minister from April 1967 to April 1976, made really self-confident use of these expanded possibilities during his last three years in office. His successor, Marshal Ustinov, a mechanical and construction engineer by training, who could tip the scales with an additional twenty-four years of experience as Minister of Armaments and re-organizer of the armaments industry, as well as eleven years experience as CC secretary for armaments industry. He undoubtedly had already played an important part in the decision for military intervention in Afghanistan made in late fall of 1979. After Brezhnev's death, he championed Andropov's appointment as Party leader with energy and success. By all appearances, the foreign policy course of the Soviet Union in the twenty months from April 1983 to the death of Ustinov in December 1984 was decisively determined by a troika consisting of Gromyko-Ustinov-Ponomarev.

The majority of the Politburo apparently preferred then 73-year-old Marshal Sokolov to younger, more profiled and ambitious contenders when refilling the vacancy. This can be interpreted as an attempt to reduce the influence of the defense portfolio on the process of foreign policy decisionmaking (but also on the distribution of budgetary appropriations, etc.). The decision of the CC plenary session of April 1985 also fits into this: Sokolov was admitted to the Politburo as a "candidate member" only while KGB-chief Chebrikov simultaneously rose from "candidate" to full member of the Politburo, and CC secretaries Ligachev and Ryzhkov were directly appointed full members of the Politburo.

The linkage of the Ministry of Defense to the CPSU apparatus is guaranteed (among other things) by the simultaneous attachment of the Main Political Administration of the Armed Forces to the CC Secretariat as a special department. This main administrative unit, or CC department, is regularly headed by a general. His area of responsibility encompasses primarily the ideological training of officers, noncommissioned officers, and enlisted men, as well as the system of political control within the armed services.

The State Security Service (KGB)

The Committee for State Security (KGB) participates in three major ways in the process of foreign and security policymaking. First, through its intelligence service, said to employ hundreds of thousands of agents abroad,[5] it provides important additional information. This information forms the basis for the decisionmaking of the "leadership collective." Second, several KGB departments have a hand in influencing the opposition side using disinformation and other secret service activities. Third, the KGB chief himself, provided he is a full member of the Politburo, can continuously influence the process of foreign policy decisionmaking with his active participation in the pertinent deliberations of the Party leadership or of the Defense Council. He can, no doubt, easily get the better of other participants thanks to exclusive KGB information or simply superior knowledge of facts. Since 1967, Andropov had been a "candidate member," and since the April 1973 plenary session, a full member of the Politburo. As early as the mid-seventies he was depicted as a member of the Politburo who was particularly competent on domestic and foreign policy, intellectually towering above most other colleagues—and feared by some.

From May 1982 to April 1985, the KGB was not represented by a full member in the Politburo, other than the Party leader himself, namely Andropov. For 15 years he had been successful in the role of KGB chairman. There can be no doubt that the new KGB chief Chebrikov, who assumed this office in December 1982 and moved up to candidate member of the Politburo a year later, was consulted regularly when major foreign and security policy decisions were to be made at the center of power. With Chebrikov's promotion to full member of the Politburo at the CC plenary session of April 1985, the KGB essentially was restored to the strong position it had previously occupied for a decade, starting in April 1973. The armed forces fared less well since their highest-ranking representative, Marshal Sokolov, had to make do at the same time with the rank of candidate member of the Politburo.

The CC Secretariat and Its Foreign Apparatus

For a long time the West failed fully to appreciate the importance of the part played by the CC Secretariat and its foreign departments in the system of foreign and security policy decisionmaking. The CC Secretariat, which currently once again consists of ten CC secretaries, prepares the final version of all foreign policy proposals to be submitted for decision to the Politburo. Furthermore, the CC apparatus often furnishes members of the Politburo with supplementary information and documentary material for their orientation and as an aid in their decisionmaking process. Even files originating in the Ministry of Foreign Affairs, or brought to the point of decision there, have to be transmitted to the Politburo through the CC Secretariat. The very fact that it—in conjunction with an informal Politburo steering committee in part composed of CC secretaries—sets the respective agenda for the weekly sessions of the Politburo, can block individual initiatives on formal grounds and using miscellaneous other interventions, enables the CC Secretariat to guide, or better, manipulate the decision process.

Thus, the CC Secretariat constitutes the "final link" in the preparatory phase. But frequently it is also already involved in the initiation of foreign policy initiatives and exerts strong influence, especially in its advisory function. With its control over the implementation of foreign and security policy decisions taken by the Politburo, it assumes decisive importance.[6]

Under the conditions of "collective leadership," the secretary general has always assumed ultimate responsibility for foreign policy questions inside the CC Secretariat. This applied to Khrushchev and Brezhnev, as well as to Andropov and Chernenko, though at times their supreme leadership authority over foreign policy was outwardly contested by other members of the Politburo with greater expertise. Brezhnev, long eclipsed by Kosygin and Suslov in this respect, gathered well-versed foreign policy experts (such as A.N. Aleksandrov, A.I. Blatov, K.V. Rusakov, A.Ye. Bovin) in his "personal secretariat" to make up for his own deficiency.[7] This practice was continued by Andropov, Chernenko, and Gorbachev, who even took over some of the same experts: Thus, Aleksandrov, who outlasted all changes at the top in his influential assistant's position, belongs to Gorbachev's advisory staff again, without any change.

Because of his precarious state of health, Andropov required from the very outset the support of his "personal secretariat." The less he was capable of discharging his responsibilities in his Muscovite office in an orderly manner, the more dependent he became on his assistants. Later it was said that de facto he really "ruled" for just nine months, that is, from December 1982 to late August 1983. The ensuing five-and-a-half months until Chernenko assumed office were an interregnum—an interregnum of Andropov-deputies (Chernenko, Gorbachev, and on occasion probably Ustinov, too), the secretariats (CC Secretariat, "personal secretariat" of the secretary general), and the great apparatuses (Party apparatus, foreign ministry, military apparatus, KGB, Tikhonov's economic administration).

At the time, it seems, the troika of Gromyko-Ustinov-Ponomarev assumed command in foreign policy and continued to set the tone after Chernenko's advancement to secretary general. On the other hand, in speeches and in interviews on foreign policy, Chernenko repeatedly underscored, as best he could, that as far as he was concerned (and notwithstanding his lack of professionalism and health handicaps), he had no intention of relinquishing his predecessors' claim to setting the foreign policy guidelines in the CC Secretariat, nor with regard to the Politburo either. In this, he could also rely on his chancellery's staff of experts and on the apparatus of the CC Secretariat. Given a similarly unfavorable starting position, the considerably younger "bearer of hopes," Gorbachev, does dispose of significant advantages, compared with Chernenko—advantages rooted chiefly in his personality structure, and these should facilitate his relatively quick rise to the secretary general's traditional role in the area of foreign policy, as well.

The framework of the CC apparatus endows two departments of the CC Secretariat in particular with foreign policy responsibilities: the International Department (head: CC Secretary B.N. Ponomarev) and the Department for Relations with Communist and Workers' Parties in Socialist Countries (head: CC Secretary K.V. Rusakov). In this context, the Department for Foreign Information (head: L.M. Zamyatin) and the Department for Foreign Cadres also ought to be mentioned.[8] In charge of coordinating the propagandistic-ideological foreign activities with domestic propaganda is the CC secretary for ideology and propaganda, M.V. Zimyanin, who together with Ponomarev and Rusakov participates regularly in the frequent conferences of the CC secretaries for ideology and the foreign work of all governing parties of the WTO-CMEA system.

The Comintern veteran, Ponomarev, (born in 1905) must be regarded as the pivotal figure proper in this multifaceted "foreign apparatus" of the CC Secretariat. This finds partial expression in the fact that he—the most senior of all CC secretaries (since 1961)—as a candidate member of the Politburo outranks CC secretaries Rusakov (born in 1909) and Zimyanin (born in 1914) in the nomenklatura. Moreover, he holds the office of chairman of the Foreign Policy Commission of the Soviet of Nationalities at the Supreme Soviet of the USSR, of which Rusakov, Zimyanin and Zamyatin (Commission Secretary) are members. Ponomarev's first deputy V.V. Zagladin, incidentally, is secretary of the Foreign Policy Commission of the Soviet of the Union.

From 1955–1957, Ponomarev was head of the international department and was responsible for the governing "sister parties" in the Socialist states, for the non-governing CPs and also for national and social revolutionary "liberation movements" in the Third World. Though after the 1957 reorganization, Andropov took charge of the newly created "liaison department," which henceforth specialized on cultivating special relations between the CPSU leadership and the leadership apparatuses of the governing CPs, Ponomarev by no means withdrew from co-responsibility for this area of the international communist party system. Characteristically, the CPSU delegation, which was supposed to negotiate the end of the schism with representatives of China's CP in the summer of 1963, originally consisted of Suslov, Ponomarev, Andropov, Ilyichev (then CC secretary for ideology and propaganda), and Chervonenko (ambassador of the USSR in Peking). Subsequently it was enlarged by the two Khrushchev followers Grishin (trade union president) and Satyukov (editor-in-chief of *Pravda*) as counterweights to the preponderant Suslovites (Suslov, Ponomarev, Andropov).

Ponomarev never ceased to speak out authoritatively on basic questions from the "socialist camp."[9] He is superintendent of important leading organs in the international communist movement (including the governing CPs) such as *World Marxist Review* (Prague) and *New Times* (Moscow). Also, he regularly attends the Eastern-bloc conferences of CC secretaries for ideology and foreign work. His influence on foreign policy, always substantial, grew further under Andropov and Chernenko. After Andropov's departure, there remained only one other member of the CPSU leadership with comparable foreign policy experience and international acquaintances, namely Foreign Minister Gromyko.

While Ponomarev, in co-operation with Gromyko and Ustinov, set out to take on the role as Soviet foreign policy's "grey eminence," he left the direction of the International Department largely to his first deputy Zagladin. This department, with an estimated staff of 200, has a very broad scope of tasks assigned to it. Routinely, it stays in touch with about 100 non-governing CPs in ninety-five countries. It finances and directs numerous crypto-communist front and auxiliary organizations. Time and again, it launches large-scale campaigns of agitation and propaganda in "capitalist" and developing countries, backing them for months and years. It maintains information and working contacts with numerous parties and organizations on the non-communist left. It provides tangible support for dozens of "liberation movements" in developing countries, and furthermore assures cooperation at the party and government levels with fifteen to twenty developing countries of "socialist orientation." At the same time, its leading theoreticians constantly busy themselves designing ideological-political strategic conceptions for the CPs of Western industrialized states (Zagladin et al.) and of developing countries (K.N. Brutents et al.) as well as for national, or, better, social-revolutionary, "liberation movements" and for developing countries of "socialist orientation" (R.A. Ulyanovsky, Brutents), propounding them, explaining them, and occasionally re-adjusting them to the course of time.[10]

Meanwhile, Ponomarev's main attention has been focused for several years now on the political configuration of East-West relations, i.e., primarily on Soviet policy vis-à-vis the US and the other NATO states. To his desk come proposals, reports and analyses from the Ministry of Foreign Affairs, from the KGB, from the Ministry of Defense, from the Party's foreign apparatus, and also materials from the media and propaganda apparatus, controlled by Zimyanin, as well as contributions by the various research institutes of the Academy of Sciences of the USSR. Ponomarev, who as a rule personally conducts the negotiations with the ministers, with the KGB chief, with the other CC secretaries, and with the directors of the research institutes, is reputed to have a good, albeit far from conflict-free relationship with Gromyko. The close cooperation of the International Department and the KGB looks back on a long tradition. Many secret service documents for Politburo deliberations on impending foreign policy decisions continue to be produced jointly by the International Department of the CC Secretariat and the KGB.[11]

More often than not, Ponomarev is also the recipient of requests by the secretary general's "personal secretariat" (as has become customary since the Brezhnev era) for the formation of ad hoc committees to work out specific foreign policy positions. Ordinarily, the task of making the requisite organizational preparations and assembling the results—be it into a finished draft of an official document, be it into a memo with alternate proposals, be it into a recommendation for a foreign policy course correction—falls upon the International Department. Ranking and particularly knowledgeable representatives of the Party's foreign apparatus, the foreign ministry, and the KGB are regularly called upon to participate in the deliberations, as occasionally are representatives of the Ministry of Defense and other portfolios as well as experts from the research institutes. At times such closed meetings last days or even weeks. The results are then submitted to the Politburo for decision.[12]

The CC Secretariat's Department for Liaison With Communist Parties in Socialist Countries routinely sees to the cultivation of special relations between the CPSU and the leading apparatuses of the "sister parties" of the WTO-CMEA system comprising Poland, the GDR, the CSSR, Hungary, Romania, Bulgaria, Cuba, the Mongolian People's Republic, and Vietnam. Relations between the USSR and these member states of the closer "community of socialist states" consist at least as much of party-relations as they do of state-relations. Among other things, this is corroborated by the fact that without exception Soviet ambassadors in the capitals of the above-listed countries are members (full members or "candidate members") of the CC of the CPSU. The respective ambassadors, incidentally, are often CPSU functionaries of long standing from the Party's central apparatus, or former regional secretaries. They are also authorized by the CPSU leadership to exercise control functions and are required to report not just to the Ministry of Foreign Affairs but also to the "liaison department" of the CC Secretariat.

The head of the department, CC Secretary Rusakov, himself gained experiences as ambassador to the Mongolian PR (1962–1964). In 1965 he was appointed first deputy head, and in 1968 head of the "liaison department." In the period from 1972–1977, while on the staff of Brezhnev's "personal secretariat," the then CC secretary responsible for governing CPs, K.F. Katushev, also functioned as head of the department. In 1977, he was replaced in both positions by Rusakov.

In addition, the "liaison department" daily looks after the political interests of the USSR in the Warsaw Treaty Organization (always in close touch with the Ministry of Foreign Affairs and the Presidium of the Council of Ministers of the USSR). Finally, it is in charge of routine communications with the governing parties of other socialist states—especially Laos, Yugoslavia, and North Korea—as well as the continuous observation of developments in the PR of China and in Albania. On the other hand, the developing countries of "socialist orientation"—among them for instance Afghanistan, Syria, South Yemen, Ethiopia, Angola, Nicaragua—fall under the jurisdiction not of this, but rather of the International Department.

The Department for Foreign Cadres is headed by S.V. Chervonenko (born in 1915), formerly ambassador to the PR of China (1959–1965), the CSSR (1965–1973) and France (1973–1983), and a full member of the CC since 1961. This department is mainly responsible for filling positions at embassies, consulates, trade missions, and USSR delegations in international organizations, and furthermore for all personnel issues related to the cadres abroad in its charge, and for Party work at all foreign missions. However, it is neither responsible for KGB agents abroad nor for those of the military intelligence service GRU, nor for the foreign correspondents of the Soviet press, the wire service TASS, or Soviet television. All active journalists are instead subordinate to the Propaganda Department, which also assigns them to foreign duty.[13] CC Secretary Zimyanin, who is in control of this department, was himself able to gain experience abroad as ambassador (1956–1957 in North Vietnam, 1960–1965 in the CSSR).

The head of the Department for Foreign Information, newly established in February 1978, CC member L.M. Zamyatin (born in 1922) started his career in the Ministry of Foreign Affairs where he took charge of the press department in 1962. He was director general of TASS from 1970 to 1978. The job of the CC department he heads consists primarily in coordinating Soviet foreign propaganda. At the same time it is apparently under orders to participate decisively in the coordination of the presentation of Soviet foreign policy on radio and television as well as in other mass media, for the benefit of the domestic audience.[14] For a time, Zamyatin also acted as foreign policy adviser, or as public relations manager for Brezhnev's trips at home and abroad.

The Relationship Between the Party Apparatus and the Ministry of Foreign Affairs

As explained above, the personnel amalgamation of the foreign apparatus of the CC Secretariat and of the USSR's foreign service is far more compact and variegated than is generally assumed. Operative cooperation also seems to function extraordinarily smoothly and effectively in numerous areas. The same applies to the interplay of both apparatuses in the execution of foreign and security policy decision processes.

Of the 470 CC members and candidate members elected at the Twenty-sixth Party Congress (1981), twenty-four were active foreign service officers, among them seventeen full members and seven "candidate members." The first group included Minister of Foreign Affairs Gromyko and his first deputies Korniyenko and Maltsev as well as the ambassadors to the US, France, India, Japan, Algeria, Afghanistan, Yugoslavia, Poland, the GDR, the CSSR, Hungary, Romania, Bulgaria, and Cuba. The second group consisted of Deputy Minister of Foreign Affairs Ilyichev and the ambassadors to the Federal Republic of Germany, Italy, Ethiopia, North Korea, Vietnam, and the Mongolian PR. In addition, there were five members of the Central Auditing Commission: Deputy Minister of Foreign Affairs N.S. Ryzhov, Chief Delegate to the UN O.A. Troyanovsky and the ambassadors to Great Britain, the PR of China, and Lebanon. With an essentially unchanged pattern of composition, this inventory has since undergone only minimal alterations.

Moreover, it must be borne in mind that the CC Secretaries Rusakov and Zimyanin, the department heads Zamyatin and Chervonenko, plus several deputy heads of departments (such as Rusakov's deputies O.B. Rakhmanin and G.A. Kiselyov as well as Chervonenko's deputy N.N. Chetverikov) also either started out in the foreign service or were temporarily attached to it as ambassadors. Inversely, the Ministry of Foreign Affairs has for some twenty years been in the habit of employing permanent staff of the International Department of the CC apparatus in various positions (mostly as embassy counsellors) at the USSR's foreign missions. A defectors' report indicates, for instance, that in 1969 a six-member working group from the International Department that was headed by an embassy counsellor had formed at the Soviet embassy in Cairo.[15]

Cooperation between the International Department and the Ministry of Foreign Affairs also extends to the weekly *Novoe Vremya* (New Times). In the West, because of its focus on political themes, it is still widely taken for a publication primarily subordinated to the Ministry of Foreign Affairs. In fact, this leading CPSU organ for current political questions was established in 1943 and published in nine languages, and it has been supervised by the CC Secretariat from the very beginning. According to credible reports by KGB defector S. Levchenko, who in 1974 had been assigned to the Moscow bureau of *Novoe Vremya* for a year, only some 30 percent of contributions at the time were from the pens of the journal's genuine staff members. Another 30 percent was contributed by members of the International Department, 20 percent by the KGB's disinformation service, and the remaining 20 percent by officials of the Ministry of Foreign Affairs.[16] It became evident that Ponomarev and the International Department were also decisively behind the journal, inter alia, from its massive polemical participation in the disputes on "Eurocommunism" in the seventies.

The journal *Novoe Vremya* is a textbook example of the tight cooperative amalgamation of the interests of the Party's foreign apparatus and the Ministry of Foreign Affairs, as well as the KGB. It was no coincidence that the Soviet revanchism campaign was started in early April 1984 with an article in *Novoe Vremya.*[17] Only two weeks later, a statement on "concepts endangering peace" that "place into question . . . the borders of European states and are directed against the political-territorial realities that have developed in Europe" found its way into the communique of a conference by the WTO-foreign ministers.[18] In the 27 July 1984 edition of *Pravda*, L. Bezymensky warned GDR leadership using horror stories of the "Kohl/Genscher government's" policy of revenge for disengaging from the "joint strategy" of resistance to the "attacks" levelled against "the countries of the socialist community" by contemporary American and West German "crusaders." Bezymensky is notorious in Bonn as a *Novoe Vremya* commentator of long standing on policy towards Germany, and he is known to have close ties to the Soviet Ministry of Foreign Affairs and the KGB. This article by Bezymensky in particular and the anonymous and bitter follow-up attack in *Pravda* on 2 August (entitled "The Wrong Way") cast into sharp relief the deeper motives behind the major offensive against Bonn's alleged policy of revanche.

This campaign was engineered jointly by the CPSU's propaganda apparatus and the Soviet Ministry of Foreign Affairs. It was designed first of all to stir up patriotism and nationalism in the Soviet Union proper for purposes of resisting the "American Challenge."[19] By associating Pershing-II deployment with German revanchist desires, it was also meant to awaken old historic feelings of fear and hate. Second, by reviving antiquated enemy images that had faded in the period of detente, it was to contribute to effectively stemming particularist tendencies within the WTO-CMEA system and to restoring bloc-discipline in the USSR's Eastern European buffer zone.[20] Finally, it was well suited to the "diplomatic" punishment of the Federal Republic of Germany and its government;[21] for it was perceived in Moscow, not without a certain logic, as among those most to blame for the implementation of the deployment part of NATO's 12 December 1979 "dual track decision," which began in December 1983, after the offers contained in the negotiation part had failed to produce the desired disarmament and arms limitation agreements.

The Defense Council and the "Military Factor"

The Defense Council plays a fairly mysterious part in the Soviet Union's foreign and security policy decision system, shrouded as it is in particularly strict secrecy. It was presumably established in its current form around 1973, in terms of composition and objective probably continuing along the lines of the Supreme Military Council (*Vysshiy Voyennyi Sovet*) of the Khrushchev era. The Soviet press mentioned the new Defense Council for the first time in April 1976. But details of how it fits into the decision process are unknown. There is considerable evidence that all important security policy proposals are deliberated on in this body, prior to final decision by the Politburo. Some experts believe the resolutions of the Defense Council carry such weight in certain cases, that they in fact anticipate the ultimate decision to be made by the Politburo.[22]

Little is known about the Council's membership, either. According to previous practice, the chair is restricted in principle to the CPSU secretary general. Presumably the title of a Supreme Commander of the Armed Forces, with which Brezhnev and Chernenko officially adorned themselves, is also a derivative of this privilege.

The configuration of the membership may perhaps be inferred from the composition of the presidium of a commanding officers' convention that took place on 27 October 1982 in the Kremlin, shortly before Brezhnev's death.[23] The presidium included: the secretary general (Brezhnev) the Chairman of the Council of Ministers (Tikhonov), the Minister of Foreign Affairs (Gromyko), the Minister of Defense (Ustinov), two CC secretaries in charge of cadre policies and of the Party's foreign apparatus (Chernenko and Andropov), the Chairman of the Commission for Armaments Industries at the Presidium of the Council of Ministers (L.V. Smirnov), the Chief of the General Staff (Marshal Ogarkov), the Supreme Commander of the WTO forces (Marshal Kulikov), the third First Deputy of the Minister of Defense (Marshal Sokolov), and the head of the Main Political Administration of the Armed Forces, as such also head of department in the CC Secretariat (General Yepishev). However, two important office holders were missing, who, on the basis of much evidence, must also be regarded as ex officio members of the Defense Council: the KGB chief (then V.V. Fedorchuk as a transitional figure) and the CC secretary responsible for the armaments industry (a position vacant between 1979 and 1983).

Projecting from this function-based pattern, the twelve to thirteen member "core" of the Defense Council presumably consisted in April 1985 of the following: Gorbachev, Tikhonov, Gromyko, Romanov, Ligachev, Chebrikov, and Smirnov, plus the marshals Sokolov, Kulikov, and Petrov, as well as General Yepishev. Seven full members of the Politburo faced five ranking representatives of the military apparatus, although it would certainly be wrong to assume irresoluble permanently conflicting interests between the representatives of the political leadership and the military spokesmen. Rather, according to its basic concept, the Defense Council assembles the political experience and authority of the most competent members of the Politburo and the CC Secretariat and the military expertise of leading members of the armed forces' high command for the purpose of pertinent advice and harmonious decisionmaking. For the rest, there is much evidence that Party leadership can rely on the loyalty of the marshals and generals, i.e. any "Bonapartist" leanings on the part of individual military men would currently stand no chance of success.[24] Nevertheless, Party leaders let no opportunity go by (and that also includes the institutionalization of cooperative relations) to reaffirm strongly the precedence of the political leadership over the military high command.

Presumably, the Defense Council participates regularly in the foreign policy decision process whenever security policy, military-strategic, military-technical, and armaments policy aspects of certain foreign policy options suggest thorough consultation with the military. Certainly, crisis management in Afghanistan and Poland repeatedly and intensively occupied this circle. Just as surely, the problems hidden behind the formula of the course followed by the state as a whole to "further strengthen the Soviet Union's economic and defensive power" are discussed here in detail—since 1981 the issue has been a Soviet counter-program to the Reagan administration's "policy of strength." Leading politicians and the USSR's military unanimously consider Reagan's policy an attempt to restore a clear global-strategic superiority for the US. By all appearances the military, usually represented by Ogarkov, demanded in this connection larger resource allocations and more rigorous measures of economic mobilization than the politicians were prepared to grant. Viewed from this angle, the politicians at the commanding officers' convention of 27 October 1982 evidently sought to appease the disgruntled marshals and generals.

As early as July 1982, the military and politicians had agreed on uncompromising rejection of all NATO offers at the Geneva INF negotiations, which caused Nitze's "walk-in-the-woods" initiative of 16 July to miscarry.[25] The waves of confrontational excitement also carried Andropov on to victory over his competitor Chernenko in his bid to succeed Brezhnev, whereby (as one could hear it said in Moscow) Ustinov and Gromyko provided cover fire by referring to the dangerous international situation. Ustinov sided unequivocally with the political leadership that had settled on the oppositional course all the way to breaking off the Geneva and Vienna disarmament, or better arms control, negotiations, but was unwilling to embark upon a suicidal acceleration of arms escalation.

This seems to have been at the core of the conflict between Ustinov and Ogarkov. The Politburo after much vascillation put an end to this conflict in early September 1984 with the removal of the chief of the general staff. Not valid is the interpretation of this lengthy controversy—which evidently touched on many areas—as a tug-of-war between the champions of a concept viewing nuclear war as feasible and winnable, and the advocates (allegedly represented by Ustinov) of the principle of deterrence who, according to this interpretation, kept the upper hand.[26] Now as then it remains the task of the Soviet Armed Forces to safeguard effectively the nation's defense, that is, to arm adequately for active waging of war against any "aggressor," up to the ultimate victory.[27]

Marshal Ogarkov's dismissal was unofficially explained by his lack of political instinct and "behavior contrary to Party interests."[28] Semi-official word was that he was assigned an important task as commander-in-chief of the operations zone West. His part in the downing of the South Korean airliner KAL-007 which was intercepted on 1 September 1983 near Sakhalin by Soviet fighters, apparently contributed to his sacking. As announced by the editor-in-chief of *Pravda*, Afanasyev, as early as 18 September in a BBC interview, the catastrophe that claimed 269 lives resulted among other things in reprimands for some ranking military, though the politicians, for instance Gromyko and Ustinov, defended before the world public the methods used by the commanders in charge. Andropov, to be sure, did not refer to the downed Jumbo until four weeks later, and then only incidentally, in connection with another issue.

Ogarkov's dismissal occurred during Chernenko's tenure, and it was certainly taken as a penalty by the generals. The full extent of the demotion was plain to everyone following Ustinov's death late in December 1984. While Marshal Akhromeyev signed the obituary as the first representative of the armed forces in 29th place, Ogarkov's name does not appear until 70th place, and only as the 19th among the military.[29] On the one hand, this case conveys a notion of how much room for argument and action the Party leadership grants its top military. But it also demonstrates how jealously mindful the Politburo is to guard its authority against subversion, especially in periods of evidently weak leadership and diffusion of power.

The Politburo Decides Everything Jointly

Is it possible for the newly appointed CPSU secretary general, soon after coming to office, to fully recast his country's foreign policy, as can the president of the US, and perhaps even give it a whole new direction? The framework conditions awaiting him at his accession render this improbable. Gorbachev, too, will have to pay tribute to such realities and the same would apply to a Party leader more focused on foreign policy aims than he is.

The reality of the Soviet system is such that a new secretary general as the de facto head of government gets a "cabinet" (i.e., a Politburo) already formed under his predecessor. He cannot replace members at his discretion. This fact, amplified by the firm roots of Politburo members in certain apparatuses and patronage cartels, as a rule makes for immobility in foreign policy and consequently more continuity than change. Though it is incumbent on the secretary general to chair weekly sessions of the Politburo, he does lack a clearly defined power to determine policy guidelines. He is expected first and foremost to organize or "program" consensus since the principle of consensus is normally applied (only in rare exceptions are disputes resolved by votes).[30]

The secretary general's backing flows primarily from his strong position at the head of the CC Secretariat, which assists him in controlling the preparation of all proposals and the implementation of all decisions. He can also protect his initial majority in the Politburo, which lifted him into the saddle, through pragmatic alliances with other members or groups, and he can later gradually increase his own following through adroit deals on the occasion of new admissions. Otherwise, though, his daily grind consists in presenting the "leadership collective" time and again with proposals suitable for compromise since he is dependent on the voluntary cooperation of the other oligarchs. Normally, to be sure, all important issues come before the Politburo for decision, but the secretary general does not make the decision there; rather, the Politburo decides everything jointly.

All this must be qualified, however, because there are some privileged members of the Politburo who make up an informal "permanent committee" usually composed of five "main oligarchs." This inner circle sets the agenda for the sessions, invites extraordinary participants (experts and other reference persons and attempts to work out in advance proposals allowing for smooth decisionmaking. As a rule, the body consists of full members who reside permanently in Moscow and have special qualities (experience, competency, influence). For the most part, the CC secretaries predominate. The General Department of the CC Secretariat manages the business of this steering committee—and of the entire Politburo.[31]

Hence, to the extent that the secretary general also wants to put his own new concepts into practice in foreign and security policy, he must begin by trying to come to terms with his committee colleagues. The widely divergent composition of the body alone suffices to make this a difficult undertaking. Under Andropov, the other members of the committee of five consisted of Tikhonov, Chernenko, Gromyko, and Ustinov. Then Chernenko, Tikhonov, Gromyko, Ustinov, and Gorbachev made up the circle. The new composition with which Gorbachev is forced to "govern" is as yet not discernible to outsiders. So far, a public announcement has not been the rule.

In late summer of 1983, shortly after the downing of the South Korean Jumbo KAL-007, Gromyko, then the world's most senior foreign minister by far, had become the real helmsman of Soviet foreign policy, and renewed subordination should certainly not be easy for him. His latest book on the theme of monopoly capital and imperialist expansion, with which he evidently meant to prove himself a sound Leninist, is written from the vantage of an ultra-conservative, blinker-wearing dogmatist.[32] This did not spare him reproaches from domestic critics that his recall of the Soviet negotiating teams from Geneva and Vienna in November and December of 1983 violated elementary principles of Leninism in the practice of foreign policy. Gromyko then surprised many observers by his flexibility in correcting this error. On 12 March 1985, the Geneva negotiations with the US were reopened at three levels—of intercontinental strategic, continental strategic, and space weapons—by the Soviet Union in a truly Leninist spirit.

In foreign policy discussions Gromyko can rely mainly on three candidate members of the Politburo who distinguish themselves by great expertise in foreign and security policy: the CC secretary in charge of the Party's foreign apparatus, Ponomarev (born in 1905), the first deputy chairman of the SS Presidium, Kuznetsov (born in 1901), and on Marshal Sokolov (born in 1911), Minister of Defense since December 1984. Even without voting rights, all three can bring their manyfaceted experiences fully to bear at foreign policy deliberations of the Politburo. Otherwise, only Full Member V.I. Vorotnikov, an industrial manager who was temporarily assigned to Cuba as ambassador for three years (1979–1982), commands limited expertise in foreign policy.

As the principle of consensus rules in the Politburo, Gromyko could at all times prevent foreign policy decisions he considers doubtful, even without help. As long as he is on the steering committee, he has additional means of blocking proposals unacceptable to him. Furthermore, he is by no means isolated. At least half of the thirteen full members back him as a matter of principle in foreign policy questions; and beyond that during debates he can rely on assistance from the phalanx of experts, Ponomarev-Kuznetsov-Sokolov. Gorbachev would have to alter this constellation fundamentally should he intend to assume for himself the part of chief foreign policymaker of the "collective leadership."[33]

Notes

1. On this, cf. the detailed description of the foreign and security policy decision system of the USSR by B. Meissner, in: *Aus Politik und Zeitgeschichte: Beilage zur Wochenzeitung "Das Parlament,"* B 43/83, pp. 31–45.

2. L.D. Trotsky (1917–18), G.V. Chicherin (1918–30), M.M. Litvinov (1930–39), V.M. Molotov (1939–49), A.Ya. Vyshinsky (1949–53), V.M. Molotov (1953–56), D.T. Shepilov (1956–57), A.A. Gromyko (1957–85), E.A. Shevardnadse (as of 2 July 1985) succeeded each other as Minister of Foreign Affairs.

3. Since the toppling of Khrushchev, who was both Party leader and (after 1958) chairman of the Council of Ministers, there has been strict separation of these two offices, as an inviolable fundamental element of the principle of "collective leadership."

4. Since 2 July 1985, Politburo and CC Secretary Ye.K. Ligachov.

5. On this, Astrid von Borcke, "The Role of the Secret Service," in this volume, Chapter 5.

6. Cf. B. Meissner, op. cit., p. 36.

7. Alexandrov and Blatov had previously held responsible positions on the German desk of the Ministry of Foreign Affairs Rusakov started in the CC Department for Liaison with Governing Communist Parties (1962–72) and returned there in 1977. Bovin had previously belonged to the advisory staff of the same CC department.

8. Cf. E. Teague, in: *RL*, 27 October 1980 (special edition: *The Foreign Departments of the Central Committee of the CPSU*); J.F. Hough, in *Studies in Comparative Communism*, No. 3, (1982), pp. 167–183. The impending disbandment of the

Department for Foreign Information and the probable assignment of Samyatin to the foreign service was reported by *W* 16 July 1985.

9. Cf. the contributions by Ponomarev in *PFS*, No. 1 (1975), pp. 4–17, and No. 9 (1984), pp. 1155–1166.

10. R.V. Kitrinos, in *Problems of Communism*, No. 5 (1984), pp. 47–75; R.F. Staar, ibid., No. 2 (1985), pp. 92–96; in addition V.V. Zagladin, in *Pr*, 5 June 1984. Further, Wolfgang Berner, "States with a Socialist Orientation: A Soviet Model of Partnership," Chapter 28.

11. R.V. Kitrinos, *op. cit.*, p. 50, pp. 59ff; in addition, J. Barron, *KGB Today: The Hidden Hand* (New York, 1983), p. 446f.

12. Cf. J.F. Hough, *op. cit.*, p. 182, and V. Petrov, in *Orbis*, No. 3 (1973), p. 830.

13. Cf. E. Teague, *op. cit.*, p. 6; J.F. Hough, *op. cit.*, p. 172f.; V. Petrov, *op. cit.*, pp. 824ff.

14. Vf. E. Teague, *op. cit.*, pp. 25ff, p. 47; in addition the description of the tasks by K.U. Chernenko, in *Pr*, 15 June 1983 (speech at the CC plenary session). The disbandment of the Department for Foreign Information has apparently been pushed forward since early 1983 among others by Ponomarev; cf. on this note 8.

15. W. Spaulding, in *Problems of Communism*, No. 5 (1984), pp. 74ff.

16. *Sp*, No. 28 (1984), p. 110 (according to J. Barron, *op. cit.*, p. 82). NT contributions by Zagladin appear under the pseudonym of Boris Vesnin.

17. A. Tolpegin, in: *Novoe Vremya*, No. 15 (1984), pp. 21ff.

18. *ND*, 21 and 22 April 1984.

19. On this, see Manfred Görtemaker, "Soviet Policy Vis-à-vis the United States," in this volume, Chapter 21.

20. On this, Wolfgand Berner/Christian Meier et al., "The Soviet Policy of Hegemony and the Crisis of Authority in Eastern Europe," in this volume, Chapter 24.

21. On this, Fred Oldenburg, "Relations Between the USSR and the Federal Republic of Germany," in this volume, Chapter 23.

22. More details in B. Meissner, *op. cit.*, p. 41ff.

23. *Pr*, 28 October 1982; *KZ*, 28 October 1982.

24. On this, Peter Kruschin, "Military and Political Decisionmaking Processes," in this volume, Chapter 4.

25. Cf. P. Nitze, in *Department of State Bulletin*, No. 2089 (1984), p. 36.

26. This thesis is advanced by G. Weickhardt, in *Problems of Communism*, No. 1 (1985), pp. 77–82.

27. On this, Gerhard Wettig, "Arms Limitation and Arms Control in Soviet Policy Towards the West," in this volume, Chapter 22.

28. Cf. *NYT*, 13 September 1984.

29. *Pr*, 22 December, 1984.

30. More details in B. Meissner, *op. cit.*, p. 43f.

31. *Ibid.*, p. 44.

32. On this H. Brahm, *Aktuelle Analysen des BIOst*, No. 31 (1984).

33. The appointment of Gromyko as Chairman of the Presidium of the Supreme Soviet on 2 July 1985 and his replacement in the position of Minister of Foreign Affairs by E.A. Shevardnadse can be interpreted as an important step in this direction. The preceeding day, Shevardnadse had been promoted from "candidate member" to full member of the Politburo.

21
Soviet Policy Vis-à-vis the United States

Manfred Görtemaker

The transitional phase in Soviet politics, following the death of Brezhnev on 10 November 1982, also represented a period of insecurity and indecision for the development of Soviet-American relations. Hopes that the leadership change in the Kremlin might bring about a renewal of the dialogue among the world powers soon proved disappointing. The continuing disputes over Soviet intermediate-range armament in Europe, the discussion of modernization as part of the NATO dual-track decision of 12 December 1979, the persisting Soviet presence in Afghanistan, the situation in Poland, and the difficulties in East-West trade repeatedly gave rise to new mutual accusations and charges. And the domestic political conditions in the US and in the USSR hardly promoted an intensification and improvement of Soviet-American relations either.

Under President Reagan the US had returned to a policy of containment by strength in January 1981. This policy was reminiscent in many ways of President Truman's containment policy after 1947.[1] Reagan sought to launch an era of conservative reflection and patriotic renewal in order to stay the decline of America's world power position that had been observable since Vietnam and Watergate. He wanted to reconsolidate the global position of the US in terms of armaments policy, economics, and ideology, and to check the Soviet-Cuban advance using a determined policy of "neo-containment." Only subsequent to the restoration of American strength was the thread of negotiation to be picked up again. Consequently, the emphasis on antagonism moved to the fore; advocates of a new detente initially and for the foreseeable future remained without appreciable influence.

The Soviet Union, by contrast, had already fallen into mounting political stagnation in the closing phase of the Brezhnev era, and this also affected relations with the US. The deteriorating state of the secretary General's health practically prevented a flexible and decisive policy. This changed very little after Brezhnev's death since his successor, Yuri Andropov, also turned out to be seriously ill. He stayed hidden from the public for at least six of the fifteen months during which he functioned as secretary general (12 November 1982–9 February 1984). He was evidently largely incapable of adequately conducting his government business. Others, like Defense Minister Ustinov—and with him the military apparatus—as well as Minister of Foreign Affairs Gromyko gained a degree of importance they would hardly have achieved under a secretary general able to act. The resulting diffusion of the decisionmaking process and of responsibilities and distribution of power impeded the flexibility of Soviet policy so persistently that it was less and less capable of an innovative role.[2]

Thus, both in the US and in the Soviet Union the overall conditions for an improvement of bilateral connections and of East-West relations were not propitious in the early eighties. Only with the approach of the American presidential elections of 6 November 1984 did signs increase that indicated a return to dialogue and a turnabout in Soviet-American relations. On the one hand this was caused by the willingness of the US to renew talks with the Soviet Union from its regained position of strength, and on the other hand by the realization apparently taking hold of the new Soviet leadership under Chernenko that after the failure of the INF negotiations and the beginning deployment of American medium-range weapons in Europe it was necessary to overcome the deep rift between the two countries in order to reduce dangerously escalated tensions. The fact that Reagan stood for reelection as president in 1984 and that his remaining in the White House beyond 20 January 1985 was to be expected probably contributed to this development.

Reagan's re-election secured the Republican administration a term lasting until at least 1989; the appointment of 54-year-old Gorbachev as the new secretary general of the CPSU following Chernenko's death on 10 March 1985 marked the transition to a new generation of Soviet leaders; and the re-opening of the Geneva arms-reduction negotiations by the US and the Soviet Union on 12 March 1985 all underscored emphatically the signs of change on both sides. For the first time after a decade of tensions, the consolidation expressed bore the chance for a gradual improvement of Soviet-American relations. This could well usher in a new era.

Continuing Confrontation Under Andropov

Up to this point, Soviet-US relations had been marked for nearly a decade by a high measure of confrontation and readiness for conflict. The policy of detente that had temporarily brought about an improvement of relations during Nixon's presidency had entered a crisis as early as the mid-seventies—something which is frequently overlooked—from which it never recovered. This was so because between 1975 and 1979 the Soviet Union made use of the fact that the US world power's capacity to act had been limited by the Vietnam trauma and the Watergate affair. The Soviets tried to advance their own sphere of influence and aroused growing doubts in the US about whether continuing the policy of cooperation aimed at detente still made sense in view of uncooperative Soviet behavior.[3] The end of detente in the wake of the invasion of Afghanistan by Soviet troops, did not mean a relapse into Cold War; but it did initiate a phase of sharpened confrontation and aggressive rhetoric on both sides so that agreement on issues central to East-West relations was no longer possible.

When on 12 November 1982 Andropov was elected the new secretary general of the CPSU, many began to hope that there was a possibility of surmounting the stagnation of Soviet politics and of a rapprochement between the US and the USSR. These hopes were fuelled when Andropov immediately manifested his interest in a reduction of East-West tensions and stated in his inaugural address to the plenum of the CC of the CPSU on 22 November that the policy of detente was by no means over, but that the future belonged to it. The Soviet Union advocated "seeking a sound base acceptable to both sides to solve the most complex problems, particularly, of course, the problems of limiting the arms race both in nuclear and in conventional weapons."[4]

In fact, the hopes attached to the change of leadership in the Kremlin soon proved illusory. To be sure, the release of L. Wałęsa on 12 December 1982 as well as the lifting of martial law and the termination of internment for numerous members of the Polish opposition at year's end in 1982 brought a certain stabilization to the Polish situation, and this also relieved Soviet-US relations. But hopes beyond this remained unfulfilled. There was no progress either in Afghanistan (then KGB chief Andropov is said to have cautioned the Soviet Politburo in 1978 against entanglement in that country) or in Africa or Central America. And even Andropov's offer on 21 December 1982 at the Geneva negotiations failed to produce results because Moscow continued trying to prevent installation of US intermediate-range weapons in Europe while itself refusing to dismantle a significant portion of its SS-20 rockets aimed at Western Europe. The Geneva negotiations on intermediate-range missiles called for the USSR to reduce its intermediate-range weapons including the SS-20 in the European theater to the number of British and French intermediate-range missiles (about 160), provided NATO abandon the projected deployment of Pershing-II and cruise missiles.[5]

Consequently, the US did not deem the signals by the new secretary general at the turn of 1982/83 sufficient to warrant a change of course in US policy vis-à-vis the Soviet Union and, for instance, work towards a summit meeting of Reagan and Andropov. New Soviet proposals in January 1983 to forego the first use of nuclear weapons and conclude a general treaty on the renunciation of force as well as to create a 500–600 kilometer-wide nuclear-weapons-free zone in Central Europe[6] were also rejected by the US since in its view, they merely constituted propaganda maneuvers designed to divert attention from the real problems of the disarmament negotiations. Thereupon, Andropov accused the US (as early as 1 February 1983 in a *Pravda* interview) of leading "the Geneva negotiations deliberately into failure;" a few weeks later Minister of Defense Ustinov and Minister of Foreign Affairs Gromyko made corresponding utterances.[7]

By contrast, the US president, on 8 May in a speech in Orlando (Florida), again rejected a "freeze" of nuclear weapons since this would remove any incentive for the Soviet Union to negotiate seriously at the Geneva INF and START talks. In a radio and television address on 23 March, since known as the "Star-Wars-speech," he further demanded the application of existing and novel technologies to create by the end of the century an effective anti-missile system, capable of protecting the US and its allies from nuclear attack.[8]

To Soviet leadership, President Reagan's statements were just new proof of the US intent to continue rearming. Conversely, the US continued to eye Soviet behavior with great suspicion since the announcements in November and December 1982 were not followed by deeds. Hence, the hoped-for improvement of Soviet-US relations did not materialize.

In this climate of persistent confrontation and continuing suspicion, even the US proposal that took its bearings from West European wishes met with firm rejection from Moscow.[9] (The US proposal was to strive for a "transitional solution" at the Geneva INF negotiations based on partial concessions by both sides instead of the immediate removal of all nuclear intermediate-range systems in Europe, "zero option"). Reagan therefore felt convinced that Moscow would only be prepared for serious negotiations on intermediate-range weapons after the scheduled start of INF-deployment in Western Europe at the end of 1983.[10] In a government declaration on the "rearmament policy of the US," the Soviet Union announced countermeasures on 28 May in case the decision to start deploying new US missiles in Europe were to be implemented.

Among the few positive aspects during this phase was the April 12 suggestion by US Secretary of Defense Weinberger to reduce the risk of unintentional nuclear war by improving communication links with the Soviet Union and to this end to modernize the existing teletype line—the so-called "Hot Line"—between Washington and Moscow,[11] as well as the 22 April announcement by President Reagan that his government had proposed to the Soviet Union the conclusion of a long-term grain supply agreement. Talks on the refurbishing of the hot line got under way in the fall of 1983 in Moscow and eventually resulted in the signing of a corresponding agreement on 17 July 1984. As early as late July 1983, both sides had come to terms on a new grain supply agreement limited to five years. This increased Soviet minimum purchases by 50 percent to 9 million tons per annum, and the US undertook to permit exports of the agreed amounts and not even to interrupt supplies should a possible shortage at home suggest such an intervention.[12] The agreement was signed on 24 August in Moscow and entered into force on 1 October 1983. The rapid conclusion of the negotiations, though, was largely attributable to domestic political pressure in the US. For negotiations on the renewal of the 1975 long-term grain agreement had expired in 1981 and had previously been put off due to the situation in Poland. Only the stipulations then in effect had twice been extended by one year. The US portion of Soviet grain imports had declined from 74 percent in 1978/79 to a mere 19 percent in 1982/83 owing to this partial embargo.[13] Consequently, the US farmers' lobby had prevailed upon President Reagan and Agriculture Secretary Block to dismantle the "grain weapon."

Downing of the KAL-Jumbo and Effects of Pershing-II Deployment

Despite the new grain agreement and some progress in negotiating a new cultural agreement, there was remarkable accord in Washington and Moscow in the summer of 1983 that Soviet-US relations had "not improved."[14] In particular, there was no progress in the disarmament talks. Reservations about new contractual agreements with the Soviet Union in this area actually increased in Washington when it came to be known that the Soviet Union had possibly violated the terms of the SALT-II agreement that was being adhered to informally, and the ABM-treaty of 1972. Investigations by an expert commission installed in late April had concluded that in contravention of SALT-II the Soviet Union had apparently readied several SS-16 missiles near Plesetsk in the Arkhangelsk region and tested two new intercontinental missiles—the PL-5 and the SSX-24—even though the SALT-II terms permitted tests of only one new missile in this category. Beyond that, large new radar installations had been noted in Siberia that could be used for anti-missile purposes, counter to the ABM-terms.[15] These insights were in crass contrast to the numerous "peace initiatives" that the Soviet Union had been launching time and again. So, just shortly before (on 18 August 1983) at a reception for US senators, Andropov had cautioned against an "extension of the arms race to space" and demanded a renunciation of all "use of force both in space as well as from space against earth."[16]

Therefore, in the summer of 1983, it rather fit into the US picture of Soviet leadership as simultaneously dishonest and unscrupulous when on 1 September Soviet fighter planes shot down a South Korean Boeing 747 airliner out of Anchorage. The airliner had 269 people aboard (240 of them passengers) and had strayed into Soviet airspace over Kamchatka and Sakhalin. The Chief of the General Staff, N. Ogarkov, explained the downing at a press conference on 9 September by maintaining that it "had been proven irrefutably that the intrusion by the Korean airplane had been a deliberate and carefully planned intelligence operation."[17] US Secretary of State Shultz, by contrast, said that as far as the US was concerned, there was no justification whatsoever for shooting down an unarmed airliner, whether or not it violated national airspace. President Reagan demanded a Soviet apology for the action; besides, the "chasm between words and deeds of the Soviet government," he said, had become obvious to all. By way of reaction he announced the non-renewal of the bilateral transportation agreement, confirmation of a landing prohibition for Aeroflot, the call for an investigation of the occurrence by the International Civil Aviation Organization (ICAO), and the discontinuation of several bilateral negotiations. The disarmament talks, however, were not to be interrupted.[18]

But, to be sure, the atmosphere surrounding these talks was even less propitious after the Soviet downing of the Jumbo than before. Both sides again submitted new proposals at the Geneva INF-negotiations shortly before the beginning of the planned Western deployment; but agreement was not reached. For to the very end Soviet efforts were designed to keep all US intermediate-range missiles capable of reaching Soviet territory out of Europe, but to maintain as far as possible the respective Soviet potential to threaten Europe, and in any case not to dismantle it completely. Just once, within the terms of the compromise formula of the "walk-in-the-woods" on 16 July 1982, did the Soviet side temporarily back down from its basic position not to grant the US any reinforcements for its European INF potential. This formula envisaged reducing the SS-20 arsenal from a total of 333 to seventy-five missiles in Europe, plus ninety in Asia, with 495 war-heads in all and the new deployment of seventy-five US launchers for 300 cruise missiles with one war-head each in Western Europe. However, shortly afterwards, both the Kremlin and the US repudiated this formula.[19] Instead, all recent Soviet proposals again amounted to a contractual fixation of unilateral Soviet advantages and were hence unacceptable to the NATO countries. Their governments and parliaments, therefore, had little choice but to endorse deployment according to schedule, as for instance the German Federal Government and the *Bundestag* did on 22 November 1983.

After that, the Soviet chief delegate at the INF-negotiations, Yu. Kvitsinsky, declared that the talks would not be continued; a reopening of negotiations was made contingent upon a reversal of the Western missile deployment. START and MBFR negotiations, too, were indefinitely adjourned, but not broken off. By contrast, the Conference on Confidence-Building Measures and Disarmament in Europe (CCDE), envisaged as a continuation of the CSCE-process, began as planned on 17 January 1984 in Stockholm.

Beginnings of a Change of Course Under Chernenko

The failure of the INF negotiations and the interruption of the START and MBFR talks in late 1983 marked a low point in Soviet-US relations. However, for the US the start of Western INF deployment was proof of Western strength and resolution. It took its place in a modernization program that completed American measures of stabilization initiated with Reagan's inauguration three years earlier. Based on the restored position of US world power, the realization of the second part of the Reagan administration's long-term foreign policy program could now be undertaken: renewing the framework for talks with the Soviet Union.

Therefore, it was far from a mere tactical manoeuvre in the election campaign when on the eve of the opening of the CCDE, (on 16 January 1984), President Reagan announced in a television address what amounted to an about-face in US policy vis-à-vis the Soviet Union, proclaiming: "We must and will involve the Soviets in a dialogue which is as earnest and constructive as possible and will serve the promotion of peace in the troubled areas of the world, reduce the level of armaments, and create a constructive working relationship."[20]

Andropov replied in a *Pravda* interview on 25 January that the Soviet Union was prepared to "make use of any real opportunity for negotiations to achieve practical agreements on a limitation and reduction of nuclear armaments, based on the principle of equality and equal security."[21] However, a dialogue would have to be conducted on the basis of equality, not a position of strength as proposed by Reagan. Andropov again rejected reopening the INF negotiations, as long as the US missiles had not been withdrawn again.

The Soviet leadership stuck to this line even after Andropov's death and Chernenko's election as his successor on 13 February 1984. Yet, Chernenko obviously went further than Andropov in his proposals to pick up the thread of cooperation with the US. Thus, in an election speech on 2 March the new secretary general spoke of the possibility of a "genuine turnabout" as well as the "Soviet Union's desire to bring on a real, drastic change in Soviet-US relations."[22] It fit into this context that the interrupted MBFR-talks in Vienna were taken up as early as 16 March.

Calls for a renewal of the Soviet-US dialogue were now the order of the day on both sides. However, the Soviet side in particular mostly combined manifestations of readiness to talk with criticism of the opponent's armaments policy. Probably primarily as a retaliation for the American boycott of the Moscow Olympic Games in 1980, the Soviet Union stayed away from the 1984 Summer Olympic Games in Los Angeles, though "solely the slack security and the intensified anti-Sovietism" in the US were proffered as reasons.[23]

But in any event, no serious reopening of negotiations between the US and the USSR was to be expected at that time, since in November 1984 the US presidential election was impending, and this would determine whether Reagan would continue on his course or whether a new president would recast US foreign policy. Given the resultant uncertainty, all new initiatives met with considerable reservation in this phase. Thus, negotiations on anti-satellite and space weapons could not be brought about, even though on 15 June President Reagan took up corresponding Soviet proposals, submitted since Andropov's overture at a reception for US senators on 18 August 1983. According to the US interpretation, negotiations on the subject were to begin in September 1984 in Vienna and include both space weapons and the systems previously addressed in INF and START. Consequently Moscow suspected—probably correctly—that in this way the US was trying to move the Soviet Union back along the space track to negotiations on strategic and Euro-strategic weapons, and refused.

At the same time, an exchange of unequivocally positive signals took place: the signing of the agreement on the upgrading of the hot line on 17 July, the partial lifting of US sanctions against Poland on 3 August, as well as Reagan's decision of 11 September to raise the upper limit for Soviet grain purchases in the US for the second year of the long-term agreement of 1983, beginning on 1 October, to 22 million tons (as opposed to 9 million tons 1983/84). Most important, though, the first meeting in a long time of Minister of Foreign Affairs Gromyko and Secretary of State Shultz came to pass at the thirty-ninth session of the UN General Assembly in late September. On 28 September Gromyko and Reagan met for the first time at the White House.

The very fact that the conversation between Gromyko and Reagan took place more than a month prior to the presidential elections was revealing, even though by accounts on both sides it produced rather meager results. The Soviet leadership was evidently bent on easing relations with the US even though it must have known that the new president would again be Ronald Reagan. His demonstrative invitation of Gromyko to the White House reaffirmed the seriousness of his intent to contribute to a fundamental improvement of relations with the USSR. This convergence was also expressed in an interview Chernenko gave the *Washington Post* on 17 October as well as an important keynote speech by Secretary of State Shultz on 18 October in Los Angeles.[24]

Perspectives

Both sides having paved the way for a return to dialogue even prior to the US presidential election, Reagan's landslide victory on 6 November 1984 was no longer experienced as a shock in Moscow. Rather, in a speech on the occasion of celebrations on the sixty-seventh anniversary of the October Revolution on election day, Minister of Foreign Affairs Gromyko again advocated an improvement of relations with the US because the international climate depended on it. In Washington, the President re-elect affirmed the readiness of the US to make progress in the area of arms control and termed the avoidance of the nuclear threat a central task of his future policy.[25]

In fact, both sides agreed as early as January 1985 to reopen the disarmament talks in Geneva on 12 March. Contrary to its previous attitude, the Soviet Union was now willing to talk not only about those systems formerly treated at START, but to include the Euro-strategic weapons as well. The scales were apparently tipped towards Soviet conciliation by the newly acquired realization that US plans for a space-based anti-missile system ("Strategic Defense Initiative") had to be taken very seriously.[26] The Soviets were anxious lest the unhindered realization of pertinent research and development programs by the US detract decisively from the military value of Soviet missile systems, possibly already in the near future. This was probably accompanied by the fear of being drawn into a novel, technologically demanding, and financially expensive arms race with the US, the outcome of which would be uncertain. In any event, it might turn into a dangerous burden for the Soviet economy, strained as it was. Yet the fact that the two superpowers returned to the bargaining table boded well, the more so since the political backdrop brightened in no small measure.

Hence, perspectives for Soviet-US relations were considerably more hopeful at the outset of President Reagan's second term than in the preceding years. The renewal of the Soviet leadership with Gorbachev's election as secretary general of the CPSU upon Chernenko's death on 10 March 1985 fuelled already existing hopes. However, in the US, there were warnings about exaggerated optimism; the existence of a collective leadership in the USSR was said to hem in somewhat the secretary general's room for action; far from being a "liberal," Gorbachev was a product of the old, existing leading caste to which he had always accommodated himself; and Soviet foreign policy continued to be determined chiefly by Gromyko.[27] Still, a certain relief was unmistakable—both regarding the generational change that had finally been effected at the apex of the Soviet leadership, as well as regarding the prospect of being able again after a long time to enter into personal, direct contact with the Soviet secretary general. Therefore, on 13 March, while attending Chernenko's funeral ceremonies, US Vice-President Bush handed the new secretary general a message from Reagan in which the latter declared himself prepared to meet with Gorbachev as soon as possible—this was also a signal for the turnabout, discernible since early 1984.

Notes

1. Cf. M. Görtemaker, in *OE*, No. 6 (1981), pp. 445 ff.
2. Cf. B. Meissner, in: *EA*, No. 24 (1983), pp. 747 ff.
3. Cf. N. Podhoretz, *The Present Danger* (New York, 1980); see also Gerhard Wettig, "Arms Limitation and Arms Control in Soviet Policy Towards the West," in this volume, Chapter 22.
4. *Pr*, 23 November 1982, in German in *EA*, No. 1 (1983), pp. D 12–19.
5. Cf. G. Wettig, in *The Soviet Union 1982–83*, pp. 288 ff.
6. Cf. *Pr*, 28 January 1983.
7. *Pr*, 23 February 1983.
8. Cf. *Weekly Compilation of Presidential Documents*, No. 12 (Washington, D.C., 1983), pp. 442–448.
9. Cf. Gromyko's press conference of 2 April 1983, in *Pr*, 3 April 1983.
10. Interview with six foreign television correspondents of 26 May 1983, in: *Weekly Compilation of Presidential Documents*, No. 2 (Washington, D.C., 1983), p. 781.
11. Cf. *EA*, No. 9 (1983), p. Z 81.
12. *NZZ*, 31 July 1983.
13. *FAZ*, 25 August 1983.
14. *FAZ*, 30 August 1983.
15. J. Voas, *CRS Report* No. 84-160 F, Washington, D.C., 10 September 1984; *TIME*, 3 December 1984, p. 31 ff.
16. *Pr*, 19 August 1983.
17. *Pr*, 10 September 1983.
18. *EA*, No. 19 (1983), p. Z 173.
19. *TIME*, 5 December 1983, pp. 16–22.
20. *EA*, No. 4 (1984), pp. D 110 ff.
21. *Pr*, 25 January 1984.
22. *Pr*, 3 March 1984.

23. According to M. Gramov, Chairman of the National Olympic Committee of the USSR, at a press conference in Moscow, *Pr*, 15 May 1984.

24. *Wireless Bulletin from Washington* (Bonn), No. 196, (1984), pp. 2ff.

25. TIME, 19 November 1984, pp. 20ff.

26. On this the series of articles entitled "Weapons in Space," in NYT, 3 March–8 March 1985.

27. On the reactions in the US see NYT, 12 March 1985.

22

Arms Limitation and Arms Control in Soviet Policy Towards the West

Gerhard Wettig

The Problem of Arms Control

According to conventional US notions of arms control, widely accepted in the West, it is imperative to safeguard the security of East and West alike. Both sides are to enjoy the best possible guarantee that they will not become embroiled in war against each other. A military balance seems a suitable basis that leaves neither side the option of going to war with the promise of its own survival and a military victory. As this philosophy of war prevention has it, the risk of incurring unacceptable damage and the improbability of success bear the optimal guarantee of a renunciation of military threats by both sides. Consequently, the following seem to be required:

- Both sides renounce endeavors for military superiority and work towards a stable relationship of balance. Accordingly, each side strives to thwart the respective other side's option of waging war with its own military capacity, which also implies the willingness to relinquish that option oneself.
- The mutual deterrence from war assumes the capacity and the will to keep the other side from the inadmissable option of waging war because in case of contravention, one would certainly put the threatened consequences into effect by military means. At the same time, however, it must be clear that no threatening initiative is intended. With regards to the eventuality of war, preparations for defensive military behavior seem appropriate, the more so since offensive operations are believed to necessitate the availability of superior forces.
- The renunciation of offensive military planning brings with it the renunciation of the element of surprise. This appears correct not solely for military reasons. It is at least an equally momentous consideration that in case of a war-threatening crisis, neither side be attempted to attack "in anticipation of" a possibly expected war, as this would render illusory any success for efforts aimed at the prevention of war.

The aforementioned three postulates presume agreement among the potential opponents, since this is the only chance that the required military restraint be mutually respected. Ordinarily, negotiations seem the best way to achieve such an understanding. Accordingly, the US and the USSR, or the NATO and Warsaw Pact member states respectively, have repeatedly engaged in negotiations for the mutual limitation of military potentials.

The Problem of the Strategic Balance of Forces in SALT and START

In 1965, the US government first suggested to Moscow a treaty on mutual renunciation of anti-missile systems. Such an arrangement was to secure permanently the condition of "mutually assured destruction" of the two world powers as the foundation for a mutual inability to wage war against each other. The Soviet leadership evaded the US initiative. Unlike the US, the USSR had two anti-missile installations at the time around Moscow and Leningrad.

Three years later, the Soviet rejection caused the administration and Congress in Washington to decide in turn on the construction of an anti-missile system that would be "thin" at first. This produced anxiety in the Soviet capital for the US was believed capable of rapidly developing a system technically far superior to the relatively primitive Soviet installations. After that, the Soviet leadership pressed Washington for a treaty renouncing anti-missile systems. This became part of the US-Soviet SALT-I treaty of May 1972.

In the late sixties, the US government and public worried lest the global-strategic balance be unhinged by other means. The USSR was deploying intercontinental missiles at a rapid pace. In 1964, after the United States had stopped at 1,000 missiles, plus fifty-four older ones and was determined to continue this self-imposed limitation, the perspective of being overtaken by the Soviets loomed larger. Experts in Washington perceived the emerging danger that the USSR, with a considerably larger potential of offensive missiles, might achieve military superiority over the US. Particularly menacing seemed the heavy SS-9 missiles the nuclear payload of which was equivalent to many megatons of TNT.

The US government demanded from Moscow that on this issue also mutual limitations be negotiated. Given its interest in restrictions on anti missile systems, the Soviet government felt compelled to accede to the demand. However, it kept procrastinating on this part of the negotiations until it had armed to about one-and-a-half times numerical superiority in intercontinental missiles, and thereafter carried the point by achieving a freeze agreement that was limited in time. Likewise, it achieved a settlement that accepted as fixed its monopoly in "heavy missiles." Beyond this, it secured the possibility of modernizing the existing 309 SS-9s in the future and further increasing their payload in the process.

Notwithstanding these asymmetries in Moscow's favor, the SALT-I treaty overall amounted to a codification of the balance between the two world powers at the global-strategic level. Both the US and the USSR acted in full consciousness that they were unable to do away with their mutual global-strategic vulnerability, that they were therefore forced to avoid a war at this level, and that consequently both benefitted from an appropriate stabilization agreement.[1]

In much the same way Soviet leadership approached the SALT-II negotiations that were to bring about the final settlement, due as of 1977, regarding a limitation of all intercontinental weapons. From Moscow's perspective, the US Senate vote that a further SALT agreement must not again envisage unequal limits for the two sides, impeded the course of the talks. Moscow had always deemed unreasonable demands for reductions—unilateral ones at that—in existing military assets. The Soviet negotiators responded to the US demand for such renunciations by calling for compensations. Thus additional asymmetries entered the SALT-II treaty, which was not concluded until June 1979.

Much to the disappointment of committed SALT-advocates in Washington in particular, numerical upper limits were also set at a level only about 10 percent below that of the Soviet arsenal. In the US view, this was insufficient to satisfy the claim of being a genuine arms limitation measure and live up to an arms control notion of a balance based on minimal deterrence. Still, the agreement indicated once again that the two world powers had resigned themselves to their inability to reasonably wage a global-strategic war against each other.[2]

From the very beginning the SALT-II treaty was controversial with the US public. Aside from specific disadvantages accepted by the government, a decisive part in making it so was played by widespread doubts about Soviet arms-control willingness. US and British specialists on the Soviet Union have claimed ever more emphatically since the mid-seventies that the USSR took a dim view of Western arms control philosophy and acceded to the agreements reached only on account of the military advantages thus acquired.[3]

This led many politicians and journalists to the conclusion that entering arms control agreements with Moscow is always senseless because the presumed community of arms control purposes was lacking. Frequently, the Soviet leadership's motive was seen as seeking to open a SALT-II based "window of vulnerability" towards the US, i.e., they sought to acquire a capacity for a debilitating first strike against the land-based US intercontinental missiles. This danger, it was then said, had to be met by a rejection of the limitations arising from the SALT-II treaty in order to create the requisite defensive options. US indignation at the USSR's military intervention in Afghanistan in December 1979 caused the last opportunities for a ratification of the SALT-II agreement by the US Senate to wane.

It took nearly two years before interest in agreements on global-strategic arms control with the USSR took shape again in Washington. The Reagan administration coupled this with sharp criticism of the concept pursued by preceding US governments. Word was that the issue must no longer be to codify more or less prevalent conditions. Rather, what mattered were substantial arms reductions and qualitative changes in armaments. Henceforth, therefore, "strategic arms reduction talks" (START) must be held.

The Soviet leadership, which up to that point had unswervingly called the implementation of SALT-II the indispensible precondition for additional measures, felt compelled to respond to the new US line. Viewed from Moscow, no stone was to be left unturned to limit contractually as much as possible the input of superior US technology into the global-strategic armaments of the US. Hence, a clear Soviet effort to arrive at specific results was felt in START from the very beginning. Moscow, however, could not be reconciled to Washington's demand to shift the missiles out to sea so as to prevent any capacity for a debilitating first strike by either side. Unlike the US, for the USSR this would have entailed large-scale and costly changes.

This decisive difference notwithstanding, the course of START gave rise to some optimism. When the Soviet leadership broke off negotiations anyway in November 1983, this had nothing to do with the START problems. It was meant to punish the US government for the deployment of INF missiles in Western Europe. Those missiles are of decisive importance to the Kremlin's security policy. Furthermore, the Kremlin apparently entertained doubts as to the extent of the US government's general interest in a stabilization of the reciprocal relationship. From his conversation with President Reagan in late September 1984, Minister of Foreign Affairs Gromyko gained the impression that the US side was serious about it. This resulted in a new beginning for negotiations on strategic arms limitation.

Forward Based Systems and Armed Forces Reduction in Central Europe

The global-strategic balance as such does not yet guarantee that no power could afford a war in Europe, either. Accordingly, NATO's security policy aims at extending war-preventing deterrence to the European theater. This purpose is to be served not least by the deployment of US intermediate-range systems. The point is to make plain to the USSR that the US has the option of nuclear-strategic escalation and that consequently a war that the Soviet Union might perhaps deem fit to wage on NATO brings with it the risk of extending the ravages of war to Soviet territory.

Since the beginning of SALT-I, Soviet leadership had tried time and again to prevail upon the US side to renounce its "forward based systems," i.e., its intermediate-range nuclear aircraft stationed in Europe and elsewhere. It explained in the process that, after all, it did not have at its disposal either corresponding systems capable of reaching North American territory. Thus, it tacitly staked out a claim to unilateral possession of INF weaponry to threaten allies of the US because these were not directed against the other world power.

The Soviet effort to uncouple the European theater from the relationship of deterrence between the two world powers became especially evident in

1972. Minister of Foreign Affairs Gromyko and Secretary General Brezhnev, in negotiations on an agreement for the prevention of nuclear war, sought to persuade the US government to come to an understanding according to which, in the case of war between NATO and the Warsaw Pact, nuclear weapons should be used only against each other's allies, but not against each other's territories proper.[4]

When the deployment of US Pershing-II missiles in Western Europe became of current importance in the late seventies, Moscow tried to prevent this at all costs. Soviet propaganda sought to convince Western Europeans that the measure envisaged by NATO served US interests exclusively and was detrimental to the security of Western European countries. Soviet representatives addressed the US side with the allusion that the deployment planned for the benefit of the Europeans merely threatened to entangle the US in a potential European war. At the bottom of this was Moscow's assessment that the deployment of Pershing-II and cruise missiles was a significant factor extending the global-strategic balance of deterrence between the two world power to the European theater.[5]

The question of whether Europe would stay coupled to the war-preventing balance between the US and the USSR or be detached from it was of particular importance in light of the military imbalances generally assumed to exist there. In the early seventies, the NATO states pressed Moscow for negotiations on "mutual balanced forces reductions" (MBFR) in Central Europe. The proclaimed purpose was to bring about a reduction in prevailing military imbalances. Consequently, the WP-states were to agree to larger reductions than the NATO-countries. Soviet leadership resisted this demand and could be brought to the negotiating table only by a linkage with the Conference on Security and Cooperation in Europe (CSCE) that it desired.

Initially, the USSR and its allies were mainly anxious to fend off the Western demand for disproportionate Eastern reductions with MBFR. According to their line of argument, it was inadmissable for one side to seek advantages from the projected agreements. In informal conversations, Soviet diplomats occasionally explained that their country required certain military compensations in Central Europe for military and political disadvantages existing elsewhere. Secretary General Brezhnev summarized the position saying, "the power relations that have developed in Central Europe and on the European continent generally" must not "altered."[6] Moreover, the Soviet line of argument indicated that just like leaders of Western governments, leaders in the Kremlin assumed an existing Soviet preponderance.

The Soviet position brought forth a negative echo in the Western public. This caused Moscow to alter its political line. In 1976, Soviet negotiators at MBFR submitted a description of the military power relations in Europe resting on the thesis that near parity already existed between the two alliances. In January of the following year, Secretary General Brezhnev issued a new statement. According to that statement, the USSR does not strive for "superiority in armament," but restricts itself to the requirements of its defense.[7]

Nevertheless the Soviet side thereafter assumed the same positions at MBFR as before—with the sole exception that what had previously been defended as the "prevalent power relations" was now declared an inviolable "prevalent balance." The ensuing negotiations continued to pivot on the differential numerical data about the Eastern European armed forces. In the process, it proved impossible to determine in detail what criteria Moscow had applied to count the Warsaw Pact troops in Central Europe—the result being that the strength of Eastern military units could not be compared with the strength of Western military units.

Negotiations on Transparency-Building Measures in Europe

In the Western view, the threat emanating from Soviet military might is increased to no small degree by Soviet planning foreseeing a rapid offensive advance by the Warsaw Pact against Western Europe. The great importance attributed to the element of surprise seemed especially dangerous. Militarily and politically great problems were seen to flow from this. Should the Soviet leadership decide on a sudden attack, the NATO states might not have enough time to adequately organize their defenses. Insofar as such an eventuality had to be taken into account, it could not but weigh heavily upon any potentially developing East-West crisis. Should the Western side on suspicion attempt early precautionary measures against a possible Eastern attack, this would inevitably have to exacerbate the situation and escalate the dispute.

Considerations along these lines led to the conclusion that the point was to counteract the sense of threat by creating more transparency. Each side was to afford the other insights enabling it to ascertain the groundlessness of its worries. The parties were to undertake certain obligations to expose their respective military behavior. The refusal to afford the insights envisaged by the treaty was then to be taken as evidence of threatening intentions.

This philosophy was at the bottom both of the Western proposals for "accompanying measures" at MBFR and of the Western-neutral concept of "confidence-building measures" at CSCE and CCDE. Soviet leadership's reaction to all these proposals was fundamentally negative. At MBFR, Soviet negotiators saw to it that the "accompanying measures" played no major part in the deliberations. At CSCE and the follow-up meeting in Belgrade, all proposals aiming at real insights into the military dispositions of each side foundered on Soviet resistance.

At the Madrid negotiations, after much ado, representatives of the Western, neutral, and non-aligned states managed to achieve concessions on a mandate for CCDE because Moscow was urgently interested in holding the conference. When CCDE began deliberations in Stockholm in 1984, however, Soviet delegates assumed the position that the projected "confidence-building measures" were to be understood and implemented as a Moscow-type declaration on security. Soviet leadership evidently remained unsympathetic to the creation of military transparency. Seen from its vantage, regulations of this kind could only be disadvantageous. After all, the Eastern side alone had at its disposal an offensive military option in the European theater that could be improved by means of surprise. Thus, if greater transparency came to pass, the possibilities for action by the USSR would be reduced unilaterally.

Soviet Notions of Security

Soviet leadership starts out with the premise that East-West relations are antagonistic in nature. While in certain cases both sides may cooperate pragmatically, they are still condemned to insurmountable rivalry due to the prevailing systemic antagonism. From this it follows that war between NATO and the Warsaw Pact remains a constant possibility, even though the Kremlin may strive to avoid it. Therefore, it seems fully inadequate to Soviet leadership to bet all their chips on war prevention. The security of the USSR must stand the test also, and especially in the case of war. The country may be deemed safe only to the extent that it is able to weather a war with the Western alliance.

Consequently, the idea of deterrence has no place in the Soviet way of looking at things. "Defense" is the key term of Soviet security policy. But defense means waging war. This results in wide-ranging practical effects. Soviet politicians and the military have made it clear which military capabilities must be regarded as necessary:

- The enemy, who must pass for the "aggressor" in all cases, must be prevented from entering one's own sphere of power. What matters, then, is that from the outset he be forced back into the depths of his own territory.
- In the event of war, the functioning of the political and social order on Soviet territory must remain unconditionally safeguarded. This applies in principle also to a nuclear war.
- The enemy's "aggression" must be terminated by a Soviet victory.

Assuming a sufficiently large military potential, these three aforementioned requirements can be fulfilled, but only in a conventional and tactical-nuclear conflict. Should Western states, mainly the US, commit long-range nuclear weapons that would descend on Soviet territory, then unforeseeable, devastating destruction must be expected in the USSR. Regardless of whether its armed forces then still advance to the Atlantic, there can be no question of a fully functioning Soviet political and social order.

Here, then, lies the motive for Soviet leadership both to come to terms with the global-stategic balance and to aspire to uncouple Europe from this balance. As seen from Moscow, there is no chance for the time being of turning total nuclear war with the US into an acceptable risk. Fortunately, there also seems to be no reasonable ground for the two world powers to embark upon such a mutually destructive duel.

Repercussions on Security Notions in the United States

Conventional US arms control philosophy was founded on the assumption that the Soviet leadership was guided by similar ideas or would gradually accede to the US way of thinking. However, in view of numerous disappointments caused by Soviet behavior, there were growing doubts in the US during the second half of the seventies as to the justification for the basic assumption that the Kremlin engaged in arms control policy the same way the West did. Numerous experts concluded instead that Soviet thinking and action was determined by a "strategy for the conduct of war," tied to the motive of nuclear-strategic "damage limitation," if not even to ambitions of a nuclear-strategic "first-strike-capacity" vis-à-vis the US. Many became convinced that Soviet leadership considered an East-West-war—in the European theater or also at the global-strategic level—as one that could be waged and won. Especially the USSR's continuing massive efforts in the areas of aerial defense, civil defense, and offensive weapons aimed at US missile sites contributed decisively to this evaluation.

What is more, since the early eighties US doubts have increased, regarding the observance of the 1972 ABM-treaty on the part of the USSR. Reconnaissance findings have given rise to the suspicion that certain anti-aircraft missiles, designed so that they can later be committed as anti-missile missiles have been increasingly deployed in the Soviet Union. In addition, there was the installation of a large radar system in the Kraznoyarsk region, possibly conceived as the nucleus for a country-wide Soviet anti-missile system (prohibited by the AMB-treaty). It was also learned that the USSR had begun to develop a novel, mobile anti-missile system, capable of being moved rapidly to any location, and to test components of anti-aircraft and anti-missile systems. All this fueled the suspicions of leading personalities in the Reagan administration that the Soviet Union was striving for nuclear-strategic superiority; especially its policy of active and passive damage limitation in respect to US intercontinental missiles included both preparations for a debilitating first strike and precautions to shield the USSR against the second-strike missiles, then still left to the US.

It is not entirely clear to what extent these realizations and fears were already playing a part when on 23 March 1983 President Reagan, in a televised speech, for the first time elaborated on the concept of a US anti-missile system which, among other things, was to be space-based. The public, in any event, was not coherently informed about the observations until late 1984/early 1985.[8] In public discussions, advocates of the "strategic defense initiative" (SDI) justified their insistence by alleging that, unlike the US, the USSR had never neglected its research and development and had even prepared a country-wide deployment of anti-missile systems.

For Reagan an essential consideration was that the new concept seemed suitable for pulling the rug out from under protests against the current NATO strategy of nuclear deterrence. These protests had been ever more vocally articulated on both sides of the Atlantic since 1979. He was largely in agreement with those critics of the principle of "mutually assured destruction" (MAD), who rejected such a security policy as immoral, inimical to life, and perilous to the extreme. With the assistance of a non-nuclear anti-missile shield in space, Reagan hoped to be able to replace the current principle with the prospect of "mutually assured survival." Future space weapons were to "destroy missiles, not kill people."

The Kremlin responded to these announcements and the ensuing steps by the US, which elucidated Reagan's emphatic insistence on a drastic conceptual change in US security policy, with virulent reproaches reflecting surprise and anxiety. In Soviet propaganda, the polemics against Reagan's alleged "star-wars" plans soon relegated the topic of US intermediate-range missile deployment in Europe from first to second place. The prevention of the American research program became the priority objective of Soviet policy. At the arms limitation talks, resumed in Geneva on 12 March 1985, the USSR made any agreement on other questions conditional upon US renunciation of SDI research.

Notes

1. This is, for instance, evidenced by numerous statements by Soviet experts at the conclusion of the SALT-I treaty. Cf., *inter alia*, G.A. Arbatov, "Sobytie vazhnogo mezhdunarodnogo znacheniya," in *SShA*, No. 8 (1972), pp. 3–12; G.A. Trofimenko, "Sovetsko-amerikanskoe soglashenie ob ogranichenii strategicheskikh vooruzheniy," in: *SShA*, No. 9 (1972), pp. 3–16.

2. As far as Moscow is concerned, this can again be derived from Soviet statements; cf., *inter alia*, the Document by the Politburo of the CPSU, by the Presidium of the Supreme Soviet of the USSR, and by the Council of Ministers of the USSR, rendered in: *SShA*, No. 7 (1979), pp. 3ff.; "Imperativ razryadki," in *SShA*, No. 7 (1979), pp. 5–7; A.A. Platonov, "Krupneyshee dostizhenie v oblasti ogranicheniya vooruzheniy," in *SShA*, No. 9 (1979), pp. 11–23; V. Zurkin, OSV-2: vazhnyi vklad v ukreplenie mira, in *Mirovaya ekonomika i mezhduna-rodnye otnosheniya*, No. 8 (1979), pp. 3–12.

3. Cf., *inter alia*, R.W. Barnett, "Trans-SALT: Soviet Strategic Doctrine," in *Orbis*, Summer, 1975, pp. 533–561; J. Erikson, "The Chimera of Mutual Deterrence," in *Strategic Review*, Spring, 1978, pp. 11–17; S. Sienkievicz, "SALT and Soviet Nuclear Doctrine," in *International Security*, Spring, 1978, pp. 84–100; F.W. Ermarth, "Contrasts in American and Soviet Strategic Thought," in *Interntional Security*, Fall, 1978, pp. 138–155; cf. also Manfred Görtemaker, "Soviet Policy Vis-à-vis the United States," in this volume, Chapter 21.

4. H. Kissinger, *Years of Upheaval* (London, 1982), pp. 236–239.

5. J. Barry, "Geneva Behind Closed Doors," in *T*, 31 May 1983.

6. Speech on 26 October 1973 (*Pr*, 27 October 1973).

7. Speech on 19 January 1977 (*Pr*, 20 January 1977).

8. C.W. Weinberger, speech on 19 December 1984, in *Wireless Bulletin from Washington*, No. 237 (1984), pp. 7–15; government statement: "The President's Strategic Defense Initiative," *ibid.*, No. 2 (1985), pp. 1–22. See also L.I. Barrett, "How Reagan Became a Believer," in *TIME*, 11 March 1985, p. 120.

23

Relations Between the USSR and the Federal Republic of Germany

Fred Oldenburg

Though of eminent significance to the USSR's leadership as in previous years, Soviet policy towards Germany more than ever remained subordinate to relations with the other superpower, the US, on the one hand, and to the safeguarding of Soviet hegemony over an Eastern Europe that was growing increasingly self-confident (including the GDR) on the other.[1] For all that, Soviet policy vis-à-vis the Federal Republic has always operated on two parallel levels—the diplomatic one and the ideological-propagandistic one. It must, moreover, be taken into account that following Brezhnev's death there were at times three competing orientations of Soviet policy towards the West, represented by the pairs Gromyko-Ustinov, Chernenko-Tikhonov, and Andropov-Gorbachev.

For the representatives of the first school, the unequivocal priority of the global conflict with the US and of arms competition with the NATO states was never in doubt. Those of the second school, while sharing the same ambitions of equality and parity in foreign and armaments policy, still tended to place considerably more emphasis on Soviet interest in political and economic cooperation with Western industrialized states. The third school was more intent on active exploitation of conflicts within the "capitalist camp." Such exploitation is meant to reduce the external pressures on the Soviet empire, combining a tendency to place their chips on cooperation with the West Europeans with the all-out exclusion of economic cooperation from the political confrontation between the USSR and the US.

Throughout the entire Brezhnev era and Andropov's fifteen-month transitional rule, a dominant tendency in Soviet foreign policy was to talk the Federal Republic into a favorable approach to Moscow's policy towards the West, and to throw Bonn's international weight onto the scales for the ascendancy of Soviet positions, especially vis-à-vis Washington. In the Brezhnev era, this was done predominantly by wooing; under Andropov wooing and threats alternated. Finally, during Chernenko's thirteen months in office the elements of threat predominated. Remarkably enough, throughout the past thirty years Soviet leadership has never used the bait of German reunification. They preferred instead to play upon the geopolitical situation, the national and economic interests of the Federal Republic, as well as the Germans' deeply rooted fears of a third world war, and to make them operative by skillfully exerting influence on different strata of the population.

Already prior to the last Brezhnev visit in November 1981, the political dialogue was shifting increasingly to the uncertainty regarding Western rearmament and to Soviet countermeasures. This also affected bilateral relations, though the relationship of economic cooperation was left all but undisturbed. In order to maintain regional military superiority over Western Europe, Moscow's main objective up to the confirmation of the Federal Government's decision for deployment by the Bundestag on 22 November 1983 and beyond was to prevent or interrupt the planned installation by 1988 of 108 American Pershing-II, and 96 cruise missiles. Because this failed in spite of all threats, Soviet leadership tried to isolate the Federal Republic as of 1984, and, bypassing it, establish by early 1985 alternative centers of gravity. This seemed the more urgent since several Eastern European countries, immediately following the break-down of the Geneva INF-negotiations (23 November 1983), communicated their desire to contain damage to East-West-relations. At the same time, the USSR, quite to the contrary, was intent on making the most of the countermeasures and reprisals it had announced earlier.

Until the autumn of 1985, this Soviet policy of punishment met with procrastinating resistance, especially on the part of the SED leadership, which could refer to another strategy in the policy towards Germany aimed at dialogue and presumably agreed on in May 1983 with Andropov. In fact, during the lengthy Soviet succession crisis, the GDR showed itself quite ready to present its very own line in the area of foreign policy and, for the first time, in security policy as well.[2] Ultimately, though, Soviet leadership once again proved itself strong enough to exact sufficient loyalty from the GDR.[3] Thus, in September 1984, Party leaders and heads of state in the GDR and Bulgaria were urgently advised to cancel visits to the Federal Republic of Germany, planned for that very month. After Chernenko's death on 10 March 1985, Honecker immediately signalled his continuing interest in closer economic and security cooperation with Bonn. Apparently, he assumed that new Secretary General Gorbachev, who had already earlier been placed in the Andropov-wing of the Politburo of the CPSU, would again grant the GDR greater German-German room for maneuver. However, already by late April it was becoming obvious that the SED leader had again misjudged his posibilities for action.

Political Relations

During 1984, the Federal Republic of Germany forfeited the role of a preferred partner, intended for it by Brezhnev upon the conclusion of the 1970 Moscow Treaty. This became apparent both during Chernenko's brief tenure in office and in the purely formal treatment accorded Chancellor Kohl by Secretary General Gorbachev at the funeral ceremonies for Chernenko on 14 March 1985. While Soviet leadership does not intend to undermine the substance of political—much less economic—relations with Bonn, it still expects the Federal Republic to pay more heed to its security interests and to keep greater distance from the United States. It was also irritated by the fact that the coalition of CDU/CSU and FDP, governing since October 1982, once again declares, more adamantly than before, the German question to be open. Thereby, differential emphases in Bonn, particularly in statements regarding the Eastern borders, provided fuel for Soviet propaganda which, after some delay, launched a revanchism-campaign against the Federal Republic in May 1984.[4] Presumably, the issue was not so much a fear on the part of Moscow that Bonn intended to question the post-war order; it was rather the revival of old enemy images, for the purpose of legitimizing Soviet hegemony over the peoples of Central and Eastern Europe.

There had been critical comments about the West German *Ostpolitik* even prior to Andropov's meeting in Moscow with Chancellor Kohl and Foreign Minister Genscher, from 4 to 7 July 1983.[5] Thus, in late June 1983 Soviet Prime Miniter Tikhonov warned then Minister of Economic Affairs Lambsdorff of the negative consequences of US missile deployment on bilateral trade exchanges.[6] This admonition was repeated in autumn of 1983 by individual media, but was not reiterated by Soviet politicians at high-level bilateral meetings.

After the death of Brezhnev, the Soviet-German summit of July 1983 in Moscow was Andropov's first encounter with a Western head of government; this indicated the then high ranking of the Federal Republic in Soviet strategy towards the West. Two months earlier, Andropov had received Honecker and settled on flexible tactics vis-à-vis the Federal Republic. In June 1983, he even replaced Ambassador Abrasimov, disliked in East Berlin, thereby facilitating contacts between Bonn and East Berlin.

Impending NATO rearmament and deteriorating Soviet-US relations already cast a shadow over Andropov's encounter with Kohl on 5 July 1983, that had actually been aimed at a strengthening of relations. In the process, Andropov, Tikhonov, Gromyko, and Ustinov, and also then Chief of Staff Ogarkov, repeatedly warned against the consequences of the deployment in Europe of US intermediate-range missiles. They would negatively affect the Soviet-German relationship, they warned, and dramatically raise the dangers to the Federal Republic. At the same time, the Soviet side solicited support for its disarmament initiatives toward the US. The Soviet leaders linked this encouragement to positive assessments of German-German relations to which they attributed a stabilizing role in the East-West relationship. Due to clear differences in positions on security matters, and due also to the brusk Soviet rejection of German requests for more emigration permits for Soviet citizens of German extraction, no joint communique was signed at the time.

The second half of 1983 was marked by Moscow's attempts to influence public opinion in the Federal Republic and West Berlin by the appearance of Soviet "travelling cadres." At the diplomatic level, Ambassador Semyonov warned the chairmen of the political parties represented in the Bundestag, as well as members of parliament, foreign service officers, and journalists as late as November 1983 against deployment of US missiles to which he attached "fundamental significance" as it was a "step hostile to the cause of peace." The ambassador held the members of the Bundestag personally responsible for the continuation or failure of the Geneva INF-negotiations. Eventually the Federal Government felt these activities to be so objectionable that the West German Minister of Economic Affairs told the Chairman of the Council of Ministers, Tikhonov, in Moscow at the twelfth session of the joint economic commission, that Semyonov's behavior was an "unfriendly act of pressure" and, moreover, counterproductive for Soviet policy.[7] Yet, Andropov also tried to intervene in Bonn's decisionmaking, with several personal letters to the chancellor between August and November.

The problems of rearmament eventually also weighed down the total of eleven hours of talks by the two foreign ministers on 15 and 16 October 1983 in Vienna.[8] Here Gromyko and Genscher attempted once more to expound the positions of the two alliances. While the German Minister of Foreign Affairs tried in vain to move the Soviet side to dispense with including British and French missile systems in the Geneva negotiations, his Soviet colleague placed particular emphasis on describing the US proposals as thin and insincere. He requested that the Federal Government make representatives in Washington, pleading for a postponement and ultimately renunciation of Western rearmament, but at the very least for an extension of the Geneva talks. Immediately thereafter, Gromyko journeyed to East Berlin in order to commit the SED leadership to the continuation of the deployment of Soviet SS-21, 22, and 23 intermediate-range missiles that had already started in the GDR. Their deployment was finally announced in late October by the Soviet Ministry of Defense, the National Defense Council of the GDR, and the CSSR-government.[9]

Gromyko had used strong words in East Berlin when he warned the SED Politburo against Western European politicians who made themselves "accomplices against peace in Europe." This was presumably intended to boost those forces previously already indirectly critical of Honecker's line of continuing the German-German dialogue even after the beginning of deployment, anticipated for the end of the year. But Soviet leadership had to take cognizance of Honecker's explanation at the seventh plenary session of the CC of the SED on 25 November 1983 that Soviet countermeasurs elicited "no joy" in the GDR. Rather, the SED leader committed the GDR to a policy of "damage limitation" in East-West relations, which Hungarian CC Secretary Szürös had already supported in October of that year and which in the following months led to covert coordination of Budapest's and East Berlin's policies towards the West.[10]

The continuing Soviet succession crisis presumably interfered in the fall and winter months of 1983/84, with greater pressure on the GDR leadership and with a sharper pace vis-à-vis the Federal Republic. When newly appointed

Secretary General Chernenko met with Kohl and Genscher at the funeral ceremonies for his predecessor on 14 February, he underscored again "the Soviet Union's position on principle regarding the effects of the deployment of US missiles."[11] However, in the brief exchange of views on basic questions of bilateral relations as well as on the situation in Europe, Chernenko avoided taking a firm stand regarding the consequences. The first meeting of Kohl and Honecker that took place on 13 February in the Soviet government's guest house in Moscow's Lenin Hills, was more fruitful. Like the Chancellor, the GDR's Chairman of the State Council advocated at that meeting a contribution by both states to the improvement of the political climate in Europe, and both came out in favor of a continuation of the East-West dialogue.

However, this policy of the GDR and other Eastern European states vis-à-vis the West aimed at conciliation and readiness to talk, evidently ran counter to the Soviet leadership's intentions. Having threatened a new "ice age" as a result of the missile deployment, Soviet leaders did not want to lose face. The antagonism between Moscow and important Eastern European capitals caused the CPSU, and especially its CC department for governing communist parties under K.V. Rusakov and O.B. Rakhmanin, to kindle a discussion on the principles of the relationship between "things national and things international" (its line of argument, to be sure, being supported only by the Prague communists).[12] When it became ever more evident that several Warsaw Pact states balked at Moscow's confrontation course—above all, presumably, out of economic interests in maintaining economic contacts with the West, but also out of security policy considerations—Soviet propaganda as of April 1984 sought to revive the enemy image of the "neo-Nazi and renvachist" Germans. To this end, the 40th anniversary of the victory over Hitler's Germany (8 May 1985), in particular, provided numerous points of departure.

The German Minister of Foreign Affairs was made to feel the hardening Soviet position in his conversations with Chernenko and Gromyko from 20 to 22 May 1984. Gromyko expressed to his German colleague Soviet anxiety at U.S. rearmament and foreign policy.[13] He not only blamed the US altogether for the arms race, but also accused it of kindling all the world's major crises—from Nicaragua to Lebanon and all the way to the Iran-Iraq conflict. What allegedly mattered to the Reagan administration was to force the US will upon the world, Gromyko stressed. To counteract Washington's plans, the time was now ripe for the Federal Government to cast its weight onto the "scales of East-West relations" in the interest of a "proper understanding of peace" and cooperation. Bonn was flatly called upon to urge the President of the US to forego his "ambitions in space." But at the same time Gromyko refused to attend an expert meeting on the issue of the destruction of chemical weapons, planned for 12 to 14 June in the Westphalian city of Münster. However, the Soviet Minister of Foreign Affairs emphasized simultaneously the USSR's continuing quest for fields of mutual cooperation. Surprisingly, he assessed the quality of relations as "good or at least satisfactory." He expressed readiness henceforth to intensify economic, technological, and cultural cooperation. In this context, the USSR agreed to participate in the European environmental conference held in Munich from 24 to 27 June 1984.

Following the Gromyko-Genscher meeting, the Soviet leadership apparently reached the conclusion that the desired disciplinary effects in Eastern Europe could only be achieved by further stepping up the defamatory campaign against the Federal Republic. Preparatory to 8 May 1985, then, two accusations were recurrently leveled in numerous media contributions: (1) In the Federal Republic of Germany, revanchist, militarist, and partly also neo-Nazi forces, intent on reversing Germany's defeat after the deployment of US missiles, were said to be gaining momentum with the connivance of the government; and (2) With the Bonn coalition falling in with the US course of confrontation—rearmament plus rejection of the status quo, allegedly determined at Yalta in 1945—West German foreign policy was also said to be increasingly bent on questioning the post-war order, the existing boundaries, the sovereignty of the GDR, and ultimately on turning away from the Eastern treaties of the seventies.

Honecker's visit to the Federal Republic of Germany was announced in March 1984, and in early May it was set for late September. To impede this visit, Chernenko personally committed the SED secretary general, in an encounter accompanying the CMEA summit on 14 June 1984, to the Soviet view. According to that view, the "reinforcement of preparations for war on the part of NATO is conducive to activating extreme right-wing circles in the FRG."[14] Three days later a CC decision was published in Moscow, devoting much space to the preparations of the victory celebrations in May 1985.[15]

The presentation of protest notes to the governments of the US, Great Britain, and France also served as reminders of the former war-time allies' joint responsibility towards Germany. In the notes, the USSR objected to the Council of the Western European Union's decision on Genscher's application in mid-June 1984 to lift restrictions on the production of conventional weapons that had been imposed on the Federal Republic. The notes maintained that the West Germans were now permitted to develop "long-range offensive weapons" that posed a threat not just to neighbors, but also to "distant states."[16] On 15 July a similar diplomatic note to the Federal Republic's foreign office claimed that the decision by the Western European Union was in contravention of the specific stipulations of the Potsdam Agreement, of the CSCE Final Act, and of the Moscow Treaty of 1970. Poland and the CSSR joined in the Soviet protest.

When, even after the CMEA summit and the intensified revanchism campaign, the GDR was reluctant to support Moscow's policy of partially isolating Bonn, and when aside from Honecker also T. Zhivkov and N. Ceauşescu, the party leaders and heads of state of Bulgaria and Romania, announced their visits for September and October 1984, Soviet media pressure increased even further. Already in late August, it was leaked in

East Berlin that the GDR Chairman of the State Council, assisted by influential partners in Moscow, was trying to defend his policy of "damage limitation" and the German-German "community of responsibility," but it was to be expected that the envisaged visit to the Federal Republic was unlikely to be carried out. Honecker's definite cancellation was conveyed on 4 September, Zhivkov's on 9 September. Only Ceauşescu did not yield: On 15 October he arrived in Bonn for a three day visit, shortened though it was.

When in September 1984, Genscher met with Gromyko at the UN General Assembly, the latter affirmed continuing Soviet interest in a dialogue with Bonn. At the same time, the German Minister of Foreign Affairs again found himself sharply criticized. Gromyko emphasized that, viewed from Moscow, the "course of the Bonn government aimed at transforming the FRG's territory into a US deployment area for nuclear missiles, and supporting the objectives of certain circles that cast doubt upon the post-war boundaries was incompatible with the interests of European and international security."[17] Prime Minister Tikhonov took the same position on 3 November 1984 in a meeting with Genscher in New Delhi on the occasion of the funeral ceremonies for Indian Prime Minister Indira Gandhi.

Immediately before the re-opening of the Geneva arms control negotiations, there was a further meeting of the Soviet Minister of Foreign Affairs and his German collegue on 4 March 1985 in Moscow where Genscher stopped over on his way to Helsinki, Warsaw, and Sofia. During this conversation that lasted four and a half hours all together, Gromyko not only commented positively on the utility of such encounters, but once again asserted the USSR's wish to expand bilateral relations both in the political and the economic arenas. Curiously, the news agency TASS manipulated these remarks so as to attach a far more negative meaning to them.[18] The Geneva negotiations and the US's "Strategic Defense Initiative" were the main themes. In this context, the Soviet Minister of Foreign Affairs termed Bonn's alleged support of the US space projects "irresponsible;" but he certainly did not accuse the Federal Government of being an "accomplice" to the violation of the ABM-treaty, as asserted by TASS. Rather, with regards to SDI, he imputed economic motives to Bonn. Beyond that, Gromyko criticized the Federal Government's foreign policy only in bilateral relations. Specifically, he addressed the "revanchism" of certain circles. Though selecting flexible formulations, the Federal Government was nonetheless paving the way for a revanchist policy. In this context he found particular fault with Bonn's insufficient respect for the sovereignty of the GDR.

On 7 March Gromyko briefed the Politburo on this meeting. Pertaining to that, it was said that the Soviet leadership endorsed the "development of mutually advantageous cooperation on the basis of the Moscow Treaty and other Soviet-West German agreements." The decisive element was and remained the question of security.[19]

Secretary General Gorbachev struck similar notes in his first contact with Chancellor Kohl in the Kremlin on 14 March, following Chernenko's funeral. He termed respect for the existing territorial-political realities one of the foundations of Soviet-German relations. Like Gromyko before him, he underscored that the further development of the relationship between Moscow and Bonn depended on which "policy the FRG pursued with regards to the security interests of the Soviet Union and her allies."[20]

For all that, in the spring of 1985, Soviet leadership occasionally intimated that it had no intention of diverting its own foreign policy and that of other Warsaw Pact countries around officials in Bonn indefinitely. This was further corroborated when CC Secretary Zimyanin announced his visit to Bonn for mid-March 1985. The projected meeting with Bonn parliamentarians, however, failed to materialize due to Moscow bereavement. Zimyanin had to return to the Soviet capital as early as 10 March after a day's sojourn in Hamburg. The visit was returned in mid-April 1985. As early as 18 December 1984, the Soviet government had invited the President of the Bundesrat, L. Späth, to the USSR sometime during 1985. During Späth's visit (22–29 March), a "National Exhibition of Industry and Technology from Baden-Württemberg" (19–27 March 1985) was open to visitors in Moscow's Sokolniki Park.

Problem Area: Berlin

Despite much international and bilateral stress, there were no significant difficulties concerning the Berlin question, but there was no progress either. Since the USSR continues to reject full inclusion of West Berlin in agreements on scientific-technological cooperation, legal assistance, or in a two-year program for cultural exchanges, the accords, otherwise ready to be signed, remain frozen. However, at the 13th session of the Joint Economic Commission in late January 1985, the Soviet Union displayed greater interest again, at least in an agreement on scientific-technological cooperation.

Threats directed at West Berlin by then Soviet Ambassador to the GDR P.A. Abrasimov threatened West Berlin immediately before his replacement in June 1983. These threats turned out to be Abrasimov's work alone. Abrasimov had warned about effects on the situation in Berlin, should US intermediate-range missiles be deployed. But evidently those considerations ultimately won the day in Moscow, which assumed that any pressure exerted on West Berlin would inevitably result in Western European solidarity with the Federal Republic.

There was no change in the Soviet position that West Berlin is not a part of the Federal Republic and must not be governed by it. The presence of West German politicians, meetings of Bundestag caucuses, as well as rallies by West German parties or youth organizations, have always been routinely accompanied by Soviet protests. Already prior to the UEFA decision in March 1985 granting the 1988 European soccer championships to the Federal Republic, the sports organizations of the Warsaw Pact states made this conditional on no matches being held in West Berlin.

Apparently there were no problems in 1984 with the transfer of the West Berlin city railway (whcih is to be distinguished from the BVG-run metro) from the East Berlin Deutsche Reichsbahn to the West Berlin Berliner Verkehrsbetriebe (BVG). This transfer was made for financial reasons. Soviet interests were safeguarded to the extent that the transaction's premise was that the previous status of Berlin's transportation routes would be maintained. On the negative side, Soviet pressure presumably forced East Berlin to back down from the inclusion of West Berliners in an eleven-point agreement on humanitarian questions. This agreement was made in late August 1984, and the Federal Chancellery had originally expected it. It had been established in the early seventies that West Berliners as compared with West Germans were not to be discriminated against during visits to East Berlin.

Human Rights Issues

Among the problems weighing especially heavily on bilateral relations ever since the early eighties is Soviet restrictions on emigration requests by Soviet citizens of German national origin. Between 1955 and 1982, after all, 91,616 Germans residing in the USSR and Soviet citizens of German extraction were allowed leave for the Federal Republic. However, a low point was reached in 1983, with 1,447 resettlers, and in 1984 with a mere 864. In January 1985, only forty-two Germans were allowed to leave the Soviet Union, and only twenty-seven in February.[21]

Even in earlier years, the Soviet government had contended that the number of emigration requests was of course declining, as a result of previous resettlements. But in fact, 87,000 emigration requests are still in the hands of the German Red Cross. As a rule, applicants are subject to harassment. Minister of Foreign Affairs Genscher has repeatedly pointed to this unsavory situation, but the Soviet side proved particularly unreceptive during the bilateral contacts in 1984. Even in the context of humanitarian questions, the USSR criticized the German government's allegedly unconditional support of US policy, as well as what it called growing "neo-Nazi and revanchist machinations" in the Federal Republic of Germany.

The possibility of reciprocal visits for family matters was made more difficult. On the other hand, direct telephone lines to company representatives accredited by the Soviet Union, which had been discontinued in 1981, were restored in 1983. However, long-distance calls are permitted only in the direction USSR-Federal Republic. Journalists and non-accredited companies remain without direct-dial long-distance telephone service. Finally, on 1 August 1984, the USSR suspended procedures for the advance payment of import duties, ostensibly for technical reasons. Previously West German senders of parcels could prepay customs duties levied in the USSR, thereby relieving the Soviet recipient of the cost.

Economic Relations

Soviet endeavors to free trade relations from the deterioration of the bilateral relationship were the more conspicuous. Again in 1984, the Federal

Republic remained the USSR's most important Western trading partner, ahead of Finland, Italy, France, the US, Japan, and Great Britain. What is more, exports to West Germany are the most important Soviet source of foreign exchange. Intra-German trade aside, the Soviet Union was the Federal Republic's most significant partner in Eastern trade, with a share of 51.5 percent in 1984.

Some troubling factors notwithstanding, the overall development of bilateral trade relations was positive. However, in 1984 the USSR once again imported considerbly less than in the preceding year and achieved a surplus of 3.6 billion marks. Soviet exports expanded by 22.1 percent to 14.4 billion marks, while imports shrunk by 4.3 percent to 10.8 billion marks. According to Soviet data, though, the USSR increased its exports by only 11.5 percent to 4,536.1 million Rbl. and even expanded imports by 0.5 percent to 3,375.9 million Rbl. According to that, trade returns grew by just 6.5 percent.[22] At some 90 percent of total value, natural gas, oil, and oil products constituted the bulk of Soviet exports. Contrary to some expectations, these exports were even increased. On the other hand, the Soviet Union reduced imports of steel tubing and sheet metals. Large-scale projects shoudl continue to be the supporting pillar of cooperation in the near future. Closer cooperation in the energy sector is under discussion. Soviet foreign trade organizations have sounded out the German side regarding the construction of complete chemical plants.

The thirteenth session of the German-Soviet Joint Economic Commission held in Bonn from 21 to 22 January 1985 struck positive notes. In a joint communique, both sides affirmed that bilateral economic relations should continue to "develop in the spirit of agreements reached in Helsinki and at the Madrid meeting." However, the new Soviet copresident, A.K. Antonov, stressed that the dynamics of economic relations hinged on the political situation. In this context, he was especially criticial of the gradual expansion of Western trade restrictions (Cocom).[23] The Commission's next session will, in rotation, be held in Moscow in April 1986. The focus will be on cooperation in the consumer goods sector.

Perspectives

Since 1970, both Brezhnev and Andropov had always treated the Federal Republic of Germany as a preferred partner in the framework of their policy towards Western Europe. In the process, the Kremlin endeavored to encourage Bonn to present its own interests more vigorously within the Western alliance. Soviet leadership was probably aiming less at detaching the Federal Republic from the US shield. At best, that is one of Moscow's long-term aspirations. Rather, the point was to move the Federal Republic into spontaneous adjustment to Soviet interests on the one hand, and to exacerbate differences of opinion between Bonn and Washington on the other. When the campaign of fear that was to prevent deployment of US intermediate-range missiles failed, and Chancellor Kohl decided on different emphases in his *Ostpolitik* from those of his predecessors (in regard to the safeguarding of German legal positions), the Federal Republic began to lose its status of preferred partner in the course of 1984.

Under Chernenko it seemed for a while as if Moscow wanted to isolate the Federal Republic in foreign policy terms and, in its own policy, to circumvent Bonn. The revanchism campaign, kindled after a considerable lag in April 1984, was the prime instrument of discreditation, designed on the one hand to save face following the start of deployment in late 1983, while on the other serving to forestall the policy of "damage limitation" projected by the other East Europeans, and in particular the GDR. Not until early 1985 did relations between Moscow and Bonn relax again. CPSU Secretary General Gorbachev is also likely to remain committed to continuity in Soviet policy towards Germany, although in Soviet policy vis-à-vis the West, he will presumably place greater emphasis on the Europeans' common interests.

First signals from East Berlin indicate that Honecker again expects the new personnel constellation in the Kremlin to allow increased elbow-room in intra-German relations. Soviet leadership has stressed the idea that a turn for the better in relations between Bonn and Moscow depends on allowances for the security interests of the USSR and its allies. Independent of that, it can be assumed that after 8 May 1985, detente in Soviet–West German relations will come about only gradually. At the same time, it will continue to remain a primary function of Soviet-US relations, but it will be less apt to be reduced to that than it was during Chernenko's brief tenure.

Notes

1. W. Berner, *Berichte des BIOst*, No. 20 (1984); G. Wettig, *Berichte des BIOst*, No. 10 (1982).
2. F. Oldenburg, *Aktuelle Analysen des BIOst*, No. 16 and No. 19 (1984); *Deutschland Archiv*, No. 5 (1984), pp. 491–496, and No. 8 (1984), pp. 834–843; B. v.Plate, in *Aus Politik und Zeitgeschichte*, supplement to the weekly *Das Parlament*, B 15/84, pp. 27–39.
3. W. Seiffert, *Deutschland Archiv*, No. 10 (1984), pp. 1043–1059.
4. Examples in *Pr*, 16, 17, and 21 May 1984; *LG*, 16 May 1984; *TASS*, 17, 18, and 27 May 1984; *KZ*, 18 May 1984.
5. Cf. *Pr*, 18, 19, and 29 May 1983; *TASS*, 7 June 1983; *RM*, 30 May, 3 June, and 7 June 1983.
6. *FAZ*, 29 June 1983.
7. *dpa*, 15 and 16 November 1983.
8. *TASS*, 16 October 1983; *Pr*, 17 October 1983.
9. *Pr*, 19, 20, and 25 October 1983; *ND*, 25 October 1983.
10. *ND*, 26/27 November 1983; G. Józsa, *Berichte des BIOst*, Nos. 4 and 5 (1985).
11. *Pr*, 15 February 1984.
12. In detail on this, see W. Berner, *Berichte des BIOst*, No. 20 (1984).
13. *TASS*, 21 May 1984; *Pr*, 23 May 1984; *Novosti*, 25 May 1984.
14. *Pr*, 15 June 1984.

15. *Pr*, 17 June 1984.
16. *TASS* and *ND*, 13 July 1984.
17. *Iz*, 27 September 1984.
18. *Pr*, 5 March 1985.
19. *Pr*, 8 March 1985; *FAZ*, 8 March 1985.
20. *Pr*, 15 March 1985.
21. In the first half of 1985 the total was 205 (FAZ, 8 June 1985). Cf. W. Oschlies, *The Soviet Union 1982/83*, p. 105.
22. German data by *Zusammenfassende Übersichten für den Aussenhandel*, Statistisches Bundesamt, Wiesbaden, Fachserie 7, Reihe 1, No. 1 (1985); Soviet data by supplement to *Aussenhandel*, Moscow, No. 3 (1985). See also Christian Meier, "Soviet Foreign Trade Restricted by Foreign Policy?" in this volume, Chapter 19.
23. *Pr*, 13 January 1985; *SZ*, 23 January 1985.

24
The Soviet Policy of Hegemony and the Crisis of Authority in Eastern Europe

Wolfgang Berner and Christian Meier,
with Dieter Bingen, Gyula Józsa,
*Fred Oldenburg, and Wolf Oschlies**

The maintenance of the Soviet Union's predominant position in Eastern Europe, i.e., mainly the safeguarding of its own military, political, economic, and ideological control over the six buffer states—Poland, GDR, CSSR, Hungary, Romania, and Bulgaria—continues to hold first place on its foreign policies priorities scale. All these states are members of the Warsaw Treaty Organization (WTO), and together with the USSR form the real core of the economic community of the Council for Mutual Economic Assistance (CMEA). This also encompasses the socialist developing countries, Cuba, Vietnam, and the Mongolian People's Republic. The only other thing that claims the Soviet Union's foreign policy energies and economic military potential to a comparable degree is the consolidation of its position as a world power equal to the US, in the dangerously tense relationship between offensive superpower rivalism and defensive avoidance of direct military conflict between the two superpowers.

In principle, it is a fair assumption that Moscow's leaders do not by any means deem Soviet possessions in Western Europe safe and permanently secured. In this context, its attention is certainly not focused exclusively on potential external threats. As proven by a long series of attempted rebellions, open popular revolts, and emancipatory movements of various sorts, Soviet hegemony and leadership authority has also repeatedly been threatened from within, i.e., by opposition forces which, in the final analysis, the Soviet system of rule itself is constantly producing. To wit, Yugoslavia's (1948) and Albania's (1961) secession; the revolts in the GDR (1953), in Poland (1956), and Hungary (1956); Romania's emancipation in economic, foreign, and security policy (1965); the reform movement in the CSSR (1968); and the series of acute systemic crises in Poland (1956/1970/1980) that it was ultimately possible for the Soviets to contain only with a military takeover and with the imposition of martial law (1981).

The latest Polish crisis has shaken the entire WTO-CMEA system to its very foundations because it was accompanied by a powerful, grassroots movement that was critical of the system and called for social reform and national emancipation simultaneously. The negative ramifications for the partner states, which contributed considerably to the loosening of the bloc structure, even spread to the alliance's coordination and consultative mechanism as well as to the leading organs of the Council for Mutual Economic Assistance. Serious conflicts of interest appeared everywhere, fostered further by the persistently weak leadership of Moscow's decisionmaking and administrative bodies.

Moreover, there were psychological-political influences from the outside that not only irritated the supreme representatives of the Soviet hegemonial power but, in view of tendencies toward disintegration in Eastern Europe, also made them feel quite insecure. Of great significance, in this connection, was the revival of the discussion about the actual political substance of the decisions at Yalta (February 1945) and Potsdam (July–August 1945) and the maxim that called for "overcoming Yalta" and was propounded particularly by prominent US politicians. Small wonder that such statements and reflections were interpreted by the Kremlin as manifestations of a new US roll-back strategy.

The topic of keeping the "German question" open was again making the headlines in the Federal Republic of Germany. This fact was placed in the same context. As the Soviets see it, any politician insisting on the reunification of Germany based on free self-determination is a "revisionist," and anyone who regards the continuing existence of the old German *Reich* with its 1937 boundaries as more than merely a theoretical legal position is a "revanchist."

Within the WTO-CMEA system, most regimes felt all but compelled to act autonomously in the economic area because it turned out that the performance of the Soviet economy was not even up to satisfying the needs of its own population. A trend towards "particularist" concentration on "national" economic interests asserted itself in the minor Eastern bloc states. In places, even beginnings of a certain "security policy nationalism" began to emerge.

The rigid Soviet behavior in the dispute with the US on the question of SS-20 armament, which was to be balanced by the deployment of US intermediate-range missiles in Western Europe, caused some WTO states—especially Romania, Hungary, and the GDR—to distance themselves in a more or less critical fashion from the Soviet strategy of confrontation. Above all, "front line states" like Hungary and the GDR that were particularly endangered were confronted with a paradox. The Soviet Union's and their own vital security interests diverged further from each other, the more the leading politicians of these exposed small states were prepared to take at face value Soviet claims concerning US craving for nuclear war and an alleged incapacity for compromise on the US side at the Geneva INF negotiations. These negotiations were then broken off by the Soviet Union in November 1983.

These developments resulted partially from objective inevitabilities, and partially from autonomous decisions and subjective efforts. From 1982–1984 they caused that "horizontal" particularization and fragmentation in the WTO-CMEA domain that Soviet leadership noted with the greatest concern. When he assumed office as CPSU secretary general in November 1982, Andropov, by all appearances, already regarded it as among his paramount tasks to keep the smaller WTO-CMEA states from drifting apart. Regarding the East European buffer region, in February 1984 his successor Chernenko found a situation which, if anything, had deteriorated since late 1982. During his term in office, a large-scale disciplinary campaign was carried out simultaneously in many sectors, and within certain bounds. It proved remarkably successful. Still, the goal of restoring the bloc's internal coherence and unity of action in foreign policy is as yet far from achieved. Much remains to be done by Secretary General Gorbachev, who succeeded Chernenko in March 1985, before the problem can be considered solved.

Coordinated Foreign and Security Policy

The instruments of Soviet bloc coordination within the framework of the WTO-CMEA system during the tenures of Andropov (12 November 1982–9 February 1984) and Chernenko (13 February–10 March 1985) consisted mainly of three methods of conceptual and operational adjustment. Most major decisions were either reached at multilateral routine conferences (e.g., at meetings of the Political Consultative Committee, PCC, of the WTO, at CMEA council meetings, and meetings of CC secretaries) or arranged at multilateral summit meetings of Party leaders and chairmen of councils of ministers (like the WTO coordinating summit on 28 June 1983 and the CMEA coordinating summit on 12–14 June 1984), unless they resulted from bilateral consultations between the Soviet Party leader and the respective party leader from an individual partner country. Secretary General Gorbachev immediately availed himself of Chernenko's funeral ceremonies to come to an understanding with the heads of all delegations from WTO states on the imminent extension of the Warsaw Treaty of 14 May 1955.[1] Accordingly, on 26 April 1985 the top representatives of the USSR, Poland, the GDR, the CSSR, Hungary, Romania, and Bulgaria assembled in the Polish capital at an extraordinary meeting of the PCC of the WTO, to authenticate solemnly the treaty's extension by twenty years.

During the closing phase of the Brezhnev era, Soviet leaders had conspicuously refrained from using the instruments of multilateral consultation and decisionmaking according to the usual rules of procedure. Instead, Soviet unilateralism and selective bilateralism had been practiced increasingly in dealing with the alliance and cooperating partners. Among other things, this was related to the fact that the Poles (because of their emancipatory movement in 1980–1981), and (for some time already) the Romanians were considered shifty characters, and it was thought better not to confide in them at deliberations on East bloc crises.

Yet, in view of weak Soviet leadership, the centrifugal tendencies within the WTO-CMEA system had generally increased to such an extent that without hesitation as soon as he had advanced to the highest office, Andropov devoted himself to the reconsolidation of the closer socialist community of states, as a paramount foreign policy task. Right after his appointment, the new secretary general announced to the CC of the CPSU joint steps to improve cooperation among the socialist countries of Eastern Europe. Shortly afterwards he stressed that the political-organizational and institutional machinery already in place for purposes of coordination had to be used far more effectively to restore bloc discipline and unity of action by the WTO-CMEA states. To be sure, on a different occasion, he admitted to the realization that it was necessary to show appropriate consideration for national peculiarities as well as special interests in the smaller partner states.[2]

The 18th PCC conference had been convoked to meet in Prague in November 1982, when Brezhnev was still alive. There is much evidence that Andropov wanted to make this conference (which met on 4 and 5 January 1983) into the starting point for a deliberate upgrading and revitalization of the political WTO organs—an intention he was eventually unable to realize with the requisite consistency because of his illness. It was remarkable, for instance, that contrary to usual practice the Prague communique already named the venue for the next PCC meeting, that is, Sofia.

In view of the continuing Geneva negotiations on NATO rearmament in the INF area (continental strategic missiles), party leaders and heads of government of the WTO states had originally submitted a long-term program for the reduction of East-West tensions as part of the Prague Declaration of 5 January 1983.[3] Later, they complemented it at the Moscow summit of 28 June with a crash program in the form of a joint declaration.[4] It represented the point of departure for coordinated actions in the diplomatic-political, in the social, and in the journalistic realms. It was designed primarily to put pressure on the Federal Republic of Germany to take back its deployment commitments to the NATO dual track decision. When the failure of these efforts became discernible, it was also soon clear which of the Warsaw Pact's collective measures Soviet leadership had in mind as reactions to the deployment of continental strategic missiles in several Western European NATO states.

Above all, SS-21, SS-22, and SS-23 type short-range missiles with high impact accuracy were to be moved forward to the CSSR and the GDR because Pershing-II bases in West Germany can ostensibly be eliminated with such weapons most rapidly and most safely from the territory of these two WTO members. The requisite decisions on technical-military measures were made at an extraordinary meeting of the Committee of Defense Ministers in East Berlin on 20 October as well as at the committee's regular session from 5 to 7 December 1983 in Sofia. The Ministries of Defense of the USSR, the GDR, and the CSSR announced the start of preparations for the forward deployment of the missiles on 24 October in nearly identical bulletins.[5]

At least with the GDR and the CSSR, agreement on these measures had presumably been reached long before. On the other hand, there is much evidence that the Soviet decision of 23 November 1983 to end abruptly the Geneva INF negotiations with the US and to break off until further notice the other bilateral disarmament negotiations was not made in concert with the minor WTO partners. This has perhaps caused some of them to distance themselves unusually clearly and vigorously from the Soviet course of confrontation.

It is true, of course, that the Committee of Foreign Ministers of the WTO states at its Sofia session of 13 and 14 October 1983 approved the Soviet position that a continuation of the Geneva INF negotiations was possible only in conjunction with US renunciation of the start of missile deployment in Western Europe according to the NATO schedule.[6] Shortly after this approval, heads of government of the CMEA states expressly reaffirmed this position in a joint communique at the thirty-seventh council meeting in East Berlin (18–20 October).[7]

But then, the secretaries general of the SED and the CPC, Honecker and Husák, met in Prague on 24 October. It was certainly not without significance that they finally demanded not only counter measures to NATO's rearmament in the INF area, but also activation of East-West negotiations on the whole issue of limiting and reducing nuclear weapons arsenals.[8] The Federal Assembly of the CSSR, which, in a special session on 26 October endorsed missile deployment in its own country, combined this vote with a demand for a continuation of the Geneva INF negotiations.[9] Subsequently, Kádár paid Honecker a brief unofficial visit that ended without a communique. At that point, Andropov had already been forced to relinquish de facto control of Soviet foreign policy to Gromyko and Marshal Ustinov. It is a reasonable assumption that in view of this constellation, Honecker and Kádár also agreed on ways of making the divergent interest of the smaller WTO states politically effective. Maintenance of smoothly functioning Western contacts and generally an active reduction of confrontational risks are among the interests of these states.

In fact, at times Soviet leadership must have felt almost completely isolated in its intransigent position: In East Berlin, Honecker was pleading for a policy of "damage limitation" in East-West relations and for a German-German "coalition of common sense."[10] In Hungary, top functionaries of the HSWP spoke out for a more active commitment from the smaller countries and middle-powers in Europe to East-West détente. Romania never tired of developing new initiatives for the establishment of collective security in Europe and an improvement in the East-West climate. At the same time, Bulgaria, which continued to advocate a nuclear weapons–free zone in the Balkans, let it be known that it was interested in enhanced East-West cooperation but resisted inclusion in Soviet deployment plans. The "ice age" announced by Moscow inconvenienced Poland, if only because it was incapable of staying afloat economically without Western aid, including extensive private donations. Even the CSSR seemed to disapprove of the unilateral walkout from the Geneva negotiations, although it otherwise supported with conformist zeal Soviet attempts to contain particularist special tendencies. Most other Eastern bloc countries, however, were so recalcitrant that an evident lack of coordination was noticeable among WTO states at the opening of the CCDE in Stockholm on 17 January 1984 and during the conference's first round that lasted until 16 March.

The February 1984 changeover from Andropov to Chernenko as head of the Soviet Union was soon followed by a broad campaign, whose primary aim was to restore Moscow's leadership authority. By doing that, it also hoped to improve bloc discipline in the WTO/CMEA system. Gromyko, Ustinov, and CC Secretaries Ponomarev and Rusakov, who decisively determined the course of foreign policy under Chernenko, were presumably behind it. In March/April, Soviet and Czechoslovak publications launched concerted attacks on the leaders of Hungary, the GDR, and other Eastern bloc countries whom they charged with economic nationalism and security policy particularism.[11] Simultaneously the switches were thrown for other decisions that had a disciplinary effect: All WTO/CMEA states were to cancel en bloc their participation in the Los Angeles Olympics; all were to participate in a massive media-campaign against West German revisionism, revanchism, and neo-Nazism; and all were to be induced to accept an increase in economic integration.

The foreign ministers' conference of the WTO states, held in Budapest on 19 and 20 April 1984, served to attain common consent for this program, and even its communique referred to "concepts endangering peace" that "question the boundaries of European states . . . and are directed against the political-territorial realities that have developed in Europe."[12] On 14 May the Soviet Ministry of Defense announced the deployment in the GDR of additional operative-tactical missiles with longer ranges. In the second half of May, Poland, the GDR, the CSSR, Hungary, and Bulgaria (as well as Cuba, the Mongolian PR, Vietnam, and North Korea) joined the Soviet boycott of the Los Angeles Olympic Games. Only Romania did not yield to Soviet pressure. Subsequently, a joint political declaration was passed at the Moscow CMEA coordinating summit in June, committing all participants to support of the rigid Soviet policy towards the US. This entailed no offers of constructive dialogue. In return, the declaration granted the East European states freedom of movement to expand their economic and scientific-technological relations particularly with the Western European industrialized states and the EC.[13]

In July and August 1984, the smear campaign waged by the Soviet press against the Federal Republic of Germany proved that these concessions had relatively little political substance. This campaign labeled West Germany a "haven of revanchism" and included passing shots at the GDR that were designed mainly to prevent a planned Honecker visit. As a result, East Berlin postponed the trip indefinitely on 4 September, some three weeks before the envisaged travel date. Similarly, Bulgarian head of state and Party leader Zhivkov felt compelled to cancel a firmly scheduled visit to the Federal Republic on 9 September. Again, Romanian head of state and Party leader Ceauşescu was the only one to prove steadfast, as he carried out as planned a visit to Bonn that had been projected for late October.

The change of course in Soviet policy towards the US, ushered in by the Reagan-Gromyko talks on 28 September 1984, was coordinated with the other Eastern bloc countries. At a meeting of the foreign ministers of the WTO states on 3 and 4 December in East Berlin, the participants approved in principle the re-opening of arms control talks between the US and the USSR in the three areas of continental-strategic, intercontinental, and space weapons. This was done in anticipation of the pertinent agreements reached by foreign ministers Shultz and Gromyko on 8 January 1985 in Geneva. This was followed on 1 March by a consultative meeting at the level of deputy foreign ministers of the WTO states. Bilateral consultations between Gromyko and his colleagues from the CSSR and the GDR took place in early February and on 20 March respectively. The extent to which joint positions for the Geneva INF negotiations between the USSR and the US were decided on, and to what extent the WTO partners were informed on the state of the arms control talks, is unknown.

Originally, the planned extension of the Warsaw Pact for another twenty years was to have been decided on at a regular PCC session in Sofia, planned for mid-January 1985. However, the Soviet Union had to cancel the date because Chernenko's state of health was deteriorating rapidly. Meanwhile, the differences between Romania and the USSR on the time frame and form of the projected treaty extension were settled. Possibly, there were also differences of opinion on certain parts of the treaty as well as efforts to improve the WP organization on the occasion of the extension of the treaty. All of this can be deduced from a cryptic remark by the Hungarian Deputy Minister of Foreign Affairs, I. Roska.[14] By his own account, Gorbachev took advantage of his predecessor Chernenko's funeral ceremonies in Moscow in March 1985 to brush aside all such reservations and to secure from the representatives of all WTO states assembled in Moscow agreement to the intended treaty extension (with unaltered treaty text).

Coordinated Economic Policy

The summit meeting of the WTO states from 12 to 14 June 1984 in Moscow had its origins in a Romanian proposal, first submitted at the thirty-fourth CMEA Council meeting (17–19 June 1980) in Prague. After Brezhnev had adopted this suggestion at the Twenty-sixth CPSU Congress in the spring of 1981, the projected conference remained constantly under consideration, but its realization was delayed because it got caught between the millstones of the CMEA states' divergent economic interests. Nonetheless, the preliminaries for the CMEA summit were hastened along so vigorously under Andropov that the Soviet Chairman of the Council of Ministers, Tikhonov, was able to announce the conclusion of the preparations at the thirty-seventh CMEA Council meeting in East Berlin (18–20 October 1983). The summit nevertheless failed to meet until June 1984, and this was due primarily to the Soviet Union's reduced capacity to act prior to and after the change in the office of CPSU secretary general.

Nine CMEA states were represented by their Party leaders and heads of government, the tenth—Cuba—by its deputy prime minister, Politburo member C.R. Rodriguez. The results of the conference were summarized in three unanimously adopted documents. They are:

1. The "Declaration on the Main Directions of Future Development and Intensification of Economic and Scientific Cooperation Among CMEA Member Countries."[15]
2. The "Declaration" by CMEA member countries, "The Maintenance of Peace and International Economic Cooperation."[16]
3. The unpublished "Decision" on main problems of economic cooperation by the CMEA countries.

Judging by the content of the "Declaration," which attempts to harmonize differing notions held by the CMEA states about the orientation, methods, and objectives of the desired integration, the summit deliberations focused on four topics:

1. The further development of trade and cooperative relations within the CMEA.
2. The future trade and cooperative policy of the CMEA countries vis-à-vis the Western industrialized countries.
3. The institutional structures and the instruments of cooperation among the CMEA countries.
4. The economic differences in the levels and performance of the Eastern European CMEA countries and the non-European CMEA developing countries.

As for the future of intra-CMEA cooperation, the USSR agreed vaguely and without setting fixed quotas to supply the East European CMEA states with raw materials and energy. All CMEA member countries that receive raw and energy materials from the Soviet Union and essentially pay for them in kind are required to supply the Soviet market, more than in the past and in adequate quantities, with high quality products. In the future, the prices that the Soviets impose on energy and raw material shipments are to be more in tune with current world market prices. Nothing was said of a general change in Moscow's price formula, though. Increased cooperation in various areas of the agrarian-industrial complex is not only to improve quantitatively and qualitatively the supply of foodstuffs to the population in the CMEA area, but also to throttle considerably the import of grain and fodder from Western countries. The intention is to work out a complex program for scientific-technological progress, covering some fifteen to twenty years, so as to decrease decisively, in the long run, dependency on technology imports from the West and to forestall any political instrumentalization of technology transfer. The creation of an integrated transportation system is to facilitate the exchange of goods among CMEA states.

The "Declaration" expressly endorses trade and economic cooperation among CMEA states with western industrialized countries. No mention is made of any restrictions in this regard. In fact, however, the guidelines for intra-CMEA cooperation, and in particular increased Soviet demands, further restrict each country's room for maneuver in Western trade. Of course, even the Soviet Union must have an interest in smaller CMEA states having economic relations with the West. On the one hand, it cannot be keen on exacerbating their economic difficulties; on the other hand, the minor CMEA states are an important link in East-West technology transfer.

As for the perspectives for integration, the participants at the summit conference agreed, rather more formerly than in actuality, to improve the functioning of existing mechanisms. Regular summit meetings are to provide stronger political impulses. Also, the various possibilities for coordinated planning, the establishment of direct relations at the plant level etc. are to be used more effectively. Presumably the intended shaping of the integrational mechanism will foster an "integrative bilateralism," albeit enriched by improved multilateral elements. The goal of a harmonization of the economic systems and economic policies of the individual countries is farther removed than ever.

The "Declaration" clearly assigns priority to bringing CMEA developing countries like Vietnam, Cuba, and the Mongolian PR up to the performance levels of the Eastern European CMEA states. This is more important than using possibilities of enlarging the circle of CMEA members by admitting additional developing countries—such as Laos, Afghanistan, Ethiopia, Kampuchea, or Nicaragua.

The "Decision" that presumably lays down priorities and emphases for cooperation in major economic sectors was not published. But it is likely to be no more than a set of framework agreements because, according to the communique, the CMEA executive committee was ordered to "direct . . . the work of the Council organs towards the implementation" of the Moscow summit decisions. The thirty-eighth extraordinary Council session, linked to the coordinating summit, issued special instructions to this end and, in addition, set deadlines for realization.[17] The 110th and 111th sessions of the CMEA Executive Committee, held respectively on 15 and 16 June and 19 to 21 September 1984 in Moscow, specified individual tasks and discussed pertinent organizational questions.

Soviet leadership would obviously like to see the decisions of the CMEA summit carried out primarily in the form of USSR-centered cooperation.

The new "long-term programs for the development of economic and scientific-technological cooperation to the year 2000" are evidence of this, and so far the Soviet Union has agreed with Poland (5 May 1984), the GDR (6 October 1984), Cuba (31 October 1984), and Hungary (1 April 1985).[18]

The beginnings of a multilateral implementation of the cooperation agreements emerged in three of four areas of joint action at the thirty-ninth CMEA Council meeting held at Havana from 29 to 31 October 1984. Various regulations were laid down to guarantee the long-term and reliable satisfaction of the CMEA countries' needs for fuels and raw materials up to 1990 and beyond. In this connection, special emphasis was placed on the implementation of joint investment projects in certain CMEA countries. As for integration perspectives—apart from setting up a CMEA committee on cooperation in mechanical engineering—several unspecified measures were adopted to enlarge the powers of the Council in the organization of cooperation and to focus the activities of Council organs more on the resolution of the most important problems of material production. The non-European CMEA developing countries Cuba, Vietnam, and the Mongolian PR were given additional, albeit very vague, promises of aid.

Ideological Cooperation

Multilateral cooperation among the ruling communist parties of the WTO-CMEA states has been an institution since 1973, but it does not proceed with equal intensity and regularity in all areas. Viewed with these two criteria in mind, cooperation among CC secretaries in charge of ideology and international relations deserves special attention. These secretaries meet at least once annually for a regular session in the capital of a WTO/CMEA state and more frequently during important phases of development or of tension in East-West relations.

Following the Prague WTO summit in January 1983, these CC secretaries met for a regular session in Moscow on 14 and 15 March dealing above all with the translation of the proposals contained in the Prague Declaration into everyday political-ideological work.[19] As they were apparently still hoping to be able to prevent the deployment of US intermediate-range missiles in Western Europe by means of stepped-up propaganda efforts, "additional steps" for the realization of programs contained in the documents of the WTO summits in Prague and Moscow were discussed at an extraordinary conference of CC secretaries in charge of ideology and foreign policy on 20 September 1983 in Moscow.[20] In view of Pershing-II and cruise missile deployment in some Western European NATO states, the CC secretaries then felt compelled to adjust to the new situation. Thus, at a further extraordinary meeting in Moscow on 9 December 1983, they agreed to focus information and propaganda work primarily on the effects of the deployment of US missiles and concurrently to continue the advertising campaign for the USSR's security proposals.[21]

As was to be expected, the regular deliberations of the CC secretaries in charge of ideological and international tasks on 11 and 12 July 1984, held in Prague a month after the Moscow CMEA summit, directed attention to the foreign policy declaration by the CMEA states of 14 June 1984. Henceforth these were to constitute the most important basic material for international propaganda activity in the communist parties.[22]

Advance planning by the WTO/CMEA states for the 40th anniversary celebrations of the end of the Second World War opened a new sphere of action for the ideology and propaganda secretaries. The pertinent individual tasks were discussed on 6 March 1985 at a conference convened in Moscow expressly for this purpose. Then deputy secretary general of the CPSU, M.S. Gorbachev, also attended.[23]

The multilateral coordination activities of CC secretaries in charge of Party and organizational work were more limited. In Prague (30 March–1 April) in the spring of 1982, they dealt with the role of basic organizations in the "realization of economic and social policy" in socialist countries, with their role in the "ideological education of the masses," and in the "creation of a healthy political-moral atmosphere in work collectives."[24] Their next meeting in Sofia on 29 and 30 May served mainly as an "exchange of opinions and experiences on questions about the realization of the Party's leading role vis-à-vis youth organizations and current tasks in work with juveniles."[25]

Time and again, the course of the editorial conferences organized by the Prague monthly *World Marxist Review* demonstrates Soviet leadership's keen interest in including non-governing communist parties in the multilateral cooperation among governing communist parties in WTO/CMEA states. CPSU leaders, the real publishers, repeatedly made these conferences the vehicle for soliciting support for the convention of a fourth communist world conference. For this purpose, they used spokesmen from other "sister parties" who were closely associated with them. At the conference in December 1984, B.N. Ponomarev, candidate member of the Politburo and CC secretary of the CPSU, criticized previous forms of cooperation as inadequate. Among other things, he called on all parties represented on the editorial board "to speak up with one voice . . . against the threat of war and the arms race" again in the future.[26]

Poland: The Rule of Generals as a Lasting Provisional Arrangement

Polish foreign policy has long been marked by a subsidiary accommodation to the general line of the WTO/CMEA, determined by the USSR's hegemonial interests. Of course, in many ways this is merely the façade of subservience, opportunistic in part. Apart from this, so far Soviet leadership generally has little cause for satisfaction with the results of the "course of normalization," pursued by the Jaruzelski regime since the lifting of martial law in July 1983. For viewed from the angle of the "laws" of Marxism-Leninism, the real existing Polish "model of socialism" as a whole is not really acceptable to Moscow. This by itself should be sufficient grounds for the Jaruzelski government's conformity with Soviet foreign policy.

To be sure, for some time Poland's mass media have again been emphasizing the Communist Party (PUWP) as the "leading force" though in fact the military continues to be in power, taking advantage of the armed forces' greater prestige (measured against the unpopularity of the Party). By means of determined personnel policies, since 1982 Jaruzelski has expanded the influence of the army's Party cadres in the entire Party apparatus step by step. Thus, generals and staff officers have taken charge of major ministries and voivodeships, and also filled numerous key positions in the Party and in public administration. The Party's supreme leading organs (Politburo and Secretariat) are incapacitated by infighting. Instead, the officer corps, the Party apparatus of the army, and the security organs function as Jaruzelski's main pillars of power.[27]

PUWP membership declined from some 2,870,000 in mid-1981 to 2,158,700 in mid-1984 (−24.8 percent).[28] As seen from Moscow, Jaruzelski has done far too little to restore the Party's monopoly of power and its organizational-political punch. His decision to permit the exposure of the practices of the security apparatus in connection with the Toruň trial of Popiełuszko's murderers (27 December 1984–7 February 1985) presumably looks like a typical example of Polish extravagance viewed from Moscow's vantage.

The unbroken vigor of Polish Catholicism, as a counter-ideology firmly rooted in the population, as well as the contrast between the moral authority of the Church and the irreparable loss of authority by the Party, are extremely disquieting for the Kremlin. One has to accept that, as a consequence, episcopate and clergy exert great influence on Polish social life, whereas the regime's organs of repression have thus far been unable to break up the Solidarność organization—which has continued to operate illegally—and other varyingly inspired opposition groups. The murdered Chaplain Popiełuszko was a figure symbolic of popular resistance to the communist dictatorship of functionaries, police, and military, which, in turn, was concurrently fueled by religious, grass-roots democratic, and national sources.

Though consolidated, the economic situation remains precarious: Price hikes and devaluations of the Zloty alternate; the 1982 reform program is ineffective because bureaucracy and resignation have spread everywhere; the standard of living is declining; and production is contracting in many sectors. Recovery would be conceivable only if the USSR and other CMEA countries were to increase their reconstructive aid considerably, or if Poland were permitted to accept Western offers of credit and cooperation again on a large scale so as to wiggle out of the "East-West pinch."[29] The USSR, however, is already hard pressed to keep its promises. Over 75 percent of Poland's arable land (1983: 76.8 percent) is owned by individual farmers. This remains a constant starting point for Soviet criticism of the "Polish model."

Poland was especially actively committed to the media campaign against alleged German revanchism and US-German boundary-revisionism. Certainly, the regime intended in part to demonstrate solidarity and exemplary fighting spirit to the Soviet leadership. But at the same time, this behavior was dictated by its proper domestic political interest. The leadership conjured up a threat from abroad in order to generate a sense of national consensus by emotionalizing and—given the lack of true successes in its "policy of renewal"—in this way remedy its own lack of legitimacy.

The regime's mouthpieces had already reacted with alarm to the first government declaration by the new Bonn CDU/CSU/FDP coalition in October 1982. They then produced a wave of complaints about the revival of West German revanchist and revisionist tendencies that lasted until late April 1983, while similar reproaches were leveled rarely and comparatively guardedly in this phase by the Soviet side. Following a brief ebb in the summer months of 1983, Polish complaints of alleged provocations by Bonn intensified in late 1983 and early 1984, culminating in the contention that German imperialism, this time in alliance with the US, was again embarked on endangering world peace. Jaruzelski also turned a warning against "imperialist forces" in the Federal Republic of Germany into a declaration composed on the occasion of a visit by Zhivkov on 5 April 1984. An actual synchronization with the Soviet revanchism campaign did not materialize until the months of May through December 1984. Thereafter, things gradually settled down again.

GDR: The Beginnings of Independent Policies

In the period from August 1982 to September 1984 GDR leadership took advantage of the temporarily enlarged latitude, granted in the areas of foreign and German-political policies, to pursue in diverse ways certain special interests. In the process, it even permitted itself conspicuous deviations from the USSR's general foreign policy line, namely by seeking to take the drama out of the situation subsequent to the deployment of US intermediate-range missiles in Western Europe. In this context it also strove to keep German-German relations out of the threatened "freeze" instead of penalizing the Federal Republic of Germany in unison with the Soviet strategy of confrontation by a policy of sanctions, boycotts, and defamation. It must, however, be noted at the same time, that with its initiatives the SED regime did not actually question the basic ideological and military-strategic position of Soviet supremacy.

In August 1982, a meeting between Brezhnev and Honecker took place in the Crimea and was also attended by Gromyko and Chernenko. On this occasion, the principles of bilateral cooperation were agreed upon, taking into account the special opportunities and circumstances in the GDR. The GDR serves as the focal point for nineteen Soviet divisions that have nuclear weapons at their disposal. It assists the Soviet Union from the West in keeping restive Poland under control. In all this the CPSU leadership can rest entirely assured of the ideological-political reliability of SED leaders if only because in divided Germany their exercise of power rests solely on a Soviet mandate. At the same time, the GDR's economy is marked by a relatively high rate of productivity. Moreover, the GDR is absolutely the USSR's most significant trading partner. In 1984, it was especially keen on fulfilling its export commitments to Moscow, but again fell short of this mark. However, by way of intra-German trade, the GDR has greater access to Western technology than other CMEA countries, and the Soviet Union can also take advantage of these.

After Brezhnev's death, in December 1982, during his meeting with Andropov Honecker succeeded in reaching an agreement on the basic principles that had been agreed upon four months earlier in the Crimea. During another visit to Moscow in early May 1983, he probably secured additional room for maneuver. Among other things, Andropov's concessions found expression in his assent to Honecker's request to order the replacement of Ambassador Abrasimov, who was disliked in East Berlin. Presumably Andropov viewed an intensification of relations between East Berlin and Bonn as an opportunity to prevail upon the Federal Republic to back down from its obligations to the NATO rearmament program. When this failed to work out, Honecker had to fear that the threatened cooling off of East-West relationship might entail more than just serious economic disadvantages for the GDR. He certainly also had to take into account the restiveness of the GDR's population, apprehensive about an escalation of the East-West conflict because of the "pre-war propaganda" in the communist media. It is also possible that there was no clear conception in East Berlin of the power relations in the Kremlin, and that the influence of the Soviet military was perhaps overestimated.

The GDR's leadership made it plain that it had by no means joyfully agreed to Soviet "countermeasures" resolved in October of 1983. Simultaneously it applied itself to a policy of "damage limitation." Furthermore, it referred to a particular German-German "community of responsibility" concerning the maintenance of peace in (Central) Europe. In his efforts for a continuation of the East-West dialogue, but also in his advocacy of a re-opening of the INF negotiations, Honecker was actively supported by Hungary, in insinuations even by the CSSR, as well as indirectly by Romania, Bulgaria, and Poland.

After Andropov had passed away, Moscow was already reacting with agitation under Chernenko and was reproaching those who tend to place their national interests ahead of their internationalist obligations.[30] Although the GDR joined the Soviet boycott of the summer Olympics at Los Angeles and, at the CMEA summit in Moscow in June 1984 it apparently allowed itself to be prevailed upon to promise additional aid to Cuba and Vietnam. Honecker evidently still insisted in bilateral consultations with Chernenko at the summit on his continued claim to the latitude granted him by Brezhnev and Andropov. As a result, the GDR—after Bonn had become the target of Moscow's revanchism campaign—came into the firing line, with Soviet media insinuating in the summer of 1984 that East Berlin was susceptible to Bonn's temptations. Thereupon Honecker was forced to cancel his planned visit to the Federal Republic on short notice, on 4 September.[31]

At the celebrations of the 35th anniversary of the GDR's founding in October, he demonstrated complete agreement with Gromyko, the head of the Soviet delegation, on foreign policy and policy toward Germany. But when Chernenko died in March 1985, Honecker immediately used the funeral ceremonies in Moscow for direct contacts with Chancellor Kohl. He apparently hoped for a return under Gorbachev to the bilateral agreements that had applied to the cooperation between the GDR and the USSR during Andropov's period in office.

In the economic realm, the GDR's leadership displays no inclination to venture into reform experiments that might affect the existing system of the centrally planned economy. In close imitation of the Soviet Union, it prefers to bet on limited "improvements," in conformity with the system, aimed at technocratic streamlining of the organizational structures and administrative procedures. For all that, it is able to point to comparatively good economic results.[32]

In the GDR, the Catholic Church, as a diaspora church, plays no politically significant role. In contrast, the Protestant churches have gained considerably in political weight by means of partial resistance to the militarization of young people's education and by means of its support of the local "autonomous" peace movement. While the Protestant side has developed a critically constructive concept of the "church in socialism," tolerance on the part of the SED regime has increased. However, the critically positive attitude of many clergymen in the SED-state often also acts to stabilize the system—in the sense of domesticating deviant behavior.

Czechoslovakia: Moscow's Most Conforming Vassal

Since late 1968, the foreign policy of the CSSR has been subordinated in all major points to the foreign policy line of the Soviet Union and the WTO, or CMEA, decisions. Only in connection with preparations for the deployment of Soviet short- and intermediate-range missiles in the CSSR and the GDR in autumn of 1983, and in regard to the USSR's unilateral walk-out from the Geneva arms control negotiations, did the CSSR advance certain reservations. In the process, rather similar methods and signals were used by the CSSR and the GDR.

Six days after the publication of the agreement on deployment, Radio Prague announced on 30 October 1983 that this event had sparked a "lively discussion" in the population. Then, on 5 November, the Party newspaper *Rudé Právo* informed its readers that "mountains of letters" from concerned citizens had reached the editorial offices. Individual sentences or questions were quoted, among them the warning—picking up on an argument frequently used with regard to the Federal Republic of Germany—that because of the deployment, the CSSR was itself going to be turned into a missiles target. In the GDR, too, fears among the population had been registered by the publication of letters in the SED central organ *Neues Deutschland*. What is more, on 19 November Prime Minister Štrougal stated verbatim: "None of us is happy about this decision," namely the missile decision of 24 October. Similarly, Honecker affirmed repeatedly that the "Soviet" decision had caused "no joy" in the GDR (seventh CC plenary session), and he himself had by no means assented "cheerfully."[33]

At their Prague meeting on 24 October 1983, Husák and Honecker demanded not only the "countermeasures" in question, but also the continuation, indeed activation, of all arms limitation and disarmament negotiations. The CSSR Federal Assembly left no doubt about it on 26 October that this meant the continuation of the negotiations on the beginning of deployment. The communique on the Husák-Kádár talks in Prague on 10 November also favored additional negotiations, without mentioning a time limit, and underscored the conviction that "a solution to all contentious international issues" could and must "be found by way of negotiations." Finally, nine days later, Štrougal hinted that the CSSR leadership (irrespective of all Soviet threats to break off negotiations) had by no means given up hope for a continuation of the negotiations.[34]

Even though misgivings about the course taken by the Soviet Union emerged repeatedly, in the spring of 1984 the CPC leadership, side by side with the CPSU, hastened to launch a large-scale campaign to discipline those "sister parties" that had more or less openly championed a different course or a correction of the course.[35] Naturally, the CSSR joined the Soviet Olympic boycott and committed itself so vehemently to the revanchism campaign as to eclipse even Soviet and Polish accusations and suspicions. At the CMEA Council meetings of June and October 1984, Štrougal took it upon himself to plead Moscow's case by calling upon the minor CMEA member states to participate with massive investments in the expansion of Soviet oil production capacities as they would otherwise have to count on a reduction in deliveries.[36]

Characteristically, relations between Peking and Prague are even worse than those between Peking and Moscow. Of the WTO states, Romania enjoys by far the best relations with the PR China. It is followed by Hungary and the GDR, ahead of Poland and Bulgaria, behind which one would have to place the USSR. The CSSR—according to Chinese information—is definitely in last place.

After two years of negative growth (1981 and 1982) the CSSR's economy has recovered somewhat thanks to good harvests, but reaching the original targets of the five-year plan is out of the question by now. Nevertheless, there are no signs whatsoever of reform projects. In this area, too, no other WTO/CMEA state follows the Soviet example more closely than the CSSR.

Hungary: For a Steady East-West Dialogue and Cautious Reforms

The long-valid thesis that Hungary acquired its leeway in domestic politics by absolute faithfulness to the USSR's foreign policy line no longer holds without qualifications since the late seventies. Starting with the Polish crisis of 1980–1981 at the latest, Budapest has begun developing its own foreign policy concepts and standing up for its own interests. This emerged mainly in connection with the serious deterioration of East-West relations, caused by the struggle about NATO rearmament in the INF area and the "countermeasures" threatened by Moscow in the years 1983–1984. During this period, Hungarian leadership openly and vigorously championed a foreign policy concept that may be described with the phrase, "East-West dialogue despite Euro-missiles."

This Hungarian line was in clear contrast to the confrontation course taken by the Soviet Union during the same period. This ultimately led to the disruption of the Geneva arms control negotiations on 23 November 1983. The orientation of its economy towards the world market and the intent to press on carefully with the domestic program of reforms, above all, were decisive factors in Hungary's behavior. Hungarian perseverance was not least explained by the fact that the other smaller WTO partners almost without exception sympathized with the Hungarian position and in part even supported it openly.

In the spring of 1984, still prior to the Budapest foreign ministers' conference of the WTO states (19–20 April), two journals of the CC of the HSWP published an important essay by the CC secretary in charge of foreign policy, M. Szürös.[37] Apparently, the theses advanced in it seemed provocative to some orthodox keepers of the holy grail of bloc discipline. The minor countries, Szürös contended, played a significant part in arriving at compromises between the superpowers; the Cold War and the mechanical copying of the Soviet model had occasioned very negative effects for Hungary; in conflicts between national and internationalist interests there no longer was an "arbiter"; a "new type" of relations between socialist countries had developed requiring confidence, patience, circumspection, and "mutually acceptable agreements"; the so-called "universal laws" for building socialism had to be "enriched" based on more recent experiences; historic traditions and certain "circumstances" allowed for the further development of relations between individual socialist and capitalist states, even when the East-West climate as a whole was deteriorating; in the process, each socialist country was entitled to take advantage of its own particular opportunities. These opinions, shared by other ranking Hungarian politicians, even enjoy the backing of Hungary's Party leader Kádár.

The CPC's daily *Rudé Právo* responded on 30 March 1984 with sharp criticism of Szürös' theses. Szürös commented rather calmly on the reproaches from Prague in an interview that essentially repeated all Hungarian positions. The SED organ *Neues Deutschland* also printed this interview as a show of solidarity.[38]

However, it soon became evident that the critique from Prague was not an isolated, individual act, but part and parcel of a disciplinary campaign in concert with the CPSU apparatus. Similar reproaches were also published shortly afterwards by a Moscow Party journal.[39] Though some points of the attack were directed against the GDR and Romania as well, the thrust of the cross fire was aimed at Hungary's foreign policy stance as taken by Szürös.[40]

Relations between Budapest and Vienna are considerably better than those between Bucharest and Prague. There are large Hungarian minorities in Romania and the CSSR (approximately 2 million and 600,000 respectively) who have reason to complain about discrimination and harassment. Hungary maintains comparatively good relations with the Federal Republic of Germany. Therefore, great efforts were made to avoid participation in the revanchism campaign staged by Moscow.

In the economic realm, the government holds to its reform course in the face of slowing growth rates and dropping net incomes (with rising prices). New measures, decreed in the spring of 1984, which also include elements of control by the market, are being introduced step by step. Moscow seems to tolerate these experiments provided Budapest observes certain ideological principles, provided it takes into account important Soviet interests, and provided the Hungarian reform model remains essentially restricted to Hungary.[41] For all that, various developments leading up to the Thirteenth HSWP Convention (March 1985)—e.g., a campaign of repression and intimidation directed at dissidents—were evidence that the Hungarian leadership is far from being composed exclusively of progressively minded reformers.

Romania: Between Self-Assertion and Accommodation

Romania in the mid-eighties is nothing but a feeble copy of an earlier, better time when the country not only achieved high economic growth rates with Western loans and Western technology, but also derived from that the self-confidence for a separate national profile and the power for a national-communist individual, independent stance, in defiance of Moscow's will. Back then, Romania was led by a charismatic Ceauşescu, liked by the people and respected worldwide as an "honest broker." In the spring of 1985, the "Conducător" (born in 1918) had held the office of leader of the Romanian CP for exactly 20 years, and while he has raised himself and the members of his family to objects of a grotesque personality cult, the country is in desperate straits: There is a permanent supply crisis, industrial facilities are not used to capacity, private energy consumption has dropped by half, plus onerous Western debts, insecurity among Party functionaries and civil servants, and dissatisfaction among the populace.

Romania's current relations with the Soviet Union are neither particularly good nor particularly bad. It seems that both sides watch each other with due caution. Though Ceauşescu has always been close to the Eastern bloc line laid down by Moscow, he has still kept his distance. Notwithstanding Soviet assistance, like 1.5 million tons of crude oil in 1984, economic aid fell far short of the extent hoped for and needed by Romania.

At the same time, the Soviet side put considerable pressure on Ceauşescu to fall into line with Moscow's hard confrontation course, but in vain. Neither Gromyko, who visited Bucharest in January 1984, nor Chernenko, who conferred with Ceauşescu the following June in Moscow, managed to induce the Romanian "leader" to throw in his lot unequivocally with the Soviet side, on questions of particular relevance—such as the question of "countermeasures" to the deployment of US intermediate-range missiles in Western Europe. Romania did not even participate, as demanded by Moscow, in the Olympic boycott, behind which, otherwise, all WTO and CMEA countries (including North Korea) had closed ranks. Unlike Honecker and Zhivkov, Ceauşescu was not to be distracted from his scheduled visit in Bonn in the fall of 1984. In its revanchism campaign, too, Moscow had to do without Romanian participation.

Overall, Romania's position vis-à-vis the Soviet Union has been better than might appear at first blush. It can boast a positive balance of trade, it has put offers of joint ventures to the Soviet Union that embarrassed Moscow, and many of its exports are also competitive in the West. This improves its initial position in negotiations on long-term agreements. Thus, the Romanians have been able to prevail with their own "classic" stance in important questions: Even in 1983 and 1984, they neither permitted WTO troops to enter the country nor did they participate in WTO maneuvers. At the CCDE in Stockholm, they assumed a far more constructive posture in the matter of "confidence-building measures" than the Soviets. They maintain good relations to the PR of China and are on diplomatic terms with Israel. They entertain views different from the Kremlin's with regards to the Middle East and also concerning Afghanistan. They have a positive attitude towards Eurocommunism.

But above all, Ceauşescu refuses to renounce the nationalist base of his entire foreign policy. For him, a country's foreign policy is not the result of "class interests" (i.e., an instrument of Soviet hegemony in the sense of the "Brezhnev doctrine"), but is, rather fundamentally impregnated by the interests of a nation and it must therefore always align itself with the principles of international law, of equal rights, and of sovereignty and non-interference. The constant repetition of these precepts amounts to a continuous warning, addressed to the Soviet Union, not to consider Romania weaker than it currently is and not to commit the error of misinterpreting Ceauşescu's occasional concessions as indications of his imminent capitulation.

Bulgaria: Friendship Yes, But Without Soviet Missiles

Modern Bulgaria is a "country in ordered circumstances." Its economy is prospering under the banner of a "New Economic Mechanism." Certainly this is not without some elements from the Hungarian reform model, but on the whole it can be considered the realization of genuinely Bulgarian notions of reform, belated by a decade and a half. In foreign policy it has always aptly reconciled proverbial alliance—loyalty and cunningly safeguarded self-interests. Domestic and cultural policy move along quietly for the most part, though the shaping of a growing, profound sense of Bulgarian nationality has been discernible for a decade ("Bulgaria—the classic homeland, the Greece and Rome of Slavdom"). Foreign trade and agriculture make a large contribution to the relatively high standard of living since they are handled with undogmatic pragmatism. Problems appeared only in the realm of regional policy, where "traditional" Balkan frictions blend with new conflicts of interest.

Among other things, the remarkable continuity of personnel and concepts in Bulgarian domestic, economic, and foreign policy is manifested in the person of the extraordinarily vigorous head of state and Party leader T. Zhivkov (born in 1911). He celebrated his 30th anniversary as secretary general of the Bulgarian CP in March 1984. Several mysterious bomb explosions in the late summer of 1984 can be connected to Shivkov's travel plans at the time, but there is no specific evidence pointing to a certain group or motives.

Bulgaria's "secret of success" in dealing with Moscow has two dimensions: the historic one, expressed in the traditionally pro-Russian sentiment of most Bulgarians; and the pragmatic-realist one, putting up with the inevitable and making the best of it. The fact that well over 50 percent of Bulgarian foreign trade has for some time been with the USSR is not generally taken as a burden, but rather as a guarantee of Bulgaria's own development. As early as the late sixties the Bulgarians began to extract needed raw materials in the Soviet Union themselves. This gave them a certain head start over other CMEA countries, at least in "atmospheric" terms, with regard to the Soviet assessment of its partners.

In foreign policy, Sofia asks only two things of Moscow, though very emphatically so: for one, a relatively free hand in the Balkans (with due consideration to strict bilateralism, deemed indispensable by Soviet leadership), and the exclusion of Bulgaria from Soviet missile deployment for another. Already by the end of 1983, the Bulgarians had gotten their way on both counts. One result is a notably close relationship with Greece now, which has withdrawn a large part of its troops that were previously posted along its border with Bulgaria. Relations with Turkey have deteriorated on account of the harassment of Bulgaria's Turkish minority (about one million), which is subjected to name changes and Bulgarianization measures. Relations with Yugoslavia are also traditionally bad due to the irksome "Macedonian question." Under these circumstances the Bulgarian dream-vision of a "nuclear weapons–free zone on the Balkans," for which the Soviets have little use, is not likely to be realized all that soon.

Zhivkov, who had announced his visit to Bonn for mid-September 1984, preferred to bend to Soviet pressure in this dispute and postpone his travel plans to a later date. Still, he seems to have put up a remarkably long resistance until the Kremlin dispatched then deputy secretary general Gorbachev to Sofia to stress Soviet wishes. However, Bulgaria made a point of stating in Bonn that Zhivkov's cancellation was in no way intended as a vote against the Federal Republic of Germany. It fits the context that the revanchism campaign, essentially Soviet-Polish-Czechoslovakian orchestrated, also had to make do without Bulgarian participation.

Notes

*The introductory passages to this chapter were written by Wolfgang Berner. Christian Meier wrote the sections "Coordinated Foreign and Security Policy," "Coordinated Economic Policy," and "Ideological Cooperation"; Dieter Bingen wrote "Poland: The Rule of Generals as a Lasting Provisional Arrangement"; Fred Oldenburg wrote "GDR: The Beginnings of Independent Policies"; Wolfgang Berner wrote "Czechoslovakia: Moscow's Most Conforming Vassal"; Gyula Józsa wrote "Hungary: For a Steady East-West Dialogue and Cautious Reforms"; Wolf Oschlies wrote "Romania: Between Self-Assertion and Accommodation" and "Bulgaria: Friendship Yes, But Without Soviet Missiles."

1. Cf. Gorbachev's speech, in *Pr*, 24 April 1985; in addition, *ND*, 14 March 1985.
2. Cf. Andropov's speeches, in *Pr*, 23 November, 23 December 1982, and 16 June 1983.
3. Declaration in *ND*, 7 January 1982; *EA*, No. 4 (1983), pp. D 104–116.
4. *Pr*, 26 September 1983; *EA*, No. 18 (1983), pp. D 501–505.
5. *ND*, 21 October, 25 October, and 8 December 1983.
6. *ND*, 15/16 October 1983.
7. *ND*, 21 October 1983.
8. *ND*, 25 October 1983.
9. Full text Radio Hvězda, Prague, 26 October 1983; cf. note 34 below.
10. Cf. on this Fred Oldenburg, "Relations Between the USSR and the Federal Republic of Germany," in this volume, Chapter 23.
11. Cf. W. Berner, *Berichte des BIOst*, No. 20 (1984).
12. *ND*, 21/22 April 1984.
13. *ND*, 16 June 1984; *EA*, No. 18 (1984), pp. D 520–527; in addition H.-H. Höhmann/C. Meier, *Berichte des BIOst*, No. 55 (1984).
14. Rendition of a Nepszava-interview by Hungary's Deputy Foreign Minister J. Roska, in *ND*, 4 March 1985.
15. *ND*, 16 June 1984; *EA*, No. 18 (1984), pp. D 514–520.
16. *ND*, 16 June 1984; *EA*, No. 18 (1984), pp. D 520–527.
17. TASS, 15 June 1984; press communique in *ND*, 15 June 1984; *EA*, No. 18 (1984), pp. D 513 ff.
18. Similar agreements have meanwhile been concluded with the CSSR (31 May) and with Bulgaria (7 June 1985).
19. *ND*, 16 March 1983.
20. *PFS*, No. 11 (1983), pp. 1489 ff.
21. *PFS*, No. 2 (1984), pp. 171 ff.
22. *PFS*, No. 9 (1984), pp. 1194–1197.
23. *ND*, 7 March 1985.
24. *ND*, 2 April 1982.
25. *PFS*, No. 8 (1984), p. 1039.
26. *Pr*, 5 December 1984.
27. Cf. on this D. Bingen, *Berichte des BIOst*, No. 50 (1984).
28. Cf. *Trybuna Opolska*, 3 October 1984.
29. Cf. on this H.-H. Höhmann, *Berichte des BIOst*, No. 7 (1985).
30. Cf. on this W. Berner, *op. cit.*, pp. 19–27.
31. Cf. R.D. Asmus, in *Orbis*, No. 4 (Winter 1985), pp. 743–774; F. Oldenburg, in OE, No. 5 (1985), pp. 303–319 and in *Deutschland Archiv*, No. 8 (1984), pp. 834–843.

32. Cf. on this H.-H. Höhmann, *op. cit.*, pp. 3, 6, 8, 14 ff.

33. On the letters see *ND*, 22 October and 3 November 1983; Štrougal's speech in *RPr*, 21 November 1983; Honecker's statements in *ND*, 26, 27 November 1983, and 6 January 1984.

34. *RPr*, 25 and 27 October 1983 (Declaration by the CSSR Federal Assembly in abbreviated form, full text in Radio Hvězda, Prague, 26 October, 12 o'clock); 11 and 21 October 1983.

35. Cf. M. Štefaňak and I. Hlivka, *ibid.*, 30 March 1984; on this W. Berner, *op. cit.*

36. According to *RFE-RL*, No. 2 (1985), *Background Report*, No. 1, p. 13.

37. Comprehensively in *Tarzadalmi Szemle*, No. 1 (1984), pp. 13–25.

38. Cf. *Magyar Hirlap*, 4 April 1984; *ND*, 12 April 1984.

39. O.V. Borizov, in *VIKPSS*, No. 4 (1984), pp. 34–49.

40. In more detail, G. Józsa, *Berichte des BIOst*, Nos. 5 and 6 (1985).

41. Cf. H.-H. Höhmann, *op. cit.*, pp. 13 ff.

25
Soviet Policy Towards the Middle East: Minimizing Risks, New Initiatives

Gerd Linde

For nearly twenty years, from the mid-fifties to the mid-seventies, the USSR was able to gain influence in the Middle East and consolidate this influence by exploiting conflicts resulting chiefly from the maintenance of old colonial borders and from tribal rivalries. This was followed by nearly a decade of maturing conflicts among its own clients and other states wooed by Moscow. The most important examples are the Iran-Iraq war and the deep-rooted discord between Syria and the PLO. Outmaneuvered politically for a while, the Kremlin seems to have settled on a policy of trying to soothe the endemic conflicts—which is difficult—and channelling the somewhat diffuse resentments in the region at the behavior of the US, Israel, and Egypt into an anti-US and anti-Israeli direction, which is easier to accomplish but by no means without risks given the instability of power constellation.

It was not necessarily the changeover from secretary general Brezhnev to Andropov and from him to Chernenko that was responsible for a certain stagnation that emerged in Soviet policy toward the Middle East up to mid-1984, though that may have played a part. In any event, continuity was assured through Gromyko. It is more likely that this immobility was caused in part by a lack of maneuverability, and in part by a conscious and deliberate inactivity.

Maneuverability was restricted by:

- The continuing military involvement in Afghanistan.
- The option in favor of neutrality in the conflict between treaty partner Iraq and wooed Iran.
- The danger of repercussions from Syria's role in this conflict for Soviet-Syrian relations.
- The sharpening conflict between Syria and the Arafat wing of the PLO, which is also among Moscow's clients—a conflict that had escalated into armed confrontation in Lebanon and Syria by late 1983.

The Soviet Union displayed little inclination to encumber, much less endanger, its positions by intensifying relations with one or the other party to the conflicts. It preferred a wait-and-see attitude instead.

Afghanistan: Option for a Pyrrhic Victory?

A political solution to the problems brought on by the Soviet occupation of Afghanistan is no more in sight that an end to Afghan popular resistance. The talks held in Geneva between June 1982 and June 1983 ended inconclusively.

On the other hand, the warfare against the freedom fighters escalated into merciless severity. New weapons systems, e.g., armored helicopters and automatic mortars, were used just as much as the "scorched earth" technique, the destruction of living space, herds, and crops, and the expulsion of the population into exile—mostly to Pakistan.[1] The result may well be labelled "genocide by expulsion."[2] However, the commanders of the intervention forces were confronted with mounting disciplinary problems. Nor could they prevent freedom fighters from deriving a certain legitimacy from armistices concluded with them by the interventionists.[3]

Afghanistan can be destroyed. But the resistance movement is not likely ever to be completely eliminated. The only military option left to the Soviet Union is a Pyrrhic victory. To be sure, the indignation in the Arabic-Islamic region at the Soviet intervention has abated somewhat in the course of four years. Events in Lebanon—that is, both the Israeli and the US actions—probably contributed to this, as did the Gulf war, which caused many governments to look upon the Shi'ite challenge as the paramount danger. Besides, a pacification of Afghanistan by military victory would merely represent a local success for the Soviet Union. As a result, the Soviet advance would again be perceived as a real danger in the Arab region.

The Iran-Iraq War: Moscow Opts for the Lesser Evil

Soviet rapprochement with Iraq, discernible since mid-1983, was certainly influenced by the constant refusal of the Ayatollah-regime in Teheran to improve relations with Moscow and probably also by the persecution of the Tudeh Party in Iran. But additional considerations may well have played a part here: Moscow provided next to no assistance to its treaty partner Iraq from 1980 to 1983. This did little to make Moscow appear a credible ally to the capitals of other countries. Furthermore, a convergence of interests—albeit limited—of the great powers, the majority of Arab states, Israel, and probably Europe and Japan as well, was beginning to show. Preventing the collapse of Iraq seemed called for since otherwise an Iranian-Shi'ite dominated strip might cut right across the Arab Peninsula with Syria as a bridgehead. In this case, the quest for independence by the Iraqi Kurds might well receive fresh impetus, and their emancipatory movement would almost inexorably spread to the NATO member Turkey—a country with its own Kurdish problem.

The community of interests ends, of course, when it comes to the goals of the war. Most Arabs wish for an Iraqi victory. Israel would rather have two losers. The two major powers, the USSR and the US, seem to consider a draw the best solution. Neither great power commands direct influence in Teheran. Moscow makes use of the Syrian connection—without notable success, so far—as illustrated by visits to Teheran and efforts at mediation by Syrian Vice President Rifaad al-Assad.[4]

Following the Iraqi defeat at Khorramchar (May 1982), contacts between the USSR and Iraq grew closer again. The persecution, soon thereafter, of the communist Tudeh Party in Iran, which was declared disbanded on 4 May 1983, fostered this development. However, the Iraqi attitude towards its indigenous communists continued to be determined by rejection. In August 1983, the leading Soviet foreign economist Y. Ryabov visited Iraq and promised assistance for the further expansion of oil production facilities. Shortly thereafter, Foreign Minister Tarik Aziz visited Moscow. During his visit, the Soviet Union indirectly cautioned Iran against blocking the Straits of Hormuz.[5] In late April, the deputy chairman of the Iraqi revolutionary council, T.Y. Ramada, sojourned in Moscow. Currently, K. Brutents, deputy head of the International Department of the CC Secretariat of the CPSU and Middle Eastern expert, visited Iraq and Syria.[6] As early as spring of 1983, Soviet arms shipments again reached Iraq via Aqaba.[7]

In the meantime, Iraq expanded its foreign policy leeway towards the West by re-opening diplomatic relations with the US on 27 November 1984—after seventeen years of interruption. Hence, the danger of being isolated, like Syria, seems obviated for the time being.

Initially, Moscow had tried to discover progressive traits in the Khomeini revolution—the elimination of the monarchy was welcomed, as was anti-US agitation, championship of "the poor in this world," hostility to the enemies of the USSR. There had been hope that the upheavals Iran was experiencing would soon rock pro-Western Arab regimes as well. It took a long time to realize that a reactionary regime in the literal sense of the word had been instituted in Teheran. Down to its own bitter end, the Tudeh Party stood by the Khomeini regime—save for the Afghan question. This may have contributed to the Soviet misinterpretation.

As early as spring of 1983, many observers thought that Soviet-Iranian relations had been better under the Shah. The USSR was referred to in Teheran as "Satan Nr. 1." On 4 May 1983, things came to the expulsion of eighteen Soviet diplomats and a TASS correspondent who had failed to report on the use of Soviet missiles by Iraq.[8] In the summer of 1983, Khomeini accused Tudeh of espionage for the Soviet Union. By June, Moscow's criticism of the persecution of Tudeh had taken definite shape.[9]

In the spring of 1984, the Soviet Union denied Iranian claims that Moscow had supplied Baghdad with gas grenades.[10] In connection with this, the accusation was levelled that the Gulf war served Iran's purposes of persecuting progressive forces, accompanied by the obligatory polemics against the US presence in the Gulf. Teheran's contentions that Iraqi soldiers had been trained in the Soviet Union to use chemical weapons provoked a sharp Soviet denial.[11]

Officially, the Soviet Union is neutral in the conflict. It continues to publish military bulletins from both sides, the Iraqi one from Baghdad, the Iranian one from Nikosia. At the same time, however, it stresses that it considers the war senseless, and its calls upon Iran finally to allow for negotiations indicate whom the Kremlin holds responsible for the escalation of the war.[12]

The longer this war lasts, the less can be gained for Soviet regional interests. On the contrary, Moscow will probably have to accept strategic losses. All the same, an indirect gain from the Gulf war was scored when Kuwait decided to deploy Soviet weapons—in particular anti-aircraft missiles—and probably is giving thought to inviting Soviet advisors as well.[13]

Syria, the PLO, and the Lebanese Crisis: Fragile Friendships

Although there is no Arab state where Soviet influence is greater than in Syria, the bilateral relationship is still difficult. The atmosphere did not improve when in the Lebanese war Soviet weapons proved inferior to those of the Israelis. The Soviet Union felt compelled to replace Syrian losses with deliveries of modern equipment, including anti-aircraft missiles and tanks. Some 200 Soviet advisers are thought to have been killed in action in Lebanon.[14]

The rupture between Assad and the PLO caused another complication. In late 1983, Gromyko was still assuring Arafat of further Soviet support and urging him to come to terms with the Syrians. However, the schism in the PLO rather suited Assad; he made active use of it to reduce considerably Arafat's political weight not only in his own organization, but in the entire Arab world.

Syria is not likely to have welcomed the re-activation of the Soviet-Iraqi partnership. Evidence for this is President Assad's stubborn refusal to accept Soviet mediation efforts and, for instance, to re-open the oil pipeline from Kirkuk in Iraq to the Mediterranean port of Banias.[15] Inversely, Syrian efforts to get Iraq and Iran to the negotiating table probably foundered because Syria is not regarded as an honest broker by Baghdad.[16] However, the improvement of the Soviet-Iraqi relationship is likely to have had a positive influence on Jordan's course of cautious rapprochement with Moscow. Syria's domestic political situation, too, gives rise to worries in the Kremlin. Apparently, the succession struggles occasioned by the president's illness were settled by the appointment of Rifaat Assad and Abdel H. Khaddam as vice presidents in March 1984.

Still under Andropov, Soviet diplomatic activity increased in Syria as well as in Lebanon. The propaganda campaign conjuring up US-Israeli conspiracy against Syria was intensified. Shortly after Andropov's death, G. Aliyev was the first Politburo member in years to visit Syria again. An understanding was reached to fight the "enslaving agreement" between Israel and Lebanon, to resist Zionism, to stand up for the Palestinian Arabs' right to a state of their own, and to help overcome the differences of opinion inside the PLO.[17]

Aliyev met with Vice Presidents R. Assad and A.H. Khaddam, with General M. Tlass, and with CP leader G. Haoui. He was accompanied by K. Brutents and V. Polyakov, the head of the Middle Eastern desk in the Soviet Ministry of Foreign Affairs. Apparently, the Gulf war was left out of the conversations. Brutents and Polyakov also spoke with Lebanese President A. Gemayel and the leader of the Druzes, W. Djumblat.[18] These meetings were probably also in Syria's interest which is currently not at cross purposes with Soviet interests in Lebanon. After the events of the war had considerably reduced Gemayel's power base, Syria attempted to bolster him because the other Maronite leaders such as C. Shamun and F. Frem pursue a tougher policy towards Syria. Syrian support for Gemayel could drive a wedge between him and parts of the Christian militias and thus render him more dependent on Syria.

R. Assad returned Aliyev's visit almost immediately with a visit to Moscow. He was accompanied by the new Minister of Foreign Affairs, Farouk al-Sharaa.[19] Word was at that time that Moscow was planning to set up a mobile intervention force of two divisions for Syria, capable of being moved to any area of operation within eight hours.[20] On the occasion of the fourth anniversary of the signing of the Treaty of Friendship, Hafiz Assad met with K. Chernenko in Moscow (16–18 October 1984). Apparently, the two countries' main differences concerning mutual relations with the PLO, Iraq, and Iran could not be resolved as none of these problems were even mentioned in the final communique.[21]

The USSR went so far in its support of Syria in the confrontation with Israel as it possibly could under the circumstances: It extended weapons, training, and financial aid as well as propagandistic-journalistic support. Still, the effects on Soviet prestige in the Middle East were negative. Soviet hesitancy to grant more wide-ranging aid made a poor impression after the previous announcement that US-Israeli actions (this was the official Soviet wording) would not be accepted. But there were sound reasons for Soviet restraint. Actually, at the height of the Lebanon crisis, only the commitment of combat troops would have made a decisive difference in the course of events. The consequences of such a measure, however, were difficult to assess in advance, and it was not in the Soviet interest to risk a world crisis on account of Arafat, the less so since the rupture between the PLO and Syria was beginning to show. In this context, it must be borne in mind that it has always been Soviet practice to support states rather than "liberation movements." Moreover, there are few ideological affinities between Arafat and Moscow. Still, Moscow seeks to avoid an open breach as long as Arafat advocates an international conference on the Middle East with Soviet participation—a project resisted by Syria. However, the points of contact between Marxism-Leninism and the Syrian Baath ideology are also marginal.

The decision to play their cards close to the chest proved correct the moment the US contingent in the international peace-keeping force could be adduced as evidence for the onesided partisanship of the US. This, together with the massacres at Sabra and Shatila, added up to some propaganda material—also in other Arab states such as Jordan or Saudi Arabia—where irritation at US policy continues to be one of the best Soviet trump cards—to deflect attention from Soviet actions in Afghanistan. That Israeli actions met only with subdued applause in Washington played no role in this connection.

Jordan's policy stands under the banner of cultivating businesslike contacts with Moscow. However, Amman does not want to allow dependencies or a client relationship to come out of this. Lebanon attempts to follow the same course, the model having been supplied for some time by Kuwait. King Hussein's quest for Soviet weapons, of course, is also connected to the US refusal to supply him with certain weapons systems. Recently, there has been an increasingly sharp edge to his criticism of US policy. Thus, he accused the US of submitting to Israeli dictate, thereby losing its own credibility. In his opinion, negotiations with Israel are out of the question until after a complete Israeli withdrawal from the occupied territories. The USSR, he emphasized, was to be included in these negotiations, as demanded by Cairo and Beirut as well.[22] The monarch told a delegation from a US military academy that, after all, the USSR was present in the region and, besides, did advocate the implementation of Resolution 242 of the UN Security Council.[23]

In the Soviet Union, comments on Hussein's stance were favorable. It was interpreted as proof that anti-US sentiments were on the rise all over the Arab world.[24] It is noteworthy that the last (29 July 1984) Soviet proposal for a settlement of Middle East problems can be construed to mean that the USSR no longer uncompromisingly insists on the establishment of a separate State of Palestine but also deems a federation—in the final analysis possible only with Jordan—conceivable. This "Chernenko Plan" is essentially based on the "Brezhnev Plan" of 15 September 1982. However, he seems keen on meeting Arab notions by including a series of additional elements and suggestions, as specified in the Fez Plan of 9 September 1982.[25]

Egypt: The End of Isolation?

Together with partially successful attempts at overcoming its own isolation in the Arab camp, Egypt pursued détente in its relations with the Soviet Union. These relations had reached a low point with the expulsion of Ambassador V. Polyakov in 1981. To be sure, diplomatic relations had not been broken; only, the ambassadorships were left vacant for a long time. In the spring of 1984, Polyakov returned to Cairo as head of the Middle Eastern desk of the Ministry of Foreign Affairs for talks with Foreign

Minister B. Ghali on the improvement of relations.[26] Like Jordan, Egypt, too, declared that Moscow would have to be a party to a comprehensive settlement of the Middle East problem (which can be interpreted as a move away from the Camp-David agreements). The renewed exchange of ambassadors—initially announced without a target date—was an important step towards normalization, the more so since it could be interpreted as Egypt wishing to demonstrate its non-alignment, while the Soviet Union wants to enlarge its still restricted room for maneuver in the Middle East.

The noticeable cooling of Egypt's relations with Israel does facilitate Soviet-Egyptian rapprochement, but Moscow will have to make allowance for Syrian sensibilities, for Damascus is working towards a complete breach between Cairo and Jerusalem. Jordan, which also normalized its relations with Egypt and is currently well liked in Moscow, resists this Syrian policy. Albeit not yet officially, Iraq has for some time, again, been maintaining good de facto cooperative relations with Egypt.

In late 1983, Egypt and the USSR signed a trade agreement with a volume in excess of 500 million dollars. In 1984 the exchange of goods was to be increased by 25 percent. By contrast, no new arms sales are envisaged as Egypt discarded its Soviet weapons systems and is converting its armed forces to Western armaments.[27] In early July 1984, A. Belonogov was appointed Soviet ambassador to Cairo, while S. Bassiouni assumed the post of Egyptian ambassador in Moscow.[28]

The return to the diplomatic stage is the main goal of Soviet policy towards the Middle East, especially in the form of participation in an international Mideast conference. There is no discernible Soviet interest in an escalation of tensions, which would entail hard-to-assess political risks for Moscow itself. Virtually all Arab states save Syria would like to see an international Mideast conference convened. By contrast, the US, and more decisively yet Israel, reject the project. The normalization of relations with Egypt, the rapprochement with Iraq, and the improvement of relations with Jordan are important steps along this way for Moscow.

The very process, however, bears the danger of alienation from Syria, which is on bad terms with all these states and also rejects a solution of Middle East problems at the bargaining table. Damascus, however, is hardly in a position to break with Moscow because of its military-technological dependence on the Soviet Union. The Arafat-PLO, considerably weakened by the schism, is also inclined to a conference solution, in consonance with Soviet and general Arab notions, but in contrast to Syria. Thus, Arafat manages to retain a certain influence in Moscow despite his current military and political powerlessness.

Notes

1. C. Malhuret, "Report from Afghanistan," *Foreign Affairs*, Winter 1983/84, pp. 426ff.
2. *T*, 7 January 1981.

3. L. Dupree, "Afghanistan in 1983—and Still No Solution," *Asian Survey*, No. 1 (1984), p. 235.
4. *IHT*, 4 and 5 June 1984.
5. NZZ, 24 November 1983; see also *T*, 11 May 1984.
6. *Pr*, 26 and 27 April 1984.
7. *IHT*, 28 April 1984.
8. *The Christian Science Monitor*, 6 May 1983.
9. LG, 22 June 1983; see also *FAZ*, 8 December 1983.
10. *Trud*, 25 March 1984.
11. RM, 1 March 1984; *KZ*, 4 and 22 March 1984.
12. *KZ*, 22 March 1984.
13. *Pr*, 10 July 1984; *NZZ*, 16 July 1984.
14. *IHT*, 15 February 1983.
15. *IHT*, 18 May 1984.
16. *IHT*, 2 and 5 June 1984.
17. *Pr*, 14 March 1984.
18. *dpa*, 3 April 1984.
19. *Pr*, 29 and 30 May, 1 and 2 June 1984.
20. NZZ, 18 May 1984.
21. *Pr*, 17 October 1984; *ND*, 19 October 1984.
22. *IHT*, 11 March 1984; *FAZ*, 16 March 1984; *T*, 20 June 1984.
23. *W*, 9 April 1984.
24. *Pr*, 21 March 1984; *Iz*, 28 March 1984.
25. Cf. *The Soviet Union 1982/1983*, p. 319.
26. *W*, 17 April 1984.
27. Handelsblatt, 25 April 1984.
28. FAZ, 9 July 1984.

26
Soviet Policy Towards China: Détente with Setbacks

Dieter Heinzig

Up to the end of Andropov's period in office, the process of cautious détente between the Soviet Union and the PR of China that had been started in 1982, ran on the tracks laid out by the actual development launched at the time and by the course of the first three rounds of consultation at the level of Deputy Ministers of Foreign Affairs (October 1982 as well as March and October 1983).[1] This means that cooperation in such areas as science, culture, sports, technology, and tourism that has resumed since then gradually expanded. The volume of trade increased greatly, and the climate of mutual intercourse improved noticeably. No progress was discernible in the three great conflict areas of security policy—troop concentrations along the border, Cambodia, and Afghanistan.

From Andropov to Chernenko

In the first months of 1984, there were signs that both sides endeavored to endow the process of rapprochement with new momentum. Thus, the intention was to upgrade formally diplomatic relations that usually took place at the level of First Deputy Ministers, and in exceptional cases of Ministers of Foreign Affairs. This was manifested in early February by the official confirmation that First Deputy Prime Minister I. Arkhipov would take a trip to China. Shortly after that, the death of Secretary General Andropov (9 February 1984) provided the opportunity to move ahead in time the upgrading of formal relations that had been agreed upon. Unlike November 1982, when State Commissar and Foreign Minister Huang Hua was sent to Moscow for Brezhnev's burial, the funeral ceremonies this time were attended by First Deputy Prime Minister Wan Li. This was the most senior representative to travel to the Soviet Union since Zhou En-Lai's visit to Moscow in November 1964. At about that time, an agreement was signed that included an increase in trade to 1.18 billion US dollars for 1984, and hence a rise in volume of some 60 percent compared to the preceding year.[2]

A Chinese assessment of Andropov's term of office was conspicuous by its exclusively positive accents.[3] A part may have been played by the fact that Andropov, who in the view of a prominent Soviet author (Bovin) knew more about China "than Brezhnev and Chernenko taken together," had possibly applied himself more vigorously than his predecessors to a Sino-Soviet rapprochement.[4] As to the rest, both sides made it plain again shortly after Andropov's death that for the moment no progress was to be expected in the conflict areas of security policy, which the Chinese side also labelled "obstacles to normalization."[5] In the process, Peking went so far as to criticize Chernenko personally because—unlike Andropov in his time at the same occasion—in his first public statement as the new secretary general that dealt with China, he had, among other things, served up again the "third state argument." According to this argument, Moscow could not enter into any arrangements with Peking at the expense of third countries (meaning the Mongolian PR, Vietnam, and Afghanistan)—a position which seemed provocative as viewed from China.

Small wonder, then, that the fourth round of consultations (12–26 March 1984) made no headway regarding the "obstacles to normalization," but may in any case have been able to extend cooperative projects cautiously in the bilateral realm. The planned-for continuation of the deliberations in a fifth round in October was expressly noted in the communique.[6] Immediately following the fourth round of consultations, attacks against each other flared up again in the media. In spite of this, the consolidation of bilateral cooperation continued.

The Cancellation of Arkhipov's Visit: Lines Harden

The actual drastic change in climate occurred on 9 May. That day the leadership in the Kremlin cancelled First Deputy Prime Minister Arkhipov's visit to China that was scheduled for the following day and asked for a postponement.[7] Arkhipov would have been the most senior Soviet government representative to travel to China in fifteen years.

The last-minute cancellation on the grounds of not being "fully prepared" must have struck Peking as a diplomatic slap in the face, since, quite to the contrary, the visit had been long and carefully prepared. First probes apparently date back as far as the autumn of 1983. In early February 1984, the trip had been confirmed officially for the first time, and in late April it was announced for the second half of May by the Soviet side. The declared object of Arkhipov's visit was to accelerate the consolidation of relations in the areas of trade, economic cooperation, and technology, and great expectations were apparently attached to it.

The causes for cancellation of the visit cannot be documented unequivocally. Attempts at a monocausal interpretation do not appear very sensible. The analysis of the political environment suggests that the Soviet decision was influenced by the concurrence of two components. For one, China appears to have entered the ambit of a fortress mentality, which began to dominate in Moscow following the Soviet walk-out from the Geneva INF negotiations in late 1983, and which above all clouded relations with the United States (US component). For another, since late April 1984, the Soviet leadership had felt growing pressure for solidarity with Hanoi in the wake of the heaviest Chinese attacks on Vietnam since 1979 (Vietnam component).

With regard to the US component, those forces in the Kremlin leadership managed to prevail in the first half of 1984, who thought it feasible to do without diplomatic artifice vis-à-vis China. Instead, they deemed it advisable to rely once again on elements of a policy of strength. In their view it was apparently high time to drive home to the Chinese, by means of a short-term cancellation of Arkhipov's visit, Soviet displeasure at their working so nonchalantly towards ever closer relations with the US and with Japan. This policy fuelling deep-rooted fears in Moscow of the emergence of a Washington-Tokyo-(Seoul)-Peking axis. Hence, the journey to Washington in January by Chinese Prime Minister Zhao Ziyang and the visit to Peking in March by Japanese Prime Minister Nakasone had been accompanied by disapproving comments on the part of the Soviet media.

In this connection, an authoritative article in a Moscow Party journal, published in early April, made ears prick up because of its shrill pitch and the nature of its attacks on Peking's "international opportunism."[8] Indirectly, but clearly understandable in the context, it linked China to alleged efforts by "imperialism" designed to "export counterrevolution and interfere directly in the affairs of the socialist states." It reproached China—like Washington—for acting "differentially" towards the Soviet bloc countries. However, moderate positions relative to China were also advanced at about the same time.[9]

In late April 1984, matters came to a head concurrently in both areas of conflict; that is to say, in the realm of the US and of the Vietnam component. As can be deduced from the unusually sharp reactions to President Reagan's visit to China (26 April–1 May), Moscow deemed the behavior of the Chinese hosts decidedly provocative. Peking's leadership, it was said, had failed to differentiate between the imperialist policy of the US and the peaceful policy of the USSR. Deng Xiaoping allegedly even indicated his support of increased US armament efforts. Soviet irritation at the course and results of the Reagan visit must have been compounded by the fact that just at the time these events took place, on 28 April to be precise, China stepped up its attacks along the Vietnam border to an extent not observed since the "punitive action" against Hanoi of February and March 1979. It is a fair assumption that the Chinese escalation was meant as a response to the late March 1984 offensive of the Vietnamese army against the Khmer coalition in Cambodia—the biggest such offensive since 1978. It was also seen as an act of protest against Soviet landings in early April—apparently for the first time—south of Haiphong. Moscow must have been apprehensive lest it end up in an embarrassing situation should the Chinese offensive, as was to be expected, continue during the Arkhipov visit.

The climate of relations between Moscow and Peking deteriorated markedly as a result of the cancellation of the visit—though with continuation of bilateral cooperative projects. This manifested itself primarily in increasingly irritated mutual polemics regarding the other side's behavior in the Indochinese crisis area. Again, Chinese propaganda resorted to the unusual means of a personal attack on Secretary General Chernenko by the—justified—accusation that he himself had attacked China for the first time since coming to office on the occasion of the visit by a Vietnamese Party and government delegation in June.[10] Soon thereafter, on the occasion of a Laotian visit, he was said to have given proof that he stuck "obstinately by his support for Vietnam, its aggression against Kampuchea, and its provocations against China."[11] In mid-July, *Pravda* assailed the Chinese media for having exposed for some time "practically all basic aspects of the Soviet Union's international activities to rude invective."[12] In late August, Peking's *People's Daily* countered that over the past six months the central Soviet press and the news agency TASS had doubled the number of anti-Chinese commentaries as compared to the preceding year.[13]

Return to the Course of Détente

After temperatures between Moscow and Peking had thus fallen to their lowest point since the beginning of the rapprochement process in 1982, first signs were noticeable in the late summer of 1984, pointing once again to an impending thaw. If the hypothesis advanced above holds true—namely that the cooling off was caused on the one hand by the Soviet Union out of solidarity with Vietnam (which was particularly hard-pressed that spring), and on the other was set off by the suction effect of the hardening Soviet-US relationship—then, the Vietnam component had in the meantime been removed. As to the US component, Moscow had by all appearances since realized the foolishness of carrying on a dual confrontation with the United States and China.

Both circumstances evidently made Soviet leaders reconsider, and this resulted in the realization that it would be sensible to return to the course of détente in relations with Peking. In mid-August, the Deputy Minister of Foreign Affairs responsible for China, Kapitsa, announced that Arkhipov's visit to China would probably be made up for at year's end. In the same connection, word has it that after the current five-year plan, i.e., in late 1985, the Soviet Union would offer China the modernization of factories, built in the fifties with Soviet aid. Moreover, there was hope in Moscow of raising foreign trade with Peking from approximately one billion to seven billion US dollars by 1990. Strikingly, mutual polemics abated clearly as of early September.

Unprecedented six-hour-long talks held—apparently on a Soviet initiative—in late September 1984 at the UN General Assembly in New York by Ministers of Foreign Affairs Gromyko and Wu Xueqian pointed in the same direction. Wu called them the first substantial meetings of the foreign ministers from both states in at least twenty years. Though they had produced no compromise on the most important points at issue, they were still "of great significance."[14] The Chinese side apparently also took advantage of the encounter to reassure Moscow with regard to Soviet concerns about the emergence of a Washington-Tokyo-Peking axis. After President Li Xiannian had already indicated to Ceauşescu in late August that China was not about to enter an alliance with the US against the USSR,[15] Wu by all appearances assured Gromyko in New York that Peking would not conclude any agreements with Japan that would be hostile to Moscow either.[16]

The fifth round of consultations was held as scheduled from 18 October to 2 November 1984 in Peking. Although there was no visible progress in the area of security policy, by comparison to past rounds it was the first time that the communique mentioned the "readiness" of both sides to "further consolidate" contacts in the fields of economy, trade, science, and in other sectors.[17] The sixth round of consultations was set for April 1985.

In spite of the appearance of an article sharply critical of China in a Soviet periodical on foreign policy, reproaching Peking for its close cooperation with "imperialism" and its "differential policy" towards the "socialist states,"[18] the consolidation of bilateral relations advanced rapidly by the end of the year. In late November—for the first time ahead of the beginning of the term—an agreement on trade and payments was concluded in Moscow[19] that included an increase in trade to 3.6 billion Swiss francs. As was announced at the same time, this amounted to an expansion of the volume by 35.7 percent over 1984. This was precisely what the Soviets had in mind, but it fell far short of Chinese desires.[20]

The Arkhipov Visit

The actual breakthrough in the atmosphere and in the area of economic-technological cooperation that clearly signaled the Soviet return to detente with Peking came with the visit to China by First Deputy Prime Minister Arkhipov (21–29 December 1984). He was accompanied by a deputy minister and three deputy chairmen of state committees.

Arkhipov was the most senior representative of the Soviet Union to travel to China since Prime Minister Kosygin's visit to Peking in September 1969. Already prior to his arrival, the Chinese leadership took pains to create a friendly atmosphere. Arkhipov was styled an "old friend of China" who had made a useful contribution to drawing up and implementing the first Chinese five-year plan.[21] Indeed, the seventy-seven year old was splendidly equipped for his mission, having been chief counselor for economic cooperation at the Soviet embassy in Peking, charged with the coordination of the USSR's economic aid to China between 1953 and 1957, that is, precisely during the five-year plan mentioned.

By all appearances, the visit progressed from beginning to end in a cordial atmosphere unprecedented since the Sino-Soviet rift. This was attributable in part to the Old-China-Hand characteristics of the visitor. On the other hand, careful Chinese staging effectively saw to it that cordiality did not go overboard. Thus, while there were embraces by hosts and guests at arrival and departure—as far as we know a novelty in Sino-Soviet relations since the sixties—the Chinese media did not publish pictures of these scenes and refused, moreover, to make them available to foreign journalists. Though himself only a CC member, Arkhipov also met with numerous high-ranking persons, among them four Politburo members and a candidate member of the Politburo. He was still refused an encounter with the two most important Party leaders, Deng Xiaoping and Hu Yaobang.

Actual results from Arkhipov's visit were commendable. At the close of the visit, three agreements were signed that constituted a novelty since the outbreak of the Sino-Soviet conflict, namely on

- Economic-technological cooperation.
- Scientific-technological cooperation.
- Establishing a commission on cooperation in economics, trade, science, and technology.[22]

The first-mentioned agreement provided, among other things, for an exchange of production technology, for the planning, construction and alteration of industrial plants, for placing technical services at each other's disposal, and for the reciprocal training of technical personnel.[23] Within this framework the Soviet Union was apparently also prepared to modernize Soviet production installations dating back to the fifties. The visit's most important material result is likely to be an agreement pursuant to which a long-term trade agreement for 1986 to 1990—i.e., the term of the next Soviet and Chinese five-year plans—is to be concluded, permitting the coordination of these plans; preparations for this agreement are planned for the first half of 1985.[24]

Moreover, a supplementary protocol to the trade agreement for 1985 was signed during the visit. It provided for the expansion of the trade volume beyond the 3.6 billion Swiss francs agreed upon only a month earlier to 4.6 billion; in 1984, Chinese trade with the USSR amounted to about one fifth of anticipated Sino-US trade.[25] The invitation extended to Deputy Prime Minister Yao Yilin—the Chinese representative Arkhipov primarily dealt with—for a return visit to the Soviet Union in 1985 was accepted.

Arkhipov's visit undoubtedly brought a general improvement in the climate and the preconditions for closer cooperation in the economic, scientific, and technological area. Here, Soviet determination to make the visit a sure success at second try contributed significantly. There can be no other explanation for Moscow being—apparently—as unmoved by the spectacular relativization of Marxism-Leninism's applicability to the solution of contemporary problems, published shortly before by Peking's *People's*

Daily,[26] as by the increased Chinese pressure along the border with Vietnam, and the imminent first visit to China by the chief of staff of US armed forces.

On the other hand, there is no mistaking the fact that the visit evidently failed to budge the rigid fronts drawn for some time in the area of security policy. While still in Peking, Arkhipov had to take it from his closest partner in cooperation from the fifties, Member of the Politburo Chen Yun, that a normalization of Sino-Soviet relations could be brought about only after the USSR had removed the "major impediments." Similarly, an authoritative Chinese article in early 1985[27] stated that despite other successes of the Arkhipov visit these impediments remained.

Conspicuous Climatic Improvements Following Gorbachev's Accession

After Gorbachev's assumption of office (11 March 1985) the process of rapprochement received new impetus. Moscow made the first friendly gesture. In a speech to the CC, Gorbachev emphasized Soviet interest in a "serious improvement" of relations, listing China in the sole paragraph devoted to the "socialist states," and dispensing with the "third state argumentation."[28] The Chinese reacted swiftly and positively. The speaker of the parliament Peng Zhen congratulated "Comrade Gorbachev" on his election, and on the occasion of Chernenko's funeral, the two Party leaders exchanged mutual greetings through Vice President Li Peng who headed the Chinese delegation of condolence.[29]

This indicated that the process of détente was about to take on a new dimension. For the first time since the rupture of Party relations in March 1966, as far as we know, messages were again exchanged at the Party level. For the first time since those days, a CPSU member was again addressed as "comrade" by the Chinese side. After this establishment of contacts at the Party level, the reopening of formal Party relations in the short or medium term can no longer be excluded. It was by the same token that Peking simultaneously recognized the Soviet Union again as a "socialist state" and for the first time stressed readiness to develop political relations.[30]

The evidence adduced above points to the conclusion that the upswing that Arkhipov's Chinese journey of December 1984 had achieved mainly in the economic-technical sector, was not spilling over into the political-ideological realm.

Summary and Conclusions

The set-back suffered by the Sino-Soviet process of rapprochement in 1984 was definitely overcome by Arkhipov's visit to Peking and developments following Gorbachev's assumption of office. Better yet: Never since the early sixties had the climate between Moscow and Peking been as good as it was in the second half of March 1985.

In the short and medium term, a gradual consolidation of cooperation in the hitherto prevailing fields of cooperation such as trade, culture, science, technology, sports, and tourism is to be expected. It is unlikely to attain the intensity of contacts with the US, Japan, and Western Europe. What will come of readiness for political cooperation that China has declared remains to be seen. For the time being, little movement is to be expected in the three major fields of conflict in security policy. A restoration of the Sino-Soviet alliance of the fifties can be ruled out even in the long run.

Notes

1. On the development up to the spring of 1983 cf. D. Heinzig, *The Soviet Union 1982/1983*, pp. 313 ff.
2. *BR*, No. 9 (1984), p. 12; TASS, 10 February 1984.
3. *BR*, No. 10 (1984), pp. 12 ff.
4. H. Brahm, *Berichte des BIOst*, No. 15 (1984), pp. 8, 23 ff. (with references).
5. On this and on the following sentence, Deng Xiaoping on 22 February 1984, XNA (Engl.), 22 February 1984; Chernenko in a speech on 2 March 1984, *Iz*, 3 March 1984; Andropov in a speech on 22 November 1982, *Pr*, 23 November 1982.
6. *Renmin ribao*, 27 March 1984; *Pr*, 27 March 1984.
7. XNA, 9 May 1974.
8. O.V. Borisov, in *VIKPSS*, No. 4 (1984), p. 44.
9. A. Bovin in a broadcast by Radio Moscow, domestic service, 10 March 1984, and by Radio Prague, domestic service, 2 March 1984.
10. XNA from Moscow, 11 June 1984.
11. XNA from Moscow, 26 June 1984.
12. *Pr*, 19 July 1984.
13. *Renmin ribao*, 28 August 1984.
14. Wu Xueqian on 24 September 1984 in New York, *IHT*, 26 September 1984.
15. Hu Yaobang to an ICP representative in late September 1984 in Peking, *U*, 30 September 1984.
16. Diplomatic sources in Peking, *JT*, 12 October 1984.
17. On this and the following sentence *Renmin ribao*, 4 November 1984; TASS (Russ.), 2 November 1984.
18. I. Alekseyev, F. Nikolayev, in *MZh*, No. 11 (1984), pp. 33, 32 and 35, respectively.
19. Agreement of 30 November 1984, XNA from Moscow, 30 November 1984.
20. Hu Yaobang, in *U*, 30 September 1984.
21. Vice-Foreign Minister Qian Qichen to *Shijie zhishi*, Peking, No. 24 (1984), p. 2.
22. *Pr*, 30 December 1984.
23. XNA (Engl.), 28 December 1984.
24. *Pr*, 30 December 1984.
25. Supplementary Protocol of 26 December 1984, *Renmin ribao*, 29 December 1984; XNA (Engl.), 17 December 1984; *U.S. News and World Report*, 17 September 1984, p. 27.
26. *Renmin ribao*, 7 and 8 December 1984.
27. *Renmin ribao*, 4 January 1985.

28. Gorbachev on 11 March 1985 at the CC plenary session, *Pr*, 12 March 1985.

29. RP (Chin), domestic service, 12 March 1985, *Summary of World Broadcasts*, FE/7900/i; Xinhua (Engl.), 14 March 1985, *News from Xinhua News Agency* (London), 13 March 1985, p. 11.

30. *Ibid.*

27
Soviet Policy Towards Japan and Korea

Joachim Glaubitz

Preliminary Remarks

Relations between the Soviet Union and Japan depend to a large extent on the overall condition of the relationship between the two superpowers. This is one of the reasons why the climate between Moscow and Tokyo remained frosty in the first half of the eighties and occasionally dropped to the lowest level since the re-opening of diplomatic relations in 1956. The Soviet invasion of Afghanistan, the forced enlargement of the Soviet Pacific fleet, the deployment of SS-20s in the Asian part of the Soviet Union, the increasing demonstrations of Soviet military might in the immediate vicinity of Japan, the persistent stubborn refusal to recognize the existence of a territorial problem with Japan, unresolved since the end of World War II—these and other activities of Soviet policy towards Asia made Japan move even closer to its US alliance partner in terms of security policy.

The Soviet Union started a development resulting in greater security consciousness in Japan and a discussion in Tokyo of defense measures that Soviet policy allegedly strove to prevent. The policy of the Soviet Union in northeastern Asia—and not just there—is characterized by this peculiar counterproductiveness. It launches precisely those developments that it then adduces to justify its countermeasures. Thus, in the last few years an atmosphere has arisen in the relations between the Soviet Union and Japan in which political contacts atrophied, semi-official encounters were reduced, and even economic relations were not left unscathed. Since mid-1984, a cautious revival of official contacts has been noticed, though it is too early to tell whether it will lead to a thorough improvement of relations between the two states.

Territorial Question: Obstacle to Rapprochement

The major obstacle to a lasting improvement in the political climate between the Soviet Union and Japan continues to be the territorial question, i.e., the claim by both sides to four islands at the southern tip of the Kurils. The Soviets have occupied them since 1945. In a joint declaration issued on 19 October 1955 to celebrate the restoration of diplomatic relations, the USSR agreed to return the islands of the Habomai group and Shikotan to Japan following the conclusion of a peace treaty. Since the early seventies it has no longer wished to be reminded of this commitment. Today its position is that there is no territorial problem with Japan. This boundary resulting from the Second World War, like all post-war boundaries, is unchangeable. With its refusal to conclude a treaty on good neighborliness and cooperation with the Soviet Union, Japan is said to bear the responsibility for the deplorable state of the relationship. By contrast, all Japanese governments thus far have assumed the position that the objective remains the conclusion of a peace treaty conditional upon the return of the four contended islands.

In early January 1981, this dispute sharpened when the Parliament in Tokyo, its ear to the ground of Japanese public opinion, resolved to declare 7 February the "Day of the Northern Territories." On that day in 1855, Japan and Russia concluded the Treaty of Shimoda which regulated trade and shipping between the two countries and fixed the Russo-Japanese border. According to its terms, the border ran between the islands of Uruppu and Etorofu. All Kuril islands north of this line became Russian, the islands south of it Japanese territory. Though later agreements moved this border further north, it never, prior to 1945, ran farther to the south than agreed in the mid-19th century. This means that since the oldest boundary agreement between the two states in 1855 in Shimoda, the islands now claimed (and occupied) by the Soviet Union were never Russian, but always belonged to Japan.

The introduction of a "Day of the Northern Territories" induced the Soviet Union to register a formal protest with the Japanese ambassador in Moscow on 20 January 1981. A declaration by the Soviet Ministry of Foreign Affairs on 16 February 1981 says on this occasion: "We cannot but direct attention to the manifest fact that the campaign mentioned (for a solution of the territorial question—author's note) has recently assumed a character bordering on hostility towards our country."[1] Soviet media labeled the institution of the memorial day a "provocative event" and interpreted the incident as a relapse into Japan's militarist and expansionist past, which could "once more turn into a tragedy for the peoples of Asia, and primarily for Japan."[2] Aside from the institution of the memorial day, in September 1981, Prime Minister Suzuki's inspection trip to Northern Japan and to the point most proximate to the contested islands contributed to a further intensification of the territorial dispute. In this manner, a Japanese head of government manifested his support for the claim to the islands for the first time.

At the same time, moreover, cartographic publishers in various countries friendly to Japan, whose maps marked the contested islands as Soviet, were asked to correct their maps in accordance with the Japanese view.[3] This has not been done. Prompted by LDP, the Japanese governing party, the US State Department approached US map producers and recommended marking the four contested islands henceforth as Japanese rather than Soviet territory.[4] The Soviet Minister of Foreign Affairs criticized this action most emphatically in a conversation with his Japanese colleague Abe at the UN General Assembly.[5]

The Soviet side bolsters its claim in a different way, namely with the help of archeology and with military might: *Sovetskaya Rossiya* reported in mid-September 1984 on recently discovered traces of early Russian settlements on the Kurils, dating back to the early 18th century. They are supposed to be settlements established after 1713, the arrival date of Ivan Kozyrevsky. The first Russian description of the Kurils is by Kozyrevsky.[6] Remarkably, here against Japan the Soviet Union avails itself of the very arguments, based on the history of settlement, which it rejects when they are turned against the Soviet Union itself—as China does occasionally.

It is more problematic for Japan to counter the resources of military power that the Soviet Union uses to stress its determination to annex the occupied territory for good. Since mid-1978, armed forces and equipment have been deployed and gradually reinforced on three of the four islands, on Etorofu, Kunashiri, and Shikotan. In 1980, there were some 6,000, in 1984 some 10,000 troops.[7] Moreover, air force units are stationed on the islands, and especially on Etorofu. In late 1982, the Soviet Union replaced a wing of 20 Mig 17 fighters by planes of the more modern Mig 21 type.[8] Some six months later, the first third-generation fighters, i.e., of the Mig 23 type, arrived on the island, and their number grew to forty in the first half of 1984.[9] The trend, then, points to a consolidation and modernization of the military presence.

In the view of military experts, the strategic significance of the Kurils, under Soviet control since 1945, consists on the one hand of the access to the Pacific located there and on the other, of blocking off the Sea of Okhotsk: This sea has thus turned into a safe theater of operation for Soviet Delta-class submarines which—equipped with strategic missiles (ranges exceeding 8,000 km)—can reach targets in the US without having to leave Soviet waters.[10]

Conditions for a Visit to Japan by the Soviet Minister of Foreign Affairs

The massive pressure that the Soviets exert to eliminate the territorial question from political talks is illustrated by the way the vague prospect of a visit to Tokyo by Gromyko is handled. For years the Japanese government has been wooing the Soviet Minister of Foreign Affairs, who last visited Japan in 1976. Its numerous invitations have either met with procrastinating replies or undiplomatically formulated refusals. At a meeting with Gromyko at Andropov's funeral ceremonies in February 1984, Foreign Minister Abe again invited his Soviet colleague to visit Tokyo; Gromyko declined with the remark that it was still too early; conditions for a sensible visit had not yet matured.[11] Gromyko reiterated this view when the two foreign ministers met in September at the UN General Assembly in New York. In Gromyko's opinion, Japan would bring up the territorial question and thus ruin the visit.[12]

Tokyo's interest in a visit from the Soviet Minister of Foreign Affairs was presented with such undiplomatic obtrusiveness that the Soviet side was tempted to set conditions. In late September 1984 in Moscow, Deputy Minister of Foreign Affairs M. Kapitsa listed three conditions for a visit from Gromyko to an LDP member of parliament: First, the demand for a return of the islands must not dominate the talks from beginning to end; second, the visit must take place in a quiet atmosphere—i.e., without demonstrations against the Soviet guest; and third, the visit must lead to results in the areas of economic, cultural, scientific, and technological exchanges.[13] Shortly after that at the National Press Club in Tokyo, Zagladin also spoke of conditions for a visit to Japan by Gromyko.[14] I. Kovalenko, deputy head of the International Department of the CC responsible for Japan, upped the ante by telling Japanese journalists Gromyko's visit as such was no problem, but there must be the possibility of it leading to the signing of an agreement. By way of example, he mentioned, among other things, the treaty on good neighborliness and cooperation proffered time and again by the Soviet Union.[15] But one of the objectives of the treaty is to skirt the territorial problem and to let it rest for all times to come.[16] To exclude the territorial question from the relationship is a long-term objective of Soviet policy vis-à-vis Japan, the splitting of the Japanese-US alliance, and hence the weakening of Japan is another; third, the Soviet Union is keenly interested in exploiting Japanese technology and credits to tap Siberian natural resources by intensifying economic relations.

Japan could most readily meet the latter Soviet interest. Recently, there has been evidence of some movement here that might usher in a limited revival of economic relations. The first two goals, however, are unattainable in the foreseeable future. In these respects, the Soviet Union stands in its own way and just about blocks any progress in the desired direction with its own policy.

Growing Soviet Military Presence in the Far East

It has not been lost on military observers that for a decade the Soviet Union has been attaching particular importance to an expansion of its military potential in the Far East and the Pacific. Especially conspicuous in Soviet deployment policy are the reinforcement of the Pacific fleet, the deployment of SS-20 missiles, and the stationing of the "Backfire"-bomber. In early 1984, the "Novorossiysk," an aircraft carrier of 37,000 tons, reached East Asia; apparently it is to be assigned to the Pacific fleet. Thus, the fleet now includes two carriers which, however—unlike carriers in the US fleets—

can be used only by helicopters and vertical take-off aircraft.[17] These ships of the "Kiev-class" carry on board only 19 helicopters and 13 vertical take-off Yak-36s.

The continuing deployment of SS-20s met with greater attention from the Japanese public. The Japanese government regarded this mobile weapon as a dual threat: For one, a remark by Gromyko in early 1983 gave rise to the fear that SS-20s possibly withdrawn from Europe might be re-deployed east of the Urals and trained on east Asian targets.[18] Japan would thus be burdened by US-Soviet agreements in the NATO area and its security detached from that of the remainder of the Western world. Prime Minister Nakasone recognized this problem and therefore supported Western unity on security policy at the Williamsburg summit in May 1983.

The second kind of threat posed by the SS-20 is of a military nature. Here, Japan is also dependent on protection from the US. Soviet claims (Kapitsa in April 1983 in Tokyo) that SS-20s in Asia were deployed against missiles trained on the Soviet Union are an attempt to make Japan look like a hostage of US policy towards Asia and to fan fears of dangers deriving from the alliance with the US. With the decision to deploy Pershing-II and cruise missiles in Western Europe, the SS-20 issue receded in Japan, too. According to Japanese information, the Soviet Union had deployed 117 SS-20s east of the Urals by late 1983. There is no doubt that with its seventh fleet and its bases in the Asian-Pacific region, the US is still superior to the Soviet Union and that its modernization of ships, aircraft, and missile equipment as well as its deployment policy provide the Soviet Union domestically and internationally with a convenient justification for its own armament efforts. Since Prime Minister Nakasone welcomes and supports a more intensive US interest in the Pacific, he was made the target of Soviet attacks immediately upon assuming office in the fall of 1982. With flowery indignation, Soviet observers suddenly noticed that Nakasone was riding roughshod over three decades of Japanese military policy: the one-percent-of-GNP threshold for military expenditures, the 1976 framework plan for defense, the constitution with its article renouncing war, and the three principles of the renunciation of nuclear weapons.[19]

This sounds as if the Soviet Union, reassured by the existence of these guidelines, had depicted Japan as a peace-loving neighbor during the past 30 years. The opposite was the case. Since 1950 at the latest, the sound of reawakening Japanese militarism has been heard with numbing repetition. It is not without a certain irony that China's foreign minister felt compelled to defend Japan against Gromyko's warning of a potential reawakening of Japanese militarism by stating that China had noticed no such signs.[20]

What seems to have irritated the Soviet Union for some time is Japan's stronger international involvement, its clear position on the side of industrialized democracies, and its ever closer cooperation with South Korea. But, to be sure, the United States also belongs in the picture of Japan endangering peace, as painted by the Soviet Union in innumerable descriptions. The Soviet Union does not consider Japan an independent actor in international politics, but a tool of the US. The Soviet Union does not recognize Japan as a full-fledged power because it lacks the means to project power outward. An army on which the government spends less than one percent of GNP is not taken seriously by a Soviet leadership thinking in categories of military power.

Stagnant Economic Relations

In view of Soviet arrogance towards Japan it is difficult to believe the sincerity of the Soviet leadership's desire to improve relations. The most powerful motive behind these assertions is the Soviet quest for economic benefits without political concessions. But since Japan wants to treat politics and economics as one entity in its relations with the Soviet Union, i.e., since, in other words, it is not prepared to concede economic advantages to the other side without itself receiving the slightest political concessions, the growth of Japanese-Soviet trade will remain limited. The large private Japanese economic and trade delegation that traveled to the Soviet Union in early 1983 did not succeed in reviving stagnant business, nor will the Joint Japanese–Soviet Economic Committee, which met in Tokyo late in 1984 after four years of interruption, be able to achieve this.[21] The Japanese business world's interest in the Soviet Union is no longer very great even though the Japanese government—following the Western European model—has toned down sanctions imposed because of the Soviet invasion of Afghanistan.

Currently, economic cooperation is still limited to five projects: the third wood-resources project, the supply of wood chips for paper production, coke mining in Southern Yakutiya, oil exploration on the continental shelf off Sakhalin, and natural gas exploration in Yakutiya.[22] In 1983, the volume of trade fell to the low point of 4.27 billion dollars. In trade and economic cooperation with Japan, the Soviet Union has been displaced by China: In 1983, Japanese-Chinese trade reached a volume of ten billion dollars.

A certain willingness to talk on Moscow's part in 1984 somewhat prematurely nurtured expectations on the Japanese side that an improvement in relations was in the offing. This was caused by working-level talks in mid-1984 on the Middle East and on questions concerning the United Nations, the publication of a preface advocating better relations authored by Secretary General Chernenko for the Japanese edition of his speeches,[23] the first encounter in eleven years of the prime ministers of both countries at Indira Gandhi's funeral ceremonies, and the intensification of contacts by the two communist parties. In December 1984, the chairman of the CPJ, Kenji Miyamoto, conferred with Chernenko, without, however, touching on the two issues under contention between the two parties, Afghanistan and the Kurils question.[24] The exchange of visits by parliamentarians and discussion groups completed the picture. However, close scrutiny of the respective opinions exchanged leads to the conclusion that the Soviet side displayed no flexibility at all on the fundamental issues, but—and this is also illustrated by Gromyko's New Year's declaration in the daily *Asahi*—puts its own part in bilateral relations in the best light with the usual assignments of guilt to the other side and repeats the well-known proposals ostensibly meant to help secure peace, but which would in fact subject Japan to the Soviet Union's conception of a regional order.[25]

The USSR's Interests on the Korean Peninsula

The Korean Peninsula, with its two partitioned states engaged in hard confrontation with each other, is of major strategic significance to the Soviet Union. In 1961, both the USSR and China almost simultaneously concluded treaties with North Korea that promised friendship and aid and assured North Korea of military and other assistance using any means. US guarantees of South Korea's security date back to a 1953 defense agreement.

The Sino-Soviet conflict had induced North Korea to balance between the two combatants and avoid one-sided commitments. While Soviet economic aid is said to be of great significance to North Korea, occasional North Korean statements and actions are on record that must have displeased the Soviet Union: criticism of the Soviet invasion of Afghanistan, support of Prince Sihanouk, who resided for a while in Pyongyang, and the supply of weapons to Iran.

Still, the Soviet Union's interest in good relations with North Korea seems undiminished. This is corroborated by Moscow's silence on the bomb attack on the South Korean president and his cabinet, committed by North Korea in October 1983 in Rangoon, Soviet discretion in contacts with South Korea, and the dilatory stance thus far on the Olympic games planned for Seoul in 1988. Pyongyang, too, is interested in detente with Moscow. This is evidenced by Kim Il Sung's visit to the Soviet Union and Eastern Europe in May 1984. Twenty years had elapsed since his last trip to Moscow. No concrete results can be gleaned from the communique; the vague formulation "consolidation of cooperation" was chosen.

During the visit, the Soviet Union did not miss the opportunity of conjuring up the danger of military cooperation between Washington, Tokyo, and Seoul, and with the use of the term "hegemonism," covertly criticizing the policies of China, whose leaders had welcomed President Reagan in Peking a few weeks earlier.[26]

Most observers were taken aback by the news that a Soviet government delegation headed by Deputy Minister of Foreign Affairs, Kapitsa, had come to terms with North Korea in Pyongyang on the course of the thirty-two kilometers of joint border. During these consultations, both sides also agreed on cooperation between their foreign ministers for 1985 and 1986.[27]

North Korea will remain the object of Sino-Soviet rivalry; this, in turn, will closely circumscribe Moscow's and Peking's contacts with South Korea. However China, given its geo-political advantages, its good relations with the US and Japan, and its slightly more intensive contacts with North Korea (it has already approved Kim Il Sung's succession by his son) seems to enjoy slightly more leeway than the Soviet Union.

Summary and Conclusions

The state of relations between the Soviet Union and Japan since the early eighties offers little reason to expect a fundamental improvement. Soviet leadership is unlikely to decide in favor of the return of the occupied islands in the north. On the other hand, no Japanese government can relinquish its claim to these territories. A Soviet return to its 1956 promise to restore two of the four islands to Japan upon the conclusion of a peace treaty is certainly not to be ruled out forever, but there are no indications of such a turnabout—which, incidentally, would rather embarrass the government in Tokyo.

Another aspect also renders the continuation of the distanced Japanese-Soviet relationship probable: The Soviet Union, which is still wooing Japan with arguments that stress neighborliness and complementary economic systems, is no longer as attractive to the Japanese economy as it was in the early seventies. Today, Japan has found access to other, less problematic sources of raw materials (not least in China), so that there is little chance of a recurrence of "Siberian fever" in the next few years.

As the antagonism between the two world powers, the Soviet Union and the US, will continue to exist, an enhanced US interest in the Pacific region is likely to turn northeast Asia into a theater for the East-West conflict. Japan will have to adapt its defense policy to this, though consideration for critical Asian neighbors will keep it far below what might be termed substantial rearmament.

The Korean Peninsula, whose two partitioned states are engaged in hard confrontation with each other, is of major strategic interest to the Soviet Union. Still, the Sino-Soviet conflict has thus far induced North Korea to balance between Moscow and Peking and to avoid one-sided commitments. North Korea will remain the object of Sino Soviet rivalry. This in turn will narrowly circumscribe Moscow's and Peking's contacts with South Korea.

Notes

1. *Pr*, 7 February 1981.
2. *Iz*, 6 February 1981.
3. Cf. *Nihon Keizai Shimbun*, 7 September 1981, in *Daily Summary of the Japanese Press* (Tokyo), 9 September 1981, pp. 3–4.
4. *AEN*, 13 September 1984.
5. *AEN*, 5 October 1984.
6. *Sovetskaya Rossiya*, 13 September 1984.
7. *Asian Security 1983*, Research Institute for Peace and Security (ed.) (Tokyo, 1983), p. 86; *Asian Security 1984*, p. 64.
8. *AEN*, 16 and 17 December 1984.
9. *JT*, 28 April 1984.
10. *AEN*, 10 March 1983; *Asian Security 1982*, p. 57.
11. *AEN*, 16 February 1984.
12. *AEN*, 26 September 1984. On 5 July 1985, the Japanese government reiterated its invitation, until then directed at Gromyko, to the newly appointed Minister of

Foreign Affairs E. Shevardnadze. Shevardnadze paid an official visit to Japan on 15–19 January 1986.

13. *JT*, 5 October 1984.
14. *AEN*, 1 November 1984.
15. *JT*, 5 December 1984.
16. Cf. *The Soviet Union 1980/1981*, p. 294.
17. *AEN*, 12 June 1984; on the size of the fleet see *Asian Security 1984*, pp. 64ff.; *MB*, 1984–1985 (London, 1984), pp. 20ff.
18. See D. Heinzig, *Aktuelle Analysen des BIOst*, No. 7 (1984).
19. For instance V. Bunin, in *Far Eastern Affairs*, Moscow, No. 2 (1984), p. 74.
20. *AEN*, 12 October 1984.
21. *JT*, 18 December 1984.
22. *Asian Security 1982*, p. 41.
23. *K*, No. 13 (1984), pp. 3–4.
24. *JT*, 18 December 1984.
25. *Pr*, 2 January 1984.
26. *NYT*, 26 May 1984.
27. *Iz*, 22 November 1984.

28
States with a Socialist Orientation: A Soviet Model of Partnership

Wolfgang Berner

In the conceptual system of the Soviet Union's foreign policy doctrine, generally all developing countries that have taken a "non-capitalist" path to development are considered states of "socialist orientation." In the more restricted sense, they are Third World states with whose regimes Soviet leadership maintains or wants to establish special cooperative relations because of a more or less evident ideological affinity and also because of very tangible foreign and military-strategic motives. Brezhnev was the first to use the formula "states with a socialist orientation" in his report to the Twenty-fourth CPSU Congress in April 1971; the term has since been part and parcel of the ideological-theoretical standard vocabulary of all Soviet foreign policy makers and Party literati concerned with Third World problems. A core sentence of the Political Resolution by the Twenty-fourth CPSU Congress stated: "The Congress assigns special significance to the consolidation of cooperation with the countries with a socialist orientation."

In principle, Cuba—by current Soviet standards—was a "state with a socialist orientation" at a relatively low level of development in 1963 when Fidel Castro achieved the official acceptance of his guerilla-republic in the circle of "socialist countries." The organizer of the armed rebellion against the Batista dictatorship was certainly no communist in Khrushchev's view. At best he was a "revolutionary democrat" of dubious ideological credentials who had more than once in 1961 and 1962 come out with spectacular declarations first for socialism, then for Marxism-Leninism, in vain attempts to wrench from the Kremlin a solid public promise of assistance, or at least a clear recognition on the part of all communist states of a duty of socialist solidarity with Cuba. The Soviets, however, were in no hurry to respond to Castro's applications for membership. On the other hand, though, they were quick to turn the Caribbean island into a launching pad for intermediate-range missiles trained on the US. Castro's tough bargaining did not succeed until months after the October 1962 Cuban missile crisis in inducing the CPSU to count his country among the full members of the socialist camp. Because of this acknowledged membership, Havana feels entitled to Soviet assistance on preferential terms, in the name of "socialist internationalism." In July 1972, then, Cuba was finally accepted into the CMEA as a full member (after seven years of waiting with observer status).[1]

The Soviet Leadership's Cuban and Egyptian Trauma

By acceding to Castro's demands, however, the Soviet Union had embarked upon a risky and difficult partnership. In spite of its exposed geographic location, Cuba not only developed an expansionary revolutionary dynamic, but also an unexpectedly original experimental zeal as a tropical laboratory of socialism. Moreover, from year to year, Moscow had to dole out ever larger subsidies and military aid if the Cuban model of socialism was not to collapse ignominiously. These experiences apparently left the Kremlin with a trauma of enduringly deterrent effect. It was compounded by the fact that Soviet commitments to the "socialist" developing countries China, Vietnam, Laos, and North Korea proved similarly costly and problematic, in part even involving heavy losses.

The Cuban trauma in particular is at the bottom of it, when the Kremlin, with all kinds of more or less plausible arguments, deliberately refuses to admit to the closer community of socialist states for an indefinite period those developing countries "of socialist orientation" that seek assiduously to copy Castro's recipe for success. Among the most important preconditions and among the most difficult to fulfill in this connection, is the requirement to wait in each case until the irrevocability (or the irreversibility) of the respective country's devotion to socialism has been secured. Moscow is patiently intent on restricting the size of the club of Warsaw Pact and CMEA states to a minimum and on reserving for itself a monopoly of decision regarding all candidacies. Given the relative run by voluntary applicants, this is even a fairly rational procedure. With most of them—the rare exceptions confirming the rule—the Kremlin is able to establish on its own terms the special cooperative relations conducive to Soviet political interests, without having to place such partner regimes in any way (meaning especially regarding claims to protection, alimentation, and consultation) on the same footing as full members of the WTO-CMEA system.

Presumably, the demand for irrevocability manifests another Soviet trauma, namely the Egyptian trauma. In pertinent Soviet literature, one encounters Egypt as the standard example for the surprising change of course by a former preferential partner, reconverting from the "socialist" orientation back to the "capitalist" one. In the two decades from 1955 to 1974, Egypt had received military aid from the Soviet Union to the tune of 3.45 billion US dollars, and from 1954 to 1976 economic aid to the tune of 1.3 billion, i.e., a total of at least 4.75 billion dollars' worth of assistance. Understandably the Soviet Union is wary of entering into similar misinvestments again. It must be borne in mind, in this context, that the economic and military aid granted by the USSR over the same period to Guinea ($236 million), Ghana ($103 million), Mali ($96 million), Indonesia ($1.2 billion), Sudan ($129 million), Uganda ($36 million), Chile ($238 million), and Iran ($1.6 billion), a total of expenditures to the tune of 3.9 billion dollars, proved a waste of its own valuable resources from Moscow's vantage point.[2] The economic situation of the Soviet Union has meanwhile further deteriorated, its leadership today is even more careful to avoid such losses than it had been in the sixties and seventies.

What is more, expert discussion in the Soviet media, and particularly in specialized periodicals, which apparently echoed specific foreign policy efforts, has for some time reflected unmistakable pressure by influential forces in the CPSU leadership to keep a rein on undue revolutionary zeal by particularly radical Third World regimes, and this increasingly so since 1980. The excesses of the Taraki-Amin period in Afghanistan and the Maoist aberrations of the Chinese "cultural revolution" are frequently listed as warning examples.[3] The widespread discussion of numerous conditions to be fulfilled by candidates "of socialist orientation" before they can tackle the building of socialism are evidently addressed to certain target groups within the Soviet functional elites, which possibly represent more aggressive and less scrupulous tendencies. Certainly there must be members of the vast power and functional apparatuses inclined to advocate a continuous enlargement of the circle of "socialist" states in view of the many applicants. For instance, they might argue that nothing could prove the world revolutionary expansionist force of socialism/communism more convincingly than such accessions, even if additional developing countries had to be admitted to the CMEA as full members at the same pace.

This problem represents the focus of the Soviet dilemma. As long as aid to Poland, aid to Cuba, aid to Vietnam, the Afghan war etc. burden the CMEA system, it is hardly in a position to handle the inclusion of further developing countries. Consequently, the smaller WTO-CMEA countries without exception oppose new admissions. So far, even Laos, officially classified as "socialist," has been denied full membership in the CMEA.

On the other hand, it continues to be in the Soviet interest to tie Third World regimes fascinated by socialist models ever closer to its own hegemonial system, so as to possibly integrate them in the long run. One of the Soviet Union's prime motives is its need for a world-embracing network of military bases and "base countries" to enable it to enforce its claim to world power by projecting military might at any time anywhere in the world. These forward bases need to be associated as tightly as possible with the Soviet empire. It seems that Soviet leadership primarily assigns developing countries "of socialist orientation" such bridgehead and outpost functions of a global strategic character.

Voluntary Client Regimes and Desirable Candidates

Nowadays, the International Department of the CC Secretariat of the CPSU places the number of developing countries "of socialist orientation" at 15 to 20 states in Asia, Africa, and Latin America. According to the same authoritative source in 1979, in Asia and Africa alone "nearly twenty countries" were already being led by "revolutionary national-democratic parties" at "various stages in the approach to scientific socialism"; at the same time, the impression was conveyed that the number of states steering a course of "socialist orientation" was steadily rising.[4] Meanwhile, many indicators (e.g., differential formulations) point to a changing trend in the CPSU leadership's assessment of the situation. In the wake of the Afghan debacle and the Grenada coup for the US, the optimism feeding on an expansionist foreign policy, which was still dominant in 1979, has given way to a more sober, problem-conscious evaluation of the circumstances. A mere fifteen countries still qualify under the currently applicable Soviet standards for the ideological, political, and socio-economic requirements demanded of partner states of "socialist orientation." Beyond that, there seem to be another five or more states with qualifications judged deficient or questionable in Moscow.

The fifteen states securely categorized can be derived fairly reliably from Soviet publications. In this context, the following six "vanguard states" are mentioned regularly: Ethiopia, Afghanistan, Angola, PDR of Yemen (South Yemen), PR of the Congo, and Mozambique. Then, the pertinent literature mentions five other socialist-oriented developing countries of the "first generation," though they are mostly reputed not to have lived up fully to what was originally expected of them. They are: Algeria, Burma, Iraq, Syria, and Tanzania. To these must be added another four countries of the "second" or "third generation" which, measured against the first group of six, pass for less avant-garde, namely Kampuchea, Benin (formerly Dahomey), Madagascar, and Nicaragua.

Finally, seven further (candidate) countries are linked more or less closely to this grouping of fifteen states. The reference patterns, however, are not very consistent. Specifically, they are Guinea-Bissau, the Cape Verde Islands, the island republic of Sao Tome and Principe, the Seychelles in the Indian Ocean, Burkina Faso (ex-Upper Volta), Ghana (with its progressivist one-man military dictatorship), and Khadafi's Libya.

Ye.M. Primakov, the influential director of the Institute of Oriental Studies at the Academy of Sciences (AoS) of the USSR, published a typical list of countries "of socialist orientation" in the fall of 1979. In the catalogue of this probably most renowned Soviet expert on the countries of the Arab world, Libya, otherwise rarely mentioned, also figures at the end. Primakov elaborates:

> Thus, . . . it is characteristic that the elimination of the colonial system culminating in the bankruptcy of the last—the Portuguese—colonial empire, resulted, in the former Portuguese colonies, in the emergence of anti-imperialist regimes oriented towards scientific socialism . . . (W.B.'s note: To be added here are Angola, Mozambique, Guinea Bissau, the Cape Verde Islands, Sao Tome and Principe.) The revolution has triumphed in Ethiopia, and the revolutionary-democratic leadership that has come to power there also chose the path of a profound remodelling of society under the banner of socialist solutions. In Afghanistan the revolutionary movement achieved a historic victory. Revolutionary changes have intensified in the People's Republic of the Congo, in the Democratic Republic of Madagascar, in the Democratic People's Republic of Yemen, in the People's Republic of Benin, in Tanzania, Algeria, Libya, and others. . . . A dissociation from the socialist orientation is to be noted in Egypt, a turn to the right also being the case in some other developing countries.[5]

Iraq and Syria, governed by Baath-socialists, are conspicuously absent from this list. In mid-1981, another prominent Middle Eastern expert, G.I. Mirsky, a department head at the Institute for World Economy and International Relations (IMEMO) of the AoS-USSR, remarked in a similar context that regrettably only two OPEC member states belonged to those countries "that have made or declared their choice in favor of socialism"; all others were developing countries with particularly low per capita incomes.[6] There is considerable evidence that Mirsky referred to Algeria and Libya and not to Algeria and Iraq as the exceptions, because at that time relations between Moscow and Baghdad had deteriorated for a number of reasons to such an extent that an open rupture seemed imminent. Gromyko supplied a parallel in his speech before the Supreme Soviet on 16 June 1983. On this occasion, the Minister of Foreign Affairs listed among the "non-aligned countries" maintaining especially good relations with the USSR only states "of socialist orientation" which, moreover, had concluded a treaty of political cooperation with Moscow (specifically: Syria, South Yemen, Angola, Ethiopia, Mozambique, and the Congo), plus Algeria and Libya which so far had responded guardedly to Soviet treaty offers. Gromyko, too, passed over Iraq in his list, even though a treaty of friendship and cooperation has been in existence between Moscow and Baghdad since 1972.[7]

As illustrated by the example, the placement of a particular country in the Soviet lists of "states of socialist orientation" is often more dependent upon the momentary quality of its relations with the USSR than on objective socioeconomic criteria. This is also evidenced by the treatment of Somalia in Soviet writings. Since Mogadisho revoked its treaty of cooperation with Moscow in November 1977, Somalia is no longer classified as a developing country "of socialist orientation" in the pertinent literature, even though there have been few essential changes in the economic system and the socio-political course of Siad-Barreh's regime since.

Flexible Cooperation Formula with Variable Contents

The characterization of certain developing countries as "revolutionary powers of socialist orientation," in turn equated to a "revolutionary-democratic dictatorship," first appeared in the writings of leading Soviet politicians and theoreticians in the spring of 1968.[8] In June 1969, the "Main Document" of the third communist council in Moscow stated that in some developing countries that had taken a "non-capitalist path," the "socialist orientation" was now breaking the ice. At a conference on the "theory and practice of the non-capitalist path to development," jointly organized in the autumn of 1970 by the editorial board of a foreign policy monthly and the Academy of Social Sciences at the CC of the CPSU, eight of the twelve participants in the discussions cited in the conference proceedings employed the formula "states of socialist orientation." The remainder spoke of "states with a non-capitalist orientation."[9] In 1972, the foremost mastermind of Soviet policy towards the Third World since the early sixties, R.A. Ulyanovsky, deputy head of the International Department of the CC Secretariat of the CPSU and professor at the above-mentioned academy, published a book on *Socialism and the Liberated Countries* in which he made extensive use of the new term and detailed its specific meaning. However, this concise statement is from the same book: "Socialist orientation is synonymous with the non-capitalist path to development."[10]

In a manner of speaking, this book by Ulyanovsky marks the beginning of the systematic development of the identifying label "states with a socialist orientation" into the key term of a new conceptual framework for the Soviet strategy towards the Third World. The first coherent description of this strategy appeared in 1975 in the shape of an omnibus volume entitled *The State with a Socialist Orientation* (introduction by Ulyanovsky, main contributions by V.Ye. Chirkin and Yu.A. Yudin). An even more authoritative collective work, *The Socialist Orientation of Liberated Countries,* was published in 1982. Aside from two deputy heads of the International Department of the CC apparatus (R.A. Ulyanovsky and K.N. Brutents), the directors of the Africa Institute (A.A. Gromyko) and of the Institute of Oriental Studies (Ye.M. Primakov) of the AoS-USSR were among the authors.[11]

Nevertheless, expert discussion is still far from concluded, the more so since the new concept has raised a spate of difficult problems of formation and revolution theory. Thus, the question arises as to its compatibility with essential tenets of classical Marxism, especially with regard to Angola, Mozambique, Ethiopia, the Congo, Tanzania, Afghanistan, and other "states with a socialist orientation," boasting a clearly "pre-capitalist" social and economic structure. Given the extreme backwardness of the economic, technological, and educational structures of the countries concerned, even Soviet Third-World specialists are undecided on which specific development strategy to recommend to them on their chosen "non-capitalist path."

In a keynote speech on 20 October 1980 in East Berlin, the head of the International Department of the CC apparatus of the CPSU, candidate member of the Politburo and CC Secretary B.N. Ponomarev, emphasized that what matters first of all in the economic sphere for the "states of socialist orientation" is to see to a steady "improvement of the living conditions of the working population" while simultaneously "creating a new material-technical base." The "way out" consists of "advancing gradually" and in the process "avoiding any artificial acceleration of societal transformation." He advised the responsible politicians to take their inspiration in this regard more from Lenin's "New Economic Policy," rather than from the Eastern European campaigns of socialization in the period following the end of the Second World War. In any event, the "revolutionary force" must occupy the "commanding heights," Ponomarev emphasized. But once this condition is understood, it is possible to "apply different forms of economic management—by the state, state capitalism, cooperative, and private capitalist—to build the economy, to implement industrialization, to mechanize the economy, to collectivize farm lands provided the pre-conditions for it have matured and provided it is done with allowance for the level of the farmers' consciousness." He emphatically stressed Soviet interest in the self-determination of the "states of socialist orientation." On that hinges "to no small measure" the option by other states for a similar path and "in general the consolidation of the anti-imperialist positions in the world."[12]

In this respect the Soviet notion of the "state of socialist orientation" does not actually constitute a new or modified political-economic model of development for Third World countries. Its practical relevance consists mainly in establishing privileged cooperative relations with social-revolutionary regimes in the Third World and at the same time ideologically justifying the dilatory treatment of their candidacy for acceptance into the "community of socialist states" (i.e., the WTO-CMEA system). Allegedly, membership applications by Laos, Ethiopia, Afghanistan, and South Yemen (with the objective of full membership) have already been under consideration by the CMEA Executive Committee since the spring of 1979. Angola, Mozambique, and Benin are also said to have announced that they have applied for membership,[13] but all these applications have been rejected.

Viewed from the vantage of revolution theory, the new formula follows previous cooperative formulae with a similar purpose. All these have proven overly schematic and removed from reality. This is especially true of the cooperative model of the "state of national democracy" propounded in 1960. This demanded the inclusion of communists as coalition partners in broad governing alliances of the "national-democratic forces," and likewise the *ersatz*-model of the "state of revolutionary democracy." After revolutionary one-party regimes (e.g., in Egypt, Algeria, Guinea, Ghana, Mali, the Congo-Brazzaville, and others) rejected the first Soviet offer in 1963/64, this *ersatz* model accepted the partners' condition that cooperation with indigenous communists was possible only within the bounds of a unity party, that is, with their renunciation of organizational autonomy. Of course, influential communist parties such as Syria's CP and the Sudan's CP revolted against this new line.

Now, the concept of the "state with a socialist orientation" is broader and more flexible in design than earlier models of partnership. Its theoretical structure also takes into account efforts to bring into harmony with each other the older guiding principles of the "non-capitalist path to development," of the "national democracy," and of "revolutionary democracy" as elements, as variants, or even as components and developmental phases of the "state with a socialist orientation."

The new formula of partnership demands that regimes tending towards reliance on the USSR make more than a mere decision in principle for a "non-capitalist path to development." It also demands a clear commitment to "scientific socialism" and to close political cooperation with the Soviet Union as well as the creation of a (revolutionary-democratic) vanguard party that is also dedicated to Marxism-Leninism and to cooperation with "world socialism." Ethiopia's Workers' Party, for instance, founded in September 1984 after eight years of Soviet pressure, is such a party. As long as (de facto communist) governing parties like Afghanistan's Democratic People's Party take pains to adopt a positive attitude towards religion for opportunistic reasons, the CPSU leadership also classifies them, as a matter of principle, as "revolutionary-democratic" parties.

For all that, the planned "building of socialism" that is patterned on Eastern European "people's democracies," or Vietnam or Cuba, is not required, nor is the ideologically motivated option of forced industrialization (in order to create the missing industrial proletariat). Quite the contrary, the concept of the developing state "with a socialist orientation" allows for it to remain basically in the "capitalist world market." It is even called upon to pay special attention to combining the systematic consolidation of the public economic sector with the deliberate support for private entrepreneurial initiative within the framework of a primarily growth-oriented economy.[14]

The Soviet Union has concluded treaties of political cooperation (treaties of "friendship and cooperation") with eight states "with a socialist orientation" (Ethiopia, Afghanistan, Angola, Iraq, PDR of Yemen, the Congo, Mozambique, and Syria).[15] Without fail, these treaties contain consultation and cooperation clauses enabling the Kremlin in each case to exert massive influence at its own discretion upon the domestic and foreign policy of the treaty partner. By contrast, the partner states "with a socialist orientation" are as a rule far too weak themselves to insist on equal terms in these areas vis-à-vis the Soviet Union. Due to the USSR's enormous political, economic, and military preponderance, all eight cases represent one-sided patronage and protection treaties, essentially laying the foundations for a client's or vassal's relationship of the weaker to the stronger partner. It is reasonable to assume that the Soviet leadership is keen also on concluding analogous treaties of cooperation with all other "states with a socialist orientation."

Notes

1. Cf. W. Berner, "The Soviet Union and Latin America," in D. Geyer (ed.), *Osteuropa Handbuch. Sowjetunion. Aussenpolitik 1955–1973* (Cologne-Vienna, 1976), pp. 844–878, esp. pp. 856ff.

2. Cf. *The Soviet Union and the Third World: A Watershed in Great Power Policy?* (Washington, 1977), Congressional paper JX 1428 Russia A/CP-367; Surveys: Soviet Military Aid, 1955–1974, and Soviet Economic Aid, 1954–1976, in the Appendix (following p. 180).

3. Thus R.A. Ulyanovsky, in *VIKPSS*, No. 2 (1982), pp. 84–85, as well as in *Aziya i Afrika segodnya*, No. 10 (1980), pp. 2–6; N. Simoniya, *ibid.*, No. 5 (1981), pp. 14–17; A. Kiva, *ibid.*, No. 2 (1982), pp. 2–5.

4. R.A. Ulyanovsky, in *VF*, No. 4 (1984), p. 24, and in K, No. 11 (1979), p. 117.

5. Ye. Primakov, in *Gesellschaftswissenschaften*, Moscow, No. 3 (1979), pp. 90ff.

6. G. Mirsky and K. Maydanik (Latin American Expert), in *Mirovaya ekonomika i mezhdunarodnye otnosheniya*, No. 6 (1981), p. 27.

7. *Pr*, 17 June 1983; *ND*, 18/19 June 1983.

8. R.A. Ulyanovsky, in K, No. 4 (1968), p. 103.

9. Cf. MZh, No. 10 (1970), pp. 13–29.

10. R.A. Ulyanovsky, *Sotsializm i osvobodivshiesya strany* (Moscow, 1972), cited according to the German edition (East Berlin, 1973), p. 353.

11. *Gosudarstvo sotsialisticheskoy orientatsii* (Moscow, 1975); *Sotsialisticheskaya orientatsiya osvobodivshikhsya stran* (Moscow, 1982).

12. B.N. Ponomarev, in K, No. 1 (1981), pp. 31–44; German in *ND*, 21 October 1980.

13. Cf. *U*, 5 April 1979.

14. More details in E. Kridl Valkenier, *The Soviet Union and the Third World. An Economic Bind* (New York, 1983), especially pp. 97–103.

15. Cf. W. Berner, in *The Soviet Union 1980/81*, pp. 296–304.

Appendix Tables and Figures

TABLE A.1
Area and Climate

1. Area: 8,600,400 square miles (USA: 3,618,770 square miles)
   (East-West distance: 5,600 miles)

2. Climate:

	Average Temperature °C (°F)		Precipitation mm (inches)	
	Warmest	Coldest	Wettest	Dryest
Leningrad	17.6 (64)	-7.6 (18)	82 (3.2)	27 (1.1)
Astrakhan	25.2 (77)	-6.0 (21)	27 (1.1)	3 (0.1)
Verkhoyansk	15.5 (60)	-50.1 (-58)	36 (1.4)	3 (0.1)
New York	25.0 (77)	0.0 (32)	102 (4)	69 (2.7)

Note: 3,500,000 square miles have permafrost.

TABLE A.2
Population of the USSR
(1940-1984, in millions, at the beginning of the year)

	Population	Male		Female		Urban		Rural	
		(m.)	(%)	(m.)	(%)	(m.)	(%)	(m.)	(%)
1940	194.1	93.0	47.9	101.1	52.1	63.1	33	131.0	67
1951	181.6	79.9	44.0	101.7	56.0	73.0	40	108.6	60
1956	197.9	88.5	44.7	109.4	55.3	88.2	45	109.7	55
1961	216.3	97.9	45.3	118.4	54.7	107.9	50	108.4	50
1966	232.2	106.3	45.8	125.9	54.2	123.7	53	108.5	47
1971	243.9	112.5	46.1	131.4	53.9	139.0	57	104.9	43
1976	255.5	118.7	46.4	136.8	53.6	156.6	61	98.9	39
1977	257.8	119.9	46.5	137.9	53.5	159.6	62	98.2	38
1979	262.4	122.3	46.6	140.1	53.4	163.6	62	98.8	38
1980	264.5	123.4	46.7	141.1	53.3	166.2	63	98.3	37
1981	266.6	124.5	46.7	142.1	53.3	168.9	63	97.7	36.6
1982	268.8	125.7	46.8	143.1	53.2	171.6	63.9	97.1	36.1
1983	271.2	126.9	46.8	144.3	53.2	174.6	64.4	96.6	35.6
1984	273.8	128.3	46.9	145.5	53.1	177.5	64.8	90.3	35.2

Sources: Narodnoe khozyaystvo SSSR v 1979 g., Moscow, 1980 and Narodnoe khozyaystvo SSSR v 1980 g., Moscow, 1982; SSSR v tsifrakh v 1981 g., 1983 g., Moscow, 1982-1984. Encyclopaedia Britannica, Book of the Year 1985, Chicago, 1985, The World Almanack & Book of Facts 1985, New York, 1985.

TABLE A.3
Birth Rate (live births per 1,000 inhabitants)

	USSR	RSFSR	Uzbek SSR	USA
1913	45.5[a]	--	--	30.1[b]
1940	31.2	33.0	33.8	19.4
1950	26.7	26.9	30.8	24.1
1960	24.9	23.2	39.8	23.7
1970	17.4	14.6	33.6	18.4
1980	18.3	15.9	33.8	15.9
1983	20.7	17.6	35.3	15.5

Notes: [a]In the present territory of the USSR.
[b]1910

Sources: Narodnoe khozyaystvo SSSR v 1967 g., Moscow, 1968, pp. 40f.; Narodnoe khozyaystvo SSSR v 1980 g., pp. 32f.; Statistical Abstract of the United States 1984, 104th Ed., Washington, D.C., Department of Commerce; The Christian Science Monitor, 29 December 1984 to 4 January 1985.

TABLE A.4
The Politburo of the Central Committee of the CPSU (as of 1 January, 1986)

Full members	Positions
M. S. Gorbachev (K. U. Chernenko Feb. 12, 1984 - March 10, 1985)	Secretary General, CPSU Central Committee; Chairman, USSR Council of Defense
G. A. Aliyev	First Deputy Chairman, USSR Council of Ministers
V. M. Chebrikov*	Chairman, USSR Committee for State Security (KGB)
V. V. Grishin	(lost his post as First Secretary of the Moscow City Party Committee on 24 December 1985, therefore his retirement from the Politburo is to be expected)
A. A. Gromyko*	Chairman, Presidium, USSR Supreme Soviet
D. A. Kunayev	First Secretary, CC CP of Kazakhstan
E. K. Ligachev	Secretary, CPSU CC
N. I. Ryzhkov	Chairman, USSR Council of Ministers
V. V. Shcherbitsky	First Secretary, CC CP of the Ukraine
E. A. Shevardnadze*	USSR Minister of Foreign Affairs
M. S. Solomentsev	Chairman, Party Control Committee, CC CPSU
V. I. Vorotnikov	Chairman, RSFSR Council of Ministers

*Personnel changes that became known under Gorbachev.

TABLE A.5
The Secretaries of the Central Committee of the CPSU

Official Ranking	Area of Responsibility
M. S. Gorbachev (K. U. Chernenko Feb. 12, 1984 - March 10, 1985)	Secretary General: all matters of foreign, domestic and party policy
E. K. Ligachev	Ideology, personnel and organizational party work; regional party apparatus
B. N. Ponomarev	Communist parties and movements in non-socialist countries
V. I. Dolgikh	Heavy industry
I. V. Kapitonov	Consumer goods production
M. V. Zimyanin	Ideology, culture, and propaganda
K. V. Rusakov	Communist parties in the socialist countries
V. P. Nikonov	Agriculture
L. N. Zaykov*	Military-industrial complex
V. N. Yeltsin*	(became First Secretary of the Moscow City Party Committee on 24 December 1985, therefore his admission to the Politburo, connected with his withdrawal from the Secretariat of the CC, is to be expected)
Candidates	**Positions**
P. N. Demichev	USSR Minister of Culture
V. I. Dolgikh	Secretary, CPSU CC
V. V. Kuznetsov	First Deputy Chairman, Presidium, USSR Supreme Soviet
B. N. Ponomarev	Secretary, CPSU CC Chief, International Department, CC CPSU
S. L. Sokolov*	USSR Minister of Defense
N. V. Talyzin*	Chairman, State Planning Committee (Gosplan)

*Personnel changes that became known under Gorbachev.

TABLE A.6
The First and Second Secretaries of the CCs of the Union Republics (as of 31 December 1985)

	Secretaries of the CCs	
Armenia	K. S. Demirchyan	Yu. P. Kochetkov*
Azerbaijan	K. M. Bagirov	V. N. Konovalov
Belorussia	N. N. Slyunkov	G. G. Bartoshevich*
Estonia	K. G. Vaino	G. V. Aleshin*
Georgia	D. I. Patiashvilli*	B. V. Nikolsky
Kazakhstan	D. A. Kunayev	O. S. Miroshkhin
Kirghizistan	A. Masaliyev*	G. N. Kiselev*
Latvia	B. K. Pugo	V. I. Dmitriev
Lithuania	P. P. Griskevicius	N. K. Dybenko
Moldavia	S. K. Grossu	V. I. Smirnov*
RSFSR	(has not had its own republican CC organs since 1966)	
Tadzhikistan	K. Makhkamov*	Yu. P. Belov*
Turkmenistan	S. Niyazov*	A. I. Rachkov
Ukraine	V. V. Shcherbitsky	A. A. Titarenko
Uzbekistan	N. N. Usmankhodzhayev	T. N. Osetrov

*Personnel changes that became known under Gorbachev.

TABLE A.7
Departments and Personnel of the Central Committee of the CPSU (as of 1 January 1986)

Department	Position	Personnel	
Administration of Affairs	Administrator	N. E. Kruchina	Secretary General, Ye. K. Ligachev
	First deputy administrator	Yu. N. Valov	
	Deputy administrator	V. F. Beresnev	
		A. S. Kuklinov*	
Administrative Organs	Head	N. I. Savinkin	Secretary General, Ye. K. Ligachev, L. N. Zaykov
	First deputy	V. I. Drugov	
	Deputies	V. A. Abolentsev	
		A. N. Soshnikov	
Agricultural Mechanical Engineering	Head	I. I. Sakhnyuk	V. P. Nikonov, V. I. Dolgikh, I. V. Kapitonov
	First deputy	V. N. Demchenko	
	Deputy	V. N. Tkachev	
Agriculture and Food Industry	Head	V. A. Karlov	V. P. Nikonov, I. V. Kapitonov
	First deputy	I. I. Skiba	
	Deputies	A. D. Budyka	
		I. K. Kapustyan	
		A. N. Kashtanov	
		V. K. Onisovets	
		M. I. Polyakov	
		A. A. Pronin	
		S. V. Zasukhin	
Cadres abroad	Head	S. V. Chervonenko	Secretary General, Ye. K. Ligachev, B. N. Ponomarev, K. V. Rusakov
	First deputy	G. E. Tsukanov	

Note: *Personnel changes that became known under Gorbachev.

TABLE A.7 (continued)

Department	Position	Personnel	
Chemical Industry	Head	V. G. Afonin	V. I. Dolgikh, L. N. Zaykov
	First deputy	B. S. Semyonov	
	Deputies	Yu.A. Bespalov	
		N. M. Olshansky	
Construction	Head	?	V. I. Dolgikh, L. N. Zaykov
	First deputy	V. F. Isayev	
	Deputies	A. D. Dmitriev	
		I. P. Dyatlov	
Culture	Head	V. F. Shauro	Ye. K. Ligachev, M. V. Zimyanin
	First deputy head	S. P. Tumanova	
	Deputies	Yu. S. Afanasyev	
		A. A. Belyayev	
Defense Industry	Head	O. S. Belyakov*	Secretary General, L. N. Zaykov
Economics	Head	vacant	Secretary General, N. I. Dolgikh, I. V. Kapitanov, L. N. Zaykov
	First deputy	Yu.A. Belik*	
	Deputies	N. F. Lobachov	
		A. V. Skripnikov*	
General Department	Head	A. I. Lukyanov*	Secretary General, Ye. K. Ligachev
	First deputy	?	
	Deputies	S. P. Avetisyan	
		A. A. Solovyov	
Heavy Industry and Power Engineering	Head	I. P. Yastrebov	V. I. Dolgikh, L. N. Zaykov
	First deputy	V. M. Frolyshev*	
	Deputies	V. G. Arkhipov	
		V. A. Durasov	
		L. M. Kuznetsov	

TABLE A.7 (continued)

Department	Position	Personnel	
International Department	Head	B. N. Ponomarev	Ye. K. Ligachev
	First deputies	V. V. Zagladin	
		O. B. Rakhmanin*	
	Deputies	K. N. Brutents	
		A. S. Chernyaev	
		I. I. Kovalenko	
		P. I. Manchkha	
		V. S. Shaposhnikov	
		R. A. Ulyanovsky	
International Information	Head	L. M. Zamyatin	Secretary General, B. N. Ponomarev, M. V. Zimyanin
	First deputy	N. N. Chetverikov	
	Deputies	V. N. Ignatenko	
		Yu. I. Kandalov	
		A. I. Vlasov*	
Letters	Head	B. P. Yakovlev	Secretary General, Ye. K. Ligachev
	First deputy	V. I. Lobusov	
	Deputy	N. I. Zemskov	
Liaison with Communist and Workers' Parties of Socialist Countries	Head	K. V. Rusakov	Secretary General, Ye. K. Ligachev, K. V. Rusakov
	First deputy	O. B. Rakhmanin (?)	
	Deputies	O. A. Chukanov	
		G. A. Kiselyov	
		G.Kh. Shakhnazarov	
		M. N. Smirnovsky	
Light Industry and Consumer Goods	Head	F. I. Mochalin	I. V. Kapitonov
	First deputy	L. F. Bobykin	
	Deputies	A. N. Frolov	
		V. K. Kiselyov	
		A. P. Sochneva	

TABLE A.7 (continued)

Department	Position	Personnel	
Main Political Administration of the Soviet Army and Navy	Head	A. D. Lisichev*	Secretary General, Ye.K. Ligachev, M. V. Zimyanin
	First deputy	A. I. Sorokin	
	Deputies	V. S. Nechayev*	
		D. A. Volkogonov	
Mechanical Engineering	Head	A. I. Volsky*	V. I. Dolgikh, L. N. Zaykov
	First deputy	V. I. Pimenov	
	Deputies	Ye.N. Chernyshev*	
		V. L. Savakov	
CC Newspapers	Editors-in-chief	V. G. Afanasyev, Pravda	
		A. P. Kharlamov, Selskaya zhizn	
		Yu.Ya. Barabash, Sovetskaya kultura	
		M. F. Nenashev, Sovetskaya Rossiya	
		V. N. Golubev, Sotsialisticheskaya industriya	
		A. F. Rumyantsev, Ekonomicheskaya gazeta	
Organizational Party Work	Head	G. P. Razumovsky*	Secretary General, Ye.K. Ligachev
	First deputy	E. Z. Razumov	
	Deputies	N. S. Igrunov*	
		K. N. Mogilnichenko	
		N. S. Perun	
		P. A. Smolsky	
CC Periodicals	Editors-in-chief	M. P. Gabdulin, Agitator	
		V. I. Kazyanenko, Voprosy istorii KPSS	
		R. I. Kosolapov, Kommunist	
		M. I. Khaldeyev, Partiynaya zhizn	
		A. S. Vishnyakov, Politicheskoye samoobrazovanie	
		M. S. Kuryanov, Kadry selskogo khozyaystva	

Note: The following persons have been identified as deputy heads of department, their specific departments being unknown so far: V. G. Dolgin, A. V. Teterin.

TABLE A.7 (continued)

Department	Position	Personnel	
Propaganda	Head	A. N. Yakovlev*	Secretary General, Ye.K. Ligachev, B. N. Ponomarev, M. V. Zimyanin
	First deputy	V. G. Zakharov	
	Deputies	N. B. Bikkenin*	
		P. K. Luchinsky	
		V. N. Sevruk	
		P.Ya. Slezko	
Science and Educational Institutions	Head	V. A. Medvedev	Ye.K. Ligachev, M. V. Zimyanin
	First deputy	V. A. Grigoryev*	
	Deputies	P. P. Shirinsky	
		G. S. Strizhov	
		B. G. Vladimirov	
Trade and Domestic Services	Head	N. A. Stashenkov*	I. V. Kapitono
	First deputy	N. I. Bochkov	
	Deputy	V. P. Gusev*	
Transport and Communications	Head	K. S. Simonov	V. I. Dolgikh, L. N. Zaykov
	First deputy	V. I. Davydov	
	Deputy	I. P. Trofimov	

TABLE A.8
Heads of the Central Research and Teaching Institutions of the Party

Institution	Position	Personnel
Academy of Social Sciences at the CC of the CPSU	Rector	R. G. Yanovsky
Institute of Marxism-Leninism at the CC of the CPSU	Director	A. G. Yegorov
Institute of Social Sciences at the CC of the CPSU	Rector	Yu. N. Pankov
Institute for the Raising of Qualifications of Leading Party and Soviet Cadres of the Academy of Social Sciences at the CC of the CPSU	Director	A. M. Korolyov
Committee for Party Control at the CC of the CPSU	Chairman	M. S. Solomentsev
	First deputy	I. S. Gustov
	Deputies	M. A. Ponomarev
		M. G. Voropayev

Note: *Personnel changes that became known under Gorbachev.

FIGURE A.1
Organization of the Council of Ministers of the USSR

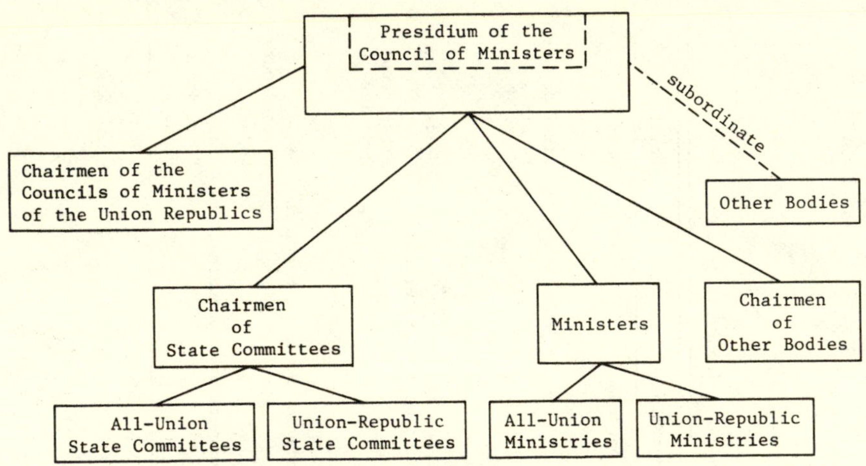

TABLE A.9
The Council of Ministers of the USSR

Department	Position	Personnel
Presidium	Chairman	N. S. Ryzhkov*
	First deputy chairmen	G. A. Aliyev
		I. V. Arkhipov
		V. S. Murakhovsky*
		N. V. Talyzin
	Deputy Chairmen	A. K. Antonov
		Yu. P. Batalin*
		G. I. Marchuk
		Yu. D. Maslyukov*
		Ya. P. Ryabov
		B. E. Shcherbina
		I. S. Silayev*
		L. A. Voronin

Department	Union Republics	Personnel
Chairmen of the Councils of Ministers of the Union Republics (ex officio members of the Council of Ministers of the USSR)	Armenia	F. T. Sarkisyan
	Azerbaijan	G. N. Seidov
	Belorussia	?
	Estonia	B. E. Saul
	Georgia	D. L. Kartvelishvili
	Kazakhstan	N. A. Nazarbayev
	Kirghizistan	A. D. Duysheyev
	Latvia	Yu.Ya. Ruben
	Lithuania	V. V. Sakalauskas*
	Moldavia	I. P. Kalin*
	RSFSR	V. I. Vorotnikov
	Tadzhikistan	I. Khayeyev*
	Turkmenistan	A. Khodzhamuradov*
	Ukraine	A. P. Lyashko
	Uzbekistan	G.Kh. Kadyrov

Note: *Personnel changes that became known under Gorbachev.

TABLE A.9 (continued)

Department	Ministry	Personnel
All-Union Ministries (as of 1 January 1986)	Automotive Industry	V. N. Polyakov
	Aviation Industry	A. I. Systsov*
	Chemical Industry	V. V. Listov
	Chemical and Petroleum Mechanical Engineering	K. I. Brekhov
	Civil Aviation	B. P. Bugayev
	Communications Equipment Industry	E. K. Pervyshin
	Construction of Petroleum and Gas Industry Enterprises	V. G. Chirskov
	Construction in the Far East and Transbaykal Regions	A. A. Babenko
	Construction, Road, and Municipal Mechanical Engineering	Ye.A. Varnachev
	Defense	S. L. Sokolov
	Defense Industry	P. V. Finogenov
	Electrical Equipment Industry	V. G. Kolesnikov*
	Electronics Industry	G. P. Voronovsky*
	Foreign Trade	B. I. Aristov*
	Gas Industry	V. S. Chernomyrdin*
	General Mechanical Engineering	O. D. Baklanov
	Heavy and Transport Mechanical Engineering	S. A. Afanasyev
	Instrument Making, Automation Equipment, and Control Systems	M. S. Shkabardnya
	Mechanical Engineering	V. V. Bakhirev
	Mechanical Engineering for Animal Husbandry and Fodder Production	K. N. Belyak
	Mechanical Engineering for Light and Food Industry and Household Appliances	L. V. Vasilyev

TABLE A.9 (continued)

Department	Ministry	Personnel
All-Union Ministries (as of 1 January 1986) (continued)	Machine Tool and Tool Building Industry	B. V. Balmont
	Maritime Fleet	T. B. Guzhenko
	Medical Industry	V. A. Bykov*
	Medium Mechanical Engineering	Ye.P. Slavsky
	Mineral Fertilizer Production	A. G. Petrishchev
	Petroleum Industry	V. A. Dinkov
	Power Mechanical Engineering	V. M. Velichenko
	Radio Industry	P. S. Pleshakov
	Railways	N. S. Konarev
	Shipbuilding Industry	I. S. Belousov
	Tractor and Agricultural Mechanical Engineering	A. A. Yezhevsky
	Transport Construction	V. A. Brezhnev*

Department	Committee	Personnel
All-Union State Committees (as of 1 January 1986)	Foreign Economic Relations (GKES)	K. F. Katushev
	Inventions and Discoveries (GOSKOMIZOBRETENIY)	I. S. Nayashkov
	Hydrometeorology and Environmental Control (GOSKOMGIDROMET)	Yu.A. Izrael
	Material Reserves	A. V. Kovalenko
	Safety in the Atomic Power Industry (GOSATOMENERGONADZOR)	I. V. Kulov
	Science and Technology (GKNT)	G. I. Marchuk
	Standards (GOSSTANDART)	G. D. Kolmogorov

TABLE A.9 (continued)

Department	Ministry	Personnel
Union-Republic Ministries (as of 1 January 1986)	Coal Industry	M. I. Shchadov*
	Communications	V. A. Shamshin
	Construction	G. A. Karavayev
	Construction of Heavy Industry Enterprises	N. V. Goldin
	Construction Materials Industry	S. F. Voenushkin*
	Culture	P. N. Demichev
	Education	S. G. Shcherbakov
	Ferrous Metallurgy	S. V. Kolpakov*
	Finance	I. S. Gostev*
	Fish Industry	V. M. Kamentsev
	Foreign Affairs	E. A. Shevardnadze*
	Geology	Ye.A. Kozlovsky
	Health	S. P. Burenkov
	Higher and Secondary Specialized Education	G. A. Yagodin*
	Industrial Construction	A. N. Shchepelnikov*
	Installation and Special Construction Work	B. V. Bakin
	Internal Affairs (MVD)	A. V. Vlasov*
	Justice	B. V. Kravtsov
	Land Reclamation and Water Resources	N. F. Vasilyev
	Light Industry	V. G. Klyuyev*
	Nonferrous Metallurgy	P. F. Lomako
	Petroleum Refining and Petrochemical Industry	N. V. Lemayev*
	Power and Electrification	S. I. Mayorets*
	Procurement	G. S. Zolotukhin
	Timber, Pulp and Paper, and Wood Processing Industry	M. I. Buzygin
	Trade	G. I. Vashchenko

TABLE A.9 (continued)

Department	Committee	Personnel
Union-Republic State Committees (as of 1 January 1986)	Agro-Industrial Committee of the USSR (GOSAGROPROM), established Nov. 1985	Chairman: V. S. Murakhovsky* First deputy chairmen: A. I. Yevlev* Ye.I. Sizenko*
	Cinematography (GOSKINO)	F. T. Yermash
	Construction (GOSSTROY)	S. V. Bashilov
	Foreign Tourism (GOSKOMINTURIST), established May 1983	V.Ya. Pavlov
	Forestry (GOSLESKHOZ)	A. I. Zverev
	Labor and Social Problems (GOSKOMTRUD)	I. I. Gladkiy*
	Material and Technical Supply (GOSSNAB)	L. A. Voronin*
	State Planning Committee (GOSPLAN)	Chairman: N. V. Talyzin* First deputy chairman: A. A. Reut*
	Prices (GOSKOMTSEN)	N. T. Glushkov
	Publishing, Printing, and Book Trade (GOSKOMIZDAT)	B. N. Pastukhov
	State Security (KGB)	V. M. Chebrikov
	Supervision of Safe Working Practices in Industry and Mine Supervision (GOSGORTEKHNADZOR)	I. M. Vladychenko
	Supply of Petroleum Products (GOSKOMNEFTE-PRODUCT)	?
	Television and Radio Broadcasting (GOSTELERADIO)	A. N. Aksyonov*
	Vocational and Technical Education (GOSPROFOBR)	N. A. Petrovichev

TABLE A.9 (continued)

	Department	Personnel
Other bodies whose chairmen belong to the USSR Council of Ministers (as of 1 January 1986)	Administration of Affairs of the Council of Ministers	M. S. Smirtyukov
	Bureau for Mechanical Engineering	I. S. Silayev
	Central Statistical Administration (TsSU)	M. A. Korolyov*
	Committee for People's Control	A. M. Shkolnikov
	USSR State Bank (GOSBANK)	V. S. Alkhimov
Bodies subordinate to the USSR Council of Ministers whose chairmen to not belong to it (as of 1 January 1986)	Academy for the National Economy	Ye.M. Sergeyev
	Allunion-bank for Financing Capital Investments (STROYBANK)	M. S. Zotov
	Committee for the Allocation of Personal Pensions	?
	Committee for Lenin Prizes and State Prizes in Literature, Art, and Architecture	G. M. Markov
	Committee for Lenin Prizes and State Prizes in Science and Technology	A. P. Aleksandrov
	Committee for Physical Culture and Sports (SPORTKOMITET)	M. V. Gramov
	Council for Religious Affairs	K. M. Kharchev
	Higher Attestation Committee (VAK)	V. G. Kirillov-Ugryumov
	Main Archives Administration (GLAVARKHIV)	F. M. Vaganov
	Main Administration of Geodesy and Cartography (GUGK)	I. A. Kutuzov

TABLE A.9 (continued)

Department	Personnel
Main Administration for Safeguarding State Secrets in the Press (GLAVLIT)	P. K. Romanov
State Arbitration Committee (GOSARBITRAZH)	E. V. Anisimov
State Commission for Useful Mineral Reserves	A. M. Bybochkin
State Committee for the Utilization of Atomic Energy	A. M. Petrosyants
TASS**	S. A. Losev

Note: **According to Pravda, 11 January 1972, TASS has the status of a state committee.

TABLE A.10
Population and Gross National Product (GNP) of Leading Countries in the World Economy in 1983

	Population (in millions)	GNP (in billion US dollars)	GNP USA=100	Per Capita GNP (in US dollars)	Per Capita GNP USA=100	GNP per employee (in US dollars)	GNP per employee USA=100
USA	234.5	3,310.5	100.0	14,120	100.0	29,400	100.0
USSR	272.5	1,843.4	55.7	6,760	47.9	13,600	46.3
Japan	119.3	1,157.0	34.9	9,700	68.7	20,000	68.0
Federal Republic of Germany	61.5	657.7	19.9	10,690	75.7	23,000	78.2
France	54.7	514.9	15.6	9,410	66.6	21,900	74.5
Great Britain	56.0	448.2	13.6	8,020	56.8	16,900	57.5
People's Republic of China	1,020.9	341.7	10.3	335	2.4	-	-
Canada	24.9	326.9	9.9	13,130	93.0	27,500	93.5
Brazil	131.3	296.8	9.0	2,260	16.0	-	-

Sources: Handbook of Economic Statistics 1984 (Washington, D.C., 1984), pp. 22 ff. (also for the methodology of calculation); Statistisches Jahrbuch 1984 für die Bundesrepublik Deutschland (Stuttgart and Mainz, 1984), pp. 658 ff.; authors' estimates and calculations.

TABLE A.11
Rates of Growth of Real Gross National Product in Leading Industrial Countries, 1981-1985

	Increase over the previous year (%) 1981	1982	1983	1984[a]	1985[b]	Average Annual Increase (%) 1971-1975	1976-1980	1981-1985
United States	2.6	-1.9	3.7	6.5	3.0	2.6	3.7	2.8
USSR[c]	2.1	2.6	3.0	2.0	2.5	3.7	2.6	2.4
Federal Republic of Germany	-0.1	-1.0	1.3	2.5	2.0	2.1	3.6	0.9
France	0.3	1.6	0.7	1.5	1.5	4.0	3.4	1.1
Great Britain	-1.3	2.3	3.3	2.0	2.0	2.1	1.6	1.6
Italy	0.1	-0.3	-1.2	2.5	2.5	2.4	3.9	0.6
Japan	4.0	3.2	3.0	5.5	4.0	4.7	5.1	3.9

Notes: [a]Provisional.
[b]Forecast.
[c]At factor cost.

Sources: Die Weltwirtschaft, No. 2 (1984), p. 15; Handbook of Economic Statistics 1982 (Washington, D.C., 1982), p. 42; Handbook of Economic Statistics 1984 (Washington, D.C., 1984), p. 37.

TABLE A.12
Gross Domestic Product at Market Prices by Origin
(percent shares, 1982)

	USA	USSR[a]	Japan	Federal Republic of Germany	France	Great Britain
Industry[b]	25.7	37.0	34.1	35.5	27.7	30.2
Construction	4.1	8.0	8.6	6.1	6.5	4.9
Agriculture[c]	2.5	14.0	3.4	2.3	4.2	2.1
Transportation		10.0				
Communications	6.4	1.0	6.9	5.8	5.2	6.3
Trade[d]	16.7	8.0	12.2	9.5	12.3	11.0
Services		20.0				
Unexplained residual	44.6	2.0	34.8	40.8	44.1	45.5
Gross Domestic Product	100.0	100.0	100.0	100.0	100.0	100.0

Notes: [a]At factor cost.
[b]Including mining, quarrying, electric power generating, water supply, and manufacturing.
[c]Including forestry and fisheries.
[d]For Western countries, including eating establishments and lodgings.

Sources: Statistisches Jahrbuch 1984 für die Bundesrepublik Deutschland (Stuttgart and Mainz, 1984), pp. 736 ff; Handbook of Economic Statistics 1984 (Washington, D.C., 1984), p. 65.

TABLE A.13
Gross Domestic Product at Market Prices by Utilization
(percent shares, 1982)

	USA	USSR[a]	Japan	Federal Republic of Germany	France	Great Britain
Private consumption	66.2	52.0	58.7	56.2	64.8	60.8
State consumption[b]	18.7	17.5	10.2	20.3	16.2	22.0
of which arms	6.5	12.0	1.0	4.1	4.2	5.3
Gross capital investment	16.6		30.0	20.6	20.5	15.4
Change in stocks	-0.4	30.0	0.5	0.4	0.9	-0.4
Exports	8.6		14.7	31.1	23.2	27.1
Imports	9.7	0.5	14.1	28.6	25.6	24.9
Gross domestic product	100.0	100.0	100.0	100.0	100.0	100.0

Notes: [a]At factor cost, authors' estimate.
[b]Total state consumption including expenditure on education and health.

Sources: For the Western countries: Statistisches Jahrbuch 1984 für die Bundesrepublik Deutschland (Stuttgart and Mainz 1984), pp. 763 ff; for arms: Military Balance 1984-1985, International Institute for Strategic Studies (London 1984), pp. 140 ff.

TABLE A.14
International Purchasing Power Comparison
(prices of consumer goods and services
in working-time units, March 1983)

Products and Services		Weekly Shopping Basket for a Four-Person Household; Minutes of Working-Time Required				
FOOD	Kg	Moscow	Munich	Paris	London	Washington
Flour	1.0	28	9	6	6	5
Bread	7.0	119	189	126	175	112
Noodles	2.0	68	32	22	28	28
Beef	1.0	123	150	119	115	69
Pork	1.5	176	150	108	117	63
Stewing beef	1.0	123	70	80	63	37
Sausage	1.0	160	75	75	51	33
Cod	1.0	47	45	118	72	61
Sugar	3.3	191	33	30	36	30
Butter	0.5	111	26	24	25	28
Margarine	2.0	222	34	36	64	46
Milk (liters)	12.0	264	84	96	108	72
Cheese	2.0	370	130	118	130	200
Eggs (number, cheapest kind)	18.0	99	22	23	29	14
Potatoes	9.0	63	36	36	27	63
Cabbage	3.0	36	21	27	30	27
Carrots	1.0	19	10	7	13	11
Tomatoes	1.0	62	28	25	32	23
Apples	1.0	92	15	15	23	10
Tea	0.1	53	10	17	5	10
Beer (liter)	3.0	48	24	21	54	33
Gin/Vodka (liter)	1.0	646	106	153	187	87
Cigarettes (number)	120.0	90	96	48	150	54
		Hours of Working Time Required				
Total of weekly shopping basket as above		53.5	23.3	22.2	25.7	18.6

TABLE A.14 (continued)

Products and Services	Minutes of Working-Time Required (unless otherwise stated)				
CLOTHING	Moscow	Munich	Paris	London	Washington
Underpants	366	18	17	18	18
Man's shirt	615	289	208	237	137
Man's shoes, 1 Pair (hours)	25	5	7	7	8
SERVICES					
Use of washing machine (12 kg)	22	50	30	16	7
Dry cleaning, man's coat	92	54	91	53	79
Ladies' hairdressing, shampoo, and set	185	126	102	73	148
PUBLIC TRANSPORTATION					
Bus ticket, 2-3 km	3	8	9	11	7
Rail ticket, 60-100 km	258	86	87	119	104
Air ticket, 300 km, economy class (hours)	14	16	17	18	11
	hours of working-time required				
HOUSING					
Monthly rent, state subsidized	12	24	39	28	51
CONSUMER DURABLES					
Refrigerator, cheapest, 230 liters	355	54	69	75	61
Automatic washing machine	165	96	56	81	47
TV set, black & white, 61 cm. tube	299	49	44	35	38
Man's bicycle, cheapest	60	22	26	22	17
	months of working-time required				
CARS					
Small car (Ford Escort)	53	6	8	11	5
Medium car (Ford Granada)	88	9	12	18	8

Sources: K. Bush, Radio Liberty Research Supplement, "Retail Prices in Moscow and Four Western Cities in March," 4 June 1982.

TABLE A.15
Output of Selected Key Products in Leading Industrial Countries in 1982

	USA	USSR	Japan	Federal Republic of Germany
Hard Coal (m. tons)	756.1	488.0	17.6	89.0
Electric Power (billion Kwh)	2,314.0	1,367.0	523.0	367.0
of which nuclear	272.0[a]	68.0[a]	102.0	64.0
Oil (m. tons)	426.7	612.6	n.a.	4.3
Gas (thousand peta joules)	19.2	17.4	n.a.	0.6
Cement (m. tons)	58.0	124.0	80.7	30.1
Steel (m. tons)	68.6	147.2	99.5	35.9
Sulphuric acid (calculated in H_2SO_4, m. tons)	29.0	23.8	6.5	4.4
Synthetic fibers and threads (m. tons)	2.6	0.6	1.3	0.7
Sawn timber (m. cubic meters)	63.6	96.0[b]	30.9	8.6
Passenger cars (million)	5.1	1.3	6.9	3.8
Trucks and buses (million)	1.9	0.9	3.8	0.3
TV sets (million)	9.9	8.3	12.8	4.2
Shoes (million pairs)	342.0	734.0	50.0	53.0
Wheat (m. tons)	76.4	87.0	0.7	8.6
Meat (m. tons)	24.4	15.2	3.1	4.5

Notes: [a]1981.
[b]Estimate.

Source: Statistisches Jahrbuch 1984 für die Bundesrepublik Deutschland (Stuttgart/ Mainz, 1984), pp. 664, 666, 674, 680.

TABLE A.16
Actual and Planned Output of Major Products in Soviet Agriculture, 1976-1990 (quantity per year in five-year averages)

	1976-1980 (actual)	1981-1985 (plan)	1981 (actual)	1982 (actual)	1983 (actual)	1984 (actual)	1986-1990 (plan)
Grain, total (m. tons)	205.0	238-243	160-165[a]	180-185[a]	190[a]	170[a]	250-255
Meat (m. tons slaughter weight)	14.8	17.0-17.5	15.2	15.4	16.4	16.7	20-20.5
Milk (m. tons)	92.6	97-99	88.9	91.0	96.4	97.6	104-106
Eggs (billion)	63.1	72	70.9	72.4	75.1	76.0	78-79
Potatoes (m. tons)	82.6	87-89	72.1	78.2	83.1	85.3	90-92
Sugar beets (m. tons)	88.7	100-103	60.8	71.4	81.8	85.3	102-103

Note: [a]Estimate.

Sources: Food Program in Pravda, 28 May 1982; USSR statistical yearbooks; plan documents; plan fulfillment reports.

TABLE A.17
Soviet Foreign Trade, Exports

Countries or Groups of Countries	1983	1984	1983	1984	1983	1984
	(million TR)		(increase over previous year in percent)		(shares, percent)	
All countries	67890.6	74383.7	7.5	9.6	100	100
Socialist Countries[b]	37714.0	41206.3	10.5	11.6	55.6	56.6
CMEA Countries[c]	34449.3	38164.6	10.6	10.8	50.7	51.3
Bulgaria	5510.8	6124.4	12.8	11.1	8.1	8.2
Czechoslovakia	5871.6	6590.8	16.3	12.2	8.6	8.9
GDR	6797.8	7481.4	5.9	10.1	10.0	10.1
Poland	5274.3	6069.2	9.6	15.1	7.8	8.2
Romania	1639.6	1807.2	15.2	10.2	2.4	2.4
Hungary	4058.0	4320.8	9.5	6.5	6.0	5.8
OECD Countries	16652.9	21349.4	4.3	8.6	28.6	28.7
EC Countries	13739.4	15288.2	3.2	11.3	20.2	20.6
Federal Republic of Germany	4066.5	4536.1	0.0	11.5	6.0	6.1
France	2422.3	2447.0	5.7	1.0	3.6	3.3
Italy	2998.3	3156.2	4.7	5.3	4.4	4.2
Great Britain	1184.8	1392.7	45.8	17.6	1.7	1.9
Finland	2483.3	2421.2	3.7	-2.5	3.7	3.3
Austria	565.7	761.1	-16.1	34.5	0.8	1.0
Japan	828.5	840.0	9.5	1.4	1.2	1.1
USA	330.5	305.9	113.5	-7.4	0.5	0.4
Developing Countries[d]	10523.7	10928.0	3.4	3.8	15.5	14.7

[a]f.o.b. values at current prices and exchange rates.

[b]CMEA countries plus People's Republic of China, Yugoslavia, N. Korea, Vietnam (after 1976 in CMEA).

[c]Bulgaria, Czechoslovakia, GDR, Cuba, Mongolia, Poland, Romania, Hungary, Vietnam (after 1976).

[d]Group figures.

TABLE A.18
Soviet Foreign Trade, Imports[a]

Countries or Groups of Countries	1983	1984	1983	1984	1983	1984
	(million TR)		(increase over previous year in percent)		(shares, percent)	
All countries	59589.2	65327.3	5.3	9.6	100.0	100.0
Socialist Countries[b]	33695.7	38220.0	9.3	13.4	56.5	58.4
CMEA countries[c]	30811.5	34587.3	11.8	12.3	51.7	52.9
Bulgaria	5053.3	5608.0	17.8	11.0	8.5	8.6
Czechoslovakia	5420.4	6016.5	14.6	11.0	9.1	9.2
GDR	6595.7	7367.2	14.2	11.7	11.1	11.3
Poland	4786.7	5296.8	16.8	10.7	8.0	8.1
Romania	1665.3	1755.2	-1.1	5.4	2.8	2.7
Hungary	4007.0	4434.4	7.0	10.7	6.7	6.8
OECD countries	18718.8	19574.1	-0.9	4.6	31.4	30.0
EC countries	8570.4	8342.0	16.5	-2.7	14.4	12.8
Federal Republic of Germany	3360.2	3375.9	15.4	0.5	5.6	5.2
France	1727.6	1777.3	36.3	2.9	2.9	2.7
Italy	1436.4	1324.6	17.5	-7.8	2.4	2.0
Great Britain	632.0	819.4	-16.0	29.7	1.1	1.3
Finland	2690.0	2307.3	-3.9	14.2	4.5	3.5
Austria	787.1	981.1	47.0	13.2	1.3	1.4
Japan	2175.5	2054.3	-25.6	-5.6	3.7	3.1
USA	1570.0	2829.0	-24.8	80.2	2.6	4.3
Developing countries[d]	7174.7	7533.2	7.0	5.0	12.0	11.5

Notes: [a]f.o.b. values at current prices and exchange rates.
[b]CMEA countries plus People's Republic of China, Yugoslavia, N. Korea, Vietnam (after 1976 in CMEA).
[c]Bulgaria, Czechoslovakia, GDR, Cuba, Mongolia, Poland, Romania, Hungary, Vietnam (after 1976).
[d]Group figures.

Sources: USSR foreign trade yearbooks; supplement to Vneshnyaya torgovlya, No. 3 (1985).

TABLE A.19
The International System of Communist Parties, 1980-1985

1. Total Membership

15 Ruling parties	approximately 75,000,000 members
Non-ruling parties	approximately 5,000,000 members
About 100 parties in all	approximately 80,000,000 members

2. Ruling Communist Parties (according to Soviet designation)

CCP	(PR China)	40,000,000	official data for Sept.	1983	RP	30 Nov. 1983
CPSU	(USSR)	18,331,000	official data for Feb.	1984	Sh	2/1984
RCP	(Romania)	3,400,000	official data for Nov.	1984	Sc	20 Nov. 1984
SED	(GDR)	2,238,283	official data for May	1984	ND	25 May 1984
YCL	(Yugoslavia)	2,200,000	official data for Feb.	1982	Ko	5 Feb. 1984
PUWP	(Poland)	2,186.000	official data for Jan.	1984	PAP	18 Jan. 1984
KWP	(North Korea)	2,000,000	official data for	1980	hor	41/1980
CPV	(Vietnam)	1,727,784	official data for early	1982	hor	15/1982
CPC	(CSSR)	1,623,000	official data for Jan.	1984	PFS	6/1984
HSWP	(Hungary)	871,000	official data for March	1985	MTI	25 March 1985
BCP	(Bulgaria)	825,876	official data for March	1981	RD	2 April 1981
CuCP	(Cuba)	414,143	official data for July	1980	PFS	2/1981
TAWP	(Albania)	122,600	official data for Nov.	1981	ZiP	2 Nov. 1981
MPRP	(Mongolian PR)	80,200	official data for late	1982	PFS	3/1983
LRPP	(Laos)	25,000	official data for April	1982	IB	9/1982

3. Non-Ruling Communist Parties: Regional Distribution

Western Europe	2,780,000	estimate for	1985	BIOst	1985
Asia and Oceania	1,200,000	estimate for	1978	STP	6/1978
Africa	70,000	official data for	1981	VIKPSS	6/1981
America, total	770,000	estimate for	1985	BIOst	1985
Latin America (incl. Cuba)	750,000	official data for	1980	hor	42/1980
North America (US and Canada)	20,000	estimate for	1985	BIOst	1985

TABLE A.19 (continued)

4. Membership of Western European Communist Parties

PCI	(Italy)	1,619,000	official data for	1984	U	20 Jan. 1985
PCF	(France)	608,000	official data for	1984	H	7 Feb. 1985
PCP	(Portugal)	200,753	official data for	1983	ND	16 Dec. 1983
PCE	(Spain)	67,808	official data for	1985	MO	4 Apr. 1985
DKP	(FR Germany)	50,482	official data for	1984	ND	7/8 Jan. 1984
KKE	(Greece)	40,000	estimate for	1985	BIOst	1985
SKP	(Finland)	33,052	official data for	1983	US	5 Nov. 1983
CPN	(Netherlands)	27,500	official data for	1978	Wa	24 Nov. 1983
KPÖ	(Austria)	16,000	official data for	1981	PFS	6/1981
VPK	(Sweden)	16,000	official data for	1978	PFS	6/1978
CPGB	(Great Britain)	15,700	estimate for	1983	FAZ	24 Nov. 1983
KKE-I	(Greece)	15,000	estimate for	1985	BIOst	1985
AKEL	(Cyprus)	14,000	official data for	1982	PFS	10/1982
DKP	(Denmark)	10,000	official data for	1983	BT	17 Nov. 1983
PCB/KPB	(Belgium	10,000	estimate for	1983	YICA	1984
PdA	(Switzerland)	5,000	estimate for	1983	YICA	1984
SEW	(West Berlin)	4,500	estimate for	1983	YICA	1984
AB	(Iceland)	3,000	estimate for	1983	YICA	1984
TCP	(Turkey)	2,000	estimate for	1984	BIOst	1985
PCSM	(San Marino)	1,040	official data for	1980	ND	8 Dec. 1980
PCL	(Luxembourg)	600	estimate for	1983	YICA	1984
NKP	(Norway)	500	estimate for	1984	YICA	1985

5. Membership of Selected Latin American and Asian Communist Parties

CP	Argentina	300,000	official data for	1983	ND	26 Sept. 1983
CP	Uruguay	50,000	official data for	1978	hor	24/1978
PSU	Mexico	40,000	official data for	1983	hor	20/1983
PPP	Panama	36,000	official data for	1982	ND	7 May 1982
CP	Colombia	25,000	official data for	1980	hor	49/1980
CP	Bolivia	20,000	official data for	1980	hor	11/1982
CP	Japan	480,000	official data for	1984	A	26 Jan. 1984
CP	India	470,000	official data for	1985	hor	2/1985
CP	India (M)	270,000	official data for	1983	B	4/1983

TABLE A.20
The Council for Mutual Economic Assistance (CMEA)
(as of July 1985)

Status	Country
Full members (Founding members) (established on 25 January 1949)	USSR PR Bulgaria Hungarian PR PR Poland SR Romania (formerly PR Romania) Czechoslovakia SR (formerly Czechoslovakian Republic) PR Albania (since 23 February 1949; has taken no further part since December 1961)
Full members (Later members)	GDR (since 29 September 1950) Mongolian PR (since 6/7 July 1962; observer status since May 1958) Republic of Cuba (since 10-12 July 1972; observer status since early 1965) SR Vietnam (since 27-29 June 1978; observer status since May 1958)
States with observer status at the CMEA	Democratic PR Korea (North Korea) (since June 1957) PR Angola (since July 1976) People's Democratic Republic of Laos (since July 1976) Ethiopia (since June 1978) People's Democratic Republic of Yemen (South Yemen) (since June 1979) Democratic Republic of Afghanistan (since June 1980) Nicaragua (since September 1983) The PR China participated as an observer between 1956 and 1961
States participating on the basis of special agreements	SFR Yugoslavia (on the basis of an agreement with the CMEA on the participation of Yugoslavia in the work of the CMEA organs, of 17 September 1964; observer status between 1956 and 1958) Republic of Finland (on the basis of an agreement on cooperation with the CMEA of 16 May 1973) Republic of Iraq (on the basis of an agreement with the CMEA of 4 July 1975) United States of Mexico (on the basis of an agreement with the CMEA of 13 August 1975)

TABLE A.20 (continued)

Date	CMEA Council Sessions Since 1969 (since the assignment to draft the "complex program")	
23-26 April 1969	XXIII.	(Extraordinary) Council Session in Moscow
12-14 May 1970	XXIV.	(Extraordinary) Council Session in Warsaw
27-29 July 1971	XXV.	Council Session in Bucharest (Adoption of the "complex program")
10-12 July 1972	XXVI.	Council Session in Moscow
5-8 June 1973	XXVII.	Council Session in Prague
18-21 June 1974	XXVIII.	Council Session in Sofia
24-26 June 1975	XXIX.	Council Session in Budapest
7-9 July 1976	XXX.	Council Session in East Berlin
21-23 June 1977	XXXI.	Council Session in Warsaw
27-29 June 1978	XXXII.	Council Session in Bucharest
26-28 June 1979	XXXIII.	Council Session in Moscow
17-19 June 1980	XXXIV.	Council Session in Prague
2-4 July 1981	XXXV.	Council Session in Sofia
8-10 June 1982	XXXVI.	Council Session in Budapest
18-20 Oct. 1983	XXXVII.	Council Session in East Berlin
12-14 June 1984		Economic consultations by CMEA member countries at the highest level in Moscow
14 June 1984	XXXVIII.	(Extraordinary) Council Session in Moscow
29-31 Oct. 1984	XXXIX.	Council Session in Havana
25-27 June 1985	XL.	Council Session in Warsaw

TABLE A.21
Chronology of the Development of the Warsaw Treaty Organization (WTO)

14 May 1955	Conclusion of the Warsaw Treaty (Treaty of Friendship, Co-operation, and Mutual Assistance Between the People's Republic of Albania, the People's Republic of Bulgaria, the Hungarian People's Republic, the German Democratic Republic, the People's Republic of Poland, the Romanian People's Republic, the Union of Soviet Socialist Republics, and the Czechoslovakian Republic)
17 Dec. 1956	Treaty on the Stationing of Troops Between the USSR and the PR Poland
12 March 1957	Agreement on the Stationing of Troops Between the USSR and the GDR
15 April 1957	Agreement on the Stationing of Troops Between the USSR and the PR Romania (Soviet troops were withdrawn from Romania in 1958)
27 May 1957	Treaty on the Stationing of Troops Between the USSR and the PR Hungary
13 Sept. 1968	Albania withdraws from the WTO
16 Oct. 1968	Treaty on the Stationing of Troops Between the USSR and the CSSR
17 March 1969	Creation of a Standing Committee of Defense Ministers of the WTO Member States and setting of new principles regarding the Joint Armed Forces and the Joint Command
24 April 1973	Signing of a Convention on the Legal Capacity, Privileges, and Immunities of the Staff and other Command Organs of the Joint Armed Forces of the WTO Member States
26 Nov. 1976	Creation of a Committee of Foreign Ministers and of a Joint Secretariat attached to the PCC

TABLE A.22
Meetings of the Warsaw Treaty Organization, 1983-1985

Year	Date	Place	Meeting	Purpose	Source
1983	4-5 January	Prague	PCC meeting	Declaration on current international questions	ADN
	11-13 January	Prague	Regular meeting of the Committee of Defense Ministers of the WTO member states	Questions regarding practical activities of the Joint Armed Forces	ADN
	6-7 April	Prague	Ordinary meeting of the Committee of Foreign Ministers of the WTO member states	Exchange of views on questions concerning the realization of the Prague Declaration	ADN
	26-28 April	Bucharest	Scheduled meeting of the Military Council of the Joint Armed Forces	Current questions concerning the activities of the Joint Armed Forces	ADN
	28 June	Moscow	Meeting of the Leading representatives of the WTO member states	Joint declaration on international questions	ADN
	30 August - 1 September	Moscow	Consultations of Deputy Foreign Ministers of socialist UN member states	Exchange of views on questions concerning the XXXVIII Session of the UN General Assembly	ADN
	13-14 October	Sofia	Regular meeting of the Committee of Foreign Ministers of WTO member states	Current questions regarding the international situation, relative to the Prague Declaration and the Moscow Joint Declaration	ADN
	20 October	Berlin (East)	Extraordinary meeting of the Committee of Defense Ministers of the WTO member states	Questions regarding developments in the military-political situation in Europe	ADN
	26-29 October	L'vov	Scheduled meeting of the Military Council of the Joint Armed Forces	Questions concerning current activities of the Joint Armed Forces	TASS

TABLE A.22 (continued)

Year	Date	Place	Meeting	Purpose	Source
1983	5-7 December	Sofia	Regular meeting of the Committee of Defense Ministers of WTO member states	Questions concerning practical activities of the Joint Armed Forces, relative to the situation that has developed in Europe	ADN
	20-21 December	Warsaw	Consultative meeting of the Deputy Foreign Ministers of the WTO member states	Questions preparatory to the CCDE	ADN
1984	19-20 April	Budapest	Regular meeting of the Committee of Foreign Ministers of the WTO member states	Current questions of the security policy situation in Europe	ADN
	17-19 October	Sofia	Scheduled meeting of the Military Council of the Joint Armed Forces	Questions regarding the implementation of decisions taken by the PCC and the Committee of Defense Ministers of the WTO member states	TASS
	3-4 December	Berlin (East)	Regular meeting of Committee of Foreign Ministers of the WTO member states	Exchange of views on current international questions, particularly military detente and disarmament	ADN
	3-5 December	Budapest	Ordinary meeting of the Committee of Defense Ministers of the WTO member states	Questions concerning current activities of the Joint Armed Forces	MTI
1985	21 January	Prague	Extraordinary meeting of the Committee of Defense Ministers of the WTO member states	Questions relative to the strengthening of the defensive capacity and military cooperation	CTK
	1 March	Moscow	Consultative meeting of the Deputy Foreign Ministers of WTO member states	Questions regarding Soviet-American negotiations on cosmic and nuclear weapons	TASS
	13 March	Moscow	Meeting of the leading representatives of WTO member states	Current questions regarding the security situation in Europe and cooperation by WTO member states	TASS

TABLE A.22 (continued)

Year	Date	Place	Meeting	Purpose	Source
1985	26 April	Warsaw	Meeting of the leading representatives of WTO member states	Signing of a protocol extending the Warsaw Treaty of 14 May 1955	TASS
	20-23 May	Budapest	Scheduled meeting of the Military Council of the Joint Armed Forces	Questions regarding the practical work of the Joint Commands	ADN

TABLE A.23
Treaties of Alliance, Cooperation, and Friendship of the USSR

TREATIES OF MILITARY ALLIANCE

Treaty Partner	Date Concluded	Renewed/Extended	Renewed/Extended
a) Treaties of Assistance on the Basis of Socialist Internationalism			
Czechoslovakia	12 December 1943	27 November 1963	6 May 1970
Poland	21 April 1945	8 April 1965	
Mongolia	27 February 1946	15 January 1966	
Romania	4 February 1948	12 May 1967	
Hungary	18 February 1948	7 September 1967	
Bulgaria	18 March 1948	7 July 1970	
North Korea	6 July 1961		
GDR	12 June 1964	7 October 1975	
b) Other Treaties of Assistance			
Finland	6 April 1948	19 September 1955	6 June 1983

TREATIES OF POLITICAL COOPERATION

Treaty Partner	Date Concluded
India	10 August 1971
Iraq	9 April 1972
Angola	8 October 1976
Mozambique	31 March 1977
Vietnam	3 November 1978
Ethiopia	20 November 1978
Afghanistan	5 December 1978
South Yemen	25 October 1979
Syria	8 October 1980
Congo (PR)	13 May 1981
North Yemen	9 October 1984

Acronyms and Abbreviations

A Akahata, Tokyo
ABM Anti-Ballistic Missile
ADN Allgemeiner Deutscher Nachrichtendienst (East German News Agency)
AEN Asahi Evening News, Tokyo
AFP Agence France Press, Paris
AP Associated Press, New York
B Beiträge zur Geschichte der Arbeiterbewegung, Berlin (East) (Contributions to the History of the Labor Movement)
BIOst Bundesinstitut für ostwissenschaftliche und internationale Studien, Cologne (Federal Institute for East European and International Studies)
BIS Bank for International Settlements
BT Berlingske Tidende, Copenhagen
CC Central Committee
CCDE Conference on Confidence-Building Measures and Disarmament in Europe
CDE Conference on Disarmament in Europe
CDU Christlich-Demokratische Union (West German Christian Democratic Party)
Cheka Vserossiyskaya Chrezvychaynaya Komissiya (All-Russian Extraordinary Commission)
CIA Central Intelligence Agency
CM Cruise Missile
CMEA Council for Mutual Economic Assistance
CoCom Coordinating Committee
CP Communist Party
CPC Communist Party of Czechoslovakia
CPCh Communist Party of China
CPSU Communist Party of the Soviet Union
CSCE Conference on Security and Cooperation in Europe

CSU	Christlich-Soziale Union (Bavarian Christian Democratic Party)
ČTK	Československá Tisková Kancelář (Czechoslovak news agency)
ddp	Deutscher Depeschen Dienst, Bonn (West German news agency)
DIW	Deutsches Institut für Wirtschaftsforschung, Berlin (German Institute for Economic Research)
dpa	Deutsche Presseagentur, Hamburg (West German news agency)
DS	Dŭržavna Sigurnost (Bulgarian State Security Service)
EA	Europa Archiv, Bonn
EKO	Ekonomika promyshlennogo proizvodstva, Novosibirsk
FAZ	Frankfurter Allgemeine Zeitung, Frankfurt/Main
FBS	Forward Based Systems (US nuclear-armed aircraft in Europe)
FDP	Freie Demokratische Partei (West German Liberal Party)
FYP	Five-Year Plan
GNP	Gross National Product
GPU	Gosudarstvennoe Politicheskoe Upravlenie (State Political Administration)
GRU	Glavnoe Razvedyvatelnoe Upravlenie (Central Administration for Military Intelligence)
H	l'Humanité, Paris
hor	horizont, Berlin (East)
HSWP	Hungarian Socialist Workers' Party
IB	Informationsbulletin, Vienna
ICBM	Intercontinental Ballistic Missile
IHT	International Herald Tribune, Zurich
IIB	International Investment Bank (Comecon)
IISS	International Institute for Strategic Studies (London)
INF	Intermediate Nuclear Forces
Iz	Izvestiya
JT	The Japan Times, Tokyo
K	Kommunist, Moscow
KGB	Komitet Gosudarstvennoy Bezopasnosti (Committee for State Security)
Ko	Komunist, Belgrade
KPSS	Kommunisticheskaya Partiya Sovetskogo Soyuza (=CPSU)
KZ	Krasnaya Zvezda, Moscow
LCY	League of Communists of Yugoslavia
LG	Literaturnaya Gazeta, Moscow
M	Le Monde, Paris
MB	The Military Balance IISS, London
MBFR	Mutual Balanced Force Reduction
MIRV	Multiple Independently Targetable Reentry Vehicle
MO	Mundo Obrero, Madrid

MTI	Magyar Távirati Iroda (Hungarian wire service)
MVD	Ministerstvo Vnutrennikh Del (Ministry of the Interior)
MZh	Mezhdunarodnaya zhizn, Moscow
N	Népszabadság, Budapest
NATO	North Atlantic Treaty Organization
ND	Neues Deutschland, Berlin (East)
NfA	Nachrichten für Außenhandel, Cologne
NKGB	Narodnyi Komissariat Gosudarstvennoy Bezopasnosti (People's Commissariat for State Security)
NKVD	Narodnyi Komissariat Vnutrennikh Del (People's Commissariat for Domestic Affairs)
NYT	The New York Times, New York
NZ	Neue Zeit, Moscow
NZZ	Neue Zürcher Zeitung, Zurich
OE	Osteuropa, Stuttgart
OECD	Organization for Economic Cooperation and Development
OGPU	Obyedinennoe Gosudarstvennoe Politicheskoe Upravlenie (Joint State Political Administration)
OPEC	Organization for Petroleum Exporting Countries
P2	Pershing 2
PAP	Polska Agencja Prasowa (Polish press agency)
PCC	Political Consultative Committee
PFS	Probleme des Friedens und des Sozialismus, Prague/Berlin (East) (German language edition of World Marxist Review)
PLO	Palestine Liberation Organization
Pr	Pravda, Moscow
PR	People's Republic (or People's Democratic Republic)
PUWP	Polish United Workers' Party
PZh	Partiynaya zhizn, Moscow
Rbl	Ruble
RCP	Romanian Communist Party
RD	Rabotnichesko delo, Sofia
RFER	Radio Free Europe Research (Munich)
RL	Radio Liberty Research Bulletin, Munich
RM	Radio Moscow
RP	Radio Peking
RPr	Rudé právo, Prague
RS	Radio Svoboda Issledovatskiy byulleten, Munich
RSFSR	Russian Soviet Federative Socialist Republic
SALT	Strategic Arms Limitation Talks
Sc	Scinteîa, Bukarest
SED	Sozialistische Einheitspartei Deutschlands (East German Socialist Unity Party)
SFR	Socialist Federative Republic
Sh	Sowjetunion heute

SISMI	Servizio per le Informazioni e la Sigurizza Militare (Information and Military Security Service)
SIss	Sotsiologicheskie issledovaniya, Moscow
SLBM	Submarine Launched Ballistic Missile
SN	Salzburger Nachrichten, Salzburg
Sp	Der Spiegel, Hamburg
SPD	Sozialdemokratische Partei Deutschlands (West German Social Democratic Party)
SR	Socialist Republic
SRV	Socialist Republic Vietnam
SSSR	Soyuz Sovetskikh Sotsialisticheskikh Respublik (Union of Soviet Socialist Republics)
START	Strategic Arms Reduction Talks
STB	Statní Tajná Bezpečnost (State Secret Security)
STP	Sozialismus, Theorie und Praxis, Moscow
SZ	Süddeutsche Zeitung, Munich
T	The Times, London
TANJUG	Telegrafska Agencija Nove Jugoslavije (Yugoslav news agency, Belgrade)
TASS	Telegrafnoe Agentsvo Sovetskogo Soyuza (State News Agency of the Soviet Union)
TRbl	Transfer-Ruble
U	l'Unità, Milan-Rome
UPI	United Press International, New York
UuS	Uusi Suomi, Helsinki
VE	Voprosy ekonomiki, Moscow
VF	Voprosy filosofii, Moscow
VI	Voprosy istorii, Moscow
VIKPSS	Voprosy istorii KPSS, Moscow
VT	Vneshnyaya torgovlya, Moscow
VVS SSSR	Vedomosti Verkhovnogo Soveta Soyuza Sovetskikh Sotsialisticheskikh Respublik, Moscow (News Bulletin of the Supreme Soviet of the USSR)
W	Die Welt, Hamburg
Wa	De Waarheid, Amsterdam
WP	Warsaw Pact
WSJ	Wall Street Journal, Brussels
WTO	Warsaw Treaty Organization
XNA	Xinhua News Agency, Peking
YICA	Yearbook on International Communist Affairs, Stanford (Calif.)
ZiP	Zeri i Popullit, Tirana

Research Reports of the Institute Relating to Subjects Covered in This Book

1983

2. Gerhard Simon, *Zeitgeschichtliche Phänomene, die es gar nicht gibt. Methodische Überlegungen zum Nationalismus in der UdSSR* (out of print).
3. Heinz Timmermann, *"Proletarischer Internationalismus" aus sowjetischer Sicht. Eine historisch-politische Analyse* (out of print).
4. Gerhard Wettig, *Konstanten sowjetischer Außen- und Sicherheitspolitik: das Erbe Breshnews* (out of print).
6. Astrid von Borcke, *"Kapazitäten," "Intentionen" und politischer Prozeß: Bestimmungsfaktoren der sowjetischen Sicherheits- und Rüstungspolitik* (out of print).
7. Heinz Timmermann, *Aktuelle Tendenzen im kommunistischen Parteiensystem. Zerfallsprozesse und Neuorientierungen* (out of print).
8. Astrid von Borcke, *Partizipationsprobleme und Parteiregime in der Sowjetunion. Grenzen des bürokratischen Autoritarismus* (out of print).
10. Hans-Hermann Höhmann, *Von Breschnew zu Andropow. Bilanz und Perspektiven sowjetischer Wirtschaftspolitik* (out of print).
11. Eberhard Schneider, *Social Backgrounds and Careers of the Members of the Council of Ministers of the USSR. An Empirical Study* (out of print).
12. Hans Bräker, *The Implications of the Islam Question for Soviet Domestic and Foreign Policy* (out of print).
13. Wolf Oschlies, *Die Deutschen in der Sowjetunion. Versuch einer Bestandsaufnahme* (out of print).
14. Astrid von Borcke, *Zwischen Revision und Reaktion: Die Sowjetunion und der Machtwechsel* (out of print).
17. Paul Roth, *Die neue Weltinformationsordnung. Argumentation, Zielvorstellung und Vorgehen der UdSSR (II)* (out of print).
18. Gertraud Seidenstecher, *Sowjetische Wirtschaft 1982/83* (out of print).
20. Dieter Bingen, *Die Rolle der Sowjetunion in der Polen-Krise 1981–1983* (out of print).
21. Gerd Linde, *Friedenssuche in Mittelost—Tauziehen am Gordischen Knoten* (out of print).
22. Ferenc Majoros, *Die Rechtshilfeabkommen der osteuropäischen RGW-Staaten. Part I: Bestandsaufnahme und Gesamtanalyse* (out of print).

24. Dieter Heinzig, *Die Sowjetunion in südostasiatischer Sicht.*
25. Heinz Timmermann, *Pekings "eurokommunistische" Wende. Zur Wiedereinschaltung der KP Chinas in das internationale kommunistische Parteiensystem* (out of print).
27. Gerhard Wettig, Die Rolle von Bedrohungsvorstellungen in der sowjetischen Westpolitik (out of print).
28. Gerhard Wettig, *Wege zur Kriegsverhütung und Friedenssicherung* (out of print).
30. Heinz Brahm, *Andropow ante portas* (out of print).
32. Helmut Dahm, *Marx-Lenin-Andropow. Ideologischer Lagebericht nach dem Führungswechsel in Moskau.*
33. Siegfried Schultz/Heinrich Machowski, *US and Soviet Trade and Aid Relations with the Third World* (out of print).
34. Ferenc Majoros, *Die Rechtshilfeabkommen der osteuropäischen RGW-Staaten. Part II: Die Abkommen in Strafsachen.*
35. Helmut Dahm, *Die verschlissene Ideologie. Was ist nach hundert Jahren Marx-Gedächtnis von seiner Lehre noch übrig?* (out of print).
38. Gerhard Wettig, *Psychoanalyse, Friedensbewegung und Sicherheitspolitik* (out of print).
39. John P. Hardt, *East-West Economic Relations: Alternative Scenarios for the Atlantic Alliance* (out of print).
41. Hans Raupach, *Notwendigkeiten und Grenzen von Wirtschaftsreformen in Staaten des realen Sozialismus* (out of print).
42. Gerhard Wettig, *Kräfteverhältnis, Kriegsverhütung und Kriegführung in sowjetischer Darstellung* (out of print).
43. Gerd Linde, *Andropow-Assad-Arafat: Wer mit wem?*
44. Hans-Hermann Höhmann, *Richtung und Grenzen neuer Wirtschaftsreformen in der UdSSR* (out of print).
45. Gerhard Wettig, *Zum Abbruch der INF-Verhandlungen.*
46. Joachim Glaubitz, *Die Sowjetunion und Japan 1980–1983.*
48. Heinrich Machowski, *Sowjetischer Außenhandel: Tendenzen und aktuelle Probleme.*
49. Gerhard Wettig, *Die Funktion der westeuropäischen Friedensbewegung in sowjetischer Sicht* (out of print).

1984

2. Heinz Brahm, *Andropows Wahl zum Generalsekretär* (out of print).
4. Gerd Linde, *Afghanistan, Iran und Camp David als Problem sowjetischer Mittelostpolitik.*
5. Ferenc Majoros, *Die Rechtshilfeabkommen der osteuropäischen RGW-Staaten. Part III: Die Abkommen in Zivilsachen* (out of print).
6. Gregory Grossman, *Die "zweite Wirtschaft" und die sowjetische Wirtschaftsplanung* (out of print).
8. Heinz Timmermann, *Das Kominform und seine Folgen in den sowjetischen Außenbeziehungen. Eine historisch-politische Analyse* (out of print).
10. Willi Möllemann, *Zu Lebens-, Arbeits- und Leistungsbedingungen sowjetischer Ingenieure.*
11. Gerhard Wettig, *Information und Sicherheit in sowjetischer Sicht* (out of print).
14. Hans-Hermann Höhmann, *Hoffnung auf die Produktivkraft Wirtschaftswissenschaft: Politische Ökonomie der UdSSR in Selbstreflexion und Parteikritik.*
15. Heinz Brahm, *Retuschen am Andropow-Bild* (out of print).
16. Gerd Linde, *Sowjetische Counter-Guerilla am Beispiel Afghanistan.*

18. Karin Schmid, *Zum neuen Grenzgesetz der UdSSR.*
20. Wolfgang Berner, *Reformdruck, Machtfragen und Partikularismus im osteuropäischen Vorfeld der UdSSR 1980–84.*
21. Gerhard Simon, *Nationalitätenprobleme und die Regierbarkeit der Sowjetunion* (out of print).
22. Astrid von Borcke, *Perception of the Soviet System.*
25. Dieter Heinzig. *Sowjetische Asienpolitik in den siebziger und achtziger Jahren. Eine Bilanz.*
26. Franz-Lothar Altmann, *Der Moskauer RGW-Wirtschaftsgipfel vom Juni 1984.*
27. Peter Hübner, *Schwarzhandel mit Büchern in der UdSSR. Part I: Bücherdefizit als Voraussetzung des schwarzen Marktes.*
28. Hans-Hermann Höhmann, *The Soviet Economy on the Eve of the 12th Five-Year Plan: Developments, Policies, Perspectives.*
30. Eberhard Schneider, *Die osteuropäische Wirtschaftskrise als innenpolitisches Problem: Polen, UdSSR und DDR* (out of print).
31. Lázsló Csaba, *Economic Policy Coordination in the CMEA.*
32. Barbara Dietz, *UdSSR: Wie weiter mit der "Vervollkommnung" der Wirtschaftsplanung?*
37. Hans Bräker, *Die islamischen Turkvölker Zentralasiens und die sowjetischchinesischen Beziehungen* (out of print).
39. Gerhard Wettig, *Modelle der zwischenstaatlichen Sicherheit. Part I: Sicherheit durch Rechtsetzung.*
40. Joachim Fesefeldt, *Der Warschauer Pakt auf dem Madrider KSZE-Folgetreffen und auf der KVAE (ohne Rumänien)* (out of print).
41. Gerhard Wettig, *Modelle der zwischenstatlichen Sicherheit. Part II: Sicherheit durch Rüstungsveränderung.*
44. Dieter Heinzig, *Sowjetisch-chinesische Beziehungen in den 70er und 80er Jahren: Vom Kalten Krieg zur begrenzten Entspannung.*
45. Gerhard Wettig, *Modelle der zwischenstaatlichen Sicherheit. Part III: Sicherheit durch militärische Macht.*
46. Gerhard Wettig, *Modelle der zwischenstaatlichen Sicherheit. Part IV: Schlußfolgerungen.*
47. Anneli Ute Gabanyi, *Rumäniens eigenwillige Positionen auf dem Madrider KSZE-Folgetreffen und auf der KVAE.*
48. Boris Rumer, *Current Problems in the Industrialization of Siberia.*
49. Karl Schlögel, *Ökologiediskussion in der Sowjetunion.*
52. Ulrich Weißenburger, *Umweltprobleme und Umweltschutz in der Sowjetunion. Part I: Umweltverschmutzung und -zerstörung als Problem der Wirtschaftspolitik.*
53. Ulrich Weißenburger, *Umweltprobleme und Umweltschutz in der Sowjetunion. Part II: Die Umweltplanung und die institutionellen Zuständigkeiten für den Umweltschutz.*
54. Heinz Timmermann, *Demokratischer Zentralismus heute. Zur Diskussion über Organisationsprinzipien und Modellfunktion kommunistischer Parteien.*
55. Hans-Hermann Höhmann/Christian Meier, *Wirtschaftslage, Außenwirtschaft und Außenpolitik in Osteuropa: Zur Politischen Ökonomie der RGW-Gipfelkonferenz.*
56. Gerhard Wettig, *Die Sowjetunion und die Rüstungskontrolle.*
58. Thomas Kussmann, *Die Psychologische Fakultät der Moskauer Lomonosov-Universität.*
59. Gertraud Sedenstecher, *Leistungsprobleme der sowjetischen Eisenbahn. Part I: Die Tragfähigkeit der technischen Basis.*

60. Gertraud Seidenstecher, *Leistungsprobleme der sowjetischen Eisenbahn. Part II: Probleme des Eisenbahnbetriebs.*

1985

1. Franz Walter, *Zur amerikanischen Neueinschätzung des Trends der Verteidigungsausgaben der UdSSR. Zuverlässigkeit und Aussagekraft der Schätzungen.*
2. Karin Schmid, *Einschränkungen des grenzüberschreitenden Informationsaustausches in der UdSSR. Part I: Propagandistische und administrative Maßnahmen.*
3. Otto Luchterhand, *Menschenrechtspolitik und KSZE. Part I: Die politischen und rechtlichen Grundlagen.*
4. Otto Luchterhand, *Menschenrechtspolitik und KSZE. Part II: Belgrad, Madrid und die Perspektiven.*
7. Hans-Hermann Höhmann, *East-European Economies 1981–1984: Growth, Reform, and Foreign Trade Problems.*
12. Ulrich Weißenburger, *Umweltprobleme und Umweltschutz in der Sowjetunion. Part III: Die Maßnahmen für den Umweltschutz.*
13. Heinz Timmermann, *Die UdSSR unter Gorbatschow: Perspektiven einer Neuorientierung?*
14. Wolf Oschlies, *"Weltfestspiele der Jugend und Studenten," Geschichte, Auftrag und Ertrag kommunistischer Jugendfestivals.*
15. Robert L. Hutchings, *Foreign and Security Policy Coordination in the Warsaw Pact.*
16. Eberhard Schneider, *Der Ministerrat der UdSSR unter Andropov und Tschernenko.*
20. Hans-Hermann Höhmann, *Sowjetische Wirtschaft am Ende des 11. Planjahrfünfts: Hoffen auf Gorbatschow.*
22. Karl E. Birnbaum, *Die KVAE als Spiegel der Großmachtpolitik: das erste Jahr der Stockholmer Konferenz.*
24. Christian Meier, *Sowjetische Außenwirtschaft unter außenpolitischer Restriktion?*
25. Helmut Dahm, *Die Ideologie als Chiffre der Politik. Das sozialökonomische und das geistig-kulturelle Krisenbewußtsein in der Sowjetunion und seine politische Verfälschung.*
26. Karin Schmid, *Einschränkungen des grenzüberschreitenden Informationsaustausches in der UdSSR. Part II: Strafrechtliche Maßnahmen.*
28. Heinz Timmermann, *"Kommunistische Weltbewegung": Das Ende eines Mythos.*
29. Eberhard Schinke/Karl-Eugen Wädekin, *Die sowjetische Landwirtschaft an der Wende zum 12. Planjahrfünft: Produktion, Verbrauch, Außenwirtschaft.*
30. Gertraud Seidenstecher, *Infrastrukturprobleme der UdSSR: Engpaß Transportwesen.*
31. Sigurd Boysen, *Vertrauensbildende Maßnahmen in der sowjetischen Außenpolitik.*
33. Hans-Hermann Höhmann, *Zum Stellenwert von Wirtschaftszielen in der sowjetischen Politik.*
35. Eberhard Schneider, *Gorbatschows Pesonalschub. Die Neubesetzung der Spitzenpositionen in Partei und Staat.*
36. Thomas Kussmann, *Die Sowjetische Psychologische Gesellschaft. Aufgaben in Forschung und Anwendung.*
37. Bernd Knabe, *Der Kampf gegen die Trunksucht in der UdSSR.*
38. Heinz Timmermann, *Gorbatschow zeigt außenpolitisches Profil Kurskorrekturen oder Konzeptionswandel?*
39. Gerhard Wettig, *Die kleineren Warschauer-Pakt-Staaten in den Ost-West-Beziehungen.*
40. Michael Rühle, *die strategische Verteidigung in Rüstung und Politik der UdSSR.*

41. Hans-Hermann Höhmann, *Wirtschaftsreformen in Osteuropa: Was ist neu an neuen Entwicklungen?*
44. Philip Hanson, *Economic Relations Between Communist and Capitalist Nations in Europe.*
45. Hans-Hermann Höhmann, *Sozialistische Wirtschaftsplanung: Grundlagen, Probleme, Reformperspektiven.*
46. Jochen Bethkenhagen, *Die sowjetische Energiewirtschaft an der Schwelle zum 12. Planjahrfünft (1986–1990).*
48. Peter Hübner, *E. Čazov—ein "ganz integrer Mann"?*
49. Dieter Heinzig, *Die Volksrepublik China zwischen den Supermächten 1949–1985. Zur Genese eines strategischen Dreiecks.*